Economic Efficiency—
Democratic Empowerment

Economic Efficiency— Democratic Empowerment

Contested Modernization in Britain and Germany

Edited by
Ingolfur Blühdorn and Uwe Jun

LEXINGTON BOOKS

A division of
ROWMAN & LITTLEFIELD PUBLISHERS, INC.
Lanham • Boulder • New York • Toronto • Plymouth, UK

LEXINGTON BOOKS

A division of Rowman & Littlefield Publishers, Inc.
A wholly owned subsidiary of The Rowman & Littlefield Publishing Group, Inc.
4501 Forbes Boulevard, Suite 200
Lanham, MD 20706

Estover Road
Plymouth PL6 7PY
United Kingdom

British Library Cataloguing in Publication Information Available

Library of Congress Cataloging-in-Publication Data

Economic efficiency—democratic empowerment : contested modernization in Britain
and Germany / edited by Ingolfur Blühdorn and Uwe Jun.
    p. cm.
  Includes bibliographical references.
  ISBN-13: 978-0-7391-1210-6 (cloth : alk. paper)
  ISBN-10: 0-7391-1210-4 (cloth : alk. paper)
  ISBN-13: 978-0-7391-1211-3 (pbk. : alk. paper)
  ISBN-10: 0-7391-1211-2 (pbk. : alk. paper)
  1. Great Britain—Economic policy—1997– 2. Germany—Economic policy—1990–
3. Democracy—Great Britain. 4. Democracy—Germany. 5. Economic development—
Political aspects. I. Blühdorn, Ingolfur. II. Jun, Uwe. III. Title: Modernization in Britain
and Germany.
  HC256.7.E27 2007
  338.941—dc22   2006034175

Printed in the United States of America

Contents

Acknowledgments

The origins of this book date back to a research seminar on the topic of societal modernization in Germany and Britain that was held at the University of Bath in the Autumn of 2003. The event had been kindly sponsored by the Anglo-German Foundation for the Study of Industrial Society (AGF), and we would like to take this opportunity to thank the AGF for their seed corn funding.

Since its early days, the project has evolved quite considerably and political debates have moved on. In Britain, the general elections in May 2005 have resulted in a historic third term in government for the Labour Party, but the era of the father of *New Labour*, Prime Minister Tony Blair, is coming to a close. In Germany, the federal elections of September 2005 have put an end to the Red-Green coalition government under Chancellor Gerhard Schröder. However, the pressure for ever new and ever more rapid modernization of social, economic, political, and administrative structures has not disappeared in either country. Nor have the social controversies which have evolved around the respective reform agendas. Time and again, these controversies center on the question for the compatibility of the desires for more democracy and more efficiency. The contributions to this book seek to capture and analyze these tensions. Editing this book has been a long but pleasurable process. We are far from having brought this ongoing research to its final completion. But we would like to thank all contributors to this volume for taking part in the project. Furthermore, we would like to thank Britta Ganswindt and Selina Klüppelholz at the University of Trier for their invaluable assistance in getting the manuscript ready for publication, and staff at Lexington Press for their swift and competent support.

List of Figures and Tables

FIGURES

TABLES

INTRODUCTION

1

Reform-Gridlock and Hyper-Innovation: Germany, Britain and the Project of Societal Modernization

Ingolfur Blühdorn and Uwe Jun

Economic globalization, demographic shifts, and the simultaneous regionalization and internationalization of politics have exposed European societies to unprecedented pressure for modernization. In a much more comprehensive sense than environmentalists could ever have hoped to achieve this, even major European economies have come to acknowledge that there are *limits to growth* and that many of their established social, economic, and political practices are no longer sustainable. In the face of fierce economic competition, high unemployment rates, overstretched welfare systems, ecological crises, and political cynicism, comprehensive societal modernization seems more urgent than ever, yet it seems more difficult than ever to devise and implement socially acceptable modernization strategies. In an attempt to cope with these pressures, governments are reviewing the relationship of, and the distribution of responsibilities between, the state, the market, and civil society. Whether the reform strategies which are being adopted are really conducive to securing, at least for the medium term, economic, social, political, and ecological stability still has to be verified in what is essentially a large-scale societal experiment with uncertain outcomes. Yet, what is certain is that determined modernizers who, as British Prime Minister Tony Blair once said about himself, have "not got a reverse gear" (Blair 2003) are not exactly popular with their constituencies and tend to trigger resistance within their own parties, anxieties in the wider public, and at times protest rallies in the streets. The reform policies which leaders such as Blair or former German Chancellor Gerhard Schröder have imposed on their countries have been greeted with considerable skepticism. And there are, of course, good reasons to be defensive about established certainties, securities, and provision, and apprehensive

about any claims that the *reforms* which are being prescribed and implemented now can stabilize the economic, political, administrative, and social
systems for any length of time, let alone safeguard or secure them for the
long-term future.

This book focuses on two major European countries, Britain and Germany, and the controversies and struggles surrounding their agendas of social, economic, and political modernization. It sets out from the assumption
that there are two *main* challenges which the two countries are confronted
with, and that these are both if not caused by then at least accelerated by the
processes of globalization which have become particularly visible and viru-
lent since the end of the bipolar world order of the Cold War: The first of
these main challenges is the combination of sluggish economic growth, high
unemployment, and ever-tighter public budgets which are supposed to cater
for ever-rising public demands. The other is the problem of declining public
confidence in, and satisfaction with, the established institutions and procedures of democracy.

The former has a lot to do with the economic progress of many countries
in Asia, Eastern Europe, and elsewhere, and the relative lack of competitiveness of western European countries with these rapidly developing economies.
Structural adjustment programs, *efficiency revolutions* in the economic system, and the systems of public administration and welfare provision, belong
to the preferred strategies by means of which western European governments
are trying to respond. The latter, i.e., the problem of declining public confidence in democratic institutions and procedures, has been caused not least by
the fact that the development of democratic structures has failed to keep pace
with the internationalization or even globalization of politics. It materializes,
on the one hand, in political cynicism and apathy which translate into legitimation crises for national governments and, on the other hand, in the rise of
forms of political articulation and activism which are no longer prepared to
rely primarily on the structures of representative democracy. What is required
is, therefore, something like a *democratic revolution*, or at least comprehensive democratic *renewal* which may restore the citizens' sense of political efficacy and public confidence that in the era of globalization democratic structures are still a suitable mechanism for resolving the societal issues that need
to be addressed. Thus, efficiency revolutions and democratic renewal are two
central dimensions of the modernization agendas in European societies; and
efficiency and democracy—as well as the relationship between the two—are,
therefore, the focus of this volume.

The book links into ongoing debates about the most suitable organization
of public affairs. *Traditional public management* tended to be dominated by
political and administrative elites and was not sufficiently oriented towards

the needs of citizens. The paradigm of *new public management*, on the other hand, was too exclusively geared towards the market and economic efficiency and underestimated the irreducible significance of politics. So the search is on for a "third way" in which variable networks of, and partnerships between, stakeholders including the full range of political actors and bodies in the public sector, private sector, and voluntary sector cooperate in forging and delivering public policy. The book also links into debates on the *performance of democratic systems* which have recently become strikingly prominent in many established democracies. *Comparative* performance assessment, in particular, has become a major issue (e.g., Roller 2005), and there are a number of reasons for this: First, following the collapse of the communist systems in Eastern Europe, comparison *within* the community of democratic states has replaced the earlier focus on comparison between democratic and nondemocratic systems. Second, low economic growth rates in many established democracies have rendered economic performance and competitiveness a key concern. Third, in a climate of growing political apathy and cynicism political elites have to provide evidence of their actual effectiveness in order to regenerate public trust and electoral support. Fourth, there is increasing uncertainty whether democratic systems are really capable of dealing effectively with problems such as unemployment, social security, environmental degradation, international migration, or terrorism. And fifth, the pervasiveness in late-modern societies of images, presentations, advertising, rhetoric, and political spin-doctoring nurtures the desire to *touch base*, i.e., to review what the major societal function systems are actually delivering, and to establish reliable points of reference (benchmarks) which may provide orientation for programs of further modernization.

What is explored and measured as the *performance* of democratic systems has at least two dimensions: On the one hand there is the question whether or to what extent institutionalized democracies actually fulfill the promises which are implied in the normative ideal of democracy. On the other hand there is the question what the economic system, systems of public administration, health systems, education systems, and so forth are actually delivering in terms of measurable output, and how efficiently they are delivering this. In both respects democratic systems have come under pressure: The established democratic structures and processes are increasingly perceived as failing to fulfill the citizens' expectations both in terms of self-determination and self-realization, and in terms of economic, social, and environmental security. International bodies such as the OECD or the EU are, therefore, putting considerable emphasis on exercises of performance measurement, performance assessment and performance enhancement. Comparison and competition are assumed to improve output and standards. Germany's response to the PISA study, for example, which measured and compared a range of skills in school children across several countries, demonstrated the stirring effect of perceived performance deficits, particularly in economically relevant policy areas such as education. Britain, for better or worse, is the country in the EU that is most passionate about performance measurement and assessment. The Blair government has introduced targets, inspectors, audits, rankings, league tables, and five-year plans for just about any sector from schools, universities, and hospitals, to city councils, police forces, prisons, and government departments. Yet, whether such strategies can really improve the citizens' quality of life and democratic experience remains contentious. Performance is notoriously difficult to measure and assess. Increasing the empirically quantifiable *outputs* of specific processes or systems is not synonymous with achieving qualitatively better *outcomes*. Also, attempts to improve performance in the sense of *systemic* outputs may well negatively affect performance in terms of *democratic* ambitions. Indeed, familiar strategies for the achievement of efficiency gains, such as increased reliance on scientific experts, on market principles, or on the private sector as provider of public goods, have triggered vociferous complaints about increasing *democratic deficits*. In the era of international economic competition the old question of the relationship between democracy and efficiency has gained new significance: democratic structures and processes are not necessarily efficient; and efficient arrangements are often rather undemocratic.

DEMOCRACY AND EFFICIENCY

The democratic ideal of government *by the people for the people* has exerted its magic ever since its inception in the ancient Greek city-states, but it is also common wisdom that *Viele Köche verderben den Brei!—Too many cooks spoil the broth!* Indeed there is a long and well-established tradition of political thought which suggests that democratic decision making is disadvantageous, firstly because ordinary citizens may lack the information and intellectual resources which are required to deal with complex or specialized issues, secondly because democratic processes require a lot of time and other resources which may be in short supply, and thirdly because most citizens are not well positioned to adopt an encompassing and far-sighted perspective that reaches beyond their personal and present-oriented interests. Democracy may be all well and good if no major problems are looming at the horizon and no major challenges need to be addressed. But particularly in situations of crisis, so the argument runs, democracy must give way to elite rule. Issues of foreign policy and war, for example, have therefore always been regarded as beyond the scope of democratic procedures. But there are also a range of other issues, such as ecological problems, where serious doubts have been articulated already in the 1960s and 1970s whether democratic structures are suitable for effectively addressing them. In the present era, issues such as terrorism further expand the list of policy areas where democratic structures seem inappropriate. And as regards economic competitiveness, it seems that for this objective, too, clear hierarchies and decisive leadership are much more effective and efficient than participatory and egalitarian structures.

In advanced modern societies, however, democratic values and procedures have become sacrosanct, and wherever questions are raised about the suitability of democratic principles this tends to trigger reflexes of defense. Not only have emancipatory movements from the era of Enlightenment to the new social movements since the late 1960s deeply rooted the belief in autonomous self-determination and individuality, but the economic system of consumer capitalism vitally depends on democracy: Only democracy produces the individualized, differentiated, autonomous, diversified consumer which the capitalist economy needs, and only democracy generates legitimacy for a socioeconomic system that, while serving individual preferences, is from a collective point of view not necessarily efficient, legitimate, and in the interest of the common good. And there are a number of reasons beyond this which call for the further deepening and widening of democracy: First, the implications and effects of many issues which contemporary societies need to address (e.g., biotechnology or nuclear energy) are so wide-ranging and important that, many believe, they cannot be left to small decision-making elites. Second, in the era of globalization democracy needs to be reinvented to suit the emerging patterns of multilevel governance. Third, democratic renewal is required because nation-states and their institutions are no longer able to deliver on the rising expectations of their citizenry. Fourth, as was indicated above, national governments need to address the problems of political apathy and the legitimacy crises which may emerge from them. Fifth, there are ever new minorities which pursue their political emancipation and demand self-determination. And sixth, in the arena of international and global politics, democracy is supposed to lead to international stability, prosperity, and peace.

These are all very different but equally compelling reasons for deepening and broadening democratic structures. Yet at least within well-established liberal democracies, the question emerges how the corresponding agendas of democratic renewal affect the agenda of efficiency gains. If, as has been suggested above, democratic structures tend to be inefficient and efficient structures tend to be undemocratic, will it be possible to pursue both objectives at the same time? Will it be possible to achieve an efficiency revolution in the economy and public administration and at the same time a democratic revolution that responds to demands for more citizen empowerment, minority emancipation, and political self-determination? The question whether and how in already highly differentiated and complex societies, democratic procedures might be able to retain and further develop diversity but at the same time avoid losses in effectiveness and efficiency is one of the key problems of democratic theory. Many have argued—and this will be explored in some detail in chapter 3 of this volume—that inclusiveness and effectiveness, i.e., responsiveness to the demand for participation and self-determination and responsiveness to the demand for effective decision making and policy delivery, cannot be maximized at the same time. The more a democratic system is trying to take into account the preferences articulated by its citizens at the input side, the higher are the costs—monetary and nonmonetary—of the decision-making process, and the lower is responsiveness at the output side. The higher the degree of differentiation and the level of complexity, the smaller the common denominator of the actors involved, and the bigger the danger of sclerosis, paralysis, and deadlock.

In the 1990s, there was considerable optimism that in the *stakeholder society* efficiency gains and democratic gains can be achieved at the same time. In the contemporary context, however, it seems more probable that the process of societal modernization implies an irresolvable dilemma: On the one hand, democratic deliberation and participation are widely regarded as essential for increasing the quality, legitimacy, and effectiveness of public policy decisions. Projects of *civic empowerment* and *capacity building* are supposed to overcome growing disengagement from politics and enable civil society to play a more active role in democratic self-governance. On the other hand, democratic participation and accountability can easily turn into obstacles to economic, administrative, or political efficiency. Increasingly they are recognized as obstructing decisive societal modernization and efficient societal management: Democracy slows down cycles of innovation and erects obstacles to the realization of potentials for growth. If economic growth and competitiveness require fast production of economically relevant ideas, low regulation density for the realization of these ideas, and low costs in the phase of practical implementation, democratic procedures are indeed likely to be unhelpful. They tend to be detrimental in all three respects (see Ian Welsh's discussion of biotechnological innovation in chapter 11 of this volume). Unsurprisingly, the argument that opportunities for democratic intervention and codetermination ought to be managed more carefully, or indeed curtailed, is gaining ground.

So the recognition that democratic structures and processes are often inefficient while efficient arrangements often lack democratic legitimacy is by no means new. However, in a condition where countries with strong democratic traditions are exposed to direct competition with less democratic or nondemocratic systems, the tension between the two objectives becomes particularly painful. Democratic systems are per definition pluralistic, oriented towards compromise, and comparatively slow in making and implementing policy. In less democratic or nondemocratic systems, in contrast, major strategic decisions can be taken and implemented more swiftly, political and economic objectives can be pursued more single-mindedly, and the demands of citizens can be managed more effectively. Global competition, however, takes place first and foremost in the arenas of the economy rather than democracy. Established western democracies therefore come under considerable pressure not only to place the emphasis of their reform agendas on the efficiency side but beyond this, to actually reduce the complexity of democratic procedures where these seem to impair economic efficiency and competitiveness. In Britain, in particular, sweeping reform programs in the labor market, the public sector, and the welfare system have been inspired by the desire to increase the efficiency of the established structures. With some delay and much more hesitantly, Germany has embarked on a similar process. But what exactly does *efficiency* actually mean? And how exactly does its pursuit affect the objective of *democratic renewal*, which is, in fact, an equally ambiguous term? The political struggle about the definition of, and relationship between, these two key parameters in the modernization debate is the recurring theme in all contributions to this volume. Focusing on a variety of political actors, structures, and strategies in Germany and Britain, the individual chapters trace how the tensions between the objectives of democracy and efficiency surface, how the definitional struggles surrounding these ideals are being managed, and how new syntheses between the two parameters are being forged. In the most general sense the question then is, of course, what *modernization* may actually mean beyond technical innovation, narratives of the knowledge economy or media democracy, and consecutive waves of restructuring at all levels of society.

ON THE COMPARABILITY OF TWO VERY DIFFERENT COUNTRIES

The two countries which are being investigated here, Germany and Britain, are very different indeed, not only because Germany is still deeply caught up in the unfinished project of its unification which represents a historical challenge larger than anything that any other western European country recently had to confront. There are also significant differences in the economic, political, and social systems as well as in terms of cultural traditions. The British economy is, for example, much more oriented towards the postindustrial service sectors than its German counterpart. The British liberal welfare state is based on different normative foundations and is less concerned about high levels of social inequality than Germany's postwar corporatist-conservative *social state* (see Elmar Wiesendahl's discussion of this concept in chapter 9). As regards the political system, Britain's tradition of centralized adversarial majority democracy has given rise to a political culture that is clearly distinct from Germany's federal system of consensual *negotiation democracy* (see Lewis Baston's and Sven Jochem's analyses in chapters 4 and 6). And in cultural terms, the long Anglo-Saxon tradition of empirical pragmatism and individualist (market) liberalism contrasts sharply with the continental European and German tradition of idealism and socially oriented collectivism. This cultural and institutional incongruence restricts the direct comparability between these two countries. At the same time, however, exploring these two countries' modernization agendas is interesting exactly because their respective political, economic, and social systems display significant differences. Neither individually, nor as a collection, the contributions to this book aim to provide a systematic comparative analysis, but they do shed light on the contemporary struggle between the Anglo-Saxon model of market liberalism and the continental-German model of the social market economy. For a long time, the German model had been highly successful and much envied, but in the era of globalization, it is widely criticized as old-fashioned and doomed to decline while the Anglo-Saxon model proudly presents itself as the model for the future.

Indeed, Britain and Germany have a long history of taking each other, or being presented to each other, as models for social, economic, or political modernization. In the postwar decades, British civic culture and democratic stability seemed superior to Germany's still unsettled political culture. In the 1970s, Britain enviously marveled at the successful German economy and generous welfare state. In the era of Thatcherism, Germany's consensualism and incrementalism appeared much more socially benign than British radical market-liberalism. From the mid-1990s then, Britain seemed to be significantly more innovative and dynamic than Germany, and much better positioned to cope with the challenges of economic globalization. In both countries, Social-Democratic governments were voted into office in the second half of the 1990s on the promise that they would modernize their country in a socially acceptable way, i.e., that they would reconcile the pressure for economic competitiveness and budgetary restraint with the commitment to securing (Germany) or achieving (Britain) an acceptable level of public provision, social justice, and quality of life. In both countries the main obstacles to efficient societal change have been identified in the "conservatism" of specific political actors (such as trade unions), in a bloated public sector, and in over-developed legal and administrative structures which suffocate reform initiatives, render social institutions inefficient, and stifle the entrepreneurial spirit. In order to increase their countries' competitiveness in the global market, the respective governments have introduced a range of reform policies (e.g., health, education, labor market). The situation of the two countries differed considerably insofar as Germany was—and is—struggling with the unaffordability of a highly developed system of public provision, while Britain was—and is—struggling to achieve acceptable standards in key areas such as education, health, pensions, public transport, and so forth. But as regards the demands for labor market flexibilization, tax reduction, budgetary consolidation, and improved international competitiveness, public debates in the two countries display considerable similarities.

Since the ascendance to power of *New Labour* in 1997, in particular, German modernizers have been fascinated by Tony Blair's reform enthusiasm, leadership, and stamina which so far no political party or charismatic leader in Germany has been able to match. Britain has pursued a trajectory of *hyper-innovation* (Moran 2003). It has pioneered changes in terms of economic organization, welfare arrangements, and institutional structures which have turned the country into a point of orientation for advocates of cross-national policy learning. Germany in contrast has for some considerable time been paralyzed by what some perceive as a *crisis of hyper-stability* (Kitschelt and Streeck 2003: 28). Germany is still one of the strongest European economies, yet it is widely regarded as a reform-laggard whose commitment to the ideals of social justice and the welfare state is slowing down economic recovery in the Euro zone. Therefore, since Tony Blair's government has managed to add a social dimension to Margaret Thatcher's market radicalism, Britain has become an important source of inspiration for German reform policy makers. At the same time, Britain is also an important point of reference for all those who have remained skeptical about market-oriented reform agendas: Over the past two decades Britain has already undergone the process of radical structural adjustment that Germany, according to market liberals, still has to confront. It can therefore help to envisage and illustrate the empirical outcomes of the large-scale societal experiment that was referred to above.

Unsurprisingly, Tony Blair's reform agenda has triggered considerable uncertainty and anxiety in the British public. Indeed, the pursuit of economic growth and international competitiveness has at times triggered fierce resistance both within the Labour Party and in the general electorate. Just like the German government under Gerhard Schröder, Tony Blair, too, has been confronted with public anger about the perceived incompetence of a self-serving *political class* who refuse to listen to the electorate and consistently fail to provide convincing political visions. Indeed, both Britain and Germany have experienced a collapse of public confidence in the respective government's committedness to the social-democratic ideals of equality, solidarity and social justice. In both polities there is considerable skepticism about the suitability of strategies of privatization, flexibilization, and liberalization as key instruments for the provision of the common good. And in both countries the Social Democrats have, after an initial phase of public enthusiasm, been hit by major electoral setbacks, an exodus of party members, and severe strains on the relationship with traditional allies such as the trade unions (see chapters 2 and 10 of this volume). In Germany these tensions have culminated in the early elections of September 2005, in which Schröder's coalition with Alliance 90/The Greens was replaced by a Grand Coalition between the Christian Democrats and the Social Democrats under Chancellor Angela Merkel. In Britain, where general elections were held a few months earlier, Blair's Labour Party won a historical third term in office, but this was indicative not of widespread public support for his reform policies but of the fact that, as the *Economist* (30 April 2005) put it on the cover of its preelection issue, "there is no alternative": Since the ascendance to power of New Labour, the Conservative Party had seen a quick succession of party leaders, but had consistently failed to develop an attractive and convincing party profile.

Indeed, as table 1.1 shows, the results of the British elections in May 2005 and the German elections in September were surprisingly similar. In both countries the Social Democratic parties lost quite substantially in comparison with the previous elections, and in neither of them the main competitors, i.e., the Conservatives and the Christian Democrats, respectively, were able to translate these losses into significant electoral gains for themselves. In Germany, the Christian Democrats actually lost votes as well (3.3 percent), and in both countries the Liberal Democrats—in Germany also the postcommu-

Table 1.1.   General Elections in Britain and Germany 2001–2002 and 2005

	British general elections		German federal elections	
	2001	2005	2002	2005
Social Democratic	40.7%	35.3%	38.5%	34.3%
Conservative	31.7%	32.3%	38.5%	35.2%
Liberal	18.3%	22.1%	7.4%	9.8%
Left			4.0%	8.7%
Green			8.6%	8.1%
Other	9.3%	10.3%	3.0%	3.8%
turn out	59.3%	61.3%	79.1%	77.7%

nist left—benefited from widespread disaffection with the major parties. Despite these similarities, however, press reactions to these election results could not have been more different. After the German elections the British press unanimously reported that the country was now even more deeply in crisis than before. The Guardian diagnosed "Paralysis in Berlin" (19 September 2005: 26). The Financial Times reported of "Election deadlock in Germany" (19 September 2005: 1) and opined: "Pace of reform agenda set to slow" (ibid.: 7). And the Economist spoke of "Germany's nightmare" (24 September 2005: title page) and saw "A system in crisis, a country adrift" (ibid.: 45). On their annual party congress in Blackpool the week after, the British Liberal Democrats were sharply criticized for being in favor of replacing the British electoral system (First Past the Post) by a system of proportional representation which in Germany had just caused "post-election paralysis" (ibid.; see Lewis Baston's discussion in chapter 4).

Undeniably, the British elections a few months earlier had a much less ambiguous outcome, even though the Labour Party had obtained only marginally better results than its German counterpart (1 percent). Yet, the British elections triggered a debate of a very different kind: As only 61.3 percent of the British electorate had actually cast their vote, and only 35.3 percent of these had voted for the Labour Party, Tony Blair came out as the winner who had been backed by a mere 21.6 percent of the electorate. While the German elections raised the question whether it would be possible to form a stable government that was able to run the country in an efficient manner, the British elections raised the question to what extent Blair's ambitious reform agenda actually had democratic legitimacy (see chapter 4). Indeed, in the 2005 elections, the Labour Party did not gain a single new constituency but lost 47 of the ones it had held before. In terms of electoral turnout Britain is at the very bottom of the old EU-15, and considerably lower than most of the 2004 accession states. As regards the government's share of the votes, there is not a single country in the EU-24 where the government has as little electoral endorsement as in Britain. Despite all this, however, the British government can pursue its reform agenda in a way that prior to the German elections and in eager anticipation of an overwhelming *Bundestag* majority, Angela Merkel described as *durchregieren*: efficiently and effectively, without major opposition and compromise. Germany, in contrast, has a government that could quickly decay into infighting and instability, and that forces the major parties into consensus and compromise. But for all these disadvantages, it is a government that represents the overwhelming majority of the electorate and that is a fairly accurate reflection of the deep uncertainties and hesitations which are prevalent in the German electorate. The trade-off between efficiency and democracy could not have been illustrated in a more timely and appropriate manner. Given that—contrary to widely held beliefs—Germany's economy is today actually both competitive and profitable (witness its export figures), one might somewhat cynically say that Germany's primary problem, her "nightmare," "crisis," and "paralysis," is that the country is actually passionately democratic. Britain, in contrast, may have the potential to modernize more effectively and efficiently, but it is, as Lewis Baston discusses in more detail in chapter 4 of this volume, what Lord Hailsham once called an *elective dictatorship* (also see chapter 12).

Their respective national elections brought considerable continuity for both countries. Since May 2005 Tony Blair and his Labour Party have continued their agenda of market-oriented reforms, and it was not before the latter half of 2006 that the Conservatives' rebranding process under new party leader David Cameron turned the Tories once again into a serious competitor. In Germany, the new Grand Coalition of the Christian Democratic Parties (CDU/CSU) and the Social Democratic Party (SPD) sucessfully engineered an impressive swing in the public mood from general depression and pessimism towards a new forward-looking optimism, yet in the second quarter of 2006 the optimism quickly evaporated and the quality and pace of agreed reform policies remained far behind what market liberal reformers had been demanding for some time. Put positively, it seems that in the struggle with the Anglo-American model of individualism and competitiveness, the German tradition of social equality and integration may once again prevail. Put negatively, one might also say that the new government has—despite some obvious reform initiatives—prolonged the condition that is widely described as *reform gridlock (Reformstau)*. To provide a broader context for the analyses offered in the individual chapters throughout this book, this phenomenon of *Reformstau* as well as Britain's recent reform enthusiasm ought to be discussed in some further detail.

REFORMSTAU FOREVER? THE GERMAN MALAISE

It was a decade ago, in 1997, that the venerable *Gesellschaft für Deutsche Sprache* (Society for the German Language) voted *Reformstau* the word of the year. But at the time the issue was by no means new as an item at the very top of the political agenda, and in the present debate it still has not lost much of its topicality (e.g., Rothacher 2005)—even though at the beginning of 2006 opinion pollsters found signals of a more optimistic outlook (Infratest dimap 2006). Already in the mid-1970s, when Helmut Schmidt had succeeded Willy Brandt in the office of Federal Chancellor, Germany's progress-oriented mood of economic recovery and social reform began to metamorphose into a much more conservative mood of stability and protection. The German trademark of *incrementalism* became the expression of both a strong commitment to social and economic standards that had been achieved, and a fundamentally skeptical attitude towards the uncertainties and risks which are invariably implied in agendas of modernization and societal change. By the early 1980s, a period that was otherwise marked by concerns about nuclear apocalypse and ecological disaster, it had become generally accepted that what the Social Democrats had proudly called "model Germany" (*Modell Deutschland*) would, in a context of declining economic growth, not easily be sustainable. Indeed, the need of comprehensive reforms had become glaringly obvious. In 1982, in his first programmatic speech as Federal Chancellor of Germany, Helmut Kohl declared that his "new government had become necessary because the old one" had "proved unable to jointly combat unemployment, to safeguard the net of social security, and to sort out the devastating condition of public finances." Kohl emphasized that his new government "started its work in the most severe economic crisis since the foundation of the Federal Republic of Germany," but promised that his "coalition of the center" would "lead the country out of the crisis," which in his view was not simply an economic crisis, but a much more profound "cultural-cum-political crisis" that necessitated a "cultural-cum-moral turnaround" (*geistig-moralische Wende*) (Kohl 1982).

This announcement could be—and has been—understood as both a promise or threat. In the 1983 elections Kohl was confirmed in office because his rhetoric of a *geistig-moralische Wende* spread a sense of optimism and departure without suggesting any radical policy changes which might have jeopardized the achievements of the previous decades. Throughout the 1980s, then, the details and direction of Kohl's supposedly radical societal modernization remained obscure. Despite some social and economic reforms, the economic indicators, unemployment figures, labor productivity and the state of the social security systems continued to deteriorate (Dyson 1999: 226). Yet, historical coincidence provided Kohl, whose Conservative-Liberal government was at the time actually widely perceived as a spent force and due for replacement, with a new lease of life as "Chancellor of unification." After the cultural-cum-moral *Wende* (turnaround) which had never materialized, the Berlin *Wende* became the new source of societal optimism and the substitute for a comprehensive modernization agenda. In an adventure of devastating institutional conservatism, the exhausted *model Germany* was extended to five new federal states (Wiesenthal 2003). A brief spell of postunification economic recovery was followed by a long paralyzing debate about Germany as a location in an increasingly globalized economy (*Standort Deutschland*). But the country still remained unable to launch a comprehensive reform agenda.

In his famous Berlin *Ruckrede* speech of April 1997, then Federal President
Roman Herzog reprimanded the country and its government for its "lack of
courage" and for "revelling in crisis scenarios." He spoke of the "loss of economic dynamism" and the "ossification of German society." Herzog warned
that "a mood of paralysis" had "descended upon our society" and that the
dominant "triad in minor" of "anxiety, *Angst* and pessimism" was completely
inappropriate at a time when "economically and socially" the country was
"confronted with the largest challenges for 50 years" (Herzog 1997). In the
following year, sixteen years after the *Wende* in Bonn, many academic observers commented that "virtually all data" were "significantly worse than in
1982/3" (Wewer 1998: 23). In a way, the fact that Helmut Kohl had, in an era
when Thatcherism and Reaganomics had radically restructured Britain and
the United States, managed to sustain the *Modell Deutschland* for another sixteen years, and even extended it to the former GDR, may be regarded as an
impressive achievement. Yet for his successor this just implied that the task
was even more unmanageable. In 1998 it was for the first time ever that the
German electorate itself removed an incumbent government from office.

In the 1998 election campaign, Schröder had successfully presented himself as the long-awaited dynamic manager of radical societal change. His
electoral success, however, was not based on any clear-cut and calculable
agenda of reform but, on the contrary, on the strategic avoidance of just such
an agenda. Schröder professionally played on the paradoxical simultaneity of
a widespread desire for radical change and widespread concerns about possible cuts into established rights and patterns of welfare provision. From the
outset, he reassured the electorate that he had no intention of doing "everything differently" from his predecessors. He merely wanted to "do many
things better." Much to the dislike of many Social Democrats, Schröder
aimed to take inspiration from the way in which Tony Blair had reformed
British social democracy. Yet in contrast to Blair who had begun to reform his
own party well before he was elected into office, Schröder still had the task
of party reform ahead of himself. Even more importantly, exactly at the point
of time when the ideas of the traditional progressive left were elsewhere regarded as increasingly outmoded and detrimental to the project of societal reform, Schröder's party received a fresh injection of egalitarian leftist thinking
from both the Greens and his own then party chairman Oskar Lafontaine.
More easily than Schröder himself, his junior coalition partner, Bündnis
90/Die Grünen, identified and successfully occupied a dimension of societal
reform—ecological and social modernization—that was widely regarded
as necessary, thoroughly realistic and, above all, associated with the further
extension, rather than reduction, of social rights and the quality of life. The
unequal partners soon began to compete for the role as the "reform motor" in

the coalition government (Blühdorn 2004a). Yet, the effectiveness of this motor always remained subdued, and in general, the ecological-postmaterial project that the coalition started to implement in the late 1990s was at least a decade late and out of synch with the perceived priorities of the time (Egle et al. 2003).

As chapter 2 will demonstrate in more detail, the first Red-Green legislature was, despite all reform rhetoric, once again, marked by political continuity rather than change. A series of well-mediatized reform projects melted down to little more than PR exercises which did not contribute much to the required restructuring of Germany's economic, social, administrative, and political systems, but often generated considerable confusion. With none of its initiatives the Red-Green government managed to break the German reform gridlock. While a comprehensive vision and clear direction for the modernization process remained as absent from Red-Green politics as it had been from the Christian Democratic–Liberal coalition, the main political actors in Germany remained wedded to the established structures and procedures. A combination of exceptional circumstances secured its reelection in 2002 (Blühdorn 2004b), but immediately after the elections opinion poll ratings slumped even further than they had done after the elections in 1998. In March 2003, Schröder's *Agenda 2010* was supposed to finally initiate the groundbreaking reforms which the country had been awaiting for several decades, yet as will be discussed in some detail below (see chapters 2 and 9), the agenda immediately triggered fierce resistance from the trade unions and the SPD's traditional electoral clientele (also see chapters 6 and 10). Schröder not only had to confront the ritualized attacks of the opposition parties and the criticism of an infuriated public, but even within his own party there was considerable resistance both against his *Agenda 2010* and against his increasingly presidential style of government. On several occasions Schröder could secure his own governing majority only by threatening to resign if the party refused to lend him their undivided support. Yet when the early elections in September 2005 put an end to the Red-Green government, the diagnosis that Helmut Kohl had made in 1982, and that Herzog had reconfirmed in 1997, was *mutatis mutandis* as valid as it had been at the time.

Angela Merkel's new government was thus confronted with the task of having to address a problem that has built up over several decades. Whether she will finally manage to break Germany's long-lasting reform gridlock remains to be seen. In certain respects her Grand Coalition is undoubtedly in a better position than its predecessors. Perhaps most significantly, Merkel's government not only commands a comfortable majority in the *Bundestag*, but also has no strong opposition in the second chamber of parliament, the *Bundesrat*, which since the beginning of the 1990s had essentially been the chamber of the opposition and a major stumbling block for any significant reform policy. Nevertheless, the so-called *German disease* may still prove difficult to cure because it is triggered by a complex combination of *institutional causes* such as the federal structure, the electoral system (as discussed by Frank Decker in chapter 5) and strong interest group representation (as explored by Josef Schmid and Christian Steffen in chapter 10), and *cultural causes* such as Germany's consensus culture, the commitment to social equality and justice, or the deeply rooted appreciation of long-termism, stability, and security (see Elmar Wiesendahl's discussion in chapter 9). The attempt to address the structural mismatch that exists between Germany's institutionalized culture of continuity, consensus and caution, on the one side, and the contemporary imperatives of flexibility, innovativeness, and speed, on the other, is therefore a genuinely Herculean task. And this task is even further complicated by the general problems that, firstly, in differentiated and media-driven excitement democracies strategic coordination and political steering have become more difficult than ever before (see chapter 8 for a detailed discussion) and that, secondly, as Ingolfur Blühdorn argues in chapter 3 and Elmar Wiesendahl in chapter 9, convincing and attractive perspectives of modernization are generally short in supply. While progress and modernization once implied the promise of more opportunities, better provision and higher quality of life for all sectors of society, modernization in the contemporary sense invariably implies improvement only for some which tend to be achieved at the price of cuts and reductions for others.

"WE ARE THE CHANGE-MAKERS": HARD ROADS TO ANYWHERE?

At the time when Helmut Kohl delivered the policy speech that was quoted above, critical observers of British politics noted that Britain had "acquired so many strong organisations and collusions that it suffers from an institutional sclerosis that slows its adaptation to changing circumstances and technologies" (Olson 1982: 78). The country's employers' associations, trade unions, and political parties were regarded as no longer "capable of engaging in any dialogue about removing obstacles to economic growth," because "their very purpose was to maintain those obstacles in order to protect the *status quo* for their members" (ibid.). At the time, Britain was widely referred to as the *English patient*, yet in contrast to their German counterparts, British institutions and society have in the meantime been comprehensively reshaped. Having identified an over-inflated public sector, high taxation, and the irresponsible exercise of power by the trade unions as the prime causes of Britain's poor socioeconomic condition, the Thatcher government in the 1980s initiated a rigorous program of deregulation, privatization, tax cuts, and reduction of trade union power. Then after eighteen years of Tory government, and a year before his German counterpart, Tony Blair was voted into office. The way he stylized himself as a radical reformer of his own party and then British society at large set the example that Schröder later wanted to emulate. At least initially, Blair's *New Labour* was defined more strongly in terms of what it was against—*Old Labour* and Thatcherism—than what it was for. The talk of the compassionate society, the stakeholder society, the enabling state, social inclusion, and opportunity for all suggested that Blair was committed to the social democratic project and would, as he himself declared, "govern for the many, not for the few." Blair's missionary zeal and the notion of a *Third Way* (see chapter 2) between traditional social democratic statism and Thatcherite market liberalism renewed the promise of social justice and raised expectations for significant improvements in public provision and the quality of life. In a way that was at times reminiscent of socialist planned economies, Blair's government set performance targets for a whole range of policy areas. Left-wing critics had considerable doubts whether his *Third Way* was really more than a kind of neoliberalism in disguise (e.g., Hay 1999; Callinicos 2001; Lawson 2005), but public enthusiasm for Blair and the "new Britain" that he promised was, at least initially, overwhelming.

Indeed, the Blair government did manage to stabilize macroeconomic conditions and promote economic growth, even at a time when most other European economies were performing poorly. Its "welfare to work" policy reduced unemployment to the lowest level since the mid-1970s. The growth of the service industries facilitated the creation of new jobs in the postindustrial low-skill and low-wage sector, and additional investment in the education system, the National Health Service (NHS), and the Police Service allowed for the recruitment of new teachers, nurses, and police officers. Budgetary restraint at the beginning of New Labour's reign led to household surpluses and a reduction in public debt. Furthermore, the introduction of a minimum wage, various family tax credits, and additional allowances for pensioners improved the situation of the poorest sectors of British society. Thus, Blair's modernization policies remedied a range of unacceptable social side effects of Thatcher's market radicalism, but in some respects Blair's government also continued rather than reversed the politics of its Conservative predecessors. Many observers noticed a "dramatic convergence towards the policy positions of the Conservatives in every economic and social arena" (Panitch and Leys 1997: 250). In fact, the new government embraced central features of Tory politics to such an extent that the oppositional Conservatives were plunged into an identity crisis from which they have not fully recovered since. It is, therefore, perhaps not surprising that many social democratic hopes and expectations remained unfulfilled.

In the press, Blairite politics quickly acquired a reputation of empty managerialism, control freakery, and dependence on political spin. Blair was criticized for betraying long-established Labour values and parts of the electorate soon felt that the government was losing touch with its own voters, that it refused to listen—or at least did not hear. In 2001 the Blair government was reelected by only 24.1 percent of the British electorate and in 2005 the figure was, as quoted above, even lower than this. At the beginning of his third term in office, Blair still presented himself as the "change maker" (Blair 2005), and believed that continental European economies such as France and Germany should urgently follow the British example. As he had been doing throughout his premiership, he was urging his party, his country, and indeed Europe at large "to go faster and further" on his reform trajectory (Blair 2003), and he continues to believe that, as he had phrased it in 2002, "we are at our best when at our boldest" (Blair 2002). There is still a lot of talk of "tough decisions" and "hard roads" which Labour will have to take. Yet, after nine years in government, it has not become much clearer where the accelerated pace of modernization is supposed to take the country, or how Blair's reform agenda is supposed to fulfill the promises of security, social justice, solidarity, and opportunity for all. Indeed, many of the government's performance targets had to be tacitly withdrawn. Incrementally, ever new announcements of radical restructuring and "biggest ever shake-ups" took the place of a goal-oriented and coordinated process of modernization. Change and innovation gradually seemed to turn into an end in themselves. And while the private sector is obtaining an ever larger role in the delivery of public goods, and the principles of the market are reshaping policy areas such as health and education, Britain is consolidating a system that provides excellence for prosperous elites, and rather basic security for major sectors at the bottom of the social pyramid.

Blair has announced that he will step down as Prime Minister some time in 2007. Despite undeniable achievements, the backlog of unresolved problems which he will leave for his likely successor, Gordon Brown, remains long. Even the favorable combination of comparatively low wage levels, a highly flexibilized labor market, diminishing costs of borrowing, a buoyant property market, and sustained consumer spending well beyond the consumers' actual means, has not generated economic growth rates of the kind that one might have expected. Indeed, recently there have been increasing concerns about the future stability of Britain's economy. The manufacturing sector, in particular, has been ailing for a long time and does not show any signs of a future recovery. The lack of proper apprenticeships and the educational focus on soft and transferable skills has given rise to the so-called "skills gap," i.e., a major shortage of well trained and qualified workers. High job mobility and flexibility further contribute to the process of de-skilling. With almost a third of each cohort leaving full time education and training at the age of sixteen, Britain does not compare favorably to many of its continental European partners. Sustained underfunding has undermined the quality of the school and university system. Similarly, the National Insurance system is, despite low unemployment figures and thus a high number of contributors, not able to provide a satisfactory level of security for all British citizens. Despite additional investment into the health system, the quality of health provision has not improved to the expected level and several NHS trusts are experiencing serious debt crises, forcing them to lay off hundreds of staff. Furthermore, following the closure of numerous final salary pension schemes, Britain is confronted with a severe pensions crisis that, according to Lord Turner's Pensions Commission (2005), can be remedied only by a combination of incrementally raising the pension age to at least 68, increasing the state pension (in 2005–2006 £82.05 per week), and introducing a new government-administered semicompulsory savings scheme.

Other areas of widespread concern include the public transport system, spiraling local taxes raised by underfunded city councils, and the mounting problems of private debt. High levels of crime and antisocial behavior, an unrivalled density of CCTV surveillance in public spaces, and the strict social segregation of residential areas indicate a decline of social cohesion. Blair's fiscal and social policy has improved the situation of the poorest sections of British society, but rather than reducing the level of overall social inequality, they have merely increased the number of those living just above the nationally accepted minimum for income, benefits, and care. Indeed, a 2003 IDS report noted that in the period since 1990, the "strongest rise" in income inequality in Britain "has been in the years since 1997" (IDS 2003). As earnings in the upper quartile have increased at a much faster pace than in the bottom quartile, about "two-thirds of full-time employees now receive less than the average gross weekly earnings" (ibid.). Thus, in comparison to his German counterpart, Tony Blair is undoubtedly a strong agenda setter, but his market-oriented reform policies have not had the expected effect. In the spring of 2006, the Economist suggested that "if Britain's Prime Minister is not thinking of stepping down, he should be" and judged that his "main achievement has been to consolidate the promarket reforms begun by Margaret Thatcher" and "to extend them into health and education" (The Economist, 18 March). If Schröder was accused of having developed a presidential style of government, Blair's style of leadership that has marginalized Parliament and imposed very specific views about what is best for the people can be categorized as "command premiership" (Hennessy 1999: 1; also Heffernan and Webb 2005). Unsurprisingly, this has undermined public trust in the government and confidence in its ability to achieve social justice, solidarity, and cohesion.

From the British perspective, the talk of a German *malaise* can, therefore, only be taken with a pinch of salt. Despite unification and several decades of paralyzing debate about the unattractiveness of Germany as an economic location and about the country's inability to move beyond its reform gridlock, Germans still enjoy a high quality of life, public services which in comparison to the UK are better resourced, and levels of security and welfare provision which are still enviable. While living expenses are lower in Germany than in the UK, the average household income is higher. At the same time Germans work shorter hours than their British counterparts. The personal allowance for tax-free annual earnings is higher in Germany than Britain, and employees still enjoy a high level of legal protection and job security. Even after the introduction of the controversial Hartz reforms (see chapters 2, 6 and 9), unemployment benefits in Germany remain more generous than the Jobseekers Allowance in the UK, and despite the ongoing debate about Germany's unsustainable pensions system, German pensioners are still well off. Thus, at least for the moment, Germany's much-lamented reform gridlock still provides a quality of life that is on average higher than what Britain has achieved through its program of hyper-innovation.

CROSS-NATIONAL POLICY LEARNING?

So, this book looks back onto Gerhard Schröder's chancellorship in Germany and—although Blair has not yet stepped down—on Tony Blair's premiership in Britain. One of the questions which invariably arise is what lessons there are to be learned with regard to the modernization goals of efficiency and democracy. Even a cursory view at the British experience reveals that the UK, too, is confronted with fundamental problems of modernization. There is no reform gridlock in the German sense, but the modernization process and the related policy programs are no less contested than in Germany. The structural adjustment program that has, by means of privatization, deregulation, flexibilization, tax reduction, welfare retrenchment, wage restriction, welfare to work policies, and so forth, reconfigured British society, has secured a measure of economic growth, reduced unemployment, and generated favorable conditions for the socially better-off. However, not only have the hopes for security, stability, and equality remained unfulfilled, but Britain is far from having achieved a condition of social, economic, political, and environmental sustainability. The British model has secured economic growth and efficiency gains by dismantling public provision and pushing a significant proportion of the labor force into highly flexible and disposable low-wage and often low-skill jobs. Neither the state nor the economy are providing the investment that is required to regenerate the public infrastructure and the social resources on which the economy relies (education, health, cohesion, etc.). Private provision and self-responsibility are supposed to replace this investment, yet not all sections of society have the means to make provision for themselves; and as a matter of principle, their investment into their private good can never compensate for public noninvestment into the public good.

The comparative perspective, therefore, sheds doubt on suggestions that Germany should pursue a structural adjustment program similar to that of the UK. It would of course be absurd to suggest that Germany should, or even could, avoid a major restructuring of its welfare system and labor market. But Germany would be well advised if it were to engage in a broader discussion about the meaning of *efficiency*. The modernization policies which have been implemented in Britain in pursuit of this goal have not had the promised effect, or at least they have promoted efficiency in a very reductionist sense. In particular, they have not secured social and economic sustainability. Having gone through even more radical changes than those which are currently being debated in Germany, the British public is still confronted with essentially the same demands for further flexibilization and efficiency gains that are causing so much anxiety in the German public. This suggests that Germany is not simply facing a one-off effort of radical restructuring which may take a decade but will eventually give rise to a new condition of stability, or even a new economic miracle providing the basis for more welfare for all. Instead, the British example seems to indicate that even after a radical structural adjustment program the pressure for further reforms will still persist.

Furthermore, comparison with the UK suggests that Germany's modernization problems do not simply originate from overly democratic structures and procedures. Undoubtedly, the political system in Germany provides favorable conditions in which political entrepreneurs can cultivate public controversies, mobilize political protest, and obstruct efforts for societal modernization. However, the less participatory British system does not necessarily compare favorably. Of course, it offers fewer veto points, and there are fewer veto players. Also, despite recent policies of devolution, British politics is much more centralized than in Germany. The party system is less fragmented and the electoral system does not give rise to coalition governments. Furthermore, the Westminster system generally favors executive control and *responsible* rather than *representative* government, and the British public is used to an *announce and implement* style of politics which the German electorate would regard as unacceptably undemocratic. Theoretically, all this should have provided the British government with exceptionally favorable conditions for the efficient implementation of a reform agenda for both economic efficiency and social justice, equality, and solidarity. In practice, however, a modern and sustainable society that provides security, stability, and an appropriate quality of life to all its citizens has not been achieved. Instead, social imbalances have increased. This sheds doubts on any suggestions to improve the efficiency of the German system by reviewing its structures of democratic participation and control.

THE STRUCTURE OF THIS BOOK

This introduction has touched upon a wide range of issues which deserve to be analyzed in much more detail. This is the task of the chapters throughout this book, and to some extent the thematic emphasis of the individual contributions has already been indicated. Each of the chapters may be read as a self-standing entity, i.e., each of them pursues its own analysis and argument. But beyond this, they also all contribute to a joint agenda which is to explore the tensions between the objectives of economic efficiency and democratic renewal as the two main dimensions of the project of societal modernization. The next two chapters are devoted to broadening the context that has been sketched so far, and to providing some conceptual tools for the analysis of the democracy-efficiency relationship. First Uwe Jun outlines, analyzes and compares the reform policies of the Blair- and Schröder-Administrations (chapter 2). Then Ingolfur Blühdorn shifts the focus to the conceptual level and investigates the changing meaning and implications of, as well as the tensions between, the three major players in the modernization debate: *democracy, efficiency,* and *futurity* (chapter 3). In the contemporary era, he argues, the traditional emancipatory concept of modernization is giving way to an entirely new notion of modernization that centers on systemic imperatives.

The following set of chapters then focuses on the structural frameworks within which, and strategic approaches through which, the social democratic governments under Blair and Schröder have sought to pursue their respective modernization projects. In chapter 4 Lewis Baston discusses the constitutional reforms which were implemented in the early stages of the Blair government and highlights the importance of electoral reform as a means of reengaging the disenchanted British electorate. Chapter 5 describes the institutional settings in Germany and investigates the main reasons for Germany's reform gridlock. Rejecting calls for a more centralized and less participatory system, Frank Decker suggests that developing more elements of direct democracy could actually be a more promising path towards an efficient and more democratic German political system. Chapter 6 centers on the noticeable shift of emphasis in German politics from tripartite corporatist consensus politics to the politics of expert commissions. Taking Chancellor

Schröder's *Alliance for Jobs* as a case study, Sven Jochem investigates to what extent this shift may be interpreted as a reduction of democratic qualities in the name of more efficient policy making. He concludes that the transition from tripartite concertation to the politics of commissions has reduced the legitimacy but by no means increased the efficiency of reform politics. In chapter 7 Matthew Flinders focuses on Tony Blair's favorite tools of policy reform, the *private finance initiative* (PFI) and *public interest companies* (PICs), and uses these examples to critically examine common assumptions regarding trade-offs and conceptual tensions between democracy and efficiency. The last chapter in that section of the book then turns to the growing importance of a coherent communication strategy for the efficient implementation of reform policies. Comparing Tony Blair's complex public-relations machine with Gerhard Schröder's much less successful communications strategy, Uwe Jun demonstrates that in "media democracies" professionalized campaigns and communication efforts that bridge the gap between policy makers and the citizenry have a significant impact not only on the public perception of government policies but also on the content of reform agendas.

The third set of contributions explores the role of major actors which help to shape the project of societal modernization. Elmar Wiesendahl starts off by investigating how external structures of opportunity and limited inner-party capabilities for action restrict the capacity of Germany's political parties to play a leading role in the modernization process (chapter 9). He concludes that, in its current shape, German party democracy is neither efficient nor sufficiently open to make sure that the agendas of societal modernization accommodate and reflect the legitimate concerns for all social groups. In chapter 10 Christian Steffen and Josef Schmid argue that Germany's trade unions, although they are still much more influential than their British counterparts, have in the last decade lost much of their political power. The chapter describes the strategic options available to the unions as well as the strategic dilemmas which lead to a comprehensive transformation of the role that trade unions have traditionally played in German politics. Chapter 11 then turns to social movements and protest networks as increasingly important political actors in both Britain's and Germany's reform debates. Ian Welsh focuses on biotechnology in the widest sense, and the mapping of the human genome more specifically, as a key area of science-driven innovation and modernization. He argues that the ways in which civil society networks contribute to the social negotiation of such contested issues may appear protracted and *inefficient* in the short term but that, given the centrality of the consumer in neoliberal market societies, policy makers are well advised to pay closer attention to the concerns they voice. In the concluding chapter, finally, Ingolfur Blühdorn suggests that in the contemporary era of globalization, societies such as Britain and Germany are not just involved in a process of modernizing their economic structures and social systems, but that they are experiencing a fundamental transformation of their democratic politics. What he conceptualizes as *the post-democratic revolution* and the transition to *simulative democracy* may point towards a new synthesis of democracy and efficiency.

REFERENCES

Blair, Tony (2002): "At our best when at our boldest." Speech to the Labour Party Conference. Blackpool, 1 October 2002.

—— (2003): "I want us to go faster and further." Speech to the Labour Party conference. Bournemouth, 30 September 2003.

—— (2005): "We are the Change-Makers." Speech to the Labour Party Conference. Brighton, 27 September 2005.

Blühdorn, Ingolfur (2004a): "New Green Pragmatism in Germany. Green Politics beyond the Social Democratic Embrace." *Government and Opposition* 39, no. 4: 564–86.

—— (2004b): "Red-Green and Beyond. The German Green Party after the 2002 Elections," in: Winnett, Adrian, ed.: *Towards an Environment Research Agenda. Volume III*. Houndmills/New York: Palgrave Macmillan, pp. 149–71.

Borchert, Jens (1995): *Die konservative Transformation des Wohlfahrtsstaates. Großbritannien, Kanada, die USA und Deutschland im Vergleich*. Frankfurt/Main/New York: Campus.

Callinicos, Alex (2001): *Against the Third Way*. Cambridge: Polity

Dyson, Kenneth (1999) "German Economic Policy after Fifty Years," in: Merkl, Peter H., ed.: *The Federal Republic of Germany at Fifty. The End of a Century of Turmoil*. New York: New York University Press, pp. 219–30.

Egle, Christoph, Ostheim, Tobias, and Zohlnhöfer, Reimut, eds. (2003): *Das Rot-Grüne Projekt. Eine Bilanz der Regierung Schröder 1998–2002*. Wiesbaden: Westdeutscher Verlag.

Hay, Colin (1999): *The Political Economy of New Labour. Labouring under False Pretences?* Manchester: Manchester University Press.

Heffernan, Richard and Webb, Paul (2005): "The British Prime Minister: Much more than 'First Among Equals,'" in: Poguntke, Thomas and Webb, Paul, eds.: *The Presidentialization of Politics, A Comparative Study of Modern Democracies*. Oxford/New York: Oxford University Press, pp. 26–62.

Hennessy, Peter (1999): *The Blair Centre, A Question of Command and Control*. London: Public Management Foundation.

Herzog, Roman (1997): "Aufbruch ins 21. Jahrhundert." Speech delivered in the Adlon Hotel in Berlin on 26 April 1997, Bundespressearchiv.

IDS (Incomes Data Services). Report 874. February 2003.

Infratest dimap (2006): "ARD DeutschlandTREND März 2006." http://www.infratest-dimap.de/print.asp (accessed 17 March 2006).

Kitschelt, Herbert, and Streeck, Wolfgang (2003): "From Stability to Stagnation: Germany at the Beginning of the Twenty-First Century." *West-European Politics 26*, no.4: 1–34.

Kohl, Helmut (1982): "Regierungserklärung vom 13. 10. 1982." *Verhandlungen des Deutschen Bundestages.* 9. Wahlperiode, Stenographische Berichte, Vol. 122, 7213–29.

Lawson, Neal (2005): "What can the European Left Learn from New Labour?" *Social Europe, The Journal of the European Left* 1, no. 3: 82–85.

Moran, Michael (2003): *The British Regulatory State. High Modernism and Hyper-Innovation.* Oxford/New York: Oxford University Press.

Olson, Mancur (1982): *The Rise and Decline of Nations.* New Haven: Princeton Universiy Press.

Panitch, Leo, and Leys, Colin (1997): *The End of Parliamentary Socialism. From New Left to New Labour,* London/New York: Verso.

Pensions Commission (2005): *A New Pension Settlement for the Twenty-first Century. The Second Report of the Pensions Commission*, http://www.pensionscommission .org.uk.

Roller, Edeltraud (2005): *The Performance of Democracies. Political Institutions and Public Policy.* Oxford/New York: Oxford University Press.

Rothacher, Albrecht (2005): "Crisis or Cure: No Hope for Germany?" *European Political Science Review* 4, no. 4: 464–75.

Wewer, Göttrik, ed. (1998): *Bilanz der Ära Kohl.* Opladen: Leske+Budrich.

Wiesenthal, Helmut (2003): "German Unification and 'Model Germany': An Adventure in Institutional Conservatism." *West European Politics* 26, no. 4: 37–58.

CONTEXTS AND CONCEPTS

2

Radical Reformers—Defiant Electorates?
Reform Policy and International Competitiveness
under Schröder and Blair

Uwe Jun

In party democracies such as Great Britain or Germany reforms are the means by which political parties are able to realize their objectives. "Policy-seeking parties" in particular try to use reforms to translate their political vision into societal reality; they try to use generally binding decisions to implement political measures. In general terms political reforms can be seen as attempts to change existing structures and to modify policy or political objectives. The agents of reform are political actors—in parliamentary democracies primarily political parties and governments. Hence, this chapter takes a closer look at parties in government, especially the major political parties, in their capacity as initiators of, and participants in, political reform processes. In Germany and Britain political parties may actually be described as three different, though interlinked, actors which are involved in the reform process:

- Party members with a portfolio in government, i.e., essentially cabinet members,
- the relevant majority party in parliament which acts in tandem with the government,
- the party, as affiliation-based membership organization, which has a minimum level of influence on the political decision-making process.

Within governing parties these three actors, which are only rarely functioning in perfect harmony, enjoy differing degrees of influence on reform processes, which depend on a variety of factors including power structures within the party, an individual's perception of his or her area of competence, and competition between politicians. Since each actor is a potential source of resistance, successful reforms require a minimum of consensus between the three. In order to achieve the best possible integration of actors and improve a party's chances of asserting itself in the reform process it would appear sensible to create a *strategic center* where all three actors can express themselves and be directly involved in decision making. In the present context, a *strategic center* is understood as an informal network of three to five people in positions of leadership and specially placed to determine the strategy of a party (Raschke 2002: 218). By forming a strategic center the major organized parties, in their incarnations as loosely coupled anarchies, attempt to integrate the different dimensions of the organization as a whole and give it orientation beyond day-to-day tactics so that it may react quickly and as coherently as possible to the ever more complex demands created by the evolution of the media and societal change in general.[1] Since a strategic center can only function as such if it has the necessary decision-making competences, it should neatly dovetail with the official leadership of the party, their informal aides and the strategic apparatus. In the planning and negotiation of reforms it acts as a coordination center for both content and application, that is, it is equally responsible for both the planning and realization of reforms and the marshalling of support for the program. Planning and implementing reform packages has to be seen in the light of the increasingly professional communication systems available to political parties, and the strategies and instruments that they use in their attempts to generate public awareness. This is because political success in media democracies[2] depends on the parties' ability to communicate. Given the reduced significance of traditional interpretation patterns and political orientations, the importance of any political activity covered by the media rises sharply and influences in its turn the form and content of further activity. For political parties this means not only that they are under double pressure to be both media-competent and credible on issues, but these two factors should also be working in concert if electioneering is to be effective. Reforms are only successful if they integrate the complex interdependency of governance, public opinion, and the strategic ability of the government and the governing parties, and if the latter are, furthermore, perceived as trustworthy in the eyes of the electorate (cf.Mangels-Voegt 2003: 33).

This chapter concentrates on reforms in economic and social policy, because these two policy areas are at the heart of any social democratic government. They form the basis for the improvement of social and economic life along with the emancipation of underprivileged social groups, for the argument of solidarity concerning social living conditions, and for the equality of opportunities in life, as well as the protection of political rights. Through their social and welfare state policy, social democratic parties set themselves apart from their competitors in the party systems of liberal democracies, but these policies also had a formative influence on the way they saw themselves and their identity in the past. Minimizing the costs of capitalism for the individual and attempting to reduce inequalities in power and affluence can be seen as the core of social democratic policy along with keeping the liberal state under the rule of law. Their fundamental political values and their perception of specific social interests are centrally expressed in the areas of social and economic policy and the welfare state. The responsibility for the control of the economy by society as a whole can be perceived as one major criterion that distinguishes the social democratic approach from conservative and liberal parties. This outstanding significance of the welfare state and economic-political mechanism of redistribution will be taken into account in this chapter. At the same time, it will be pointed out what forms of interaction there were between the aforementioned actors in the reform process of the Labour Party and the SPD-led federal government until the year 2005. It is essential to analyze how successful the respective party's strategic centers were in generating acceptance and overcoming resistance. Particular attention will be devoted to those actors who took a critical stance towards the reform process, which consisted largely of "top-down" reforms.

THE *THIRD WAY* AS A FRAMEWORK FOR NEW LABOUR'S REFORMS IN THE FIRST TERM

The Labour Party's reform process dates back to the second half of the 1980s, when Neil Kinnock had taken over the leadership and the party organization seemed to have been consolidated. Analysis of the new direction under Kinnock reveals that from 1987 onwards great efforts were made to modernize in reaction to the policy of the Conservative government under Margaret Thatcher and the changed conditions associated with globalization, economic competition, supranational structures of governance, altered social structures, and greater cultural diversity. As such the changes in the Labour Party program should be regarded first and foremost as the party's response to the Conservative four consecutive victories in the parliamentary elections from 1979 until 1992 and to the history of internal, external, and political changes in Britain during the period of the Conservative government: "What made it possible finally to transcend Labour's old identity and politics was the success of Margaret Thatcher" (Coronin 2004: 31). These political changes led to the review of Labour principles, concluded in 1990, the so-called "Policy Review." This comprehensive review of the party's program resulted in "the adoption of a 'post-revisionist' social democracy" (Shaw 1994: XIV; cf. Shaw 1994: 81ff.),[3] a social democracy that moves away from traditional Croslandite social democracy and accepts the principles of a market economy, a restrictive fiscal and finance policy and a partial renunciation by the state of macroeconomic control alongside its retention of the principles of social justice.

The altered stance of the Labour Party is the product of a number of different reform papers drafted by the party and was to a large degree inspired by Anthony Giddens' (1998, 2002) ideas regarding a *Third Way* (see Leggett 2004; Jun 2004a: 213–22; Surender 2004; Meyer 2005: 501ff). Based on the recognition that economic as well as cultural globalization, radical changes in the job market and the more fragmented society have substantially altered the starting point for any political strategy, the *Third Way* is a concept for the renewal of Social Democracy. Common to the drafts is the fundamental acceptance of market economy principles and private ownership and a commensurate and rigorous renunciation of state ownership of property and state control over the economy—a so-called *enabling state* oriented towards stability and having considerably reduced competencies. This direction was taken further under Blair's leadership and found symbolic expression in the revision of Clause Four of the party's constitution, whereby Labour ended its policy of nationalization. The *enabling state*, also referred to as the *infrastructure state* or *social investment state* (see Lister 2004), is now to intervene only in cases where market processes have broken down, and to exert influence only in isolated areas where the laws of the marketplace are unable to offer an efficient solution. These latter areas include education and training, science and technology, research and development, health, social services and social security, the environment, and transport. In all other cases the idea was to establish or improve Britain's infrastructure in a way for companies to become competitive in the international marketplace, and for a high level of employment to be attained or safeguarded. In Tony Blair's words "a framework that allows market forces to work properly is essential to economic success" (quoted by Wickham-Jones 2003: 37). By means of a transparent financial and tax policy and a supply-oriented economic policy the state was to create conditions favorable to investment, productivity, and competition. The state did not attempt to intervene further. The significance of the state as an economic and political actor with considerable powers of control has been reduced.[4] Keynesian instruments for influencing demand had long ceased to play a significant role in the economic ideals of the Labour Party.[5] New Labour's programmatic changes can be seen as a "principled response to a global economy and a fragmented society" (Seyd and Whiteley 2004: 48–49).

Government policy is anchored in the acknowledgement that individual fortune is unequally allocated. It is the task of the state to even out this uneven distribution as far as possible. In the marketplace, individuals are meant to improve their social situation and play their part in making the economy more efficient. It is also incumbent upon the state to create the best possible conditions for economic endeavor and raise the employability of the individual.[6] All individuals are to be helped to a position from which to get a start in the labor market, whereby education and training opportunities are particularly important in bringing this about. Education and training are the crucial instruments by which people's employability is raised and equality of opportunity in the job market created.[7] The emphasis on welfare reforms was geared towards shifting people from benefits into work.

The formula is as follows: More education/training = greater employability = a higher degree of equal opportunity (see Stephens 2001: 196).

The key principles are equality of opportunity and fairness of outcome (Beech 2004: 90). Levels of taxation should be appropriately low; people working for the community should receive incentives; New Labour's policy should raise people to a sufficient level of income and services. As citizens they have certain political, social, economic, and legal rights, but they also have to accept responsibilities (ibid.: 95). First and foremost it is the responsibility to enter the labor market and to engage in paid employment (Lewis 2004: 212). People refusing to contribute to the community and wishing only to receive state benefits without showing a readiness to take up employment must expect disadvantages. Abuse of the social benefit system is to be heavily penalized: "Tackling fraud is a priority issue of the New Labour reform of welfare" (Annesley 2001: 215). A community ethos, social justice, and economic efficiency are closely intertwined and are seen as the ideological triumvirate in the policy of New Labour. There are distinct echoes of the idea of a communitarian society and the policy of former American President Clinton, concepts that form a central pillar of New Labour's policy.[8] But Labour's reform policy still aims to reduce inequalities by giving priority to the worst off within British society through the concept of social inclusion: "Making low-paid work more attractive" (Driver 2004: 31) and promoting the commitment to education, skills, and opportunity are the key to social inclusion and to a redistribution of opportunities throughout society (cf. Adelmann and Cebulla 2003). By the introduction of minimum incomes, welfare to work programs, wage subsidies for low incomes, the introduction of job centers, targeted tax credits such as the Working Families Tax Credit or the Integrated Child Credit, education and training opportunities, and educational allowances, New Labour is reducing poverty and pursuing more equality of opportunity. But with regard to divergent market results, the party's leadership is willing to "increase incentives and to reduce welfare dependency" (Hickson 2004: 131). Social justice was concerned with directing benefits only to those in greatest need. In-work benefits and enhanced access to child care within a national child care strategy should address the problems of low pay and child poverty in the tax and benefit system (see Lister 2004).

THE REFORM OF THE PUBLIC SECTOR: A KEY OBJECTIVE FOR *NEW LABOUR'S* SECOND AND THIRD TERM IN GOVERNMENT

As mentioned above, New Labour's *Third Way* considers access to education and training to be the most important tool with which to establish equal opportunity. Public and private investment in training and opportunities for life-long learning are designed to help obtain qualifications for the labor market and improve people's chances (see more in detail Ainley 1999). Underpinning this is the conviction that education improves an individual's chances in the labor market and thereby helps to reduce social injustice. Lifelong learning is designed to give individuals the skills necessary to compete successfully in the labor market. This policy stems from the recognition that rapid technological transformation of the marketplace has imposed a high degree of flexibility on the individual and made it essential to adapt one's knowledge and skills to the ever-changing conditions. In highly industrialized economies, in particular, high priority is given to education and training as a means for self-determination of life in a global economy. At the same time, the individual's chances to self-fulfillment in life are improved. The Blair government has made this connection and considers education and training to be components of both economic and social policy. They have come to symbolize the convergence of both areas of policy in the Labour government: On the one hand, they serve as a means for improving and allocating individual opportunities, with the state guaranteeing to provide this for each person. The potential of individuals is to be promoted and allowed to flourish to the extent that they can gain access to the job market in a globalized economy offering adequate professional prospects.[9] This so-called "human capital strategy" (Driver 2004: 32) is an attempt to redistribute market outcomes by enhancing the tradable skills of less qualified individuals and improving their position in the labor market.

On the other hand, education and training are supposed to supply the British economy with a sufficiently qualified labor force as it competes with other economies. In 2005, the industrial association CBI still complained that the standard of apprenticeship in Britain would not be adequate in international comparison, which would manifest itself in decreasing productivity (FAZ, 30 September 2005).

The high priority given to education in the Labour Party program is reflected in the marked increase in expenditure in the education sector (see Blair 1997). There was also a significant increase in expenditure on health and public transport over the same period, but in these two areas, Britain had to catch up with the West European average, while in the area of education it had already been well positioned. From 2000 onwards, following its first two years in office after 1997, during which the Labour government had kept all its election promises and had adapted the Conservatives' budget proposals for its own purposes, a change of policy meant that more money was devoted to the public sector while simultaneously preserving financial stability (see tables 2.1 and 2.2).[10] In its second term Blair's government was striving to revitalize and strengthen the public sector without actually dismantling the state administrative bureaucracy.[11] These reforms can be understood as a reaction to the shift in public mood which by now is not against higher taxation if the government supports public sector investment, especially for the NHS, the railways and schools (Norris 2001: 20).

At the forefront of reforms in the public sector are not the interests of the suppliers of public services but the interests of the consumers of these services. The new design of the public sector is also set to be geared to the individual: consumers are to be given quantitatively and qualitatively more choice and the opportunity to compare merchandise to national norms. Meanwhile the suppliers are to become more flexible and more open to innovation (Wickham-Jones 2003). Considerably more funds were earmarked for areas in which heavy losses had been made and which had largely been neglected in the Thatcher era, such as health, education, public transport (especially the railway system), and regional development—here primarily to improve the infrastructure of problem zones in the north of England. For each of these sectors in the budgetary periods from 2001 to 2004 Gordon Brown allocated net annual funding increases in excess of six percent. These three years saw an

Table 2.1.   General Government Primary Balance in Germany and Britain 2001–2004

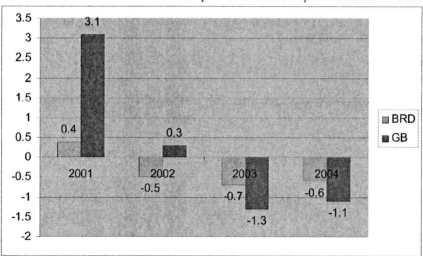

Table 2.2.   General Government Gross Debt in Germany and Britain 2001–2004

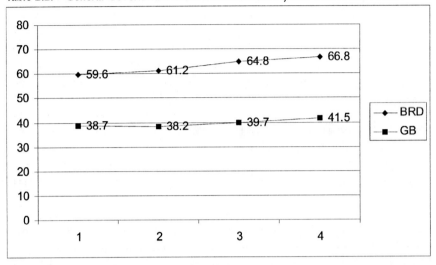

extra 71 billion pounds in total going to the funding of the reform of the public sector and especially the health and education sectors. Since 2002 the Labour government has increased its expenditure on the National Health Service from 96.8 billion Euros a year to 156.5 billion Euros in the year 2007. Offsetting this was the 1 percent increase in social insurance contributions for both employers and employees from 2003 onwards. Chancellor Brown was planning for the share of GDP, accounted for by public expenditure, to rise from 39.8 percent in 2002–2003 to 41.8 percent in 2005–2006. For example, in 2001 Gordon Brown announced a 40 percent rise in health expenditure (inflation adjusted) to hire thousands of nurses and doctors and to construct forty new hospitals.

Also, the Labour government promised in its White Paper on *The Future of Higher Education*, published in 2003, to widen access for students from poorer sections of society and to increase the overall proportion of young people experiencing higher education from 40 percent in 2003 to 50 percent within a few years. For that reason universities got the permission to charge students fees up to £3000 a year compared to previous £1000, but under the condition also to increase bursaries for students from poorer backgrounds.

In setting these targets Blair and Brown are not only relying more strongly on the national purse in the light of improvements in the economy's fortunes but also on so-called *Public-Private Partnerships* (PPP), and the favorite among them—*Private Finance Initiatives* (PFI),[12] a policy which was launched in Britain by the Conservatives after their victory in the general elections in 1992, and which was supposed to increase the investment of private capital to public schemes (also see chapter 7 in this volume). But Labour, which extended the role of PPPs in renewing and improving infrastructure, wants to establish these partnerships to overcome "the fragmentation produced by neo-liberal reforms [. . .] in which they draw on both public and private sector approaches. They thus apparently transcend the dualism of 'market vs. hierarchy' (Newman 2004: 71). Through market and contracted mechanisms coupled with decentralization and devolution of services, Labour wants to dismantle state hierarchies (ibid.: 74) and establish innovative instruments of governance. One result of this policy is that the boundaries between market and state have become considerably blurred, in particular with the idea of Public Interest Companies (see more in detail Prabhakar 2004), which in contrast to private companies are not permitted to make profit or to grant dividend payments.[13] Contrary to the Conservatives, who preferred only privatization and competition, the Labour government set up an ownership agenda beyond private or state ownership and counted on local forms of public ownership, for example with foundation hospitals (for more detail see Matthew Flinders' chapter) or new types of school administration in cooperation with private firms. Blair's personal advisor and former health secretary Alan Milburn sees PPP programs "as a new model of social ownership in British politics" (cited in Prabhakar 2004: 365). The PPPs with the most important consequences are the Independent Sector Treatment Centers (ISTC) which are private organizations treating patients from the NHS or private patients on a contractual basis with health authorities and primary care trusts for specific services to reduce the waiting lists of the NHS.

PFIs are playing a key role in the partnership idea of delivering services in a more efficient way to solve problems that require long-term investment and bring more economic efficiency into the public services, with the objective not to attack but to invigorate public services. The idea behind them is relatively simple (see also Shaw 2004: 64–67): *Private Finance Initiatives* refer to the financing of public services or buildings by private companies which then rent the premises to the state on often long-term leases, e.g., in the case of hospital or school construction, road construction, and other infra-structural projects. The private sector does not only carry the cost of the construction project including the risk of running out of budget, but is also responsible for the administration and fitting of the building. Moreover, in individual cases private service providers are sometimes able to complement public services in public institutions or even partially replace them as the ISTCs are doing. This is designed to cast a spotlight on competition structures and criteria for measuring efficiency, including performance in public service. This entails the privatization of parts of the public sector. The aim is to increase investment in public infrastructure that would not otherwise have been possible, to improve the quality of public services and to get greater value for money: "For Gordon Brown the PFI is justified where it can harness the efficiency that comes from contestability and deliver quality public services that remain in public control" (Gray and Jenkins 2004: 275).

With their coordinated approach and long-term investment Public Private Partnerships offer a means of developing solutions to complex social, educational, and welfare problems. With the introduction of PPPs the Labour government recognizes the limits of public service in terms of finance and provision on the one hand, but on the other hand also renews its commitment to public services.

The unions, in particular the public sector unions, have not welcomed this development (Ludlam and Taylor 2002). The declared aim of the reform of the civil service is to improve the quality of education, transport, and the health service in particular and gauge their performance according to standard economic criteria. The intention is also to provide improved services to people at the lower end of the income scale. The unions, however, fear a subordination of public interests to the interests of private enterprises and are afraid of the development of a "two-tier workforce, as public sector staff on better terms and conditions work alongside private sector employees on lower pay and less secure contracts" (Quinn 2005: 185). The licensing of privately run hospitals and clinics within the National Health Service (foundation hospitals) and the raising of tuition fees as a way of improving university resources has also proved to be extremely controversial amongst Labour MPs and the rank and file of the party. In the wake of the war in Iraq, with the Blair government under considerable pressure over its stance and the ensuing Kelly affair, it was quite conceivable that the loyalty shown by Labour backbenchers towards the government during its first term in office[14] had waned further than on several occasions during the second period of government. Up until then, MPs and the party membership had seen their role as that of a sounding board and had forced the government to back-pedal only in isolated cases;[15] the backbenchers had always managed to negotiate compromises with their own government (Cowley and Stuart 2003). But to the government's evident dismay, sixty-two Labour MPs voted against foundation hospitals and more than thirty abstained: "The bill survived only through a last minute compromise with the Lords" (Hindmoor 2004: 321). Also, the party leadership had to suffer a defeat at the Party Conference concerning foundation hospitals, the domestic policy issue that divides the government and the party most strongly. These results were particularly disappointing to New Labour's modernizers because they see foundation hospitals as an innovative third way "between state run public and shareholder-led private structures" (former Health Secretary Milburn, cited in Hindmoor 2004: 321; see also Greenaway et al. 2004: 517).

Criticism from the general public, the backbenchers, the party membership, and the unions on the government's plans for reforms of the public sector has been heavy. Apart from the critique of a reform overload from the concerned groups, six main objections can be identified (see also Rouse and Smith 2002: 46ff.; Shaw 2004; Hindmoor 2004).

- The individual reform projects lack coherence and clarity of vision. Multifarious steps and measures are being initiated in isolation from one another. There is no overarching vision: "The PFI, in short, is New Labour pragmatism in action" (Shaw 2004: 67).[16]
- There is inadequate coordination between planning and implementation of reforms. Local institutions charged with carrying out the reforms were not sufficiently integrated into the process. The Labour government had increased control at the national level, so that the Audit Commission in 2003 asked for *new localism* in target setting with local Public Service Agreements responsible for setting targets and guaranteeing greater local involvement.
- The government's own desire to achieve its ambitious goals as soon as possible has inflated the bureaucratic apparatus. Centralization and the rigidity of vertical control structures are in conflict with the actual intention of giving citizens and local officials responsibility for the realization of the reforms that affect them: "Too much checking, not enough doing" (Gray and Jenkins 2004: 269). By the setting of targets and goals and a proliferation of agencies concerned with audit and inspection, the Labour government created "a new process of coordinating and controlling the fragmented array of agencies and actors that are produced by the reform itself" (Newman 2004: 74), so that the words *control freakery* or *inspection overload* indicate that there are doubts concerning the efficiency of the reforms.
- The reform has intensified social imbalances without seeing a corresponding improvement in the efficiency of resource utilization. Despite the injection of resources into the health service and the transport and education sectors, there have not been any improvements in the conditions experienced by patients, passengers, pupils, and students. Hindmoor notes regarding foundation hospitals: "As their performance already secures these hospitals a great deal of effective autonomy, foundation status may not mean much more in practice than a new sign above the public entrance" (Hindmoor 2004: 322). Shaw notices there is no evidence that PFI provides higher quality public services (Shaw 2004: 72–73) (also see Flinders' analysis later in this volume).

- The relatively long duration of the PFI contracts will be a massive constraint for future governments in their ability to decide on how to respond to changing political and social needs or on how to set new priorities.
- Business risk is relatively low. Even if the contractor fails to provide the required public services, the public sector is still responsible for delivering them. In the end, this might lead to higher costs for consumers or to new public debts.

A BRIEF SUMMARY: NEW LABOUR'S ECONOMIC AND PUBLIC SERVICE REFORMS SINCE 1997

To sum up, New Labour's four main elements of its social democratic liberalism can be characterized as follows:

- The principle acceptance of the market economy and adaptation of international economic forces with an emphasis on macroeconomic stability, supply-side measures for growth and a flexible labor market providing employment and economic opportunities, and the strengthening of the British economy to improve in international competition.
- The maintenance of a selective welfare state with paid work as the main factor of social inclusion. Core services such as the NHS or primary education are still freely provided and financed. Others are means tested benefits to prevent abuse of the social systems. New Labour prefers investment in human capital and a welfare policy that is responsive to new types of family formation and gender roles and that is more attuned to balancing work and family than to just a consumerist approach on welfare policy.
- The avoidance or reduction of poverty and social exclusion as well as the promotion of equal opportunity and a cohesive society with rights and responsibilities for all of its citizens.
- The upholding of a large public sector, but one which increasingly has to incorporate market structures and commercial standards to fulfill its public tasks with the extension of markets and consumer choice. A system of target setting, control, and restricted autonomy should guarantee a new public service ethos.

Government policy in these areas can be seen as relatively successful: As the diagrams below illustrate, the average unemployment rate (less than 5.5 percent, see table 2.3) and the inflation rate are relatively low (see table 2.4), the average growth of gross national product is one of the highest within the

European Union and much higher than in France, Germany, or Italy (3.2 percent in 2004 compared to 2.0 in the Euro-countries, see tables 2.5 and 2.6), and in addition to this, national debt is relatively low (see table 2.2). Even if critics are not convinced that "social justice can only be secured by economic efficiency" (Lawson 2005: 84)—and there is no doubt that the Blair administration was more successful in economic than in social terms—it seems evident that in the age of international economic competition, a comprehensive welfare state is not achievable without a high degree of economic efficiency. The British Labour Party recognized this much earlier than the German SPD.

Table 2.3. Unemployment Rate in Germany and Britain 2001–2004

Table 2.4. Inflation Rate in Germany and Britain 2001–2004

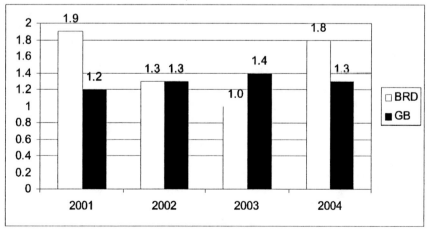

Table 2.5.   Economic Growth Rate in Germany and Britain 2001–2006

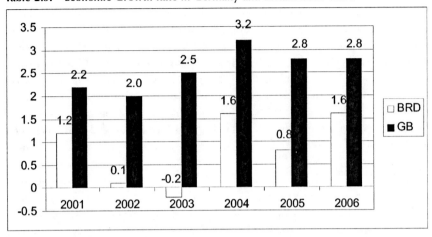

Table 2.6.   Gross Domestic Product per Capita in Germany and Britain 2001–2006

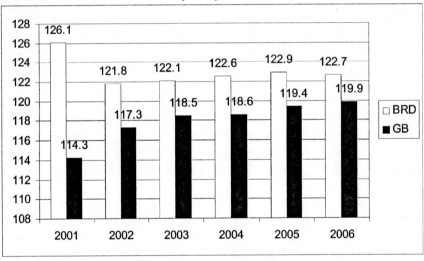

PROGRAMMATIC AND POLICY CHANGES IN
THE FIRST TERM OF THE SCHRÖDER GOVERNMENT

Within the SPD, Giddens' idea of the *Third Way* has had a much smaller impact on the programmatic discussion than in the British Labour Party. It was not until the publication of the *Schröder-Blair-Paper*[17] in the spring of 1999 that a public discussion on the *Third Way* got under way. However, this discussion subsided fairly soon after it had emerged. Since then, the programmatic discourse of the SPD has been held almost exclusively within the party, without attracting much media attention until 2005. Suddenly in April 2005 the SPD's then chair Franz Müntefering surprised the public with remarkable criticism of the market economy in a speech given at a conference discussing some ideas concerning the values of a new basic program, which the SPD was intending to decide upon at the end of 2005. Müntefering declared that the increasing power of the international financial markets and a total orientation towards economic questions would result in short-sighted profit-seeking which ruthlessly reduces the state's capacity of action. As a consequence the state dramatically loses its reputation with its citizens because it is becoming unable to fulfill the citizens' expectations. From his point of view the international profit-maximizing strategy endangers democracy because it unscrupulously uses social and political structures only for its own advantages (see FAZ, 14 April 2005). Müntefering's speech found much resonance and heavy media attention: It met with almost unanimous approval in the SPD, but was strictly rejected by the parliamentary opposition and trade associations (see FAZ, 18 April 2005). It was controversially debated in German newspapers and on television. The wider German public seemed to be irritated because there was an obvious gap between Münterfering's programmatic anticapitalism speech and the declared policy of the government: In an interview given in September 2004, Chancellor Schröder had emphasized that it should not be allowed to play off social justice against economic efficiency. From his point of view, economic efficiency and social justice seemed to imply each other (cf. FAZ, 22 September 2004). Schröder seemed to indicate that only economic growth guarantees social justice, i.e., welfare systems depend on economic necessities. Obviously, Schröder as agent of the government had a different perspective than Müntefering who wanted to strengthen the image of the SPD as the working-class party because the party needed its traditional supporters to win the important regional elections in North-Rhine Westphalia in May 2005. Müntefering's rhetorical efforts failed: the SPD lost the election, and with it the party once again lost the electorate's confidence. Up to the present, the SPD is still searching for a new programmatic and political identity that incorporates the principles of social justice, liberty, and solidarity at its core. The conception of justice in particular is supposed to be newly defined and balanced with the equality of opportunities and liberty in the new program of principles (see Meyer 2004a). Here justice of equal chances and of participation should play a bigger role than justice of distribution without sacrificing the accentuation of a concept of justice interpreted as egalitarian.

The Berlin Program (*Berliner Programm*) from 1989, which is still effective, is in the eyes of its critics no longer in keeping with the times. It is incoherent and has, from the moment of its adoption, always been outdated. It has therefore been unable to serve as a compass for politics in the united Germany.[18] The Berlin Program was an attempt to reconcile the old and the new Left. It combines the traditional social democratic values of the labor movement with the ecological and postmaterialist values of left-libertarian movements which arose from the student protests of the late 1960s. It also incorporated new ideas concerning the role of the welfare state in the era of globalization. Political scientists seem to concur in the view that the Berlin Program was "bereft of any impact" (Walter 1997: 1318). As Keynesian ideas were abandoned, so was the traditional aim of economic growth, and the program failed to fill the void with a new consistent strategy of social and economic policy. The SPD remained in a position between modernization and tradition.

Economic modernization and social justice (*Innovation und Gerechtigkeit*) were the main themes of the SPD in 1998 and 2002. The ecological impetus of the Berlin Program with its skeptical implications concerning economic growth and modern technology was taking a back seat. With the resignation of Lafontaine as party chairman the modernizers and the supporters of the pragmatic "New Politics group" (Padgett 1993: 36) were prevailing over the Left. These groups were more unequivocally oriented towards gaining and maintaining power than the other factions within the SPD. From their perspective, the parliamentary elections in 1998 and 2002 were an indication that they had chosen the better strategy because the party won votes from the most diverse segments of the electorate without losing support from its traditional clientele. While at the time of writing the program commission of the SPD is still working to develop its new program on general principles—now under the executive direction of the new party chairman Matthias Platzeck—this chapter only considers the SPD's policy directions and discussion papers until 2005 and its government policy during the years of the Red-Green coalition.[19]

As the party of the *Neue Mitte*, the SPD adopted some ideas arising from Anthony Gidden's *Third Way*, yet they were not been integrated systematically into the party's programmatic concepts nor into its governmental policy. Classic social democratic concerns such as traditional labor policy, a reform of codetermination structures between employers and employees, more protection against unlawful dismissal, legal claims to part-time working arrangements, and an extension of jobs that require contributions to the different social insurance funds (health, pensions, unemployment) were mixed into the tentative *Third Way* thinking. For instance, a change in law increased the payment of replacement wages in cases of sickness to one hundred percent (see Sven Jochem's analysis in chapter 6). It is in this context that Schabedoth

(2001: 194) concludes that the Schröder government in its first term was attempting to define traditional social democratic and trade union policies as the core interest of its electoral clientele, thereby trying to bolster the SPD's electoral base (see also Schroeder 2001).

What then were the main aspects of Red-Green policy in Schröder's first term of government? First of all, the policy of the coalition was different from that of New Labour in that it sustained adherence to the universalistic welfare state. The SPD tried to hold on to the present social insurance systems. Reforms to the system were supposed to stabilize, not to restrain it. The introduction of a state-subsidized private capital investment pension as a supplement to the public pension symbolized such a change within the boundaries of the universalistic welfare state. Because the SPD continued to conceive of social security as a basic social right, the social insurance system had to ensure economic security, and the government had to balance and regulate the market to guarantee social security to all individuals. An active government, coupled with strong public institutions and a well-developed welfare state were expected to preserve the basic values of the Left, such as solidarity and equality. In all its programmatic documents, the SPD emphasized the priority of political creative power over subordination under economic forces. Politics had to remain committed to preserving or creating solidarity within society: "Politics is the ethical heart of an alternative plan against the economy's dominating spirit, against competition that has been made absolute, and against the law of the jungle" (Schwan and Thierse 2004: 11).

A transition to an activating social investment state had only partially been achieved during the Red-Green coalition's first government term. The pensions reform with its strengthening of self-provision after retirement from the labor market was one part of the aspired encouragement of individual initiative. The SPD asked the individual to assume responsibility for him- or herself and his or her economic security. It was seen as the role of the activating social investment state to support the individual in acquiring knowledge and competence, in order for him or her to make use of income opportunities in a self-reliant and socially integrated manner. Justice was supposed to be understood primarily as access for all and equality of opportunity. The emphasis was intended to be on a new distribution of opportunities, not on equality of outcome. Accordingly, everyone was supposed to have the same access to education, work, and information because participation in society is possible only on this basis, and its implementation depends upon the guarantee of social rights and equality of opportunity. To secure participation was regarded as crucial for a forward-looking social policy. Nevertheless, the system of social security as a form of compensation for income and individual support remained almost completely unchanged until 2004; it had only been supplemented with incentives to take up a job and to obtain guidance from the Employment Office.

The SPD believed that it is the task of the welfare state to ensure access to second opportunities in the sense of "help for self-help." But the SPD's proposal did not go as far as Giddens' proposal to construct a concept of positive welfare in which inefficient and overly protective practices of the welfare state are abandoned and replaced by investment in human capital (education and training). Giddens' key value of individual responsibility and flexibility was also present in the governmental policy of the SPD and Greens, but for a long time it had not been pushed to the center of the reform initiatives.

Another main strategy of Red-Green government policy during the first term was the establishment of consensus meetings to create a result-oriented culture of dialogue between politics, science, economy, and the public (Steinmeier 2001). These reform- and result-oriented meetings, mostly initiated by the government, were intended to neutralize ideological divergence, bring the different interests closer together through a bargaining process, and generate consensus-oriented solutions in different policy areas. Norms, principles, problems, and procedures of this process were to be balanced between the different actors in order to achieve mutual accord and cooperation. Joint solutions and the potential for action was expected to be the outcome of the process. The government adopted primarily the role of a moderator that gives social actors their public space by making its organizational resources available to them.

The best known and most important forum of this kind was the *Bündnis für Arbeit* (Alliance for Jobs) which had been set up to forge trilateral agreements between federal government, employers, and employees in the areas of wage determination, labor market and economic policy, and codetermination of workers (see chapter 6 for a detailed analysis; also Fickinger 2005). From the government's perspective, the forum's overall goal was to increase the competitive capacity of Germany in the context of globalization by simultaneously increasing economic efficiency and employment (see Raschke 2001: 420). This was reflected in the fact that priority was given to paid work which was assumed to function as the basis for organizing one's life and open up opportunities in life. The government saw these trilateral discussions as an efficient means of passing joint resolutions, reducing mass unemployment, and increasing flexibility in the labor market. But conflicting strategies and a polarized atmosphere between the employers and the trade unions revealed the limitations of this corporatist strategy (see Sven Jochem's analysis in chapter 6).

While other forums such as that on immigration, the ethics commission, or the initiative for phasing out nuclear energy can be regarded as largely successful, the results from the *Bündnis für Arbeit* were modest indeed: neither could structural unemployment be reduced substantially, nor had the flexibility of the labor market been increased. Social and economic policy inertia on both sides, i.e., trade unions and employers, was responsible for this failure. The moderation capacity of the government proved to be insufficient. The obstacles, some of which can be traced back to the German political system with its various veto players (see chapter 5 in this volume), were too high to overcome. The strategy of integration and consensus between government, unions, and employers as a means for devising solutions for various political problems failed. The controversial *Hartz* reforms were a response to this failure of the *Alliance for Jobs*. They were an integral element of *Agenda 2010* and at the center of Red-Green social and economic policy during the second term of the Schröder administration.

The economic recession from 2001 further deteriorated the situation on the labor market and provided evidence that the successes of the Schröder administration were rather limited. To some extent this can be explained by the lack of coherence of SPD policy: in its governmental policy as well as in its programmatic drafts there had been various assessments and tendencies which had not been synthesized into a conclusive and comprehensive strategy.

To sum up: During its first term in government—and beyond—the SPD still preferred the traditional universalistic, corporate static welfare state without developing fundamental innovations. In principle, the party was in favor of promoting self-responsibility and social inclusion, but there were no substantial achievements in this respect. A reduction of state regulation was also hardly noticeable and unemployment rates remained high. Observers were left to ponder which social and economic actors might be able to increase employment in the future. An activating labor market policy and experiments with subsidized low-wage areas were merely supplementing measures. In accordance with the conception of the *Third Way*, governmental policy aimed at reducing the role of the state and taking on tasks such as the creation of infrastructure measures and the promotion of education and training. However, under the special conditions of Germany's federal system such policies are enforceable only in cooperation with the executives of the federal states. In the second term in office, inconsistent approaches and tendencies were still noticeable in the government's program; a coherent orientation of the government's policy could be identified only rudimentarily (Hübner 2004; Glaab and Sesselmeier 2005; Zohlnhöfer 2004): "It followed a patchwork-like policy by introducing isolated reforms without taking into account the interplay between different political arenas" (Hübner 2004: 121). As a result, there was growing dissatisfaction in the electorate with the performance of the government: In the spring of 2004, more than 75 percent of the voters were of the opinion that the government would not be able to solve the country's economic problems (cited in Glaab and Sesselmeier 2005). It is evident that the coalition government did not intend to dismantle the welfare state and that the SPD, in particular, had opted for the path of the moderate consensual welfare state, implicitly reconfirming the state's responsibility for the social security of its citizens. Cutbacks in the social security system were not only met with skepticism by a large number of people from the SPD, but up to the present attempts to tinker with the *social state* find only limited support from the electorate as a whole (see Elmar Wiesendahl's discussion of this in chapter 9).[20] Although in general terms the necessity of reforms is increasingly accepted, there is a lack of trust in politics to deal with this, and fears for the future are predominant because of the lack of political successes.

THE REFORM AGENDA 2010 AS THE MAIN REFORM POLICY OF SCHRÖDER'S SECOND TERM

Agenda 2010 began as a strategy document entitled "The Way Ahead to Increased Growth, Employment and Justice." The paper was drafted in the Chancellery in December 2002 by a small group of Chancellor Schröder's intimates led by the head of the Chancellery Steinmeier (FAZ, 4 January 2003).[21] The authors of the paper called for a comprehensive reform of the social security systems and a parallel reduction of indirect labor costs (with concomitant reduction in subsidies), a lowering of the tax burden, and the stimulation of consumer spending, particularly among well-off pensioners. At the same time, the government was asked to stay on its course of budgetary consolidation and continue to promote investment, especially in education, research, infrastructure, and the family. On the one hand, the incremental *dual transformation* of the German welfare state (Seeleib-Kaiser 2004; Bleses and Seeleib-Kaiser 2004) was to be strengthened and intensified—which implied decreasing emphasis being placed on the guarantee of the achieved living standard of workers through wage earner–centered social policies and increasing emphasis being placed on the expansion of child-care and the social service functions of the family. At the same time, public investment in the fields of education and research was to be noticeably increased.

For the first time since 1999 the paper was clearly echoing the *Schröder-Blair Paper* in which the two heads of government expressed their preference for modernizing the welfare state along market lines and asked the citizens to take on more responsibility for their own fortunes (see more in detail Jeffery and Handl 1999; Egle and Henkes 2003: 76ff.). The draft *Agenda* suggested that the federal government ought to be "building on the successes of its post-Lafontaine policy, which were interrupted by the exogenous shocks in 2001 and the tough election campaign of 2002" (FAZ, 4 January 2003). This policy document, known initially as "strategy 2010," was presented to the general public early on via informal talks with selected journalists and later publication in newspapers. Individual points raised in the document were included in the Chancellor's New Year address, in which he appealed not only to the population but also to his own party to have the courage to deal with the comprehensive changes in the social security system while strengthening the responsibility they take for their own lives.

The address delivered by Schröder in the *Bundestag* on 14 March 2003 incorporated all key points contained in the strategy paper of December 2002. Schröder suggested that the SPD had performed terribly in the then recent regional elections and polls "not because we were over-eager to push through reforms but because we were too fearful" (FAZ, 30 April 2003). This appraisal of the situation, that Schröder had first presented to his own party, was then underlined when he went on to announce fundamental reforms which were to mark a change of tack in social democratic government policy: just as Anthony Giddens' *Third Way* had done, people were expected to develop a sense of responsibility for their own fortunes and encouraged to perform better on their own account. The welfare state was no longer to revolve around what people want but what can be afforded. *Agenda 2010* was heralding a long-term transformation: in Schröder's view the welfare state could no longer serve as an alternative security system in the absence of jobs or as provision for the citizens' future, but was instead, in its role as activating social state, to give priority to helping people help themselves (FAZ, 2 June 2003). In practice Schröder's ideas implied:

- stricter rules for the unemployed encouraging them to reenter the labor market, which meant, in particular, that the long-term unemployed would have to take on any employment or accept a reduction of their social benefits;
- a shortening of the entitlement of unemployment benefits to twelve months for all, with the exception of the unemployed older than fifty-five years who would be eligible for unemployment benefits for eighteen months;[22]
- a lowering of redundancy payments to the level of social benefit;
- a larger share of health insurance premiums to be payable by the individual, along with a reduction of the benefits provided by the public health insurance;

- tax relief in the form of income tax reductions;
- and changes to the law on employment protection, not least to facilitate short-term contracts.

Furthermore, a so-called *factor of sustainability* (*Nachhaltigkeitsfaktor*) was introduced into the pensions system which was to reduce the increase of state pensions in a short term and significantly reduce the level of state pensions in a longer-term perspective. The introduction of a new taxation system for state pensions was another measure to reduce the level of state pensions from 67 percent of the average income in 2005 to 43 percent in 2040. These reforms were designed to adapt the pensions system to demographic trends including the low birth rate in Germany and the progressive ageing of German society. The pensions reform also aimed to drastically reduce the widely exploited possibilities of getting state pensions before the official retirement age.

The most controversial reform, commonly known as *Hartz IV*, aimed to, firstly, rearrange gainful employment to be more economical; secondly, make the labor market more flexible; and thirdly, optimize the process of finding employment (Giesecke and Groß 2005; also see chapters 6 and 9 in this volume). The objective was to demand more from the unemployed but at the same time offer more support. Incentives for the long-term unemployed were created in order to enable them through an active job search, but also through better efforts in finding positions by the Federal Agency for Employment (*Bundesagentur für Arbeit*), which is similar to the job centers in Britain. Also temporary "one or two Euro Jobs" as they are called (a source of minimal additional income through temporary jobs which have to be in the public interest and are available only for those who can neither find regular employment nor a place for training) were to increase the chances of transition into the formal labor market (for more details see Koch and Walwei 2005). The SPD-led government reacted with all these measures to the gradually growing fear in Germany of relatively large groups of poorly trained employees getting or staying completely and permanently locked out of the labor market. Far-reaching regulations on dismissals and supply-oriented measures of reform, as they had been demanded by a variety of economic research institutes and parts of the parliamentary opposition, were rejected by the government as a concession to the unions, the Left with the SPD, and to parts of the Greens (see Zohlnhöfer 2004: 398). Only for particularly problematic groups on the labor market (unemployed people younger than twenty-five or older than fifty-five years), simplified regulations on temporary appointments were introduced, but they soon had to be withdrawn not least because of a ruling on discrimination by the European Court of Justice.

Schröder's ideas met with skepticism and downright rejection from the left wing of the SPD and large sections of the union's leadership, and they deepened the inner-party identity crisis (see also Jun 2004b; Kimmel 2005). These groups saw *Agenda 2010* as socially imbalanced and incompatible with the campaign platform on which the 2002 general election had been contested. In the opinion of the SPD Left a number of measures were necessary in order to safeguard a social equilibrium. These included a restoration of the wealth tax, increased death duties, a system of trade tax embracing all companies and individuals, and a penalty for companies who fail to provide training places for apprentices. When the party leadership rejected the proposals of the Left, a grouping around the MPs Pronold and Schreiner attempted to force concessions. Employing the slogan "We are the party," they made use of a clause which had been inserted into the SPD constitution in 1993 that provided for the possibility of a membership poll. Ten MPs duly applied to the leadership to lodge a proposal criticizing *Agenda 2010*. At the same time, a number of regional SPD politicians demanded an extraordinary general meeting of the party to debate the document. Parallel to this, the trade unions and the party's Left continued their resistance to *Agenda 2010* and attracted considerable media attention. Their strategy was to force concessions using appearances in the media to apply pressure. As a gesture to the Left it was decided that a second proposal entitled *Paths to New Progress* was to be produced to supplement the main "Courage for Change" document, which was in essence a reflection of *Agenda 2010*. This second proposal was to deal with fundamental questions of future economic and social policy and indicate a longer-term direction for the party. It was elaborated by the *Innovation and Persistence, Growth and Jobs* committee, chaired by the former General Secretary Scholz, and embraced the opinions of all party groups. It presented a comprehensive blueprint for action at the Party Conference in November 2003. In this second proposal, which was approved together with the original proposal at the special conference on 1 June 2003, the influence of the party's Left was plain to see. It reflected a number of their demands such as: "The state must ensure that the contribution of each person in line with his/her capability reflects a just taxing of income accruing from work and wealth" (SPD-Parteivorstand 2003: 3). In concrete terms measures were suggested that levy taxes on company profits, capital gain, high incomes, and personal fortunes. The proposal also provided for the possible introduction of an opt-out penalty for those companies which are not providing places for apprentices.[23] Other demands of the Left failed to achieve majority backing at the conference.

Following this, criticism from within the party and the trade unions subsided. This can be attributed to a number of factors:

1) At the special conference Chancellor Schröder secured a clear endorsement for his reform package (the Executive Committee speaks of

90 percent approval). The reform proposals now had a high degree of legitimacy that could hardly be challenged from within the party.

2) The membership poll against *Agenda 2010* was a flop: its initiators were forced to withdraw it owing to the paltry number of signatories it had attracted.

3) The line of the party's Left was neither consistent in its composition nor strategically coherent; some people supported the membership poll while others rejected it; some favored an expansion of the welfare state, others were sympathetic to the idea of reducing social benefits.

4) In the public debate, unions and the Left went on the defensive. The trade unions had no internal strategic consensus on how to react to the government's reform policy, and tensions emerged between those unions with a more traditional attitude in social and economic policy (IG Metall, ver.di) and those with pragmatic attitudes (IG Bergbau und Chemie). DGB chairman Sommer was not successful in finding a compromise between these different opinions within the unions.

5) Schröder's resignation as party chairman in March 2004 paved the way for more consensus and stability in the SPD. His successor Franz Müntefering was, more than anyone else in the party leadership, respected by all party factions. As a "pragmatic traditionalist" he tried to integrate them all, and he was considered as a custodian of traditional social democratic values and programmatic attitudes.[24]

6) Despite widespread support for the welfare state in Germany, there was also a measure of sympathy for the government's reform policies, both among members of the public and, in particular, in the press.

7) The SPD embraced the unions' most fundamental demands and turned against the suggestions to open up area-wide collective bargaining, and to relax redundancy provisions.

Critics of the government's reform course were thus only partially successful in exploiting the disunities between government, party leadership, and MPs. Only shortly before the issue was voted on in German parliament, the SPD's own critics of the reforms were able to make their demands heard. They remained on the defensive and could take comfort in the fact that Schröder's government had only a tiny majority in parliament, and that the frontbenchers were compelled to make concessions in some areas in order to guarantee a certain degree of governing stability. Nevertheless, most of the demands of the Left were not reflected in the final reform law because— looking ahead to the *Bundesrat*—the government had been forced to find agreements with the parliamentary opposition which held a majority in the second chamber. CDU and CSU rejected the demands of the Left, and made sure that the reforms went further than the government had intended. Still, most of the government's original plans were passed by parliament.

After this agreement of the reform program with the Christian Democrats at the end of 2003, the Schröder government wanted to slow down the reform pace because there was continued resistance among important parts of the government's supporters and voters. In all regional elections the SPD had lost votes, and the party was unable to mobilize parts of its traditional electorate. In the spring of 2005, after repeated defeats in some regional elections and consistently low approval rates for the party in the opinion polls (only around 30 percent), Schröder announced some revisions to the *Agenda 2010*. This was also in response to pressure exerted by the Christian Democrats. Schröder suggested a further reduction of taxes for all enterprises, new measures to reintegrate the long-term unemployed over the age of fifty-five into the labor market, new Public-Private Partnership Programs to improve the infrastructure, and higher taxes on company shareholders. All of these measures aimed to improve the competitiveness of the German economy, and emerged against the background of the highest unemployment figures since 1945. In February 2005 the figure had gone up to an unprecedented 5.2 million. To some extent, the apparent rise in comparison to before was an implication of a new counting system, as recipients of social security benefits who are physically able to work more than fifteen hours per week now had to be included. The overall impression, however, was that none of the government's reforms which had been designed to improve the situation on the employment market were bearing any fruit, and that there was no positive impact at all.

Under the bottom line, the economic policy of the Schröder administration is judged rather critically by most observers (e.g., Hüther and Scharnagel 2005; Streeck and Trampusch 2005; slightly more positive: Eichhorst and Zimmermann 2005). The social systems which, in international comparison, are relatively generous, have not been given a solid financial basis. Furthermore, despite various measures facilitating the dual transformation of the welfare state, too much emphasis is still being placed on the consumerist parts compared with the investment-oriented parts of social policy. As regards the *Third Way* belief that more justice is achieved most efficiently through promoting gainful employment (inclusion into the labor market) and through investments into fields such as education and research, there are clearly noticeable deficiencies in the government's policies. This has given rise to a gap in justice between the generations as well as between in- and outsiders on the labor market. Only minor cutbacks in pensions, a lack of coherence in taxation policy, and high levels of national debt further increase this gap. Germany's highly complex negotiation system with its large number of potential veto-players and veto-points is, therefore, not simply perceived as inefficient and

prone to a reform policy style of "muddling through." This system is also perceived to leave insufficient room for a new conception of justice that departs
from traditional notions of justice of distribution, and places the emphasis on
political and economic participation through social inclusion and gainful employment, on equality of opportunities through education and lifelong learning, and on more efficient forms of dealing with financial resources. The individual's appropriate social security has to be proportionate to that: In this
respect, the *Agenda 2010* portrays an initial step to the "improvement of the
balance of justice" (Meyer 2004a: 186). Further steps will have to follow
since only the preservation of the principles of justice will secure sufficient
support for the SPD's reform ambitions and generate the level of public trust
which the SPD requires in order to overcome its current identity crisis. There
is no shortage of suitable proposals (e.g., contributions in Friedrich-Ebert-
Stiftung 2004). After the elections of September 2005 and the inauguration of
Germany's second Grand Coalition, it is now imperative for the SPD leadership surrounding the new chairman Beck to convert these proposals into programmatic reality.

CONCLUSION

Apart from a few obvious factors applying to both Germany and Britain, there
are a number of key differences that affect the planning and implementation
of reforms carried out by the governing British and German social democratic
parties. These differences do not only concern the dissimilar recent histories
and different internal processes of change of the respective parties, but can
also be attributed to structural and institutional factors within the political
system (cf. Egle et al. 2004).[25] Linking a party's evolution narrowly to a
clearly propounded ethos has borne fruit.[26] Both parties have come to grap-
ple with issues in their second term of office that they and their predecessors
had neglected in the past. However, where the SPD leadership has taken the
step, much more painful and controversial for a social democratic party, towards a reform of the social security systems, a freeing up of the labor market, and inroads into worker rights, all of which force its own members and
sympathizers to compromise on their values, Labour has taken the more comfortable step of modernizing public institutions and infrastructure, even if the
privatization of public institutions has proved the occasion for controversy
amid sections of the party and among the unions.

    The situation of the SPD was much trickier than that of Labour: the SPD
did not act as a one-party government as Labour does but rather in coalition
with the Greens, who on the one hand appeared as a coalition partner, largely

without public figures, that had adapted its principles to match its status in government (Raschke 2001), and that on the other hand attempted to make its discrete outlooks felt on isolated issues. An eight-member majority in parliament was a severe restriction on the government's room for maneuver and was a major reason for Schröder's plan to bring the general elections forward to September 2005. In comparison to this, Labour's parliamentary majority can tolerate a much higher number of dissenters within the own ranks.

The analysis has shown that despite all centralization tendencies within media-oriented parties (Jun 2004a) inner-party opposition against the respective reform programs has emerged. In Germany it has had a more lasting effect than in Britain. The SPD was furthermore faced with a strong *Bundesrat*, where the Christian Democrats and Liberals held the majority. This forced the Red-Green government to forge compromises with the opposition parties in the *Bundestag*, since almost all meaningful reform bills require the approval of the second chamber. In addition, the institutionalized right of individual lobby groups to participate in the political process represent a veto potential. One example are the constitutional rights of the employers' associations and the unions to negotiate their own standard wages. The structure of Germany's "negotiation democracy" coupled with the complex political relationships within the federal system is a barrier to the efficient passing and implementation of reform legislation by governing parties. In the British system, continued centralization together with a democracy of competition gives the governing party considerably more scope to come to policy decisions.

Insufficient preparation of policy contents and programmatic appeal as a party in government is another disadvantage of the SPD. The "pragmatic policy reforms" (Müntefering 2002: 3) were not based on any coherent programmatic reform made during the years in opposition. This was prevented by personnel turnover and reformatory efforts that were too ambitious. A number of drafts which had been compiled during the Social Democrats' period in opposition were not sufficient or not realizable because of administrative difficulties or inaccuracies with regard to its contents. The often changing chairmen of the party during the nineties (Engholm, Scharping, Lafontaine, Schröder) were either in charge for periods of time too short to successfully implement fundamental programmatic changes or had no deeper interest in programmatic development. One of the reasons for this attitude can be attributed to the need to overcome inner-party opposition, an undertaking that can stretch over long periods of time. Inner-party consolidation was in the foreground of the actions of the different party chairmen. Another reason underlying this behavior was the relatively strong position of the SPD in the second chamber of parliament (*Bundesrat*) during that time which gave the SPD opportunities to contribute to shaping policy, so that the use of power instruments or the solution of everyday problems in politics overlapped with the discussion of basic programmatic questions.

Hence a comparison of SPD and Labour reveals differences in the way reforms are planned and carried out. Yet there is a common danger facing both parties: with its pragmatic policy of governance the political Left is running the risk of alienating its sympathizers and voters without first establishing a new social democratic identity and a modern value system. Without a coherent and credible identity that distinguishes social democracy from other schools of party political thought and gives rise to loyalty and support, successes in the arena of political debate will be hard to achieve. If power is to be maintained in the long term, this identity has to be combined with a professional system of communications management. If the two are thought out and planned in concert success should be forthcoming. Both parties have tackled the key issues regarding their future: an all-encompassing education system, reformation of the social security systems as a way of preserving the welfare state, the expansion of the liberal constitutional state (particularly regarding immigration policy), a policy designed to safeguard and create jobs, and the creation of an efficient public sector are all issues that confer a potentially successful image on a modern social democracy. Yet in the process of reform and in inter-party rivalry Labour had the advantage over the SPD: its reform process is much more advanced and its main adversary, the Conservative Party, was in a weak position. In its reform policy, the Labour Party has continued the path of reform started by the Conservatives from a consumerist to an investment-oriented welfare state with its work-based approach towards shifting people from benefits into work. The transition to a more flexible labor market, investments in human assets, social benefits linked to gainful employment, and improved child care facilities have the effect of improved possibilities of access for the individual to the labor market. The Labour government has successfully endeavored to offer support "to those in greatest need and to address the problems of low pay and child poverty in the tax and benefit system" (Surender 2004: 5). Despite all problems, the *Third Way* has proven to be a practical way concerning the modernization of the civil service, and however its advantages and disadvantages are being judged, the reforms ought not to be dismissed as being just a neoliberal policy. In Germany, on the other hand, the consumerist part of social policy with its high pension level and comparably low incentives for taking up work, as well as its few possibilities for the individual to obtain gainful employment with compulsory social security, is still predominant.

Despite some measures of reform during the last years, no fundamental transformation of the welfare state can be noticed. On the contrary, due to high unemployment, pessimism has spread and the mentality of demanding high standards has increased (cf. Christensen 2005), which has partly caused the increase in government expenditure related to the implementation of the Hartz reforms, and which has worsened the federal budget situation. A return to more investment in human assets and research appears just as imperative as the emphasis on gainful employment. It will be interesting to see if the SPD, in a Grand Coalition with the CDU/CSU and in view of a rather strong left party in parliament, will support further reforms of the welfare state, and with this, progress on its way to a transformed identity. During the first few months of the Grand Coalition, the agreement on governmental policy with the CDU/CSU seems to indicate a continuation of the *Agenda 2010*, but with more emphasis being placed on budgetary consolidation. To keep a social democratic identity at its core and at the same time implement progressive re-form policy, this path could—following New Labour—be pursued further by the SPD. This would help the party to retain its position as a strong force within European social democracy. Until now, however, there are too few signs of the SPD developing a comprehensive and convincing reform policy which transforms the traditional German welfare state into a successful social investment state.

NOTES

1. For more detail on the position of the strategic center within parties, see Raschke (2002); Bukow and Rammelt (2003: 53ff.).

2. Media democracies are democratic states in which the political process is not determined mainly by political parties and political opinion leaders but by independent mass media. The media logic has considerable influence on party competition which reduces the significance of parties and increases the importance of the mass media (see Bürklin and Klein 1998: 183).

3. Martin J. Smith seems to be less precise when he describes the changing Labour Party as "social democracy based on capitalism, economic growth and social justice" (Smith 1992: 223). These principles are mainly in accordance with traditional social democracy and therefore with Labour's policy from the 1950s to the 1970s. Smith undervalues the declining role of the state in Labour's program already at the end of the 1980s and in the early 1990s.

4. In the eyes of Schmid and Schroeder (2001: 224) the retrenchment of the state's substantial role is *the* crucial point of Labour's policy.

5. Eric Shaw points to the view that the abandonment of Keynesianism in the "Policy Review" is a substantial departure from Labour's traditional policy (Shaw 1994).

6. See also Schmidtke (2002: 12): "The core idea here is focused on empowering people to fully use their own resources and skills before allowing the state to provide needed services. The emphasis has shifted from protecting people from the market to establishing programmes that facilitate them to successfully compete in the market."

7. See for example a speech given by Tony Blair on 18 September 2002: "Our goal is a Britain in which nobody is left behind; in which people can go as far as they have talent to go; in which we achieve true equality—equal status and equal opportunity rather than equality of outcome. It must be a Britain in which we continue to redistribute power, wealth and opportunity to the many not the few, to combat poverty and social exclusion, to deliver public services people can trust and take down the barriers that hold people back" (quoted by Shaw 2003).

8. In particular ideas of the "Democratic Leadership Council," an influential think tank of the democrats, have influenced some central policy areas (see Giddens 2002; Driver 2004).

9. Sen (1992) discusses in detail the concept of "social capability." The individual should be enabled to fully realize his/her potential in order to contribute effectively to society.

10. Giddens speaks about a "revival of Public Services" (Giddens 2002: 54ff.).

11. Mandelson (2002) specifies tax policy, the reforms of public services and the plan to join the Euro Zone as the main topics of Blair's second term in office.

12. For more detail see Giddens (2002: 56ff.) or Driver and Martell (1998: 66f., 104) who note: "There has been a shift in emphasis from the state as a monopoly provider towards partnership with the private and voluntary sectors" (ibid.: 44).

13. Prabhakar defines Public Interest Companies such as foundation hospitals or Network Rail as "organizations that display a degree of independence from the state and are charged with delivering a public service in the public interest" (Prabhakar 2004: 353). More specifically Prabhakar defines Public Interest Companies in agreement with the Public Management Foundation by nine features: They are charged with acting in the public interest; are committed to the public good; should be allowed to trade and earn their revenues by exchanging their services for money; should promote cost-efficiency and be encouraged to be entrepreneurial; are not allowed to make dividend payments; can raise money from the capital market; are accountable to different stakeholders, and they should be independent of direct political control from central government (ibid.: 355–56). He adds a minimum level of service to these nine features from the definition given by the Public Management Foundation.

14. See data given by Philip Cowley and Mark Stuart, who point to the fact that since the 1950s no Labour parliamentary party ever voted as rarely against the government as between 1997 and 2001. But at the same time the total number of MPs who voted against the government in some cases was comparatively high: "Rather, we have MPs who were prepared to rebel, and rebel in sizeable numbers, but who did so infrequently. It was behaviour not seen in any other postwar parliament. It was unique to the Blair government" (Cowley and Stuart 2003: 319). This rebellion peaked in November 2005 when the Blair government lost the vote over the antiterror law.

15. Heffernan notes: "Labour projects the party as the Blair leadership and the Blair leadership as the party. This successful strategy has served to further empower the party leadership at the expense of the party in parliament and in the country" (Heffernan 2003: 354).

16. Giddens (2002: 66) suggests: "Labour seems to lack a consistent philosophy of management within public institutions." Mark Wickham-Jones (2003: 35) notes: "As

with the Third Way, the notion of public-service reform was characterised by its uncertain nature."

17. German Chancellor Schröder and British Prime Minister Blair signed a paper which aimed to outline a guide for future social democratic policy. Most of this document had been written by the former Schröder consultant Bodo Hombach and by Peter Mandelson, one of the closest confidants of the British prime minister. It was published under the title "The Way Forward for European Social Democrats." For a closer analysis of this paper see Jeffery and Handl (1999).

18. Meyer, too, perceives the understanding of justice as it is articulated in the Berlin Programme as being too one-dimensional and as reducing the legitimacy of important parts of the Red-Green coalition's governmental policy (Meyer 2004a: 184).

19. The very character of a coalition government with the participants forced to compromise to achieve governmental cooperation gives rise to the assumption that the complete reasserting of a party's position in the government policy is nothing but an illusion. On the other hand, a government has to implement policy under more restrictive conditions than it can be formulated by political parties.

20. Eighty percent of voters reject a gradual increase of the statutory retirement age to sixty-seven years, 80 percent are against cutbacks in pensions, 68 percent disagree with higher social security contributions, and 69 percent oppose an economizing of health insurance benefits (Glaab and Sesselmeier 2005: 22). Padgett also states: "German opinion exhibits exceptionally strong resistance to welfare retrenchment" (Padgett 2005: 254). Padgett sees one explanation for this reluctance in "the historic failure of the German parties to cultivate public opinion to accept reform in the interests of economic competitiveness and employment" (ibid.: 271).

21. Participants were *inter alia* the speaker of the government Anda, chief of staff in the Chancellery Steinlein, Schröder's personal advisor Krampitz, Schröder's communications consultant Hesse, the deputy speaker of the government Steg, and the planning director of the economic ministry Cordes.

22. This measure was designed to intensify pressure on the unemployed and at the same time halt the state-supported trend towards early retirement.

23. The government successfully avoided having to apply this penalty by reaching an agreement with the employers that a sufficiently large number of apprenticeship places would be provided for all school leavers with appropriate qualifications.

24. After his election, however, Müntefering practiced strong leadership with himself and Schröder at the top of the party hierarchy at the expense of his former integrative acting. Rather than formulating any clear personal position (except the criticism on capitalism that has been discussed above), Müntefering supported the governmental policy line and thereby contributed to the rise of dissatisfaction within the party. In November 2005 he resigned from this office.

25. The authors give an overview on the different institutional factors which determine government policy regarding measures in favor of market economy. For Germany also see Zohlnhöfer 2004.

26. Hall (2002) points in his perceptive analysis of the ideas of the *Third Way* to the various common government politics of social democratic parties in Western Europe during the 1990s.

REFERENCES

Adelmann, Laura, and Cebulla, Andreas (2003): "The Dynamics of Poverty and Deprivation in the UK," in: Apospori, Eleni, and Millar, Jane, eds.: *The Dynamics of Social Exclusion in Europe. Comparing Austria, Germany, Greece, Portugal and the UK*. Cheltenham/Northhampton/Camberley: Edward Elgar, pp. 139–63.

Ainley, Patrick (1999): "New Labour and the End of the Welfare State? The Case of Lifelong Learning," in: Taylor, Gerald R., ed.: *The Impact of New Labour*. Houndmills/New York: Palgrave Macmillan, pp. 93–105.

Annesley, Claire (2001): "New Labour and Welfare," in: Ludlam, Steve, and Smith, Martin J., eds.: *New Labour in Government*. Houndmills/New York: Palgrave Macmillan, pp. 202–18.

Beech, Matt (2004): "New Labour," in: Plant, Raymond, Beech, Matt, and Hickson, Kevin, eds.: *The Struggle for Labour's Soul. Understanding Labour's Political Thought since 1945*. London/New York: Routledge, pp. 86–102.

Blair, Tony (1997): "Working Towards a People's Europe," in: Fischer, Heinz, ed.: *Die Zukunft der europäischen Sozialdemokratie*. Wien: Löcker, pp. 15–20.

Bleses, Peter, and Seeleib-Kaiser, Martin (2004): *The Dual Transformation of the German Welfare State*. Houndmills/New York: Palgrave Macmillan.

Bukow, Sebastian, and Rammelt, Stephan (2003): *Parteimanagement vor neuen Herausforderungen*. Münster: LIT.

Bürklin, Wilhelm P., and Klein, Markus (1998): *Wahlen und Wählerverhalten*. Opladen: Leske and Budrich.

Christensen, Björn (2005): *Die Lohnansprüche deutscher Arbeitsloser. Determinanten und Auswirkungen von Reservationslöhnen*. Berlin: Springer.

Clasen, Jochen, and Clegg, Daniel (2004): "Does the Third Way Work? The Left and Labour Market Policy in Britain, France, and Germany," in: Lewis, Jane, and Surender, Rebecca, eds.: *Welfare State Change. Towards a Third Way?* Oxford/New York: Oxford University Press, pp. 89–110.

Coronin, James E. (2004); "Speaking for whom? From 'old' to 'New' Labour," in: Lawson, Kay, and Poguntke, Thomas, eds.: *How Political Parties Respond. Interest aggregation revisited*. London/New York: Routledge, pp. 15–40.

Cowley, Philip, and Stuart, Mark (2003): "In Place of Strife? The PLP in Government, 1997–2001." *Political Studies* 51, no. 2: 315–31.

Driver, Stephen (2004): "North Atlantic Drift: Welfare Reform and the 'Third Way' Politics of New Labour and the New Democrats," in: Hale, Sarah, Leggett, Will, and Martell, Luke, eds.: *The Third Way and Beyond. Criticisms—Futures—Alternatives*. Manchester: Manchester University Press, pp. 31–47.

Driver, Stephen, and Martell, Luke (1998): *New Labour. Politics after Thatcherism*. Cambridge: Polity.

—— (2002): *Blair's Britain*. Cambridge: Polity.

Dyson, Kenneth (2001): "The German Model Revisited: From Schmidt to Schröder." *German Politics* 10, no. 2: 135–54.

—— (2005): "Binding Hands as a Strategy for Economic Reform: Government by Commission." *German Politics* 14, no. 2: 224–47.

Egle, Christoph, and Henkes, Christian (2003): "Später Sieg der Modernisierer über die Traditionalisten? Die Programmdebatte in der SPD," in: Egle, Christoph, Ostheim, Tobias, and Zohlnhöfer, Reimut, eds.: *Das rot-grüne Projekt. Eine Bilanz der Regierung Schröder.* Wiesbaden: Westdeutscher Verlag, pp. 67–92.

Egle, Christoph, Henkes, Christian, Ostheim, Tobias, and Petering, Alexander (2004): "Sozialdemokratische Antworten auf integrierte Märkte. Das Verhältnis von Markt und Staat, Hierarchie und Konsens." *Berliner Journal für Sozialforschung* 14, no. 1: 113–34.

Eichhorst, Werner, and Zimmermann, Klaus F. (2005): "Eine wirtschaftspolitische Bilanz der rot-grünen Bundesregierung." *Aus Politik und Zeitgeschichte* B43/2005: 11–17.

Fickinger, Nico (2005): *Der verschenkte Konsens. Das Bündnis für Arbeit, Ausbildung und Wettbewerbsfähigkeit 1998–2002: Motivation, Rahmenbedingungen und Erfolge.* Wiesbaden: VS Verlag für Sozialwissenschaften.

Friedrich-Ebert-Stiftung, ed. (2004): *Die neue SPD. Menschen stärken—Wege öffnen.* Bonn: Dietz.

Giddens, Anthony (1998): *The Third Way. The Renewal of Social Democracy.* Cambridge: Polity.

—— (2002): *Where Now for New Labour?* Cambridge: Polity.

Giesecke, Johannes, and Groß, Martin (2005): "Arbeitsmarktreformen und Ungleichheit." *Aus Politik und Zeitgeschichte* B16/2005: 25–31.

Glaab, Manuela, and Sesselmeier, Werner (2005): *Experimentierfeld Deutschland? Reformstrategien in der Sozialpolitik auf dem Prüfstand.* Bonn: Friedrich-Ebert-Stiftung.

Gray, Andrew, and Jenkins, Bill (2004): "Government and Administration: Too much Checking, Not Enough Doing?" *Parliamentary Affairs* 57, no. 2: 269–87.

Greenaway, John, Salter, Brian, and Hart, Stella (2004): "The Evolution of a "Meta-Policy": The Case of the Private Finance Initiative and the Health Sector." *British Journal of Politics and International Relations* 6, no. 4: 507–26.

Hall, Peter A. (2002): "The Comparative Political Economy of the 'Third Way,'in: Schmidtke, Oliver, ed.: *The Third Way Transformation of Social Democracy. Normative Claims and Policy Initiatives in the 21st Century.* Aldershot: Ashgate, pp. 31–58.

Harlen, Christine Margerum (2002): "Schröder's Economic Reforms: The End of Reformstau?" *German Politics* 11, no. 1: 61–80.

Heffernan, Richard (2003): "Prime ministerial dominance? Core executive politics in the UK." *British Journal of Politics and International Relations* 5, no. 3: 347–72.

Heyder, Ulrich, Menzel, Ulrich, and Rebe, Bernd, eds. (2002): *Das Land verändert? Rot-Grüne Politik zwischen Interessenbalancen und Modernisierungsdynamik.* Hamburg: VSA.

Hickson, Kevin (2004): "Equality," in: Plant, Raymond, Beech, Matt, and Hickson, Kevin, eds.: *The Struggle for Labour's Soul. Understanding Labour's Political Thought since 1945.* London/New York: Routledge, pp. 120–36.

Hindmoor, Andrew (2004): "Public Policy: But Domestic Policy Didn't Stop." *Parliamentary Affairs* 57, no. 2: 315–28.

Hörnle, Micha (2000): *What's Left? Die SPD und die British Labour Party in der Opposition*. Frankfurt/Main: Peter Lang.

Hübner, Kurt (2004): "Policy Failure: The Economic Record of the Red-Green Coalition in Germany, 1998–2002," in: Reutter, Werner, ed.: *Germany on the Road to "Normalcy": Policies and Politics of the Red-Green Federal Government (1998–2002)*. Houndmills/New York: Palgrave Macmillan, pp. 107–22.

Hüther, Michael, and Scharnagel, Benjamin (2005): "Die *Agenda 2010*: Eine wirtschaftspolitische Bilanz." *Aus Politik und Zeitgeschichte* B32-33/2005: 23–30.

Jeffery, Charlie, and Handl, Vladimir (1999): "Blair, Schröder and the Third Way," in: Funk, Lothar, ed.: *The Economics and the Politics of the Third Way*. Münster: LIT, pp. 78–87.

Jun, Uwe (2002): "Professionalisiert, medialisiert und etatisiert. Zur Lage der deutschen Großparteien am Beginn des 21. Jahrhunderts." *Zeitschrift für Parlamentsfragen* 33, no. 4: 770–89.

—— (2003): "The Changing SPD in the Schröder Era." *Journal of Policy History* 15, no. 1: 65–93.

—— (2004a): *Der Wandel von Parteien in der Mediendemokratie. SPD und Labour Party im Vergleich*. Frankfurt/Main/New York: Campus.

—— (2004b): "Sozialdemokratie in der Krise: Die SPD auf der Suche nach einer neuen Identität." *Gesellschaft—Wirtschaft—Politik* 53: 325–40.

Kavanagh, Dennis, and Seldon, Anthony (1999): *The Powers behind the Prime Minister. The Hidden Influence of Number Ten*. London: Harper Collins.

Kimmel, Adolf (2005): "Le Chancelier Schröder, l' *Agenda 2010* et la Crise du SPD." *Pouvoirs* 112: 155–66.

Koch, Susanne, and Walwei, Ulrich (2005): "Hartz IV: Neue Perspektiven für Langzeitarbeitslose?" *Aus Politik und Zeitgeschichte* B16/2005: 10–17.

Lawson, Neal (2005): "What can the European Left learn from New Labour?" *Social Europe, The Journal of the European Left* 1, no. 3: 82–85.

Leggett, Will (2004): "Criticism and the future of the Third Way," in: Hale, Sarah, Leggett, Will, and Martell, Luke, eds.: *The Third Way and beyond. Criticisms, Futures, Alternatives*. Manchester: Manchester University Press, pp. 186–200.

Lewis, Jane (2004): "What is New Labour? Can it deliver on Social Policy?" in: Lewis, Jane, and Surender, Rebecca, eds.: *Welfare State Change. Towards a Third Way?* Oxford/New York: Oxford University Press, pp. 207–27.

Lister, Ruth (2004): "The Third Way's Social Investment State," in: Lewis, Jane, and Surender, Rebecca, eds.: *Welfare State Change. Towards a Third Way?* Oxford/New York: Oxford University Press, pp. 157–81.

Ludlam, Steve, and Taylor, Andrew J. (2002): "The Political Representation of the Labour Interest: Is the British 'Labour Alliance' finished?" Paper presented at the British Journal of Industrial Relations Conference. Windsor, 16–17 September 2002.

Mandelson, Peter (2002): *The Blair Revolution Revisited*. London: Politico.

Mangels-Voegt, Birgit (2003): "Die sozialdemokratische Reformdiskussion—Kommunikationsdissonanzen in der Vermittlung der *Agenda 2010*." *Perspektiven ds* 20, no. 2: 22–33.

Meyer, Thomas (2001): "Grundwerte im Wandel," in: Müntefering, Franz/Machnig, Matthias, eds.: *Sicherheit im Wandel. Neue Solidarität im 21. Jahrhundert*. Berlin: vorwärts Verlag, pp. 13–30.

—— (2004a): "Die *Agenda 2010* und die soziale Gerechtigkeit." *Politische Vierteljahresschrift* 45, no. 2: 181–90.

—— (2004b): "Eine Theorie der sozialen Demokratie." *Perspektiven ds* 21, no. 1: 5–16.

—— (2005): *Theorie der sozialen Demokratie*. Wiesbaden: VS Verlag für Sozialwissenschaften.

Müntefering, Franz (2002): *Die Politik der Mitte in Deutschland*. Unpublished paper. Berlin.

Newman, Janet (2004): "Modernizing the State: A New Style of Governance?" in: Lewis, Jane, and Surender, Rebecca, eds.: *Welfare State Change. Towards a Third Way?* Oxford/New York: Oxford University Press, pp. 69–88.

Norris, Pippa (2001): *Britain Votes 2001*. Oxford/New York: Oxford University Press.

Padgett, Stephen (1993): "The German Social Democrats: A Redefinition of Social Democracy or Bad Godesberg Mark II," in: Gillespie, Richard, and Paterson, William E., eds.: *Rethinking Social Democracy in Western Europe*. London: Frank Cass, pp. 20–38.

—— (2003): "Germany: Modernising the Left by Stealth." *Parliamentary Affairs* 56, no. 1: 38–57.

—— (2005): "The Party Politics of Economic Reform: Public Opinion, Party Positions and Partisan Cleavages." *German Politics* 14, no. 2: 248–74.

Prabhakar, Rajiv (2004): "Do Public Interest Companies form a Third Way within Public Services?" *British Journal of Politics and International Relations* 6, no. 3: 353–69.

Quinn, Thomas (2005): *Modernising the Labour Party. Organisational Change since 1983*. Houndmills/New York: Palgrave Macmillan.

Raschke, Joachim (2001): *Die Zukunft der Grünen*. Frankfurt/Main/New York: Campus.

—— (2002): "Politische Strategie. Überlegungen zu einem politischen und politologischen Konzept," in: Nullmeier, Frank, and Saretzki, Thomas, eds.: *Jenseits des Regierungsalltags, Strategiefähigkeit politischer Parteien*. Frankfurt/Main/New York: Campus, pp. 207–41.

Rouse, John, and Smith, George (2002): "Evaluating New Labour's Accountability Reforms," in: Powell, Martin, ed.: *Evaluating New Labour's Welfare Reforms*. Bristol: Policy Press, pp. 39–60.

Schabedoth, Hans Joachim (2001): "Die deutsche Sozialdemokratie auf schwierigem Reformweg," in: Schroeder, Wolfgang, ed.: *Neue Balance zwischen Markt und Staat. Sozialdemokratische Reformstrategien in Deutschland, Frankreich und Großbritannien*. Schwalbach, Ts.: Wochenschau Verlag, pp. 187–202.

Schmid, Josef, and Schroeder, Wolfgang (2001): "Großbritannien: Vom Musterland des Konservatismus zum Mutterland der neuen Sozialdemokratie?" in: Schroeder, Wolfgang, ed.: *Neue Balance zwischen Markt und Staat. Sozialdemokratische Reformstrategien in Deutschland, Frankreich und Großbritannien*. Schwalbach, Ts.: Wochenschau Verlag, pp. 203–28.

Schmidtke, Oliver (2002): "Transforming the Social Democratic Left: the Challenges to Third Way Politics in the Age of Globalization," in: Schmidtke, Oliver, ed.: *The Third Way Transformation of Social Democracy. Normative Claims and Policy Initiatives in the 21st Century*. Aldershot: Ashgate, pp. 3–27.

Schroeder, Wolfgang (2001): "Ursprünge und Unterschiede sozialdemokratischer Reformstrategien: Großbritannien, Frankreich und Deutschland im Vergleich," in: Schroeder, Wolfgang, ed.: *Neue Balance zwischen Markt und Staat, Sozialdemokratische Reformstrategien in Deutschland, Frankreich und Großbritannien*. Schwalbach, Ts.: Wochenschau Verlag, pp. 251–74.

Schwan, Gesine, and Thierse, Wolfgang (2004): *Grundlagen unserer Politik. Impulse für das neue Grundsatzprogramm der Sozialdemokratischen Partei Deutschlands*. Unpublished paper. Berlin.

Seeleib-Kaiser, Martin (2004): "Continuity or Change: Red-Green Social Policy after sixteen years of Christian Democratic Rule," in: Reutter, Werner, ed.: *Germany on the Road to "Normalcy": Policies and Politics of the Red-Green Federal Government (1998–2002)*. Houndmills/New York: Palgrave Macmillan, pp. 123–43.

Sen, Amartya (1992): *Inequality Reexamined*. Oxford: Clarendon Press.

Seyd, Patrick, and Whiteley, Paul (2004): "From Disaster to Landslide: The Case of the British Labour Party," in: Lawson, Kay, and Poguntke, Thomas, eds.: *How Political Parties respond. Interest Aggregation revisited*. London/New York: Routledge, pp. 41–60.

Shaw, Eric (1994): *The Labour Party since 1979. Crisis and Transformation*. London/New York: Routledge.

—— (2003): "Left Abandoned? New Labour in Power." *Parliamentary Affairs* 56, no. 1: 6–23.

—— (2004): "What matters is what works: The Third Way and the case of Private Finance Initiative," in: Hale, Sarah, Leggett, Will, and Martell, Luke, eds.: *The Third Way and Beyond. Criticisms—Futures—Alternatives*. Manchester: Manchester University Press, pp. 64–82.

Smith, Martin J. (1992): "Continuity and Change in Labour Party Policy," in: Smith, Martin J., and Spear, Joanna, eds.: *The Changing Labour Party*. London/New York: Routledge, pp. 217–29.

SPD-Parteivorstand (2003): *Wege zu einem neuen Fortschritt*. Beschluss des außerordentlichen Bundesparteitages vom 1. Juni 2003 in Berlin. Berlin.

Steinmeier, Frank Walter (2001): "Konsens und Führung," in: Müntefering, Franz, and Machnig, Matthias, eds.: *Sicherheit im Wandel. Neue Solidarität im 21. Jahrhundert*. Berlin: vorwärts Verlag, pp. 263–72.

Stephens, Philip (2001): "The Treasury under Labour," in: Seldon, Anthony, ed.: *The Blair Effect. The Blair Government 1997–2001*. London: Little, Brown and Company, pp. 185–208.

Streeck, Wolfgang, Trampusch, Christine (2005): "Economic Reform and the Political Economy of the German Welfare State." *German Politics* 14, no. 2: 174–95.

Surender, Rebecca (2004): "Modern Challenges to the Welfare State and the Antecedents of the Third Way," in: Lewis, Jane, Surender, Rebecca, eds.: *Welfare State*

Change. Towards a Third Way? Oxford/New York: Oxford University Press, pp. 3–24.

Walter, Franz (1997): "Fuehrung in der Politik Am Beispil sozialdemokratischer Parteivorsitzender." *Zeitschrift für Politikwissenschaft* 7, 1287–1336.

Wickham-Jones, Mark (2003) "From Reformism to Resignation and Remedialism? Labour's Trajectory Through British Politics." *Journal of Policy History* 15, no. 1: 26–45.

Wiesenthal, Helmut (2003): "German Unification and 'Model Germany': An Adventure in Instutional Conservatism." *West European Politics* 26, no. 4: 37–58.

Zohlnhöfer, Reimut (2001): "Politikwechsel nach Machtwechseln. Die Wirtschaftspolitik der Regierungen Kohl und Schröder im Vergleich," in: Derlien, Hans-Ulrich/Murswieck, Axel, eds.: *Regieren nach Wahlen.* Opladen: Leske + Budrich, pp. 167–93.

—— (2003): "Rot-grüne Regierungspolitik in Deutschland 1998–2002. Versuch einer Zwischenbilanz." in: Egle, Christoph, Ostheim, Tobias, and Zohlnhöfer, Reimut, eds.: *Das rot-grüne Projekt. Eine Bilanz der Regierung Schröder.* Wiesbaden: Westdeutscher Verlag, pp. 399–419.

—— (2004): "Die Wirtschaftspolitik der rot-grünen Koalition: Ende des Reformstaus?" *Zeitschrift für Politikwissenschaft* 14, 381–402.

3

Democracy, Efficiency, Futurity: Contested Objectives of Societal Reform

Ingolfur Blühdorn

Democratic self-determination, the efficient provision of the means of self-realization, and the objective to reduce uncertainty and achieve security and predictability for the future have always been the key dimensions of the project of modernity and modernization.[1] *Progressive* movements since the eighteenth century, ranging from bourgeois resistance against the old feudal order, via the labor movement and the postmaterialist *new social movements*, to reform governments such as those of Willy Brandt, Gerhard Schröder,[2] or Tony Blair have always committed themselves to enhancing the democratic qualities of political structures, improving the efficiency of the different function systems that constitute modern society as a whole, and making provision for a safe and enjoyable future. Today, commitment to these goals is the defining criterion of what is commonly referred to as *good governance* or *best political practice*. Democratic effectiveness, systemic efficiency and consideration for the future are central parameters in the comparative assessment of the *performance* of democratic systems. Yet, the meaning and implications of these concepts have always been contested, and tensions between them cast doubt upon the possibility of their simultaneous realization. All three of them are abstract categories which in any particular situation and context need to be filled with concrete meaning. Hence the content and relationship of these concepts has constantly been renegotiated, and in the contemporary era they have, this chapter will suggest, been reconceptualized so rapidly and radically that an entirely new notion of modernization has emerged. Germany and Britain, whose contested agendas of societal reform are the focus of this volume are, arguably, not simply modernizing their economic, political, and social structures in order to adapt to the necessities of the increasingly globalized economy: They

69

are trying to come to terms with a comprehensive transformation of the modernization project itself. To undertake a closer analysis of the changing interpretation of democracy, efficiency and futurity, of their mutual relationship, and of the recent transformation of the modernization project is the objective of this chapter.

The analysis proceeds in five stages and places the main emphasis on the concepts of democracy and efficiency. Futurity, on the other hand, is regarded as a subordinate third dimension that was expected to reconcile tensions between democracy and efficiency. In the first section, an impressionistic overview of different ways in which the troubled relationship between democracy and efficiency has been articulated maps out the terrain. Section two undertakes a detailed conceptual analysis which first investigates in general terms the meaning of, and connection between, democracy and efficiency, then explores the democracy-efficiency relationship in the idealist tradition of modernity, and finally examines the contemporary *metaphysics of efficiency* whose emergence seems related to a crisis of the modernist ideal of the autonomous Self. Section three then reviews the attempts of the *new social movements* (NSM) to reground the abstract notion of efficiency and reconcile democracy and efficiency by reconnecting them to a revised understanding of the Self that in turn was to be grounded in the imperatives of environmental integrity and responsibility for the future. Section four explores why the NSM-agenda failed and outlines how in a process of *reflexive redefinition* the social movement ideals of democratic renewal, authentic efficiency, and responsibility for the future have been adapted to the specific requirements of late-modern society. The concluding section suggests that in their redefined contemporary understanding the concepts of democracy, efficiency, and futurity provide the underpinning for a new *system-centered* modernization that is categorically different from its *subject-centered* predecessor.

DEMOCRACY *VERSUS* EFFICIENCY: CONCEPTUALIZATIONS OF A TROUBLED RELATIONSHIP

The quality and performance of democratic systems is commonly judged by the effectiveness of democratic self-determination and the efficiency of their various function systems (e.g., Roller 2005). In public policy making and policy analysis, the faithful reiteration of the view that "political systems which are open to the inclusion of different actors and their interests are likely to perform better," and that "the policy-making system should be inclusive" because "only integration and consensual proceeding offer the best conditions for successful implementation" (Jost and Jacob 2004: 4) has become something of a matter of political correctness. The UN's *Local Agenda 21* as well as the OECD's commitment to *Engaging Citizens in Policy-making* (OECD 2001a, 2001b) provide powerful evidence that "public input generally is supposed to lead to greater effectiveness" as well as "an improved democracy, both by developing more active, engaged citizens; and by making better decisions through broader, higher quality inputs" (Parkinson 2004: 377). At the same time, however, there is an acute awareness that in many contexts the ideals of democratic governance and efficient governance are mutually obstructive. In modern democratic systems the principles of *representation* and *delegation* have been adopted not least with a view to the efficiency of political processes, even though they impair radical democratic ideals. Max Weber argued that the efficient management of complex modern societies can be secured only by comprehensive bureaucratic structures which are, however, averse to democratic scrutiny and accountability and can easily turn into an *iron cage*. Robert Michels' (1962) *iron law of oligarchy* suggests that political organizations, however much they may initially be committed to the principles of democracy, eventually adopt oligarchic structures so that they may pursue their substantive objectives more efficiently. Speaking from a contemporary perspective, Colin Crouch reconfirms Michels's view that democracy can at best be a momentary experience, and that after the "democratic moment" (Crouch 2004: 6) we have to expect an "inevitable entropy of democracy" (ibid.: 104). Thus, the prospects for achieving democracy and efficiency at the same time do not seem favorable, but prioritizing one over the other may yield undesirable results.

In the early 1970s Winfried Steffani (1973: 12) noted that "one-sided orientation towards the objective of efficiency furthers the inherent propensity of all modern industrial societies towards the authoritarian and technocratic state"; yet "one-sided orientation towards the objective of maximising participation and transparency implies a reduced understanding of democracy" that is unsuitable "for resolving the problems of complex societies" (ibid.). Arguing along the same Weberian lines Bernd Ladwig reconfirms that "the unqualified application of democratic methods would undermine the formal rationality" of political institutions "which is geared towards the performance of specific functions" (Ladwig 2002: 55). In his view a "significant measure of hierarchy" is the unavoidable price that has to be paid "for a generally advantageous level of welfare and security" (ibid.). George Tsebelis (1995, 2002) has expressed the issue in the terms of *consensus capacity* and *steering capacity*: democratic openness, while increasing a political system's capacity for consensus formation, invariably reduces its steering capacity because it raises the number of *veto players* and *veto-points*. Reversely, Tsebelis suggests, attempts to enhance a system's steering capacity, tend to be at the expense of democratic inclusiveness.

Taking a slightly different perspective, Joachim Raschke speaks of a "centrifugal drift between legitimacy and efficiency" (Raschke 1993: 30). He uses the *legitimacy-efficiency-dilemma* as a lens for the critical analysis of the German Green Party which like no other political party has been plagued by the problem that "legitimate structures are inefficient," whereas "efficient structures are not legitimate" (ibid.). Robert Dahl, too, speaks of *a democratic dilemma*. In a seminal article of 1994 he discusses "trade-offs between system effectiveness and citizen effectiveness" (ibid.: 34), i.e., between "the ability of the citizens to exercise democratic control over the decisions of the polity" and "the capacity of the system to respond satisfactorily to the collective preferences of its citizens" (ibid.: 28). Dahl conceptualizes the *democratic dilemma* primarily in terms of size: in very small political systems, he suggests, "a citizen may be able to participate extensively in decisions that do not matter much but cannot participate much in decisions that really matter a great deal." Very large systems, in contrast, "may be able to cope with problems that matter more to a citizen," yet "the opportunities for the citizen to participate in and greatly influence decisions are vastly reduced" (ibid.). As he sees no prospect for combining the advantages of both small and large systems, Dahl believes that citizens are confronted with a choice between preserving their ability "to influence the conduct of their government" and increasing the capacity of the "political unit to deal more effectively" with the issues that really matter most (ibid.: 23f.).

Indeed, public administrators seem to be facing a similar choice. Reconciling the "apparent contradictions" between "reflective policy making and effective managerialism" has become "one of the most difficult challenges" they have to confront (Hendriks and Tops 1999: 150). The paradigm of *new public management* (NPM), for example, clearly prioritizes the side of effectiveness and efficiency, and aims to achieve efficiency gains by transferring essentially political decisions to managers and markets. Implicitly, such strategies acknowledge that despite ever repeated reassurances to the contrary, there are severe doubts about the asserted link between the quality or legitimacy of policy output and the inclusiveness of democratic input into policy-making processes. The overwhelming confidence which local, national and supranational governments are investing in NPM strategies testifies to their awareness that "expanded access" may actually impair "the quality of policy-making," and that "governments may perform less well when they rely upon the quality of citizen input more than the quality of the elected representatives" and expert bodies (Dalton et al. 2003: 270f.). Furthermore, policy makers are very aware that "the costs of informed civic involvement" may be "too high to be realized by all but a few voters" (ibid.). Undoubtedly, "the expansion of communication that does not aim to keep citizens at a distance but to involve them increases the costs of political decisions" quite considerably (Sarcinelli 2003: 46).

However, the delegation of political matters to supposedly more competent and efficient expert commissions, nonmajoritarian bodies, or private sector actors raises fundamental questions about democratic legitimacy and accountability (e.g., Thatcher and Stone Sweet 2002; Lütz 2003; Moran 2003; Strøm et al. 2003; also see Matthew Flinders in this volume). It is widely acknowledged that "whilst the deinstitutionalisation of politics may lead to efficiency gains, it reinforces the impression of increasing opaqueness, . . . blurs political responsibilities and degrades Parliament to the status of a secondary political arena" (Sarcinelli 2003: 43). To some extent improved mechanisms of transparency and accountability may be able to counterbalance the loss of democratic qualities that comes with the politics of delegation. Yet Dalton and colleagues have pointed to the narrow limits for such counterstrategies: if "there is such a thing as functional secrecy, as implied in the traditional state model, there could also be dysfunctional openness" (Dalton et al. 2003: 271). "If transparency is taken to an extreme," it could "diminish government efficiency and possibly weaken legitimacy" (ibid.).

What this brief survey is intended to illustrate is that despite the constantly reasserted accord between democracy and efficiency, there is a widely shared and deeply felt perception of fundamental tensions between the two objectives. Arthur Okun conceptualizes these tensions as the "big trade-off" which means that at many points "society confronts choices that offer somewhat more equality at the expense of efficiency or somewhat more efficiency at the expense of equality" (Okun 1975: vii). Hendriks and Tops are suggesting that the agendas of democracy and efficiency can be reconciled only through a periodic shift of policy emphasis from one pole to the other. Comparing local government in Germany and the Netherlands, they note that from the 1980s to the 1990s, the trend in the Netherlands has been going "from a focus on more efficiency to a focus on more democracy, while trends in local government reform in Germany have been going the other way around" (Hendriks and Tops 1999: 133). The assumption of a similar pendulum movement seems implicit in Matthew Flinders' observation that the first New Labour government in Britain placed the emphasis on the side of democratic renewal, while the second one emphasized the side of efficiency gains (chapter 7 in this volume). In the era of economic globalization, however, there are heightened concerns that the democracy side might lose out permanently vis-à-vis the ongoing drive for efficiency. Like many others (e.g., Cerny 1999; Dryzek 2000; Crouch 2004), Robert Dahl in the above quoted article points out that so far there is little evidence of "an extension of the democratic idea beyond the national state" but considerable evidence for "the victory in that domain of de facto guardianship" (Dahl 1994: 33). This is borne out by the much discussed democratic deficits of the EU, the IMF, the WTO, and other transnational organizations. While economic globalization weakens the existing institutions of national democracy, "this new process of structural change does not at the same time create new institutional capacities for rearticulating governance at a higher, global level" (Cerny 1999: 13f). Thus, "the *de facto* level of decision-making" moves ever further away "from effective democratic control and responsiveness" (ibid.: 17).

Social movements against corporate globalization and for global justice are, therefore, vociferously demanding *A New Democracy* (e.g., Shutt 2001; George 2004; Ian Welsh in this volume) which in their view can be achieved only by "subordinating *efficiency* to the *vitality* of the system as a whole" (Dierckxsens 2000: 13; my emphasis). Within the confines of the liberal state and the hegemony of neoliberal thought they do not see much "scope for increased democratic authenticity" (Dryzek 2000: 29). In the political economy of transnational capitalism, Dryzek suggests, "the first task of all states" is "to maintain the confidence of actual and potential investors," and because "democratic influence on policy making introduces a dangerous element of indeterminacy," it "becomes increasingly curtailed" (ibid.). Adopting the perspective of ordinary citizens rather than decision-making elites Crouch adds: "Whatever aspirations might emerge from the democratic processes of politics, a population needing employment has to bend the knee to global companies' demands" (Crouch 2004: 35).

At times this kind of radical analysis is even echoed in mainstream politics: In a much noticed speech of April 2005, Franz Müntefering, then party chairman of the German Social Democratic Party, declared that "the internationally enforced strategies of profit maximisation are in the long term threatening our democracy," because "the economy is—at best—indirectly oriented towards the social human being" (Müntefering 2005). In the struggle against the "internationally growing power of capital" and for the rescue of the public good Müntefering renewed Willy Brandt's famous demand to "dare more democracy." However, despite such eruptions of left-wing populism in mainstream politics, and despite all academic optimism about the renewal of local democracy, transnational network governance (Dryzek 2000; Diani and McAdam 2003; Chesters and Welsh 2005) and the emerging era of cosmopolitanism (e.g., Beck 2002, Beck and Grande 2004; Held 2004), it still seems that efficiency and democracy are only "in theory" compatible and mutually conducive, while "in practice" there are significant tensions, with "the first goal becoming increasingly important" for contemporary agendas of modernization (Hendriks and Tops 1999: 144). Although there is a lot of declaratory commitment to democratic deepening and renewal, to *responsive* government and the removal of democratic deficits, the emphasis and priority in contemporary reform agendas invariably seems to be on achieving efficiency gains and enhancing economic competitiveness—and often this implies reducing rather than expanding the scope for authentic democracy. This raises the questions: Where exactly do the tensions between democracy and efficiency emerge? How and why has the goal of efficiency established its perceived supremacy over the objective of democracy? Detailed conceptual analysis will help to answer these questions.

CONCEPTUAL COMPLEXITIES, THE IDEALIST TRADITION, AND THE *METAPHYSICS OF EFFICIENCY*: A CONCEPTUAL ANALYSIS

A key problem with understanding the democracy-efficiency relationship is that even in the academic literature, let alone in popular debate, important differences between, for example, efficiency, effectiveness, and efficacy are very commonly blurred. Participation, accountability, and transparency, which all signify very different things and may each be interpreted in several different ways, are frequently used as if they were interchangeable and all synonymous with democracy. While in a broader sense, the above quoted authors are all exploring the relationship between democracy and efficiency, they are in fact all talking about very different issues. Steffani sets the concept of efficiency against that of *participation*. Okun, and also Ladwig, when highlighting that "the first virtue of economy and administration is efficiency," while "the first virtue of democracy is equality" (Ladwig 2002: 55), are positioning efficiency against *equality*. Raschke is talking about efficiency and *legitimacy*. Dahl is not really concerned with efficiency at all but with the *effectiveness*[3] of the political system which according to his analysis clashes with the effectiveness of citizen participation. Tsebelis, too, is focusing on effectiveness rather than efficiency, yet his opposition between steering capacity and the capacity for democratic consensus places the emphasis on the theoretical *capabilities* of political systems rather than their actual *performance*. Steffani, in turn, when emphasizing that one-sided fixation on the goal of efficiency increases "the inclination towards political apathy" (Steffani 1973: 19) is really talking about the citizens' experience of *efficacy*.[4] Dalton and colleagues, and also Sarcinelli, in discussing "the costs of informed civic involvement," are weighing the gains of participatory democracy in terms of efficacy against potential losses in epistemological as well as economic terms. And the critics of corporate globalization, finally, when they are talking about efficiency and *vitality*, are rehearsing post-Marxist arguments about the alienation, reification and commodification of human beings by the global capitalist economy.

This complexity at the conceptual level renders the analysis of the relationship between democracy and efficiency rather difficult. An additional complication is that the term *trade-off* which Okun, Dahl, Roller, and many others are using to describe this relationship has at least two different meanings: it can describe a zero-sum-game in which one side loses exactly what the other gains, but it can also refer to a choice between two or more objectives which cannot be maximized at the same time, but where prioritizing one does not necessarily come at the price of diminishing what has already been achieved in terms of the others. By way of clarification it is helpful to distinguish three different situations for which the term *trade-off* is commonly used:

- Firstly, there may be trade-offs between potentially conflicting policy areas such as social policy *versus* economic policy. Okun's trade-off between equality and efficiency falls into this category, and so do the much debated trade-offs between environmental and economic policy. At least theoretically, "joined-up thinking" and integrated policy approaches—concepts like *sustainability* or *welfare to work* spring to mind—can cure this kind of conflict. But trade-offs of this category are not the concern of the present analysis.
- Secondly, theorists of decision making may see a trade-off between the inclusiveness of decision-making processes and their effectiveness. Steffani's and Dahl's trade-off between effective participation *versus* effective government, as well as Tsebelis' trade-off between consensus capacity and steering capacity belong to this category. At least theoretically, strategies of multilevel governance and innovative forms of e-democracy can help to alleviate these problems. Such tensions between the *inclusiveness* and *effectiveness* of decision-making processes are clearly relevant for the present analysis, yet a comprehensive analysis of the relationship between democracy and efficiency needs to reach well beyond the narrow confines of decision-making theory.
- Thirdly, there may be trade-offs between democracy in the sense of effective self-determination and efficiency in the sense of the optimized performance of societal processes or function systems. It is this kind of potential trade-off that is the focus of attention in this chapter. Ladwig's opposition between the *first virtue* of democracy (equality) and the *first virtue* of administrative and economic systems (efficiency) points into this direction. Dieter Fuchs' distinction between *democratic performance* and *systemic performance* comes even closer to the core issue.[5] Although the way in which Fuchs himself defines and uses these concepts is ultimately not convincing,[6] his distinction is still useful in that it

directly positions *democracy* against *efficiency*. It thus captures what is at the center of the further analysis.

With regard to the relationship between democracy and efficiency in this sense it is useful to note that all those concepts which are commonly associated with democracy (e.g., participation, accountability, transparency) center around the political *subject* or *Self* and its claim to self-determination, whereas notions of efficiency always center around a *process* or *system* and its specific *function*. The concepts which are associated with democracy are always related to the autonomy of the Self as their ultimate objective and point of reference. They focus on the extent to which individuals and communities can, rather than being subject to the rule of externally imposed imperatives, themselves, through the political process, shape their lifestyle, life world, and social relations in accordance with their own values and preferences. There are, however, very different ways in which this ideal of autonomy and self-determination may be translated into political practice. There are very different means through which, and degrees to which, such self-determination may be desired and realized. Accordingly, there are many different models of democracy (e.g., Held 1996; Schmidt 2000; also see chapter 12 in this volume). Participation, transparency, accountability, legitimacy, and so forth are indispensable ingredients of democratic systems, yet all of them are highly flexible concepts which can be defined in several different ways.

The category of efficiency, on the other hand, measures the relationship between the *input* into and the *output* from a particular process or system, whereby input, output, and even the *boundaries and identity* of the process or system itself are highly contingent, socially constructed categories which capture, very selectively, what is actually *counted* as input, process, and output, and liberally disregard all kinds of entities and transformations which are either not measured or not valued or not perceived at all. The ecologist critique that traditional conceptualizations of the economic system externalize a wide range of social or environmental issues and have a very restricted understanding of the *resources* on which the economy depends is a well known example that nicely illustrates this contingency. Efficiency means the *resource saving* implementation of predetermined goals. Yet at this stage it remains open what counts as a resource, where and how the goal has been determined, and what normative qualities the goal may have. In other words, efficiency is a purely formal criterion that can be applied to the most diverse actions, processes, or systems, and that receives its concrete meaning from the constellation of parameters which are specific to the empirical situation in which it is applied.

Thus, both democracy and efficiency are very abstract categories, and this abstract nature implies that it is not possible to make any generally valid statement about their mutual relationship. Indeed, at the abstract conceptual level, the categories of efficiency and democracy do not have a direct and necessary relationship at all. They describe entirely different qualities and measure in entirely different units. The criterion of democracy is applicable to processes of decision making, that of efficiency is applicable to any goal-oriented system, action, or process. In other words, the category of efficiency may be applied in a wide range of contexts where the category of democracy has no relevance at all. And even in those cases where both categories are applicable, efficiency and democracy are by no means always and necessarily mutually obstructive. The enhancement of efficiency neither automatically implies a reduction of democratic qualities, nor are improvements of the latter necessarily achieved at the expense of the former. Democratic qualities may be beneficial for the efficiency of a process or system, but they may also be detrimental, or not affect its efficiency at all. They are beneficial if they enhance the ability of a system to fulfill its specific function without increasing the required inputs. They are detrimental if they either reduce the system's output, or necessitate a higher input in order to keep the output at the same level. Therefore, any talk of a direct contradiction or *trade-off* between democracy and efficiency is misleading. While there may well be a direct trade-off between the *inclusiveness* of decision making and the *effectiveness* of decision making, it would be entirely wrong to regard democracy and efficiency as opposite poles on the same scale.

In the idealist tradition of social and political thought, however, democracy and efficiency are indeed closely connected to each other. In this tradition, societal progress and modernization have come to be understood as the incremental acquisition of ever better material and cultural means, and ever more social space and opportunities for the realization of the individual and collective *autonomous Self*. Democratic revolutions on the one hand, and efficiency revolutions on the other, became the two major tools for achieving the objectives of *Self*-determination and *Self*-realization. Democratization erodes the power and privileges of established elites and authorities, grants individuals and communities the status of *subjects*, and creates the social and political space for the articulation and realization of individual autonomy and the public good. Efficiency improves the performance of society's function systems and thus social provision with the goods and services which the autonomous Self requires for its self-realization. From the modernist perspective, neither democracy nor efficiency represent intrinsic values. Neither of them is an end in itself. Both are meaningful and desirable only as means to an end, namely as means for the realization of the individual and collective Self. With regard to this objective, democracy is the *primary* condition because the democratic process defines the substantive goals which are then—ideally—pursued in an efficient way. Efficiency is a *secondary* condition which is desirable at the level of goal implementation. Put differently, democracy is a *necessary* condition for the realization of the modernist Self but not necessarily a *sufficient* one. It is supplemented by the condition of efficiency which is in itself not necessary, but renders the realization of the autonomous Self more *effective*. Thus efficiency is a means of *effectiveness*. In the modernist tradition, democracy and efficiency complement each other because they are related to the same purpose, the autonomous Self, with efficiency being no more than a tool for enhancing the effectiveness of the realization of this purpose.

However, the integration of democracy and efficiency through the link of the autonomous subject and Self rests on fragile foundations. Firstly, the process of modernization has been a process of ever increasing differentiation and fragmentation of individual and collective identities. And secondly, in *late-modern societies*,[7] the idealist notion of the autonomous Self has lost much of its original appeal both as a normative ideal of identity construction and as descriptive-analytical category in social theory. Rather than pursuing the Kantian agenda—set out in *What is Enlightenment?*—of fully developing its innate potentials for rational self-determination and emancipation from all external imperatives, the late-modern individual has immersed itself into, and has been permeated by, the logic of the market and has thereby lost the specific status of autonomy which the modernist tradition had ascribed to it. Thus, the integrating point of reference for democracy and efficiency has become increasingly volatile or has even dissolved. Yet if defined and considered in isolation from their specifically modernist purpose, democratic structures may easily appear as ineffective, and efforts to enhance the efficiency of specific processes or systems may easily be experienced as unwelcome.[8] These points warrant further exploration.

Of course the modernist idea of the autonomous Self or subject has always been, first and foremost, a philosophical ideal rather than an empirical reality or an entity that could be defined in substantive terms. But the process of modernization has been one in which notions of individual and collective identity have become increasingly differentiated and pluralized. In advanced modern societies it is becoming more and more difficult for individuals and communities to conceptualize and meaningfully articulate their ever more complex, fragmented, and fluid Selves (Bauman 2000, 2005).[9] A *common good* can be defined, if at all, only in the most abstract terms. Yet, with the modernist ideals of the autonomous Self and the common good becoming ever more elusive entities, democratic structures and practices must be perceived as ever more *ineffective*, and societal function systems, including the system of democratic politics, must appear as increasingly *inefficient*. It is in this context that we must see the widely shared diagnosis of a "continuous decline of effectiveness that undermines the confidence of citizens in the democratic regime" (Roller 2005: 1). If the *effectiveness* of democratic structures is their ability to secure the definition and realization of the individual and collective autonomous Self, this effectiveness surely diminishes in line with the increasing differentiation and volatility of the needs, interests, values, and commitments that have to be accommodated. And if the *efficiency* of societal processes and function systems is the resource-saving realization of the individual and collective Self, the elusiveness of this Self implies that the concrete meaning of efficiency becomes increasingly elusive as well. In a condition where processes of differentiation, fragmentation and ephemeralization render democratic deliberation and decision making ever more ineffective, and where due to the inability to conceptualize and articulate individual identity and the collective good substantive criteria of efficiency remain unspecified, a definition of both the Self and of efficiency in *economic* terms becomes the default position. The economic interpretation suggests itself as a capable substitute for a definition of the Self and of efficiency in terms of substantive values because it uses a medium, money, which, even though its *value* is obviously entirely contingent, is nevertheless empirically tangible and quantifiable.

At this point it is worth reemphasizing that the yardstick for efficiency is by no means *per se* the economic one. Judgments about the efficiency of systems or processes measure and value the required inputs in relation to the aspired outcomes. Of course this always implies a cost-benefit analysis, yet this is not necessarily an analysis of *economic* costs versus *economic* benefits. Indeed, even though much of the literature on this issue (e.g., Irvin and Stansbury 2004) prefers not to take this into account, the question *whether an objective is worth the effort* is very different from—and much more complex than—the question *whether an investment pays economic dividend*. In a condition, however, where the ultimate purpose and yardstick of all efficiency, i.e., the autonomous Self, is becoming increasingly difficult to define, the latter question tends to usurp the place of the former. This advance of the economic understanding of efficiency is further accelerated by the extent to which economic rationality has permeated the supposedly autonomous Self. In late-modern society, individual and collective identity as well as the common good are expressed first and foremost in economic terms. Self-construction and Self-expression have, more than anything, become a matter of product choices and consumption patterns (Featherstone 1991; Du Gay 1996; Bauman 2000; Baudrillard 2001). The idealist notion of the *autonomous Self* has been replaced by the *unique consumer profile*. The objective of self-determination and self-realization has become a matter of maximizing earning potentials and spending power. This redefinition of the

Self in economic terms elevates economic efficiency, which for the idealist Self was at best of secondary relevance, into the status of a primary goal. Efficiency, in the particular understanding of economic efficiency, metamorphoses from a means into an end. It becomes the replacement for effectiveness in the sense of the effective realization of the Self.[10] Thus, a purely formal category that in the subject-centered thinking of traditional modernity had always been subordinated to democracy and meaningful only through its relation to the Self becomes superior to democracy and, if applied to the democratic system, actually turns into its yardstick: The idealist metaphysics of the Self metamorphoses into a *metaphysics of efficiency* (see Blühdorn 2001: 183–88).

While in late-modern society the *rhetoric* of the autonomous Self, and thus the declared purpose of democracy and efficiency, has by no means disappeared, these former *tools* for the realization of the idealist Self are either turning into *intrinsic values* or they are, as tools, assigned to a *different purpose*. The former may be said to be the case in the sense that the concepts of democracy and efficiency remain in place as guiding principles of societal change beyond the point where their purpose and source of meaning, the idealist Self, has essentially been differentiated and flexibilized out of existence. The latter holds true in the sense that the idealist Self has been redefined in economic terms, and democracy and efficiency are, accordingly, turning into instruments for economic purposes. For the economically redefined Self, the enhancement of economic efficiency implies the promise of more self-realization. Democracy, however, is then desirable only to the extent that it increases economic efficiency. It is undesirable wherever it threatens to reduce economic efficiency.

Yet, despite the continuous advance of market and consumption-oriented patterns of identity construction and self-expression, the modernist vision of the *autonomous* Self neither already has completely disappeared nor does it seem likely that it will do so in the foreseeable future. For late-modern individuals and communities the claim to autonomy persists, and the political as well as the economic systems are carefully cultivating whatever remains of this modernist ideal. Even if in the late-modern condition the autonomous Self has become outdated and anachronistic, it is the only effective antidote to the characteristic *crises of self-referentiality* that plague late-modern societies (Blühdorn 2005, 2006). For this reason, this *zombie-category* (Beck 2002) cannot be allowed to die, and to the extent that the modernist distinction between the Self and the system remains in place, there continues to be a potential for economic efficiency, which is *systemic* efficiency, to be experienced as conflicting with the Self. It is from this source that calls for the reinstitution of the Self and of *vitality* continue to emerge. And it is for this reason that the new social movements' demands for authentic democracy and regrounded efficiency continue to be renewed.

AUTHENTIC DEMOCRACY, REGROUNDED EFFICIENCY: THE NSM-AGENDA

The tendency of the abstract and formal category of efficiency to develop its own dynamics and metamorphose from a secondary objective that is meaningful and desirable only in relation to the Self into a primary objective and intrinsic value, has been recognized a long time ago. In the 1940s, Horkheimer and Adorno, themselves speaking in the terms of *formal rationality* and *instrumental reason*, emphasized that the agenda of efficiency "posits no substantial goals" (Horkheimer and Adorno 1972: 89) at all and tends to "substitute formula for concept" (ibid.: 5). In the 1960s, Marcuse noted that "it projects mere form [. . .] which can be bent to practically all ends" (Marcuse 1964: 157). Since the late 1960s, the *new social movements* renewed and popularized their post-Marxist critique of modernity and modernization and demanded a radical review of both the dominant notion of efficiency as well as the established understanding of democracy (e.g., Brand et al. 1986; Roth and Rucht 1987; Burns and Van der Will 1988; Roth 1994). The two categories were to be reconnected to their original common purpose, the Self, which in turn was seen to require fundamental reconceptualization and reconstruction because in the process of modernization it had become corrupted and perverted. With their emancipatory focus on the realization and experience of the autonomous Self, the new social movements of the 1970s and 1980s may be seen as the epitome of modernist thinking in the idealist tradition. At the same time, however, the ecology movement, in particular, raised public awareness of a fundamental crisis of traditional modernity. On the one hand the new social movements established a broader than ever social base for the political demand for self-determination and self-realization. On the other hand they had become highly skeptical of the suitability of the Self as the normative centre of the modernization process. Modernity and modernization were perceived to be on a trajectory of self-destruction. For this trajectory to be readjusted, the ill-conceived individualized, consumerist and present-oriented notions of the Self that were seen to dominate western capitalist societies had to be replaced by a postmaterialist and collective Self, which in turn was to be embedded into an inclusive notion of life and nature at large. With a view to the present debate about the meaning and relationship of democracy and efficiency, the social movements' critique of efficiency, their vision of an authentic democracy and their innovative idea of *futurity* warrant some further discussion.

The social movements were rebelling against the abstract and economistic understanding of efficiency because they regarded it as the cause of tremendous *inefficiency*: this notion not only gave rise to a wasteful, conflict ridden and environmentally ruinous consumer culture, but also, instead of promoting freedom and self-realization, it only furthered Marxian *alienation* and the journey into the Weberian *iron cage of modernity*. Challenging the established dogma of productivism, consumerism and scientific-technological progress, the social movements therefore pursued what might be described as *an agenda of deliberate inefficiency*. The de-acceleration of technological and economic development was supposed to create more breathing space for precautionary risk assessment and reflective decision making (also see Ian Welsh's chapter in this volume). Subjecting the economy, science, technology, public administration and all other societal function systems which tend to develop their own dynamics and imperatives to public control; breaking down centralized, hierarchical and large-scale structures; the comprehensive politicization of previously apolitical issues and the involvement of previously uninterested and excluded citizens were regarded as important steps towards the achievement of authentic efficiency, i.e., towards the realization of both a nonalienated autonomous Self and the integrity of nature. In the sense that the *participatory revolution* (Blühdorn 2007a) was explicitly directed against those notions of efficiency that are prevalent in the system of consumer capitalism, the social movements' practices were not simply *accepted*, but actually *expected* to be inefficient in the traditional sense. At the same time they were promoting an *alternative* kind of efficiency that was grounded in substantive life world needs and identities (also see chapter 11).

Democratic renewal was a key issue especially for those strands of the emancipatory social movements which were aiming beyond single issue campaigns. It was conceptualized not simply as improved access to, or transparency of, the existing political institutions and decision making processes, but in a much more subversive sense, as the establishment of entirely new structures of *Self*-organization, *Self*-help, and *Self*-management. A new political *DIY-culture* (McKay 1998) was considered the most effective antidote against the self-imposing imperatives emerging from the institutionalized political, administrative, scientific and economic systems. Authentic democracy was seen as much more than the ritualized process of selecting between largely indistinguishable political parties, or the choice between set policy options which had been formulated by so-called elites rather than by those who would be affected by them. Very crucially, democratic renewal was expected to transcend the limitations of the liberal tradition which conceptualizes democracy as the aggregation of individualized preferences. Authentic democracy was to achieve the transformation of self-centered individuals into public-minded *citizens*. The irrational and alienating politics of strategic bargaining between self-interested actors was to be replaced by what Habermas (1987b, 1998) later described as the exercise of *communicative reason* which was supposed to cut through the distortions caused by established power relations and reveal the *force of the better argument*. In the arenas of the *public sphere* authentic democracy was to generate a broad societal consensus about the goals of modernization as well as the means of their achievement. Genuinely democratic structures and processes were to ensure that the demos can finally own up to the governance of its own present and future.

The category of futurity was a central element in the social movements' project not least because it was expected to provide the concepts of democracy and efficiency with the substantive grounding that traditional notions of the Self had evidently failed to deliver. The social movements' review of the project of modernity expanded the subject or Self that *modernization* was supposed to develop in three different ways: firstly, authentic modernization had to serve humanity at large rather than only privileged parts of it; secondly, it had to target life in general rather than just the human species; and thirdly, it had to encompass the future rather than focusing exclusively on the present. The ecology movement, in particular, had firmly embraced the idea that present generations are only borrowing their habitat from those to come and therefore have to accept responsibility (Jonas 1984) for future generations and the integrity of the natural environment. It had hoped and believed that ecological thinking would deliver and guarantee the substantive grounding for efficiency that had neither been found in any metaphysical reason nor in any transcendental subject. For ecological thinking the inclusion of nature as well as the future into the Self whose development, autonomy and integrity had to be the objective of all modernization was expected to generate substantive criteria filling the purely formal objective of efficiency with concrete meaning.

While the resistance against established notions of efficiency and expert cultures, and the campaigns for the de-acceleration of technological development, for de-differentiation, de-commodification, de-individualization, and so forth may be seen as adding up to an agenda of comprehensive *de*-modernization, the social movements were in fact pursuing a project of *selective* (Offe 1985) and *reflexive* (Beck 1992) modernization that remained firmly committed to the ideals of modernity, but acknowledged that the historical process of modernization had failed to fulfill its desired objectives and therefore needed to be redirected. Their *reinvention of politics* (Beck 1997), their *democratization of democracy* (Offe 2003), was supposed to review, reground, and reconnect the objectives of efficiency and democracy. Yet the inner tension between their emancipatory impulses and the demand for the subordination of the supposedly autonomous Self under the larger principles of the community, of nature, and of life (Raschke 1993: 854) was a challenge larger than the social movements could handle. The paradox that is implicit in the old Kantian idea of *self-imposed duty*, i.e., the idea of autonomously chosen subordination under categorical imperatives, was the root cause of the failure of their project of authentic democracy and grounded efficiency.

POST-DEMOCRACY AND *FUTURE-FITNESS*: THE RECASTING OF PROGRESSIVE POLITICS

Contemporary movements such as the antiglobalization or global justice movements remain committed to the key elements of the NSM-agenda (e.g., Callinicos 2003; George 2004). In recent democratic theory and social movement studies, deliberative democracy, transnational actor networks and cosmopolitan civil society are much debated ideas (e.g., Dryzek 2000; Andersen 2002; Diani and McAdam 2003; Offe 2003; Beck and Grande 2004; Carter 2005). Since the height of the emancipatory social movements, however, advanced modern societies have undergone significant change. *Prima facie* they seem to have fully embraced the NSM-demand for democratic renewal, authentic efficiency, and responsibility for future generations. Bringing politics closer to the people, improving the performance of democratic systems, and securing the sustainability of social and economic arrangements are key objectives for European governments promoted most strongly by those portraying themselves as truly progressive and the real "change-makers" (Blair 2005). Closer analysis, however, reveals that in a further process of reflexive redefinition, the social movements' concepts of democracy, efficiency and futurity have once again been comprehensively reinterpreted which implies "a fundamental recasting of progressive politics" (ibid.).

For the notion of efficiency, this further redefinition can most lucidly be illustrated with the example of environmental policy: Under the conceptual umbrella of *ecological modernization* (Blühdorn 2000b; Mol and Sonnenfeld 2000), the issues which the ecology movement had put on the political agenda have been redefined as technological, economic, and managerial issues, and technology- and market-based *efficiency revolutions* (Weizsäcker et al. 1998; Jordan et al. 2003) are widely presented as the most powerful policy tool. This exclusive reliance in environmental policy on the paradigm of ecological modernization reduces the ecological problematique to concerns about resource consumption and waste emissions and completely eclipses all other dimensions of the ecologist critique. Through the academic discipline of *environmental economics*, in particular, the social movements' notion of *social* and

ecological efficiency has completely been translated back into *economic* efficiency. As the discipline of economics per definition deals with the allocation
of scarce resources, it is not surprising that environmental economics has nothing to say about the *substantive meaning* of efficiency but exclusively focuses
on the management of what has *elsewhere* been defined as valuable and finite.

As regards the social movements' ideal of an authentic democracy, it is
striking how the criticism of democratic deficits and the *bottom-up* campaigns for better representation, more accountability, and stronger elements
of direct participation have recently been mirrored by *top-down* campaigns
for democratic renewal: Since the second half of the 1990s, political and administrative elites who have to address a worsening crisis of political apathy,
loss of public trust, and lack of legitimacy, and who have to square the circle
of ever increasing welfare demands and ever tighter public budgets, have dis-
covered civil society as an antidote to the problems that plague them. Engaging citizens and enhancing participation is hoped to improve the quality, legitimacy and implementation of policy decisions. Devolving responsibilities
to regional and local levels seems a promising strategy for reducing political
apathy while at the same time deflecting electoral discontent from central
governments. Decentralized and community-based welfare provision is said
to be more responsive and cost effective than centralized systems. The social
capital of local communities is seen as a vital resource for the stimulation of
new economic growth. Across Europe, lean administration, the shrinking of
the "nanny state," and the promotion of self-responsibility have, therefore,
emerged as key policy objectives. Irrespective of their party political prove-
nance political elites are calling for more freedom from state regulation, and
pledge to give citizens more power and control over their lives.

Yet, what might appear like the full mainstreaming of social movement demands actually reflects a comprehensive reframing of the ideal of democratic
renewal. Contrary to what the declaratory commitment to deliberative practices and the increasing use of public consultation exercises might suggest,
democratic renewal in this particular sense does not entail a new belief in the
bottom-up formulation of policy goals or the negotiation of visions of the future society. Instead, this promotion of *self-responsibility* means primarily the
privatization and individualization of tasks which can no longer be performed
by the cash-strapped state. In contrast to the social movements' agenda of
civic politicization and empowerment, these policies are part of an agenda of
depoliticization, delegation, and *leadership* (see chapter 12 in this volume).
This new form of civic *empowerment* means at best increased choice between
a range of service options which are designed and provided on the basis of
criteria which are themselves not subject to democratic debate. The citizen is
indeed "returning to the scene," but while for the social movements the citi-

zen was supposed to be "addressed in his role as [public-minded] *citoyen*," he is now "addressed in his role as [individualized] *consumer*" (Hendriks and Tops 1999: 145). Democratic renewal in the contemporary sense fully reverts to the tradition of democratic liberalism which sees democracy as a market for the exchange of private preferences. It has no ambition to reach beyond this understanding.

This depoliticized and managerial variety of democratic renewal redefines civil society and democratic empowerment as a *resource* for the achievement of exactly that kind of efficiency which the social movements had emphatically rejected.[11] It neither aims at nor ever achieves the social re-embedding of the abstract ideal of efficiency. "At root, public involvement initiatives" of this sort are "extensions of tools by which central government controls local agencies, not tools for local people to control central government" (Parkinson 2004: 382). While the conceptual shells of the social movements' progressive project of democratic renewal (empowerment, inclusion, participation, self-responsibility, civil society) have been saved and retained, the top-down *politics of activation* has very little in common with the bottom-up *politics of activism*. Indeed, "by reducing the participants to the status of objects rather than subjects," by turning them into "means to someone else's exercise of autonomy rather than an expression of their own" (Parkinson 2004: 385), this agenda of democratic renewal turns the social movements' project into its straight opposite. Nevertheless, any quick condemnation of this new understanding of *empowerment* would be simplistic. The process of *reflexive redefinition*, very importantly, always has to be understood as incorporating rather than excluding the experiences of the social movement era. It has been argued above that the reorientation from *social* towards *economic* efficiency may be said to reflect the changing needs and identity of the contemporary late-modern consumer Self. In the same sense, the revised understanding of democratic renewal reflects the interests and needs of late-modern citizens whose perception of democracy has, since the height of the social movements' celebration of grassroots democracy, been sobered and reconfigured by what may suitably be described as a *post-democratic revolution* (Blühdorn 2004a; Crouch 2004).[12]

The third dimension of the NSM-agenda has undergone a very similar process of appropriation-*cum*-transformation. On the one hand, sustainability has been embraced as a main policy objective by political actors from the World Bank right down to local planning authorities and business leaders. "To create an inheritance for future generations by taking the tough decisions needed to secure our future" (Blair 2005) is an explicitly declared priority not just for the British government. On the other hand, however, the social movements' notion of futurity has gone through a process of comprehensive reinterpretation. In Germany, it was as early as 1982 that the then Federal Chancellor Helmut Kohl took up the social movements' concern about the future and acknowledged that "too many have for too long been living at the expense of others: the state at the expense of citizens, citizens at the expense of fellow citizens and [. . .] we all at the expense of future generations" (Kohl 1982). In a number of respects, Kohl's societal diagnosis that led him to demand a comprehensive "cultural-*cum*-moral turn-around" (*geistig-moralische Wende*) was thoroughly comparable to the diagnosis that caused ecologists and the progressive left to call for a radical culture change. Yet what Kohl expressed in terms which he had borrowed from social movement discourses, was not so much concern about intergenerational justice and the integrity of the natural foundations of terrestrial life. Instead, he was worried about the economic base of what the Social Democrats had proudly referred to as the *Modell Deutschland*. More specifically, Kohl was concerned about the taxes that would have to be levied on the privileged sectors of German society if an egalitarian understanding of social justice and the redistributive welfare state were to be sustained.

In 1997, the then Federal President Roman Herzog in a much-cited speech reiterated essentially the same diagnosis and demands that Kohl had formulated fifteen years before (Herzog 1997). Echoing the by that time canonical definition of *sustainability* in the UN Brundtland report (Brundtland 1987), Herzog demanded "a new social contract for the benefit of the future," in which "all, really all established beliefs and practices need to be reexamined." His analysis clearly seemed to have embraced the social movements' diagnosis that the established "system is bankrupt" (Kelly 1984). Just as Kohl had done before him, and of course ecologists from their perspective, Herzog highlighted that "our real problem is one of mental attitude," and he again called for comprehensive "inner renewal." In actual fact, however, he was rather selective regarding the range of "established beliefs and practices" which he *really* wanted to see reviewed. Adopting the same perspective as Helmut Kohl had done in the early 1980s, Herzog turned Petra Kelly's *ecologist* understanding of bankruptcy into a primarily *economic* interpretation.

The ascendance to power of the Red-Green coalition in Germany in 1998 offered the first genuine opportunity for the implementation of a politics of futurity in the ecological-progressive sense. By the late 1990s, however, the once very explicit political ideals, values, and strategies of the social movement era and the early Greens had been fully reconfigured by the neomaterialist *silent counter-revolution* (Blühdorn 2002) and the *post-democratic revolution* which have been discussed above. Both the imagination of and the desire for a radical alternative to liberal consumer capitalism had largely evaporated. "Having arrived in the echelons of power, the Red-Greens no longer" had "any vision of a society as it ought to be in the future," and what was left was only the "depressive agenda of the lack of alternatives" in which "everything is reduced to a purely economic productivism" (Walter 2005: 56). While by the end of their first term in office, Alliance 90/The Greens had indeed managed to firmly establish the concept of *future-fitness* in the very center of the German reform debate, this notion has very little in common with the ecologist idea of futurity. Instead, the economic repackaging of the social movements' vision that had once been initiated by Kohl had now been adopted by the Greens themselves. While Green pragmatists were increasingly subscribing to market-liberal agendas (Blühdorn 2004c), their counterparts within their own party were much more concerned with the defensive stabilization of past societal achievements than with the radical departure from the established system which the social movements had attacked as socially and ecologically ruinous.

Indeed in the contemporary debate on future-fitness, the ecological virtues which the new social movements have rooted more deeply in German political culture than many would have believed, are now explicitly identified as barriers to the kind of societal reform that is required. Commitment to long term stability, risk avoidance, moderation of consumption, tight regulation of science, technology, and industry, and so forth: Since the paradigm of the *risk society* has been superseded by that of the *opportunity society* and by the dogma of innovation and competitiveness, these ecological virtues have turned into major obstacles for swift economic recovery and sustained economic growth. The neorealist, neoliberal, and neomaterialist understanding of progress that is central to global capitalism in the twenty-first century represents a head-on challenge to eco-political thinking. In Germany, the virtues of ecological sustainability are now commonly portrayed as one of the main causes of the "German disease" or "German defect" (e.g., Kitschelt and Streeck 2003; Geppert 2003; Steingart 2004). In Britain, the values of the traditional left have been demonized as the "forces of conservatism" (Blair 1999), and the supposedly progressive project to "secure the future" is presented as necessitating, first and foremost, "an open, liberal economy, prepared constantly to change to remain competitive" (Blair 2005). From the perspective of the social movements, however, the categorical refusal to even "debate globalisation" and the explicit acceptance that "the character of this changing world is indifferent to tradition," "unforgiving of frailty," and "has no custom and practice" (ibid.) can only be read as unconditional surrender to the very forces which progressive and emancipatory movements had set out to control.

Thus, the contemporary agenda of *future-fitness* may be understood as the market-liberal re-appropriation of the social movement heritage. The ecologist concept of futurity may be said to have first liquidized into ecological modernization and sustainability, and then evaporated into future-fitness. Once again, however, it is important to emphasize that this reconceptualization of the social movements' ideals must not simplistically be understood as imposed in a top-down fashion in violation of bottom-up demands. Instead, it reflects the transition from modern to late-modern society and from modern to late-modern needs. It may therefore be said to have a kind of democratic legitimacy. In the same sense in which it is appropriate to speak of a *silent counter-revolution* and a *post-democratic revolution*, it is also appropriate to speak of a *post-ecologist revolution* (Blühdorn 2000a; Wissenburg and Levy 2004, Blühdorn and Welsh 2007). This post-ecologist revolution has shifted the emphasis from the social movements' notion of *vitality* towards systemic, and in particular, economic *viability*. In comparison to the concept of *efficiency*, the fine but important difference of this notion of *viability* is that it no longer has any *subject-related* normative overtones but adopts an exclusively *system-centered* point of view.

SUBJECT-CENTERED AND SYSTEM-CENTERED MODERNIZATION: THE TRANSFORMATION OF THE MODERNIZATION PROJECT

The social movements' project of reconciling democracy and efficiency by reconnecting them to a revised notion of the Self and regrounding them in the notion of environmental integrity and futurity has comprehensively failed. Instead, the meaning of the three dimensions of the modernization project, the trajectory of which the emancipatory social movements had intended to correct, has changed considerably. In an exercise of reflexive redefinition the conceptual tools of the social movements' radical critique have been turned into instruments for the reproduction and stabilization of liberal consumer capitalism: The campaign for *authentic democracy* has turned into an agenda of leadership, activation, self-responsibility and consumer choice. The struggle for *genuine efficiency* has been redirected from the goal of substantive efficiency that is grounded in the needs of autonomous human beings towards formal efficiency that is defined in terms of economic competitiveness. The fight for *futurity* has metamorphosed from the rejection of the socially and ecologically destructive risk society into government-promoted campaigns for increased consumption, ever accelerated product innovation and the cultivation of an entrepreneurial culture always ready to take risks.

This reflexive redefinition of the three dimensions of the modernization project implies the transition to a completely new and categorically different form of modernization and modernity: The notion of emancipation-oriented and subject-centered modernization has given way to a new efficiency-oriented and system-centered modernization. Traditional modernity has been superseded by *late* or *denucleated* modernity in which the *metaphysics of efficiency* has eclipsed any previous recollection that democracy and efficiency do not represent intrinsic values, and in which the questions whether, where, and how substantive goals of modernization have been defined are marginalized and eventually completely abandoned. Tony Blair's managerial pragmatism is, arguably, an outstanding illustration of this condition. What Blair confidently presents as New Labour's successful attempt to make sure that "the values we believed in, became relevant to the time we lived in" (Blair 2005), might more appropriately be described as the transition to the late-modern *politics of simulation* in which *signs* are replacing the *signified*, and in which *symbols* (conceptual shells) are substituting for any substantive *referents* (Blühdorn 2002, 2003, 2004b, 2005, 2007b, 2007c). In "a world fast forwarding to the future at unprecedented speed" (Blair 2005) the idea of authentic democracy has become just as meaningless as that of efficiency. In a condition where ever accelerated innovation is not the tool of any subject-centered project of modernity but an intrinsic value and systemic imperative, it is impossible to entertain meaningful structures of democracy because neither can anything be allowed to genuinely restrict or regulate innovation, nor could democratic structures ever be able to catch up or even keep pace with its speed.

So the exploration of the relationship between democracy and efficiency culminates in the diagnosis of a radically new form of modernity and modernization. Any further development of the theory of *late* or *denucleated* modernity and its *politics of simulation* would go beyond the scope of this chapter.[13] At this stage, the emphasis has been on investigating two *essentially contested* concepts whose relationship can only be discussed if they are placed into specific social or cultural contexts which give meaning to them. For this reason, this chapter has explored a series of different contexts ranging from the tradition of idealist thought to the pragmatism of the contemporary global era. Obviously, what has been said about democracy and efficiency is in no way restricted to the two countries which are the focus of this book. The objective in this chapter has not been to make a normative case for a better or more authentic democracy. It has also not been to make a case for more authentic efficiency or better *performance*. The guiding question has neither been the one of theorists of deliberative democracy, i.e., *How do we make democracy more authentic?*, nor that of theorists of new public management, i.e., *How do we make democratic systems more efficient?* In comparison to most of the deliberative democracy literature on the one hand and the new public management literature on the other, this chapter has been very reluctant about pursuing any normative agenda. It does not give rise to any political recommendations, and raises doubts about any suggestions that things can or should be different from what they are. Instead, the objective in this chapter has been to offer a descriptive-analytical conceptualization of the changing meaning and relationship of the constitutive dimensions of societal modernization.

In conclusion it may be appropriate to ask for the benefits of such a descriptive-analytical agenda that tries to minimize its normative assumptions and articulates no political demands. Firstly, there is the academic-scholarly benefit: The explorations in this chapter might help to remove some of the conceptual confusion that in much of the relevant literature obscures the discussion of the democracy-efficiency relationship. Secondly, the exploration of democracy, efficiency, and their relationship reveals that contemporary consumer democracies have entered a new phase of modernity and modernization which is as yet poorly understood and therefore requires further research. The currently dominant social theoretical narrative of *reflexive modernity* is clearly insufficient and highly ideological. And thirdly, there is the faint idealist hope that by means of critical analysis it might be possible to trigger whatever remains of the modernist reflexes: If there is any truth in the suggestion that the contemporary discourse of democratic renewal and the contemporary talk of efficiency gains have to be understood as dimensions of a *simulated* modernization; if it is correct to say that ever accelerated innovation and ever new rounds of reform are guided by a *metaphysics of efficiency*, this might be able to reactivate something of the old modernist belief that things ought to be different.

NOTES

1. For the purposes of this chapter, *modernization* is understood not just as technological innovation and institutional or policy reform. Instead, the concept is used in the Habermasian sense of progress towards the realization of the *project of modernity* that has been formulated by the European movement of Enlightenment and has remained *unfinished* ever since (Habermas 1987a).

2. The two governments under Schröder's leadership (1998–2002 and 2002–2005) qualify as *reform governments* because of their *ambitions* and public *expectations* rather than actually implemented reform policies (see chapters 1 and 2 in this volume). Government participation of Alliance 90/The Greens, in particular, and initially widespread belief in a progressive *red-green project* (Egle et al. 2003) justify this discription.

3. The criterion of effectiveness measures the extent to which an action or process factually delivers its intended outcomes.

4. The criterion of efficacy assesses the extent to which a political actor has been, or feels to have been, able to influence a political decision.

5. For Fuchs *systemic performance* is expected from any political system, and it is measured in terms of criteria such as order, security and economic growth. *Democratic performance*, in contrast, is an additional expectation that is particular to democratic systems. It is measured in terms of specifically democratic goals such as liberty and equality (Fuchs 1998).

6. The way in which Fuchs distinguishes the two dimensions is not convincing because for him both of them ultimately measure the effective fulfilment of *human goals* rather than *systemic imperatives*. Unsurprisingly, Fuchs uses both concepts as yardsticks for *political* performance rather than using the second one for measuring the performance of systems in *systemic* terms.

7. I am using the terms *late-modern* society and the *late-modern* era or condition to describe a particular phase of modernity that distinguishes itself from earlier phases of modernity by the unprecedented degree to which economic rationality and the economic system have colonized all other forms of rationality and societal function systems, thereby threatening the viability of the dualisms that define traditional modernity (Blühdorn 2000a, 2004b, 2006, 2007c).

8. In this context it is useful to recall that while the tool of democracy is a specifically modernist invention that is useful first and foremost with regard to its specifically modernist purpose (the autonomous Self), the enhancement of efficiency may serve all kinds of purposes, including many which conflict with the modernist ideal of the autonomous Self.

9. On political articulation in late-modern societies as the *performance of identity* see Blühdorn 2005, 2006 and 2007c.

10. Unsurprisingly Fuchs, Roller, and many others who are trying to assess the *performance* of liberal democratic systems are finding it increasingly difficult to develop any "normative model of political effectiveness" (Roller 2005). See also Fuchs (1998). While they are continuing to develop empirically measurable performance indicators for the effective achievement of goals such as security, wealth, social justice, or environmental protection, their attempts to reconstruct a normative basis for performance assessment invariably fail.

11. Note the language of a recent OECD Public Management Policy Brief which describes citizen involvement as a way of *"reaping benefits"* and as "a *sound investment* in better policy-making" that "allows governments to *tap new* sources" (OECD 2001b: 1; my emphases).

12. For a more detailed elaboration of the concepts of *post-democracy* and the *post-democratic revolution* see the concluding chapter in this volume.

13. Some of these ideas will be further explored in chapter 12 in this volume.

REFERENCES

Andersen, James, ed. (2002): *Transnational Democracy. Political Spaces and Border Crossings*. London/New York: Routledge.

Baudrillard, Jean (2001): *Selected Writings*. Edited and introduced by Mark Poster. Cambridge: Polity.

Bauman, Zygmunt (2000): *Liquid Modernity*. Cambridge: Polity.

—— (2005): *Liquid Life*. Cambridge: Polity.

Beck, Ulrich (1992): *The Risk Society. Towards a New Modernity*. Cambridge: Polity.

—— (1997): *The Reinvention of Politics. Rethinking Modernity in the Global Social Order*. Cambridge: Polity.

—— (2002): "The Cosmopolitan Society and its Enemies." *Theory, Culture & Society* 19, no. 1–2: 17–44.

Beck, Ulrich, and Grande, Edgar (2004): *Das kosmopolitische Europa*. Frankfurt/Main: Suhrkamp.

Blair, Tony (1999): "Speech to the Labour Party Conference." Bournemouth, 28 September 1999.

—— (2005): "We are the Change-Makers." Speech to the Labour Party conference. Brighton, 27 September 2005.

Blühdorn, Ingolfur (2000a): *Post-ecologist Politics. Social Theory and the Abdication of the Ecologist Paradigm*. London/New York: Routledge.

—— (2000b): "Ecological Modernisation and Post-Ecologist Politics," in: Spaargaren, Gert, Mol, Arthur, and Buttel, Frederick, eds.: *Environment and Global Modernity*. London/Thousand Oaks/New Delhi: Sage, pp. 209–28.

—— (2001): "Reflexivity and Self-Referentiality: On the Normative Foundations of Ecological Communication," in: Grant, Colin, and McLaughlin, Donal (Hg.) *Language—Meaning—Social Construction*, Amsterdam/New York: Rodopi, 2001, pp.181–201.

—— (2002): "Unsustainability as a Frame of Mind—And How We Disguise It. The Silent Counter Revolution and the Politics of Simulation." *The Trumpeter* 18, no. 1: 59–69.

—— (2003): "Inclusionality—Exclusionality. Environmental Philosophy and Simulative Politics," in: Winnett, Adrian, and Warhurst, Alison, eds.: *Towards an Environment Research Agenda, Volume II*. Houndmills/New York: Palgrave Macmillan, pp. 21–45.

—— (2004a): "Future-Fitness and Reform Gridlock. Towards Social Inequality and Post-democratic Politics?" *Debatte. Review of Contemporary German Affairs* 12, no. 2: 114–36.

—— (2004b): "Post-Ecologism and the Politics of Simulation," in: Wissenburg, Marcel, and Yoram, Levy: *Liberal Democracy and the Environment. The End of Environmentalism?* London/New York: Routledge, pp. 35–47.

—— (2004c): "New Green Pragmatism in Germany. Green Politics beyond the Social Democratic Embrace." *Government and Opposition* 39, no. 4: 564–86.

—— (2005): "Social Movements and Political Performance. Niklas Luhmann, Jean Baudrillard and the Politics of Simulation," in: Haas, Birgit, ed.: *Macht—Performanz. Performativität, Polittheater*. Würzburg: Königshausen & Neumann, pp. 19–40.

—— (2006): "Self-Experience in the Theme-park of Radical Action? Social Movements and Political Articulation in the Late-modern Condition." *European Journal of Social Theory* 9, no. 1: 23–42.

—— (2007a): "The Participatory Revolution: New Social Movements and Civil Society," in: Larres, Klaus, ed.: *A Companion to Europe Since 1945*. London: Blackwell (forthcoming).

—— (2007b): "Symbolic Politics and the Politics of Simulation: Eco-political Practice in the Late-modern Condition." *Environmental Politics* 16, no. 2 (forthcoming).

—— (2007c): "Self-Description, Self-Deception, Simulation. A Systems-theoretical Perspective on Contemporary Discourses of Radical Change." *Social Movement Studies* 6, no. 1 (forthcoming).

Blühdorn, Ingolfur, and Welsh, Ian, eds. (2007): *The Politics of Unsustainability. Eco-Politics in the Post-Ecologist Era*. London/New York: Routledge.

Brand, Karl-Werner, Büsser, Detlef, and Rucht, Dieter (1986): *Aufbruch in eine andere Gesellschaft*. Frankfurt/Main/New York: Campus.

Brundtland, Gro Harlem (1987): *Our Common Future. World Commission on Environment and Development*. Oxford/New York: Oxford University Press.

Burns, Rob, and Van der Will, Wilfried (1988): *Protest and Democracy in West Germany. Extra-Parliamentary Opposition and the Democratic Agenda*. Houndmills/New York: Palgrave Macmillan.

Cain, Bruce, Dalton, Russel, and Scarrow Susan, eds. (2003): *Democracy Transformed? Expanding Political Opportunities in Advanced Industrial Democracies*. Oxford/New York: Oxford University Press.

Carter, April (2005): *Direct Action and Democracy Today*. Cambridge: Polity.

Callinicos, Alex (2003): *An Anti-Capitalist Manifesto*. Cambridge: Polity.

Cerny, Philip (1999): "Globalization and the Erosion of Democracy." *European Journal of Political Research* 36, no. 1: 1–26.

Chesters, Graeme, and Welsh, Ian (2005): "Complexity and Social Movement(s). Process and Emergence in Planetary Action Systems." *Theory, Culture & Society* 22, no. 5:187–211.

Crouch, Colin (2004): *Post-Democracy*. Cambridge: Polity.

Dahl, Robert (1994): "A Democratic Dilemma: System Effectiveness versus Citizen Participation. "*Political Science Quarterly* 109, no. 1: 23–34.

Dalton, Russell, Cain, Bruce, and Scarrow, Susan (2003): "Democratic Publics and Democratic Institutions," in: Cain, Bruce, Dalton, Russel, and Scarrow, Susan, eds.: *Democracy Transformed? Expanding Political Opportunities in Advanced Industrial Democracies*. Oxford/New York: Oxford University Press, pp. 250–75.

Dalton, Russell (2004): *Democratic Challenges—Democratic Choices. The Erosion of Political Support in Advanced Industrial Democracies*. Oxford/New York: Oxford University Press.

Diani, Mario, and McAdam, Doug (2003): *Social Movements and Networks. Relational Approaches to Collective Action*. Oxford/New York: Oxford University Press.

Dierckxsens, Wim (2000): *The Limits of Capitalism. An Approach to Globalization without Neoliberalism*. London/New York: Zed Books.

Dryzek, John (2000): *Deliberative Democracy and Beyond. Liberals, Critics, Contestations*. Oxford/New York: Oxford University Press.

Du Gay, Paul (1996): *Consumption and Identity at Work*. London/Thousand Oaks/New Delhi: Sage.

Egle, Christoph, Ostheim, Tobias, and Zohlnhöfer, Reimut, eds. (2003): *Das Rot-Grüne Projekt. Eine Bilanz der Regierung Schröder 1998–2002.* Wiesbaden: Westdeutscher Verlag.

Featherstone, Mike (1991): *Consumer Culture & Postmodernism.* London/Thousand Oaks/New Delhi: Sage.

Fuchs, Dieter (1998): "Kriterien demokratischer Performanz in Liberal Demokratien," in: Greven, Michael Th., ed.: *Demokratie—eine Kultur des Westens?* Opladen: Leske and Budrich, pp. 152–79.

George, Susan (2004): *Another World is Possible if. . . .* London/New York: Verso.

Geppert, Dominik (2003): *Maggie Thatchers Rosskur—Ein Rezept für Deutschland?* Berlin: Siedler Verlag.

Habermas, Jürgen (1987a): *The Philosophical Discourse of Modernity.* Cambridge: Polity.

—— (1987b): *The Theory of Communicative Action. Volume 2: Lifeworld and System: A Critique of Functionalist Reason.* Cambridge: Polity.

—— (1998): *The Inclusion of the Other: Studies in Political Theory.* Cambridge: Polity.

Held, David (1996): *Models of Democracy.* Stanford: Stanford University Press.

—— (2004): *Global Covenant. The Social Democratic Alternative to the Washington Consensus.* Cambridge: Polity.

Hendriks, Frank, and Tops, Pieter (1999): "Between Democracy and Efficiency: Trends in Local Government Reform in the Netherlands and Germany." *Public Administration* 77, no. 1: 133–53.

Herzog, Roman (1997): "Aufbruch ins 21. Jahrhundert." Speech delivered in the Adlon Hotel in Berlin. Bundespressearchiv, 26 April 1997 (widely referred to as *Ruckrede*).

Horkheimer, Max, and Adorno, Theodor W. (1972): *Dialectic of Enlightenment.* New York: Herder and Herder.

Irvin, Renée, and Stansbury, John (2004): "Citizen Participation in Decision Making: Is it Worth the Effort?" *Public Administration Review* 64, no. 1: 55–65.

Jonas, Hans (1984): *Das Prinzip Verantwortung.* Frankfurt/Main: Suhrkamp.

Jordan, Andrew, Wurzel, Rüdiger, and Zito, Anthony, eds. (2003): *"New" Instruments of Environmental Governance? National Experiences and Prospects.* London: Frank Cass.

Jost, Gesine Foljanty, and Jabob, Klaus (2004): "The Climate Change Policy Network in Germany." *European Environment* 14, no. 1: 1–15.

Kelly, Petra (1984): *Fighting for Hope.* London: Hogarth Press.

Kitschelt, Herbert, and Streeck, Wolfgang (2003): "From Stability to Stagnation: Germany at the Beginning of the Twenty-First Century." *West-European Politics* 26, no.4: 1–34.

Kohl, Helmut (1982): "Regierungserklärung." Speech delivered in the German *Bundestag.* Bundespressearchiv, 13 October 1982.

Ladwig, Bernd (2002): "Die politische Theorie der Frankfurter Schule: Franz L. Neumann," in: Brodocz, Andre, and Schaal, Gary S., eds.: *Politische Theorien der Gegenwart I.* Opladen: Leske and Budrich, pp. 35–75.

Lütz, Susanne (2003): "Zwischen Effektivität und Legitimität—Regulative Politik im Politikfeld- und Ländervergleich," in: Czada, Roland, Lütz, Susanne, and Mette,

Stefan, eds.: *Regulative Politik. Zähmungen von Markt und Technik*. Opladen: Leske + Budrich, 2003, pp. 241–64.

Marcuse, Herbert (1964): *One-dimensional Man*. Boston: Beacon Press.

McKay, George, ed. (1998): *DiY Culture: Party and Protest in Nineties Britain*. London/New York: Verso.

Michels, Robert (1962): *Political Parties: A Sociological Study of the Oligarchical Tendencies of Modern Democracies*. New York: The Free Press.

Mol, Arthur, and Sonnenfeld, David (2000): *Ecological Modernisation Around the World: Perspectives and Critical Debates*. London: Frank Cass.

Moran, Michael (2003): *The British Regulatory State. High Modernism and Hyper-Innovation*. Oxford/New York: Oxford University Press.

Müntefering, Franz (2005): "Demokratie. Teilhabe, Zukunftschancen, Gerechtigkeit." Speech delivered in Berlin. Willy-Brandt-Haus, 13 April 2005.

OECD (2001a.): *Citizens as Partners: OECD Handbook on Information, Consultation and Public Participation in Policy-Making*. Paris: OECD.

——— (2001b): *Engaging Citizens in Policy-making: Information, Consultation and Public Participation*. PUMA Policy Brief No.10. Paris: OECD.

Offe, Claus (1985): "Challenging the Boundaries of Traditional Politics: The Contemporary Challenge of Social Movements." *Social Research* 52, no. 4: 817–68.

———, ed. (2003): *Demokratisierung der Demokratie. Diagnosen und Reformvorschläge*. Frankfurt/Main/New York: Campus.

Okun, Arthur (1975) *Equality and Efficiency: The Big Trade-Off*. Brookings Institution

Parkinson, John (2004): "Why deliberate? The Encounter Between Deliberation and New Public Managers." *Public Administration* 82, no. 2: 377–95.

Raschke, Joachim (1993): *Die Grünen. Wie sie wurden, was sie sind*. Cologne: BUND Verlag.

Roller, Edeltraud (2005): *The Performance of Democracies. Political Institutions and Public Policy*. Oxford/New York: Oxford University Press.

Roth, Roland (1994): *Demokratie von Unten. Neue Soziale Bewegungen auf dem Wege zur politischen Institution*. Köln: bund.

Roth, Roland, and Rucht, Dieter, eds. (1987): *Neue Soziale Bewegungen in der Bundesrepublik Deutschland*. Frankfurt/Main/New York: Campus.

Sarcinelli, Ulrich (2003): "Demokratie unter Kommunikationsstress? Das parlamentarische Regierungssystem in der Mediengesellschaft." *Aus Politik und Zeitgeschichte* B43/2003 39–46.

Schmidt, Manfred G. (2000): *Demokratietheorien. Eine Einführung*. Opladen: Leske+Budrich.

Shutt, Harry (2001): *A New Democracy. Alternatives to a Bankrupt World Order*. London/New York: Zed Books.

Spaargaren, Gert, Mol, Arthur, and Buttel, Frederick, eds. (2000): *Environment and Global Modernity*. London/Thousand Oaks/New Delhi: Sage.

Steffani, Winfried (1973): "Parlamentarische Demokratie. Zur Problematik von Effizienz, Transparenz und Partizipation," in: Steffani, Winfried, ed.: *Parlamentarismus ohne Transparenz*. Wiesbaden: Westdeutscher Verlag, pp. 17–47.

Steingart, Gabor (2004): *Deutschland. Der Abstieg eines Superstars*. München: Piper.

Strøm, Kaare, Müller, Wolfgang C., and Bergman, Torbjörn, eds. (2003): *Delegation and Accountability in Parliamentary Democracies*. Oxford/New York: Oxford University Press.

Thatcher, Mark, and Stone Sweet, Alec (2002): "Theory and Practice of Delegation to Non-Majoritarian Institutions." *West European Politics* 25, no 1: 1–22.

Tsebelis, George (1995): "Decision Making in Political Systems: Veto Players in Presidentialism, Parliamentarism, Multi-Cameralism and Multi-Partyism." *British Journal of Political Science* 25, no. 2: 289–325.

——— (2002): *Veto Players: How Political Institutions Work*. Princeton: Princeton University Press.

Walter, Franz (2005): "Die Alternativlosen." *Der Spiegel* 16/2005: 54–56.

Weizsäcker, E.U.v. et al. (1998): *Factor Four: Doubling Wealth, Halving Resource Use*. London: Earthscan.

Wissenburg, Marcel, and Levy, Yoram, eds. (2004): *Liberal Democracy and the Environment. The End of Environmentalism?* London/New York: Routledge.

STRUCTURES AND STRATEGIES

4

Democratic Deficits—Democratic Renewal: Political Detachment, Constitutional Reform, and the Politics of Reengagement in the UK

Lewis Baston

This chapter aims at analyzing some of the fundamentals of the British constitution and the reforms implemented primarily in the early stages of the Blair administration in 1997–1999. It is intended as a provocative contribution to the volume; to stimulate debate and illuminate some themes that are also apparent in other chapters. It begins by contrasting two alternative analyses of the British situation in the 1970s—*elective dictatorship* and *ungovernability*—and resolving the apparent contradiction before moving on to what changed under Thatcher and in the constitutional reform program under Blair. Despite the strength and flexibility of the British state, and recent reforms, public dissatisfaction remains extremely widespread and existing methods of managing Britain are not reengaging the electorate. The concept of a *responsive* government is posited as a synthesis between efficiency and democracy, and electoral reform identified as a necessary condition for such a situation to emerge.

ELECTIVE DICTATORSHIP

Dictatorship may superficially appear a highly efficient system. It removes all the constraints that democracy imposes on the efficient conduct of government—consultation, parliamentary debate, freedom of information, amendment, opposition, media scrutiny, judicial review, entrenched human rights, federalism, and so on. It therefore allows government to act quickly and decisively.

However, actually existing dictatorship turns out to have been, for the most part, a highly inefficient system. Dictatorial government is generally badly informed government. Coercive, vertical lines of authority produce a tendency for those lower down in the hierarchy to suppress inconvenient facts when reporting upwards. The facts on which government bases its actions are therefore shrouded in fog, for instance in the compilation of economic statistics in the former Soviet Union. Rapid decision making, though efficient in a limited sense, can also be poor and hasty decision making which requires expensive and troublesome adjustment after the fact. In a market sense, competition for office between parties benefits the citizen-consumer by raising standards all round; the provision of the basic functions of government by dictatorship suffers from all the inefficiency and slowness of adaptation that monopoly providers of any service are supposed to demonstrate. When authority does not have to justify its actions to its people, political opposition, or independent media, the rationale for actions can become poorly evolved or self-interested. Dictatorial government tends to be corrupt, thanks to the lack of challenge and scrutiny, and the pervasive sense of unaccountability and coercion within the system.

Britain is, of course, not a dictatorship but a democracy, although the metaphor of dictatorship does have its uses in analyzing its political system. In October 1976 the leading Conservative lawyer Lord Hailsham coined a famous phrase. Hailsham argued that:

> The powers of our own Parliament are absolute and unlimited. And in this, we are almost alone. All other free nations impose limitations on their representative assemblies. We impose none on ours. Parliament can take away a man's liberty or his life without a trial, and in past centuries, it has actually done so [. . .]. We live in an *elective dictatorship*, absolute in theory, if hitherto thought tolerable in practice. (Hailsham 1976)

Parliamentary sovereignty has been one of the traditional pillars of British constitutional thinking. Parliament itself was originally an instrument in making monarchical government accountable if not to the people at least to the owners of land and property. With the transfer of executive power to a government and prime minister that depend on a parliamentary majority to sustain themselves in office, these roles have become fused. With the organization of MPs into party, and their dependence for the most part on party to win election, the ability of government to command the powers described by Hailsham is institutionalized.

This system has adapted itself to the mass franchise and democracy in general through the doctrines of majority rule and the mandate. A centralized, powerful government draws its legitimacy from the people through winning an election, and is held accountable for what it does with that power at the election afterwards. The manifesto that the winning party has proposed at the election is regarded as the program of action for that government, and obstruction of that has no, or only dubious, legitimacy. A party with a majority in the House of Commons faces few obstacles to the exercise of power, at least within the political system itself. External constraints such as the economic and international context do of course make themselves felt in the exercise of power in Britain, but there is relatively little that organized opposition can accomplish. Democratic values in Britain were not entrenched through constitutional provisions, but instead in an ethos of restraint in using the theoretically unlimited powers of parliamentary sovereignty. However, the concept of an ethos of restraint is an uncomfortable one in conditions that are extreme, or perceived as extreme. British governments with a secure parliamentary majority have always had the theoretical ability to restrict civil liberties or make life difficult for the opposition, but these powers have been used sparingly, for instance during the two world wars. However, it is open to governments to radically redefine the borders between state powers and individual rights without using any special constitutional procedure. In conditions of apparent urgency, as with the Prevention of Terrorism Act 1974 and the succession of antiterrorist measures since 2001, the balance can be shifted very decisively.[1]

Hailsham's phrase has had a lasting appeal as a description of parliamentary sovereignty in Britain. However, alongside the *elective dictatorship* line of analysis there also grew up what one may call the *ungovernability critique* of British politics (King 1976). This concept became current in the mid 1970s following the failure of the Heath government's attempt to regulate industrial relations through the new Industrial Relations Act, and the industrial unrest of the period culminating in the three-day week and the February 1974 election.

Ungovernability thinking highlighted the power of key groups of organized workers (and by extension other powerful groups such as the financial markets and industrial managers) and that the continued functioning of society depended on their cooperation. When groups such as miners (1972 and 1974) and foreign exchange dealers (1976) were determined to confront the government, they could win. With the unions the Heath government favored regulation, while the Labour government that followed favored a bargained arrangement that was called the Social Contract.

One heard very little about ungovernability after 1982. The possibility of unemployment leading to massive social unrest, as had seemed possible during the riots of summer 1981, receded and its effect was actually to reduce the power of organized labor. Inflation fell sharply in 1982, removing another cause of instability in industrial relations, and as economic growth gradually resumed the prospect of the Thatcher government collapsing under the strain of the crisis was removed. The spring 1982 Falklands War was seen as a reassertion of the power of government to act effectively, and the ability to ride out the 1984–1985 miners' strike without much disruption to everyday life or the national economy.

However, *ungovernability* (its reality or its reputation) had dampened the impact of the "elective dictatorship" critique because the power of a government with a parliamentary majority was so obviously contingent on external constraints. Instead of constitutional checks and balances, there existed forces outside the formal constitution, such as trade unionism between 1940 and the early 1980s, which limited government's freedom of maneuver. The difference between contemporary Germany and the Britain of the time is that the German political system possesses both constitutional checks and balances and a wider and much better organized system of social partnership than ever existed in Britain.

From 1962 until 1979 governments of both major parties attempted to share a degree of responsibility with the trade union movement and the directors of the principal industries, through the creation of "tripartite" institutions which were intended to affect policy across a range of economic and employment issues. The economic success and relative industrial peace of West Germany during this period, the high point of *Modell Deutschland*, impressed British policy makers, but tripartism never became as institutionalized or as effective as the institutions of social partnership in Germany. From time to time an attempt would be made to go further and introduce a more thoroughly corporatist system of government, but these failed not so much from the unwillingness of governments but from the incapacity of labor movement organization as it then stood to take on such functions. Britain's fragmented trade union movement, in which central authority was weak, often could not deliver on agreements reached between the leadership and the government. As outlined by Schmid and Steffen later in this volume (see chapter 10), both the German trade union movement and industrial management were remodeled after 1945, to modernize them and enable them to play a part in coordinating economic and social policy. The trade unions in particular were able to take a wider view of industrial modernization than their British counterparts, although the adjustment to a postindustrial economy poses problems that are currently apparent.

Thatcher's abandonment of even the semblance of the politics of consensus and cooperation, or even-handedness between what used to be called "the two sides of industry" created a vacuum. The attempt of some local authorities to serve as a center of opposition politics was crushed in the mid 1980s. The internal constraints no longer worked (and thanks to the weakness of the opposition vote the electoral constraint was also weakened), and all that was left were the impersonal and increasingly powerful forces of the financial markets, the United States, Europe, and the global trade system. Hailsham, ironically, served without demur in this government, which was closer to the ideal-type of elective dictatorship than any of its predecessors because it lacked the features of over-mighty barons and potential competition for office.

The powers of central government to impose its will in an "efficient" manner, and a combination of political circumstances, allowed an early neoliberal experiment to continue for an extended period after 1979. The result was a top-down imposition of an economic and social system that enabled a relatively adaptable and flexible response to the forces of globalization. Several other chapters in this volume (e.g., chapters 1, 2, and 7) explore these issues in more detail. It is not without significance that two other relatively early and complete neoliberal turns took place in other democracies based on the Westminster system—New Zealand and Australia.

Mass unemployment, the changing economic structure (the decline of large-scale industrial employment and the increasing importance of small service sector employers), and legal changes restricting trade union power, created a situation where the Thatcher government was able to dismantle institutions of social partnership. The last survivor, the National Economic Development Council (NEDC), was wound up in 1992 having lost its role several years before that. In Conservative discussions of industry at the time much was made of the "management's right to manage," and alongside this came the government's right to govern.

By the mid-1990s the costs of the elective dictatorship approach to government were becoming apparent. The Thatcher and Major governments had become remote from public opinion, making a series of gross miscalculations about the popular impact of a succession of policies from the poll tax (1990) to the forced change to economic policy and the closure of most of the coal mining industry (1992). Government itself seemed increasingly inept, inefficient, and even at the margins corrupt, but there was a democratic solution to the increasingly exhausted and sclerotic Conservative regime in the form of a renewed opposition party.

Changes Since 1997

The Blair government has been among the most radical constitutional reforming governments at least since the Liberal government of 1905–1915. That government's principal legacy was the defeat of the challenge of the House of Lords to the growth of democracy in Britain, but its attempt to devolve power to Ireland and possibly eventually to federalize the British state was frustrated. While not on the same scale, devolution to Scotland and Wales, further Lords reform, regulation of party funding, and the Human

Rights Act are all important changes. Labour came to power in 1997 with the following phrasing in the manifesto:

> The Conservatives seem opposed to the very idea of democracy. They support hereditary peers, unaccountable quangos and secretive government. They have debased democracy through their MPs who have taken cash for asking questions in the House of Commons. They are opposed to the development of decentralised government. The party which once opposed universal suffrage and votes for women now says our constitution is so perfect that it cannot be improved. Our system of government is centralised, inefficient and bureaucratic. Our citizens cannot assert their basic rights in our own courts. The Conservatives are afflicted by sleaze and prosper from secret funds from foreign supporters. There is unquestionably a national crisis of confidence in our political system, to which Labour will respond in a measured and sensible way. (The Labour Party 1997)

However, what followed was more the implementation of several disconnected measures driven by different concerns than a coherent program based on a new model of the British state. The traditional essentials survived the initial flush of reformist enthusiasm, and as Blair and New Labour became accustomed to and comfortable with power and the idea of being the establishment their interest in further reform dropped steeply.

Devolution

Scottish devolution was much discussed in the 1992 and 1997 elections, with Conservative leader John Major (and others) stressing the risks of the break up of Britain. Devolved government, it was argued, would only disrupt the functioning of British government, arouse resentment in England, and lead to ever increasing demands for full independence. The Scottish National Party's hopes were of course the same as the Conservatives' fears. In 1999 SNP leader Alex Salmond predicted an independent Scotland in 2007 and Major thought that was quite possible. Essentially, the antidevolutionists argued on efficiency grounds that a centralized state was a necessary part of the British constitutional system, and that without it there was no halfway house before "Britain" as such ceased to exist as a political entity. The principal argument of those in favor of devolution was based around democracy—that the Scots in particular wanted it and there was no strong antidevolution sentiment in England. The democratic legitimacy of devolution was cemented by the September 1997 referendum that gave strong backing to devolved government in Scotland (and a narrow acceptance of it in Wales).

However, the reality of devolution has not borne out the predictions of those who opposed it, and the SNP and the cause of independence have languished since 1999. On the other hand, neither has the institution of the Scottish Parliament itself revitalized democracy in Scotland. Turnout in the 2003 Scottish election was a disappointing 49 percent, 9 percent below what it was in the 1999 Scottish and 2001 Westminster elections. Polls tend to find general support for the institution and a belief that more powers should be devolved, but also widespread skepticism about how much it has accomplished. A 2004 poll found that 66 percent favored devolving more power and only 2 percent favored returning powers to Westminster and Whitehall (ICM/Joseph Rowntree Reform Trust 2004).

However, as a reform it has arguably increased the sustainability and efficiency of the UK constitutional system by removing a potent source of dissatisfaction with the pre-1997 order. By devolving to Scotland, the legislative burden on the Westminster parliament has been reduced, public policy made more appropriate and responsive to specifically Scottish concerns, and the role of Scotland as a public policy laboratory for the state as a whole now has legitimacy. This latter role was apparent before 1997 in areas such as the introduction of the poll tax in 1989 and single-tier local government reform in 1994, but now has a democratic basis.

The Second Chamber

The existence and nature of a second chamber offers some insight into the questions of democracy and efficiency. Like most of the British constitutional structure, the House of Lords has been fairly efficient but not democratic. Its composition relies on the predemocratic principles of patronage appointment and (for the time being) hereditary privilege. Its principal function is as a revising chamber, giving the government an opportunity to make minor improvements to the text of legislation as it passes through parliament. Its powers to obstruct are limited, and have been rarely used. As a part-time house, with relatively little legitimacy, it has been very efficient and cost-effective at its revising function without imposing much of a challenge to the smooth conduct of business.

The interim House of Lords is perhaps the most unsatisfactory result of the Blair government's constitutional reforms. It has created a second chamber whose claims to either efficiency or democracy are both suspect. Before 1958, its composition was virtually entirely hereditary. Peers sat as legislators for the most part because their ancestors had received a seat in the Lords from previous monarchs or prime ministers, for all sorts of worthy and unworthy reasons. After life peerages (individuals appointed to the House of Lords for the duration of their lifetimes, whose peerages do not pass on to their descendants) were introduced nearly all new creations fell into that category.

The size of the Lords, and the proportion of life peers, increased, but the Conservatives still maintained a strong grip on the House. Labour abolished all but 92 of the hereditary peerages in 1999 (a compromise to enable the legislation to pass quickly) and now life peers are the predominant element in the House. The 1999 reform was supposed to be stage one of a larger reform program, although stage two was put back after inconclusive parliamentary votes in 2003. The current chamber is known, with a trace of irony, as the "interim" Lords; members are conscious that the powers and composition set in 1911 were also supposed to be temporary.

In getting rid of the hereditaries, the government has removed one of the obstacles to non-Conservative governments; no longer can the Conservative Party decide at will to amend or obstruct legislation whatever the verdict of elections. The limitation of the powers of the Lords in 1911 was a necessary step before Britain could be considered a democracy. After further amendment in 1949 the remaining powers were a nuisance rather than a threat, but still mean that a constraint operated on Labour governments that did not operate on Conservative governments.

The composition of the House of Lords is now much closer than that of the House of Commons in representing the popular votes cast in the general election, although its members cannot themselves claim the legitimation of a democratic mandate. In the past, the House of Lords has been most unrepresentative of public opinion because of the preponderance of Conservative hereditary peers and the greater length of time that Conservative governments have had to appoint life peers. The removal of most of the hereditaries in 1999, and the effect of 8 years of fairly rapid creation of life peers under a Labour government, have created a new situation. This has led to a more assertive House of Lords, causing government more difficulties, and the possibility of the reassessment of the guiding convention of the use of the Lords' powers, the Salisbury Convention of 1945. The Salisbury convention (sometimes called Salisbury-Addison, after the respective Conservative and Labour leaders in the Lords at the time) was a compromise to enable the coexistence of a Conservative Lords and a Labour government. The Lords would not use their powers to obstruct items that were in the manifesto of the party that won the general election (a logical extension of the doctrine of the mandate). However, now that the composition of the Lords is so different, it can be argued that an agreement reached under different conditions need not still apply.

The Lords may be representative, in a contingent way at present, of party strengths but it is unrepresentative in a more subtle sense on issues where party politics is less relevant and in the order of priority its members attach to different issues. One criticism of the Lords in recent years has been its tendency to feel most strongly about the issues of fox hunting (preservation of) and homosexuality (suppression of). The House of Lords may no longer be large-C Conservative, but its members do tend to be small-c conservative. Its priorities are often, for good or ill, conservative—on issues of science (genetics in particular), law and the legal profession (from which so many of its members come), society and sexuality, property rights, and traditions. It tends to be suspicious of extensions of executive power (posing more of a threat to the passage of antiterrorist legislation than the Commons). Without making value judgments on the content of such changes, the conservatism of the Lords is a counterpoint to the efficient adaptation of the British model of government to economic and social change, and to threats such as terrorism.

The interim Lords is an obstacle to *efficient* government action without being democratic. A further dose of Lords reform through the introduction of direct election as the main route of entry would make it more democratic and give its powers a firm footing of legitimacy rather than a contingent link at present disguising a deeper conservatism. Most opponents of direct elections base their case on the possibility of *gridlock* between Commons and Lords, but this fear is overstated given the limited powers of the Lords. There is also the possibility that a weaker variant of the Salisbury convention could survive or even be codified, and that political compromises would be more readily made between elected representatives.

Human Rights

The Human Rights Act 1998 is a more slow-burning constitutional reform than the other two, and also still potentially reversible in a way that the Lords reform and Scottish devolution are not. It was a deceptively simple matter, essentially incorporating the European Convention on Human Rights, making it justiciable in British courts and carefully steering around conflict between judicial interpretation of the HRA and continued parliamentary sovereignty. Interpretation, where possible, of existing legislation is done on the assumption that it is compatible with the HRA, and executive actions are subject to the Act unless there is a conflict with other legislation. If there is no way of reconciling other legislation with the HRA, the judge makes a "declaration of incompatibility" and the matter is referred to Parliament to decide.

The Human Rights Act is a major statement of the rights of the citizen and a limitation on the power of the executive over the citizen that greatly extended existing trends towards making the state accountable. Cases have upheld a right to privacy not previously recognized in British law, and also removed much of the power of the Home Secretary to set prison sentences in 2003. The courts also ruled against the government's power to detain foreign suspects without trial in 2004. Some cases still go to the European Court of

Human Rights, as with the successful appeal in 2005 against the British courts' ruling that depriving prisoners of the vote was permissible. The HRA has attracted political opposition, with the Conservatives pledging to get rid of, or at least radically alter it, in 2005, and even Blair wondering about clipping its wings. The reason is essentially that it has been rather successful in changing the balance of power between state and citizen, which can be inconvenient even when, as in cases concerning terrorist suspects, the government feels it has a good case to exercise draconian powers over certain individuals. Perhaps without intending to, the government bound its hands quite tightly with the Act, and set a significantly higher bar than existed in the past to redefinition of the rights of individuals vis à vis the state. It forces the state, at the very least, to justify itself when it restricts liberties covered by the Act. It is a significant counter to the trend to circumscribe liberty in the name of security.

A PICTURE OF DISSATISFACTION

Labour's 1997 manifesto, cited above, spoke of "a national crisis of confidence in our political system" but there is no sign that this crisis of confidence has been resolved. The proportion of people believing that they can trust British governments "just about always" or "most of the time" rose sharply from its trough in the mid-1990s after 1997, but then fell back to the same level or rather below by 2003 (Bromley et al. 2004). Participation in the formal democratic system, through party membership and voting, has continued to fall—the temporary increase in Labour Party membership in 1994–1998 has been reversed. Turnout in the 1997 elections was the lowest since before 1945, but only just—the recorded level of 71.5 percent, on probably a less accurate register, was not substantially below that in some other elections such as 1970, October 1974, and 1983. But the 2001 election showed a sudden plunge in turnout, to only 59.4 percent, and the 2005 election a very minor recovery to 61.5 percent. After a long period of turnouts fluctuating around 75 percent there was a sudden drop, apparently to fluctuations around 60 percent. But it is only formal politics that seems to be affected—voluntary and self-generated activity, like writing to MPs, participating in demonstrations or the like is as high as ever, as is general interest in political issues (ibid.). Two successive British elections with exceptionally low levels of participation among the electorate show that there is a problem with this particular aspect of democracy.

The dominant perception among voters is that Britain is *fairly democratic*—a sentiment agreed with by 56 percent in 2004. This carries a suggestion that while people do not feel that Britain should be considered an undemocratic society, it may be less democratic than it should be, or than other comparable countries. Only 16 percent consider Britain *very democratic* while 19 percent think of Britain as *not very democratic* and 4 percent have the perhaps eccentric view that Britain (a country with regular competitive elections and entrenched human rights) is "not at all democratic."

The finding that the majority believes Britain is becoming *less democratic* is perhaps surprising given that reforms since 1997 have intended to increase democracy and reduce the gap between governments and governed. Devolution for Scotland and Wales does seem to have made a difference. The English feel that Britain is becoming less democratic by a margin of thirty-three points (57–24) while the Scots feel this by only a margin of nineteen points (47–28) and the Welsh (whose Assembly's powers are weaker than those of the Scottish Parliament) by twenty-two points (48–26). Devolution's democratic merits do seem to be appreciated, and the appetite for transfer of further powers suggests that it is not considered an inefficient form of government.

The reasons for the pervasive feeling, which devolution only partially ameliorates, that Britain is becoming less democratic has to do with the seeming unresponsiveness of government—that "ordinary voters" have relatively little power compared to the media, large companies, and the wishes of government ministers. In 2004, 67 percent believed that "ordinary voters" have little or no power, while 33 percent thought they had a great deal or a fair amount of power. Ninety percent thought that ordinary voters *should* have a great deal or a fair amount of power. Fully 79 percent thought the media had significant power, as opposed to 35 percent who thought this was desirable, and the balance with relation to large companies was only a little less adverse (69 percent thought they had power, 31 percent thought this desirable). The external constraints that operate on government are even less under the control of ordinary voters than the government itself.

The British system has, in mild measure, some of the flaws of dictatorship, as it has had for all its existence and particularly since 1979. Information flows upwards through the public services are being distorted not by coercion but by the mania for target-setting, which encourages a focus on the concrete measure that is being targeted rather than the principles of good service that targets attempt to encapsulate. A revealing moment of the 2005 election campaign was when the prime minister expressed puzzlement and surprise when a voter told him that she found it virtually impossible to make an appointment with her doctor. This was a paradoxical and unintended by-product of a target that people should not have to wait more than two days for an appointment. The practice managers were not booking appointments more than two days in advance, even if asked to, and all the available slots became booked up by patients as soon as they became available. The information on how the system was working in practice was obviously not reaching the people on top, although no doubt satisfactory reports were being filed in terms of the targeted variables. The diffusion of the state into a complex network of agencies and contractors has created numerous nexuses where contractual and financial relationships complicate the flow of information (see chapter 7 for closer analysis).

The strength of the centralized British state is accompanied by a form of brittleness. While dictatorships may appear strong, they are sufficiently distanced from popular feeling that when mass movements arise the regime can collapse with amazing rapidity, as happened across central and Eastern Europe in 1989. Britain, rather like France, is a centralized democratic state in which power is concentrated in the hands of relatively few people and there are few mechanisms of bringing its exercise to account. The 1990s and 2000s have seen a succession of vast demonstrations — that in support of the miners in 1992 foreshadowed the two large countryside demonstrations of 1998 and 2004 and the unprecedented size of the demonstrations against war in Iraq in 2002 and 2003. None of these had much effect on policy. On a different level was the series of refinery blockades in 2000, when farmers and road haulers caused a fuel (and political) crisis through direct action.

Public tolerance of direct action seems relatively high, with 90 percent agreeing with the statement: "If governments don't listen, peaceful protest, blockades and demonstrations are a legitimate way of expressing people's concerns" (ICM/Joseph Rowntree Reform Trust 2004). People tend to disagree rather than agree (53–38 percent) with the statement: "In a parliamentary democracy, governments should not change policies in response to protests, blockades or demonstrations" (ibid.). While on the surface Britain presents a picture of placid, strong government compared to the 1970s, the potential is still there for the disconnect between government and governed to lead to sudden chaotic events such as the fuel blockade of 2000.

Blair and the government are not unaware of the brittleness of the present order, and have sought solutions in several directions. One has been in terms of managerial politics, of anticipating challenges, and providing policy and rhetorical output that would serve to soothe the passions of mass and civil society opposition, or of changing the terms of political debate to marginalize and manage dissent. This was brilliantly successful in preventing a recurrence of the September 2000 fuel blockades — a combination of small concessions, rhetoric, media management, and (one may presume) astute use of the security apparatus of state.[2] The prevalence of polling, focus groups, and customer response research in government shows an almost desperate effort to forge further links between government and governed. In projects such as the Big Conversation[3] Labour has attempted to bridge the gap between the increasingly small and unsatisfactory intra-party system of accountability and that large part of society that considers itself nonpolitical. But both the attempts to encourage participation in formal democracy and to open new sorts of dialogue with the public and civil society have so far had little success.

Another avenue explored by Blair in recent years has been in what is termed *leader democracy*. Blair has taken the presidential role of the elective dictatorship further than before, although along a road mapped out before him by Harold Wilson and Margaret Thatcher. Blair's style of political leadership involves, as presidential systems do, an attempt at direct communication between leader and the masses, diminishing the significance of intermediary institutions such as Parliament.[4] In terms of leadership, and the skills of defining political debate to his advantage, Blair has been successful, but there is no more public confidence in leader democracy than there is in old-fashioned pluralist democracy—probably even less. Blair is still increasingly aware of his own political mortality. Blair is keen not to see his legacy washed away, as it might be given the potential in the British system for a sudden shift of near-absolute power.

The sense of a lack of power over government, a lack of accountability, is one that can be addressed in part by a more radical program of constitutional reform. In 2004 only 3 percent thought that the British system of government worked extremely well and should not be changed, while another 31 percent felt that only small changes were necessary to a generally healthy system. The more radical options of "it could be improved quite a lot" and "it needs a great deal of improvement" (ICM/Joseph Rowntree Reform Trust 2004) attracted 41 percent and 22 percent respectively, a 63–34 margin for serious constitutional reform. However, the sense of general dissatisfaction is greater than the demand for specific measures of reform. When it comes down to details rather than generalities, public opinion appears to be weakly held, vague, and sometimes even internally inconsistent (Independent Commission on Proportional Representation 2004).

The twin problems of the lack of channels for responsiveness and accountability of government, and the deteriorating effectiveness of the electoral system at legitimating government, are capable of being tackled without sacrificing the adaptability of the British system or succumbing to sclerosis. An effective second chamber is an important part of the solution. So is the revival of English local government, whether on a regional or city-district basis, with its own fiscal base and political powers. But perhaps the most important part is to alter the heart of the all-or-nothing sweepstake of British democracy— the electoral system.

ELECTORAL REFORM AND RESPONSIVENESS

Electoral reform is the great uncompleted constitutional reform of the Blair government. In its 1997 manifesto Labour promised to appoint a commission of inquiry into the electoral system for the House of Commons and hold a referendum on the outcome. The Commission was set up as promised, under the veteran Labour and Lib Dem statesman Lord Jenkins, and duly reported in 1998 in favor of introducing a more proportional electoral system (AV+)[5] (Jenkins 1998). However, the referendum did not follow and the commitment was watered down in the Labour manifestos of 2001 and 2005 as Blair became more comfortable exercising the strong powers of the traditional model of British government.

The First Past the Post (FPTP) electoral system fits in some ways with the Westminster model of accountable government. A party wins an election on the basis of its program, gains nearly untrammeled constitutional power to implement it, and stands or falls at the next election on the basis of its record. FPTP is sometimes defended on the grounds that it allows the decisive ejection of an unpopular government from power. However this is not what happened in 2005 when Labour were returned despite polling only 35.2 percent of the vote, a fall of 5.5 percentage points since 2001, and 8 points since the first election victory of 1997. By 2005, the government had shed support over its term of office as no government has done before at an equivalent stage,[6] but was still comfortably reelected. Labour in 2005 were arguably considerably less popular than in 1970, both in terms of headline support and detailed public attitudes. In the case of 2005, there was no real penalty for being an unpopular government. FPTP, especially with the systematic bias that exists at present (Labour can win a comfortable overall majority with a three-point lead in the popular vote as they did in 2005, while the Conservatives would need a lead of 11 percent to scrape an overall majority),[7] means gravely diminished accountability.

FPTP imposes an election strategy on the principal parties that serves to reduce the apparent differences between them to an even greater extent than the external constraints require. During the election campaign it was prominently reported in the *Times* (6 April) that the main parties were concentrating their efforts on the eight hundred thousand voters who would make a difference to the result. These were people living in the marginal seats who were judged on the basis of public opinion research to be likely to vote and also open to persuasion as to whom they might support. These eight hundred thousand lucky people amounted to fewer than 2 percent of the entire electorate. The premium that the FPTP electoral system puts on marginal seats means that votes most definitely do not have the same value.

The agenda of these swing voters in marginal seats has a disproportionate impact on election campaigns and on British politics in general, and has encouraged a simplistic and sloganizing emphasis on issues such as crime, immigration, and interest rates from the parties. Concentration on floating voters in marginal seats, who are not necessarily representative of Britain as a whole, has distorted the entire national debate. It is not surprising that the two main parties—despite what are reasonably significant differences in policy—sound so alike, given they are trying to win over the same people. The number of voters who believe that there are important differences between the two parties has plummeted since the days of ideological polarization in the 1980s.

The number of voters who matter is likely to be even smaller at the next election, because the overall result was closer, there are a larger number of highly marginal seats, and campaign techniques will no doubt have become even more sophisticated and able to target more precisely. After the election it was noted that there was a larger number of what the press quickly dubbed "ultra-marginal" Labour seats than before. In the 2001–2005 parliament twenty Labour MPs (4.9 percent of the Parliamentary Party) had majorities of less than 5 percent of the vote. After the 2005 election there were forty-one whose seats hung by such a narrow thread (11.5 percent). The importance of the ultra-marginal MPs is much greater now than before. Labour could afford to lose all twenty ultra-marginal MPs from the 2001 election and still have a majority of over one hundred because the party started so far ahead (majority of 165), while the loss of forty-one MPs would see Labour's 2005 overall majority of sixty-six disappear.

FPTP creates a situation where votes have unequal value in determining who sits in government. The individual voter can do relatively little to influence government in Britain unless he or she lives in one of the marginal seats. In the 2005 election, a little over half of the votes cast did not influence the result in seats, because they were cast for losing candidates. Another 20 percent of votes served only to swell the winning candidates' majorities.

The increasing fragmentation of the party system, falling turnout, and sophistication of electioneering techniques have loosened the relationship between popular support and ability to govern further than ever before. Labour's winning share of the vote in 2005, at only 35.2 percent, was lower than either main party had managed in *losing* an election from 1935 until 1983. In terms of share of the electorate, no majority government form 1924 until 1974 rested on the support of less than a third of the total electorate, and only in the last couple of elections has this share of support fallen below 25 percent.

FPTP elections are essentially choices between two alternative governments, but the electorate decreasingly sees elections in this light. At 67.5

percent of the vote, the two-party share is lower than it has been in any other general election except arguably 1918. Of the electorate, it is clear that the two-party choice is becoming a minority option. At the peak of the two-party system in 1951, the proportion of the entire electorate voting Labour or Conservative was only a whisker under 80 percent and this total did not fall below 60 percent from 1931 until 1974. The elections of 2001 and 2005 saw it plunge below 50 percent, to a record low (again possibly excepting 1918) of 41.5 percent.

The role of elections in legitimating government is therefore becoming ever more stretched and artificial. Electors are increasingly avoiding the whole process or opting out of the direct choice of government, which is supposed to be the virtue of the system. Public attitudes do suggest a readiness to consider other options, and a lack of certainty about the supposed benefits of FPTP. The 2004 State of the Nation poll found 63 percent agreeing to some extent (including 29 percent agreeing strongly) that seats in Parliament should be given proportionately to parties' votes, and 15 percent disagreeing (only 5 percent strongly). However, there was a narrow lead for the proposition "The present system of voting is the only way the country can get strong one-party governments who will get things done"—39 percent agreeing, 28 percent disagreeing, and 32 percent neutral. Following the 2005 election in Britain, the national *Independent* newspaper campaigned vigorously in favor of electoral reform, attracting over forty thousand adherents to its "Campaign for Democracy" and demonstrating some degree of groundswell on the issue. The German election of September 2005, however, gave opponents a means of arguing that PR would make forming a stable government impossible—although this neglects the fact that such a close result would probably also have created an indecisive result under FPTP. The electoral reform campaign has continued since.

A proportional electoral reform would broaden the basis of government, by necessitating an election appeal that would go beyond the few marginal seats and swing voters who are all-important under FPTP. It will be in the interests of the parties to stimulate their supporters to vote in all areas and not write off large chunks of the country as "safe" or "hopeless." Out of this should appear a more various and interesting set of issues to be discussed in election campaigns. Governments would have to be constructed from parties representing a majority, or near-majority, of voters. Depending on the model of electoral reform adopted, this might enable single-party government in particularly decisive elections such as 1979 and 1997, while necessitating minority government or coalition in others—this was the intention when the Commission under Lord Jenkins designed the "AV+" system in 1998.

Electoral reform, by increasing the level of *democracy* within the British constitutional system, might be seen to address some of the problems which exist under the current structure by injecting a greater element of *inefficiency* into that structure. However, as the preceding analysis has shown, lack of democracy and lack of efficiency are often seen together so that it must be an error to put them in opposition. However, even after reform the British central state would still have all the powers that it does currently, constrained as they are by European Union law and policy and the Human Rights Act. British government would still have efficient and direct means of taking action, but it would be required to justify itself rather more to its own citizens. The traditional *strong government* ethos of the British parliamentary system would work better, not worse, if it were more accountable and more challenged. By creating a greater degree of accountability to the electorate, as opposed to impersonal global forces, reform would do much to bridge the growing gap between government and governed.

In Hegelian terms, one can see the "efficient" dictatorial state as being a thesis, challenged in its time by the antithesis of chaotic democracy on the model of the prepartition Polish *Sejm* where all had the right of veto and nothing was able to be done. Other contributors explore whether there are modern examples of an excess of democratic veto power producing chaos or sclerosis. An antithesis by its nature is not sufficient as an organizing principle for society and is replaced by a synthesis. In this case, the answer is in the concept of *responsiveness*—the adaptability that has enabled Britain to respond to global changes needs to be extended so that the state is also responsive to its citizens, through the electoral mechanism once again as well as in midterm. The result would not be a sacrifice of efficiency, as it would offer alternative channels to the occasional sudden breakdowns of authority that take place in truly dictatorial societies as well as in the centralized *elective dictatorships* in Britain and France.

CONCLUSION

Constitutional reform, and a wider and more representative basis for government, cannot cure all the problems of governing in the early twenty-first century. There are large constituencies which oppose the dominant trends of the current age—neoliberal economics and radical social change—and it is virtually impossible to satisfy them in Britain and most other countries because what some of them demand simply cannot be delivered. Even with the best model of government, change is always difficult to manage, as other contributions in this volume make clear. Pluralist democracy on the German model has its discontents, but it also has an inclusive framework of institutions that represents and channels those discontents. However, resolving policy impasses and transcending the inbuilt conservatism of the German political establishment (and the debt-averse German consumer, and the German worker) are difficult challenges in a pluralist system.

The British tradition has been more in a series of ad hoc adaptations than in a planned framework. The lack of constitutional checks and balances has enabled rapid adaptation, but also put the system at risk from the desire of politicians to be seen to do something about problems that seem relevant at one particular time. Britain as it is does not offer a satisfactory alternative model to pluralism; public alienation from the system is probably greater than in other comparable countries and the dangers of precipitate movement are real. However, introducing a greater element of responsiveness and accountability into the UK government model is in the interests of democracy and ultimately of efficiency as well.

NOTES

1. In noting this, I do not intend to endorse the "power of nightmares" analysis that sees the current British situation as being essentially one of fear manufactured in order for politicians to cling on to and expand the power of the state. This line of argument may be more appropriate to the United States. Even the extensive constitutional safeguards of the United States have not prevented a much more radical reduction in better-established rights under the Patriot Act, driven essentially by partisan politics in a way without direct parallel in Britain.

2. There has been a rise in discussion of the "politics of managerialism." This recapitulates some debates from the 1970s relating to local government, the key text being Cynthia Cockburn (1976) about the role of local authorities and the welfare state in managing people.

3. The "Big Conversation" was part of the process of preparing the 2005 Labour manifesto. It was launched in November 2003 when Blair asked for comment and consultation from members of the public and interested groups on a series of questions. It was regarded with cynicism by most of the media and political opponents and its impact was limited.

4. For a discussion of leader democracy see András Körösényi (2005).

5. AV+ is a mixed member system like the German one, except that it would have 80 percent constituency members and 20 percent list members and be consequently less proportional. Constituency members would be elected using the Alternative Vote rather than FPTP.

6. Other governments reelected after two terms showed an increase in support of 1.4 percent (1959) and a fall of 1.6 percent (1987). Even defeated governments did better, picking up 1.0 percent in 1951 and losing only 1.1 percent in 1970 and 0.2 percent in 1979.

7. For an explanation of bias see Baston 2005. In short, the discrepancy is caused by differential turnout (turnout being much lower in safe Labour seats), the efficient distribution of the Labour vote, the Liberal Democrats taking seats disproportionately from the Conservatives and population drift causing Labour seats to have smaller electorates.

REFERENCES

Baston, Lewis (2005): *The Conservatives and Electoral Reform.* London: Electoral Reform Society.

Browley, Catherine, Curtice, John, and Seyd, Ben (2004): *Is Britain Facing a Crisis of Democracy?* CREST Working Paper 106. London and Oxford: Centre for Research into Elections and Social Trends.

Cockburn, Cynthia (1976): *The Local State.* London: Pluto Press.

Hailsham, Lord (1976): "Richard Dimbleby Memorial Lecture." *The Listener,* 21. October 1976.

ICM/Joseph Rowntree Reform Trust (2004): *State of the Nation Poll 2004.* www.jrrt.org.uk/

Independent Commission to Review Britain's Experience of PR Voting System (2003): *Changed Voting Changed Politics. Lessons of Britain's Experience of PR since 1997.* Final Report. London: The Constitution Unit.

Jenkins, Lord (1998): *Report of the Independent Commission on the Voting System.* London: The Stationery Office.

King, Anthony (1976): *Why Is Britain Becoming Harder to Govern?* London: BBC.

Körösényi, András (2005): "Political Representation in Leader Democracy." *Government and Opposition* 40, no. 3: 358–78.

The Labour Party (1997): *New Labour: Because Britain Deserves Better.* London: The Labour Party.

5

Misguided Consensualism: Prospects for Reform of the Party-Dominated Federal System in Germany

Frank Decker

The *deparliamentarization* of political systems is not only a recent issue. In fact, ever since, in Great Britain, parliamentarianism established itself as the principle of governing the modern state, it has been accompanied by debates about deparliamentarization. Extensive complaints about the decline of parliaments can already be found in the works of John Stuart Mill and Lord Bryce, partly based on the same arguments as today's criticism. That taken into account parliament has proven to be an enduring institution, which, at least in a formal way, still maintains its position at the center of the political decision-making process (Von Beyme 1997: 359–76).

Yet, this does not prove that the thesis of the growing insignificance of parliaments is inaccurate. There is now a level of consensus in political science on the reasons leading to this process. The increasing complexity of the governmental process on the one hand, and the phenomenon of denationalization as well as the growth of media power on the other, are cited as major explanatory factors. What is still disputed is only to what extent each of these different factors is responsible. While some accept deparliamentarization as an irreversible fact even in its normative implications and already talk about a new "post-parliamentary" reality of governing, others unswervingly insist on the key position of parliament. Some argue rather defiantly, as Wilhelm Hennis does, that the shift of the decision-making process beyond parliamentary institutions must be regarded as unconstitutional. Others, such as Ralf Dahrendorf, openly regret parliament's loss of its former dominant position, but they do concede that in the era of the "new democracies" this position cannot be restored.

The tendencies forming the basis of deparliamentarization can be roughly divided into two groups. On the one hand, there are developments connected to the aforementioned pluralization which increase the number of actors in the political system and, by doing so, suppress the importance of parliament in general. I shall refer to that later on. On the other hand, the distinctive features of the parliamentary system provide the sources for those tendencies. This system is characterized by a functional connection of the majority in parliament and the government, which form an operating unit. The minority of parliament confronts this operating unit as its opposition. The classical separation of powers between parliament (as a whole) and the government is thus superseded by a new form of power separation that is based on the decision principle of majoritarian, democratic competition between parties: The parties that emerge from elections as the winners form the government (or the governmental majority) while the minority plays the role of the opposition. This functional logic, however, has created a situation in which parliament's effective share of government has gradually diminished. This is most obvious to the opposition since—without the majority of votes—it cannot govern. It is harder to explain why the parliamentary parties forming the majority have effectively transferred their governmental power to the nominal government (which is appointed by them). The extensive constitutional means of the government allowing it to command obedience from its followers emphasizes the parliamentary principle. Usually these means do not need to be put into action since the parliamentary majority develops a natural interest to keep the government in office. As a result of the obligatory loyalty expected of the members of parliament, parliamentarians often bear unreasonable demands, which even brings them into conflict with the constitutionally guaranteed free mandate. Parliament's voluntary emasculation thus traditionally becomes the crucial point for the criticism of parliamentarianism that accompanies the political as well as the academic discussion until today.

Apart from this, there is a second, and more recent, line of general criticism with regard to the parliamentary system that looks at the problem from a different angle. This position assumes that parliamentary systems have drifted away from their (majoritarian) democratic principles in a manner that is deemed unacceptable. The presumed democratic merit of the parliamentary system supposedly lies in the way it assigns clear responsibilities to both the government and the opposition. The government is accountable for its actions, while the opposition wants the voter to believe that it would have performed better than their rival in the governmental function and that it will do better in the future. The dualistic party competition therefore rests on the assumption that *parties matter*, relating policy-output to those who govern. And even if this assumption turns out to be a chimera, there will at least be plenty of opportunities for the party in government to put its policies into action. For example, an electoral system, which transforms narrow election results into broad parliamentary majorities, takes care of that.

But only a few countries experience the principle of alternating governments in its purest form. Though it has been called the mother of all western democracies, the British Westminster model has remained an exception among parliamentary systems. While Great Britain continues to pay homage to the maxim of parliamentary sovereignty, the range of governmental decisions in most democratic systems is restricted by rigid constitutional rules. Instead of parliamentary sovereignty one should speak of constitutional sovereignty in this case. The latter finds its most significant expression in the judicial review of legal norms, meaning the right of an independent constitutional court to reconsider the constitutionality of a law passed by parliament and, if necessary, to overrule this law. The process of European integration implies that even the UK is now affected by this, through the back door, which gives rise to fears of a European *super state* harbored by many Britons.

The constitutional restrictions of the majoritarian principle of democracy are even more extensive in most parliamentary systems; they reach into the representational sphere where the government is forced to share its power with other actors. Different variants can be distinguished ranging from the necessity to form coalitions to the incorporation of powerful lobby groups into decision-making processes and to a federally constituted second chamber. The Dutch political scientist Arend Lijphart has introduced the term consensus (or consensual) democracy for the ensemble of such power-sharing elements, especially in contrast to the majoritarian Westminster model of parliamentarianism. But the majoritarian forms of democracy are not completely displaced by consensualism; instead they retain their effectiveness within the institutions as well as within the relations between the different institutions. In the most extreme case, however, their actual suspension can create a situation in which the parliamentary process serves the sole function of a façade, keeping the real decision-making process hidden. The examples of Austria and the Netherlands show what kind of serious legitimacy problems are produced by such a situation. Right-wing populists such as Haider and Fortuyn took advantage of this in the past.

The question of democratic quality cannot be answered only by looking at the structures of decision making. In addition to this, the efficiency of the system has to be taken into account, which can be measured by the tangible actions of the government. In this context, consensus democracy is often described as slow, generating only suboptimal results mainly because of the numerous actors taking part in the decisions. In recent academic analyses of institutions, the coactors and counter balancers, which give any parliamentary government a hard time, are therefore typically described as *veto players*. Accordingly, the dominance of veto power over positive or initiative power in consensus democracies is implied, which is certainly a correct assumption. But it should not lead to the misunderstanding that such a system inevitably creates barriers, as it is suggested by the term *veto players*. Empirical research has not yet provided any compelling evidence for this. Instead two arguments seem to challenge this assumption. On the one hand, one could argue that the whole point, or even the essence, of all politics lies in the challenge of recognizing and then overcoming barriers. Then the search for consensus would be the solution and not the problem. On the other hand—and this is even more important—the striking variety of institutional configurations which, in different political systems, moderate the majority principle in favor of other means of conflict resolution, renders it implausible to lump them together under the label of consensus democracy. Not the *if* but the *how* concerning consensus is crucial: Political actors and institutions must cooperate in favor of a reasonable result. In such an arrangement, there could emerge even greater effective chances for parliaments to influence decision-making than under the comparably restrictive conditions of a majoritarian democracy.

CROSS-SYSTEM REASONS FOR DEPARLIAMENTARIZATION

Before we turn to the German case and trace the question of which problems, concerning parliamentarianism and governance, result from the specific structures of this political system, we shall look at general (cross-system) developments reinforcing the supposed tendency of deparliamentarization. In political science textbooks usually four classical functions of parliament are mentioned: to appoint and authorize the government, to legislate, to control the government, and to foster public debates. In all four areas parliaments have lost a certain amount of effective capability. This is even correct in those areas where parliament's formal authority remains unchallenged or where it has been augmented (as in the case of its controlling competences).

Since parliamentary elections have turned into pseudo-plebiscitary prime minister or chancellor elections, the constitution of government only formally remains in the hands of parliament. This plebiscitary transformation is evident from the fact that the smaller parties usually express a clear coalition preference during their campaigns. A change of government in between elections therefore turns out to be very risky. In Germany, the liberal party (FDP) learned this lesson in 1982, when it switched sides leaving the coalition with the SPD in order to form a new government with the Christian Democrats. Because the new coalition was criticized as illegitimate, early elections were called in order to secure a mandate from the voters. Nevertheless it took half a year after the coalition change for the elections to take place, thus allowing the FDP to recover from their decline in public support.

The legislative function of parliament faces pressure from several sides. On the one hand—as already shown—it is a regular side effect of the parliamentary system that the majority in parliament cedes most of its legislative power to the government which has the necessary resources at its disposal, especially through the available body of civil servants and administration. Lacking a majority, the opposition is confined to indirect participation. On the other hand, the emigration of legislative activity away from the institutions also takes place at the governmental level. As Sven Jochem discusses elsewhere in this volume (see chapter 6), legislative processes are moved to specialized committees (e.g., coalition rounds or consensus discussions) and policy networks where experts of the various political areas work among themselves. It is self-evident that the pertinent advocates of the different interests are part of this group. Finally, the legislative power of parliaments is also weakened in a material sense, due to the fact that an increasing number of powers and responsibilities are transferred to the supranational level of the EU. While national governments take part in the European decision-making processes, the respective national parliaments occupy the role of mere spectators.

Due to the transfer of responsibilities and the inherent increase of executive importance within the legislative processes, the ability of the parliament to control or "check" the government has been limited. Due to a lack of detailed information, the activities at the European level are not only obscure, but also difficult to influence for the members of parliament. The control possibilities of the members of parliament are also reduced within the national structure because of the existence of party groups in parliament. Legislative committees as well as internal party working groups tend to be dominated by specialists. In general, the decisions prepared in these teams are usually *rubber-stamped* by the entire party group. When the committees alter or amend policy bills introduced by the executive, civil servants of national agencies are usually heavily involved in the process because in terms of gaining and processing information parliament is inferior to the executive. To illustrate this: in the Federal Republic of Germany, the *Bundestag* has about twenty-three hundred parliamentary representatives and legislative staff; the federal ministries and the chancellor's office, in contrast, have about twenty-five thousand employees. The latter also draw on extensive advisory staff and entertain regular contact with executive bureaucracies and representatives of political associations in order to coordinate policy with numerous subordinate federal agencies.

Additionally, recent developments have contributed to the decline of parliament's role in terms of political communication. In light of the shift of decision-making power in modern political systems the media have begun to focus their attention on executive institutions rather than parliament. The media, in particular television with its increasing number of channels, have encroached upon the traditional role of parliament as a forum for public debate. A publicity-seeking politician is most likely to profit more from an appearance on a talk or entertainment show than from a well-delivered speech in the *Bundestag*. Indeed, parliament in this day and age rarely stands at the center of media attention. Instances in which parliament takes the "spotlight" of media coverage include crucial parliamentary votes with unpredictable and therefore not anticipated results. Often these are "apolitical" issues or matters of conscience that create cross-party divisions, or issues where dissenters and party rebels endanger the party majority.

The examined developments support and contradict each other at the same time. The first is correct in terms of the media, for instance, which can function as an arbiter in political conflicts and thus promote plebiscitary tendencies in the governmental process. But the origin of the plebiscitary tendencies is not primarily linked to the evolution of the media system. This is rather an intervening factor. The real cause can be seen in the transformation of party competition on which the idea of alternating governments is essentially based. Its premises changed when party identities and voter loyalty became weaker, and when ideological differences became less visible. In the past the simultaneity of society's segmentation and ideological polarization secured the democratic functionality of party competition and thus worked as a safeguard against populism. Today, however, parties must court an increasingly fluctuating electorate which feels compelled by neither ideological nor sociological certainties. This in itself would not represent any major problem were it not to imply that party competition is increasingly deprived of its foundation. Indeed, today both the diminishing scope of action for national politics and the political actors' need for maximizing votes compel different parties to pursue rather similar goals and offer essentially identical solutions. In order to compete with political opponents, parties are thus left with few choices: they can focus on minor details which, however, bear the risk of boring their voters or expecting too much of them. Or they can turn to strategies of personalization or symbolic action which may lead to a depoliticization of the electorate or shift personalities rather than substantive issues into the center of politics. As regards the latter, the media have provided the parties with much welcomed assistance.

The plebiscitary transformation of party competition has two problematic consequences. First, there is a danger that the substance of politics is affected when the logic of party presentation prevails over decisions regarding actual policy content. *Political action becomes more responsive, yet, at the same time, less responsible.* Similarly, the sphere of party presentation risks to become disconnected from the actual decision-making process which, in its complexity, points well beyond the comparatively simple logic of party competition. Margaret Canovan once defined this phenomenon as the *democratic paradox* of current politics. To the same extent to which the complexity of existing problems makes the decision-making process more inclusive, consensual, and *output-bound*, it also makes it increasingly inscrutable. Populism represents a reaction to this paradoxical development. With its inclination to radical simplification it conveys a sense of plausibility and transparency, which in democratic reality has apparently fallen by the wayside. This populist countermovement is by no means limited to new right-wing challengers, but it spreads across the entire spectrum of electoral politics. *Political action becomes more introverted and, at the same time, more extroverted.*

The divergence of the two spheres raises difficult questions regarding legitimacy. The major advantage of majoritarian democracy is that it allows a clear attribution of political responsibility. In accordance with textbook knowledge, the fewer the hindrances placed in the way of political leaders in the fulfillment of their electoral mandate the easier it is for the electorate to hold politicians accountable for policy outcomes. Stronger plebiscitary tendencies are, on the other hand, the downside of party competition in representational majority democracies. Susceptibility to populist moods increases to the same extent to which the actual decision-making process distances itself from the premises of majoritarian democracy and to which party competition loses its guiding function. Nonetheless, this susceptibility is counterbalanced by plebiscitary elections taking place only in set intervals. Thus, for the duration of their mandate political leaders at least have a minimal measure of secured scope of action at their disposal.

The advantages and disadvantages of consensus democracy display a mirror image to that of majoritarian democracy. In consensus democracies the significance of competition as a control mechanism is comparatively marginal, bearing negative implications for the democratic quality of elections. Indeed, the function of elections lies primarily in the appointment of governmental personnel, rather than in the decision for a certain basic policy orientation. Consensual democratic systems also differ from competitive ones in that they give more consideration to specific interests, which, at the same time, makes them better suited for societies with structural minorities. Their antiplebiscitary character manifests itself in consensus generally being reached at the highest level of the system—namely through a trustful collaboration of political and societal elites. However, precisely in this practice also lies the problem of the consensus system. Not only are the interests of certain groups of the population consistently neglected, but in addition to this, consensus democracies are susceptible to populist counter-reactions. As the current developments in Switzerland have shown, the resulting protest can go as far as bringing the system under fire and forcing complete or partial reform.

Thus, from the perspective of the input dimension, the democratic advantages of majoritarian democracies are exactly the disadvantages of consensus democracies, and vice versa. Similarly, on the output side, no clear verdict can be met as to which of the two systems is to be regarded as preferable. The major advantage of representative majoritarian democracy is that its competition mechanisms allow for rapid changes in policy. British policy under Margaret Thatcher (1979 to 1990) and Tony Blair (since 1997) delivers telling evidence for this claim. The comparatively cumbersome processes of consensual democracies, however, do not automatically imply that they are necessarily less efficient or effective. Switzerland, Austria, Denmark, Sweden, and the Netherlands are examples for consensus democracies, which in the last one and a half decades have pursued successful reform policies. This applies to all areas of growth and employment ranging from the liberalization of labor markets to the adaptation of social systems to the reduction of national debt. Thus, these countries are repeatedly referred to as models for the Federal Republic of Germany, which has been much less successful in these areas of policy reform. The particular reform difficulties in Germany are linked to endogenous factors such as the financial burdens of reunification which clearly distinguish the situation in Germany from that of its neighbors. However, the significance of these particularities should not be overestimated. Indeed, as Blühdorn and Jun have argued above (see chapters 1 and 2), the pressing need for a reform of the social system, for example, could have been addressed in the 1990s when the country's economy was still growing. Yet, the fact that Germany has been plagued by its notorious *Reformstau* for such a long time gives rise to the suspicion that this problem might be caused by the institutional framework that determines the way in which politics is conducted in Germany.

INSTITUTIONAL VARIATIONS OF CONSENSUAL DEMOCRACY

When considering the ten distinguishing features of majoritarian and consensus democratic systems as developed by Lijphart, Germany appears to be an exemplary case for a consensus democracy. Yet, this categorization must be qualified. The three main features of Lijphart's typology—namely the concentration of executive power (one-party government) versus the division of executive power (coalition government); cabinet dominance versus the separation of executive-legislative power; and a two-party system versus a multiparty system—may be combined into a single criterion: the intensity of party competition. This competition ranges from the pole of majoritarian democracy—be it dualistically or antagonistically structured—to the extreme of a consensus democracy in which party competition is virtually suspended. While the Federal Republic of Germany in this respect formally fulfills the criteria for a consensus democracy, on a continuum it would rather have to be placed in the proximity of a majoritarian democracy. Indeed, Lijphart's criteria tend to conceal rather than explain the reality of Germany's strong antagonistic party competition. The intensity of party competition is perceivable in both the governmental power constellations, that is majority party coalitions, as well as in the nature and recurrence of changes in power brought about by the electorate.

The standard model of German governments is that of a "minimum-winning coalition" which generally faces an almost equally strong parliamentary opposition of one or more parties. Due to a lack of absolute majorities and the infrequency of Grand Coalitions—which the Christian Democrats (CDU/CSU) and Social Democrats (SPD) only turn to when left with no other political alternative—one-party governments (as in Bavaria since 1966) are the exception. Until the emergence of the Green Party in the early 1980s, a *de facto* two-party system existed in Germany. The party of Liberal Democrats (FDP) served as a "fair-weather" coalition partner for both the CDU/CSU and the SPD. It paved the way for two changes in government (1969 and 1982). With the four-party structure that had existed until the formation of the Grand Coalition in 2005, the system drew even closer to a dualistic principle: the SPD-Green party or "Red-Green" coalition stood vis-à-vis the opposition parties and "shadow government coalition" CDU and FDP.

The specific characteristics of German parliamentary majoritarian democracy point to several weaknesses in Lijphart's otherwise commendable typology. First of all, the characteristics are antithetically compared, but not empirically qualified. Secondly, Lijphart merely enumerates the criteria yet fails to weigh their specific significance, thus allowing contradictions to arise in their empirical application. And thirdly, he does not specify how the individual elements of his system relate to one another, if they reciprocally complement or rather obstruct one another in their functioning. In order to overcome such weaknesses it is necessary to systematize the characteristics and differences of majoritarian and consensus democracy, respectively, bearing in mind the logic of their specific function. German political scientist Roland Czada offered a useful suggestion. Contrary to Lijphart, Czada does not simply place the characteristics of majoritarian and consensus democracies vis-à-vis one another. Instead, the Westminster model of parliamentarian majority rule for Czada functions as both a reference case and ideal starting point in order to make the concrete variations of consensual democracy typologically evident.

Czada prefers the term *negotiation democracy* to that of *consensus democracy*. Nonetheless, both mean the same to him, namely a political system in which "essential decisions do not result from a majority vote, but emerge from a negotiation processes" (Czada 2000: 23). Czada presents the attributes —which Lijphart merely arranges as a dichotomy—in three dimensions, which describe different varieties of consensual democracy. Czada calls them consociationalism, corporatism, and constitutional interlocking politics.

First, consociationalism, according to Gerhard Lehmbruch, stands for systems which are structurally democratic and parliamentary, but display

> a dominant, specific pattern of regulating conflict between the significant political groups. The principle of majority decision is "deactivated" largely in favour of the basic principle of "amicabilis composition" found in the Treaty of Westphalia. Such "amicable arrangements" as a method of conflict resolution are generally safeguarded institutionally. Therefore, the most important societal groups are represented in the executive branch and can furthermore secure their influence on political decisions through systematic patronage based on parity. (Lehmbruch 1998: 25)

Thus, consociationalism is put into practice by means of formal or informal Grand Coalitions. Examples for such constellations are to be found in Switzerland, Austria, and formerly in the Netherlands. In each of these countries the national government attained, between 1945 and 1994, on average more than 60 percent of parliamentary votes. Consociational democracies follow the logic of proportional representation, which is why Lehmbruch once defined them as *proportional democracies*. In such systems party competition is not merely restrained, but rather almost superseded by quasi-institutionalized consensus-building committees. Thus, adjacent to—and not necessarily in place of—party competition, consensus-building emerges in a cartel of party elites.

> This system manifests itself in the Swiss *magic formula* in which, regardless of the electoral outcome, all significant parties participate in the government. The reasoning behind such a construct lies in the hindrance of structural majorities given a nonhomogeneous electoral population. [. . .] Consensual strategies should prevent the costs of political decisions from being shifted to structural minorities and, thus, thwart the erosion of the foundations of political legitimacy in a fragmented society. (Czada 2000: 27)

The advantage of such an arrangement is that no societal group has too many advantages over another; in other words, consociational democracy functions according to the rules of a positive-sum game. The disadvantage lies in the cumbersomeness of the decision-making process. In consensual democracies compromises are—if at all—often only possible on the basis of the smallest common denominator. This applies particularly to redistributive decisions, which are subject to the logic of a zero-sum game.

The second dimension of negotiation democracies is corporatism, that is the integration of organized interest groups into the decision-making process. Consociationalism and corporatist arrangements are closely interrelated. In the same way in which consociationalism encloses party competition, corporatism moderates the basic pattern of pluralistic interest organizations and the mediation of interests, which are characteristic for liberal democracies. Indeed, it is no accident that political systems with a wide coalition government and proportional representation of parties often develop corporatistic structures of interest mediation. However, as the example of Belgium, where the emergence of corporatist structures was prevented by regional conflicts, demonstrates, there are exceptions. Conversely, the Scandinavian countries show how corporatist structures can be built into systems where proportional party representation is only practiced in part and minority governments occur rather frequently.

Czada calls the third dimension of negotiation democracy constitutional interlocking politics. With this term he defines institutional arrangements and constellations "in which governmental power is formally shared by different government institutions whose representatives are accountable to the same or partly same electorate" (Czada 2000: 31). Three examples for this are: the relationship between the president and Congress in the United States—the latter consisting of two houses (House of Representatives and Senate) in which the majorities may also easily differ from one another; the dual executive in France consisting of the prime minister and his government on the one side, and the president on the other; and the dualism of parliamentary majority (in the *Bundestag*) and *Bundesrat* (or Federal Council) in the party-dominated federal system in Germany. The common feature shared by these cases is that two, and in the United States three, institutions which are democratically legitimated in a majoritarian sense are compelled by the given constitutional parameters to collaborate in order to ensure governmental efficiency. This cooperation is further complicated when the relevant institutions differ in their political orientation. Over the past decades such a constellation has occurred relatively often in all three states mentioned above. In the United States, this situation is referred to as *divided government*, in France it is called *cohabitation*. In the Federal Republic of Germany, a comparable term is yet to be found, although it has become increasingly common in Germany that the parliamentary majority must deal with an antagonistic majority in the *Bundesrat*.

The advantage of Czada's typology over Lijphart's original model is that it allows a much larger number of theoretically imaginable institutional configurations. Indeed, by making a distinction between weak and strong variations—purely mathematically speaking—eight different configurations are produced in conjunction with the three dimensions. By adding a third (medium) measure of variation for the sake of empirical specification, twenty-seven combinations are made possible. Indeed not all these combinations are equally probable and consequently to be empirically encountered. In fact this means that: the different variations of negotiation and consensual democracies—consociationalism, the corporatist integration of interest groups, and constitutional interlocking politics—in fact concur in multiple, yet by no means arbitrary, ways. Table 5.1 gives an overview of the system types, which are theoretically possible and—empirically speaking—to be found.

While corporatism clearly encourages the emergence of mechanisms of consociationalism, it is not compatible with strong constitutional political integration. Theoretically, it is perfectly conceivable that the integration of interest groups can contribute to the reduction of deadlock in decision-making, which might result from a system of "divided government." However, the opposite scenario is more likely. The reason for this is that corporatist structures require a strong government capable of acting and confronting unions as a uniform negotiation partner. If the government is limited in its scope of action by constitutional *partners* and *opponents*, a reliable collaboration between the government and the interest groups is hardly possible. However, the table shows that Germany and Switzerland are two countries with strong corporatism and equally strong constitutional interlocking, which would seem contradictory at first glance. In Switzerland this practice causes no significant problems. The institutional veto structures are enclosed in a conso-

Table 5.1. Variants of Negotiation Democracy and their Phenotypes

Consociationalism	Corporatism	Constitutional Interlocking Politics	Cases
weak	weak	weak	Great Britain, Greece, Spain, New Zealand
weak	weak	medium	France, Italy (since 1994), Canada
weak	weak	strong	Australia
weak	strong	strong	Germany
medium	weak	strong	United States
medium	medium	medium	Belgium
medium	strong	weak	Scandinavia, Austria (since 1999), the Netherlands, Japan
strong	weak	medium	Italy (until 1994)
strong	strong	weak	Austria (until 1999)
strong	strong	strong	Switzerland

ciationalist system, which restores and further safeguards government unity.[1] However, in Germany the efficacy of corporatism is undermined by the collision between intense party competition, on the one hand, and the government's institutionally limited scope of action on the other.

The table above is additionally revealing with respect to the relationship between party consociationalism and constitutional interlocking politics. Indeed, these two distinctive features are positively connected to one another—which provides further clarification: when several institutions share government power an imminent breakdown in the decision-making process can only be averted if the parties' political actors cooperate within and among the relevant institutions. While Switzerland typifies an extreme case for such an arrangement, in the United States and in France several institutional provisions make sure that deadlock situations occur rarely, and in the event that they do occur, that they are resolved comparatively swiftly. With regard to elections the United States is in fact a classical example for a majoritarian system with dualistic competition and a two-party structure. With regard to government, however, this dualism finds no counterpart. The division of power inherent in the U.S. presidential system provides for government functions to be shared between the president (administration) and Congress—effective collaboration between political actors is thus imperative. This even holds true for cases of unified government when both branches of government are controlled by the same party. In France the potential explosiveness of *cohabitation* is attenuated by mechanisms of formal and informal division of labor, which have been adopted by the president and the prime minister. While the prime minister's leading role in the context of domestic politics is unchallenged, the head of state is entitled to claim specific foreign policy rights as his *domaine réservé*. The past three *cohabitation* phases of the Fifth Republic have functioned smoothly, with both sides having made a genuine effort to respect the sphere of the other and—wherever possible—to avoid conflict. However, when disagreement arose the government could generally assert itself, and in doing so it consistently made sure that the president did not lose face.

At the opposite end of the spectrum are two countries—Germany and Austria—in which the constitutional and party political dimensions of consensus democracy diverge. However, they diverge in precisely opposite directions: While in Germany lively party competition has been able to develop despite the strict constitutional separation of power, Austria used to be a classical example of proportional representation or consociationalism until the center-right coalition of ÖVP and FPÖ assumed office in early 2000. The division of power between the two major parties was not constitutionally provided for, but was rather a direct result of societal development. The deep rift between the catholic middle-class electorate, on the one hand, and the working class, on the other hand, was to be overcome by means of co-operation between political elites. However, the problem of this system of consociationalism was that it continued to exist long after its societal foundation was in the process of dissolving. Consequently Austrian politics entered a severe crisis in the 1980s, which facilitated the electoral success of the right-wing populist Freedom Party. Ever since this party was included in the government the country has started to adopt elements of a competitive democracy—today, the current party structure (ÖVP and FPÖ versus SPÖ and Green Party) displays a strong resemblance to the power constellation that existed in the Federal Republic of Germany until 2005.

GRIDLOCK IN THE PARTY-DOMINATED FEDERAL SYSTEM IN GERMANY

Germany, on the other hand, faces adaptation problems opposite to those present in Austria. In order to overcome deadlock arising from interlocking politics, the parties' political actors should turn to intensified consociationalist practices. Nonetheless, the enduring temptations of party competition prevent this from happening. Evidently, the trend towards plebiscitary transformation—as described above—does not ease a transition from a competitive to a consensual system, but rather a shift from a consensual to a more strongly competitive system. The alternative solution of a repression of constitutional veto structures appears to be even less feasible—once established, these structures are by nature resistant to change. Indeed, in the Federal Republic of Germany the possibilities for reforming the institutional decision-making process are restricted on both sides.

In order to understand the situation, it is necessary to first examine the constitutional veto structures. Because of the traumatic experience of the Weimar Republic and of the subsequent Nazi regime, the framers of the German constitution (or *Basic Law*) stressed the notion of constitutionalism more than the concept of democracy itself. This is evident in the constitution's lack of direct democratic participation rights, as well as in its creation of a Constitutional Court—invested with the authority of interpreting laws and regulations—and both the restoration and new establishment of decentralized federalism. While in most recent times the lack of direct democracy at the national level has become subject to public debate, the position of the Constitutional Court in the political system is generally accepted and admired. As a politically neutral institution the Federal Constitutional Court is, however, not a *veto player*, as understood here. Although it exercises a pseudo-legislative function it stands above the parties and outside of democratic competition. Yet, precisely this is the source of its unassailability and high esteem.

The second potential obstructer, the *Bundesrat*, occupies a rather different position. While the Court may solely act upon appeal and is limited in its scope of action to the constitutional verification of laws and regulations already passed, the *Bundesrat* is directly involved in the legislative process. Thus it functions like a second chamber and hence takes part in party competition. The current criticism raised against the *Bundesrat* must be viewed in light of the general development of German federalism. In every federal system the division of power between the national and state level rests upon two pillars: the member states' own jurisdiction and their cooperation with respect to the jurisdiction of the central government. In the Federal Republic of Germany the first pillar has increasingly lost significance at the expense of the latter. Since the central government has claimed the jurisdiction bestowed upon it by the Constitution, the *Länder* are left with hardly any original legislative functions. However, to compensate for this loss they were conferred strong participation rights in the national legislative process through the *Bundesrat*. The basic principle of German federalism is thus not so much the specific jurisdiction of the *Länder*, but rather their "co-governing" rights shared with the central government. This is reflected in the number of laws requiring *Bundestag* consent, which has risen from an initial 40 percent of all laws to over 60 percent.[2]

As a result of the increase in decision-making capacity, the political power of the second chamber has grown. Since the 1970s the party majorities in the *Bundestag* and *Bundesrat* have tended to differ from one another. For sure, this is also linked to the particularity of German federalism. Since decisions regarding everyday life are primarily made at the national level the federal government's politics play an increasingly significant role at the state level (or *Länder*). This results in a centralization of both party competition and electoral behavior. Political parties use the *Bundesrat* as a stage to assert their goals at the national level with the help of the state governments, which they control. The voters, in turn, make use of state elections to express both their satisfaction and dissatisfaction with the central government. Because state elections do not bear direct consequences on the power constellation at the national level they represent a convenient opportunity to admonish the central government in the course of its legislation period. State elections thus generally lead to electoral losses for the central government's majority parties and, consequently, to a worsening of their position in the *Bundesrat*. Thus the social-liberal coalition in the 1970s was confronted with a permanent majority of the Christian Democrats in the second chamber. In the 1990s, as the Social Democrats gained a majority in the *Bundesrat*—the same situation repeated itself, yet, reversed. And after the victory of the Social Democrats in the 1998 *Bundestag* elections, Chancellor Gerhard Schröder took less than one year to gamble away this majority through a series of electoral defeats.

The problem inherent to the dominance of partisan politics in the German federal party system is that it attempts to bring together majoritarian and consensual decision-making patterns in the legislative process. Participatory federalism by nature rests on the principle of consensus. In order to meet decisions, the participants rely on mutuality: compromise and compensation have to be reached again and again by means of negotiations. The institutionalized manifestation of this principle is the mediation committee (*Vermittlungsausschuss*), a joint committee of an equal number of members from *Bundestag* and *Bundesrat*. On the other hand, parliamentary democracy manifests itself in party competition: a majority vote invests the government with the power to implement its legislative intentions while the parliamentary minority functions as opposition waiting in the wings as an alternative to the incumbent government.

The divergence of majority patterns in the *Bundestag* and the *Bundesrat* make the structural rupture evident: the interplay between government and opposition—which is constitutive for parliamentary government—is undermined, as the *Bundesrat* is equally involved in the legislative process through the back door of federalism. Indeed, any law that needs the consent of the *Bundesrat* requires the existence of a de facto all-party government. The necessity to reach compromise is precarious for both government and opposition. For sure this provides the opposition parties with increased influence and a chance to improve or prevent legislative action. Yet, the price for this is that the opposition has to share responsibility for government policy, that it helps to iron out the shortcomings of government policies, and that it stabilizes governmental power. If the opposition succeeds in effectively maintaining consensus and balance it helps the party in power to "look good." As a result, however, it neglects its alternative function, facing the problem of explaining to the electorate why a change in government is at all necessary at the next election.

The consequences of a dual majority are no less problematic for the government itself. Regardless of the actual role of the opposition in the legislative process, it is the government majority which ultimately remains accountable for its outcome. The reason for this lies in the higher democratic "dignity": while the *Bundesrat*—consisting of the representatives of sixteen state governments—is only indirectly legitimated, the parliamentary majority which selects the government is based upon the direct vote of the whole electorate. This endows the government the privilege of political initiative, while at the same time burdening it with the weight of responsibility. On the other hand, the opposition parties in the *Bundesrat* have the strategic advantage of—if necessary—being able to conceal their actual participation behind the back of the government. As the CDU/CSU showed by opposing the reduction of tax subsidies that the government and agreed in 2002, there is no cure against a well-conducted obstruction policy. This does not mean that logjam and deadlock are the rule in German federalism. However, the cases where this did occur are sufficiently serious to shed doubt on institutional arrangements providing for political parties to—in the words of Fritz Scharpf—collide with one another (at the national level of the parliamentary system) and, at the same time, cooperate with one another (at the federal system level) (Scharpf 1997).

The reasons for the increasing difficulties in reaching compromises in the second chamber are not only linked to constraints in party competition. They may very well be similarly associated with the differences in state interests which have increased in the same measure in which the scope of action for redistributive policies has become more limited. The changes in the party landscape exacerbate the situation even further. If only because of arithmetical reasons, in the states, coalitions differing from those to be found at the national level are becoming increasingly common. The skirmish on the tax and pensions reform in the year 2000 showed how difficult these conditions can make it for the big parties to make sure "their" representatives in the *Bundesrat* stick to a common line. By exploiting the incongruence in state interests, the government managed to "buy" several *Länder* out of their party phalanx by means of selected financial concessions and, in this way, to win the ballot vote in the *Bundesrat*. For sure, such transactions belong to the nature of political negotiations as much as the often-quoted "pork barrel" by which several matters and circumstances are merged into one legislative package. Nonetheless, it remains questionable whether this type of problem solving should be rejected outright—and whether the final outcome would be reasonable.

PROSPECTS FOR INSTITUTIONAL REFORM

There are two theoretical solutions that might help to escape or overcome institutional gridlock in the Federal Republic of Germany: a reduction of the *Bundesrat's* powers in the legislative process—which have exceedingly expanded—or a moderation of party competitiveness aimed at the establishment of consensual decision-making mechanisms at the parliamentary level.

Regarding the *Bundesrat* today, the Federal Republic of Germany has developed into a stable constitutional democracy. Its political and cultural maturity matches that of its Western neighbors by any measure. Thus, to a certain extent federalism's initial justification as a control mechanism for limiting power has become obsolete. This is all the more true in a context of the upward shift in the vertical division of power towards the supranational European Union (whose relationship to the national member states parallels the connection existing between the federal government and the *Länder* in Germany). Presently, demands for a larger measure of (inner-state) federalism are based on considerations aimed at democratization and a maximization of the system's efficiency rather than on division and decentralization of power. From a normative perspective everything militates in favor of an elimination of federalism's shortcomings.

A system-compatible solution would have to begin with considerations concerning areas of competence. A reduction of the centralizing trends and an increase in the states' scope of action would be a prerequisite for this. *Decentralization* and *re-federalization* would represent the key concepts of such a reform. In this context decentralization means that in specific policy fields the federal government and the states would not assume responsibility jointly, but individually. Re-federalization means that the states would regain competence in policy areas currently belonging exclusively to the central government or shared by central government and the states. As a compensation for that, the states could surrender a portion of their veto powers in the *Bundesrat*.

A *Commission to Modernize the Organization of the Federal System*, consisting of the sixteen heads of government (*Ministerpräsidenten*) of the German *Länder* and an equal number of members of the *Bundestag*, was created to explore such suggestions for reform. In the first attempt, the negotiations on federal reform failed due to disagreement about the distribution of powers in education policy. Further attempts were postponed until after the Grand Coalition was firmly established in 2005. However, in light of the results, it remains improbable that the reform could produce significant changes in the relationship between federal and state governments. Even if the amount of laws requiring approval of the German federal chamber, *Bundesrat*, were to decrease from currently 60 percent to 40 or 30 percent, as expected, the state executives will continue to participate with equal decision-making powers in many policies—especially concerning financial issues. Furthermore, the reform of the federal system would not have much influence on the majoritarian composition of the *Bundesrat* because no reform could reduce the effect of *Land*-elections scheduled between elections have at the national level. One could expect further tendencies toward deadlock—at least under the conditions of the existing democratic, political-partisan system.

Therefore the question arises whether the problem might be approached more successfully from the other side, namely by means of a moderation of party competition. The development of party competition in Germany—and in other countries—is subject to the contradictions described above. On the one hand, the ideological differences between political parties are decreasing while the legal complexity of society increasingly limits the scope of governance for politicians. Politics become more pragmatic and the results more consensual. On the other hand, the decline of the grand ideologies results in stronger party competitiveness, more volatile and divided voter preferences and orientations, and a much smaller number of reliable party supporters. Together these trends result in party competition becoming more and more personalized while at the same time shifting to a symbolic level. In order to survive elections parties and politicians must appear to be strong actors, albeit knowing how limited their scope of action in reality is. Precisely in this manner political actors do not only undermine the preconditions for a functioning consensus democracy resting upon compromise and accommodation, but also damage their own reputation.

The suitability of party competition in a majoritarian democracy as the basic principle of decision-making and as a guiding mechanism is questionable both with regard to legitimacy and feasibility. On the one hand, party competition alone fails to be representative since not all relevant interests can be considered, let alone included into the decision-making process. In extreme cases this can even lead to a paradox situation in which a majority within the governing party asserts its position in parliament against a de facto majority consisting of a dissenting minority within the governing party and the opposition. For instance, the overdue reform of naturalization laws was hindered during the 16 years of Helmut Kohl's administration despite wide potential parliamentary and societal support for it. In such cases majoritarian democracy functions as a de facto minority democracy. A further point is connected to this fact. Immigration is a good example for how political decisions or nondecisions can unleash dramatic social change. Issues which have the potential to turn into considerable problems at some stage in the future include, for example, demographic change, ecological problems, or the unforeseeable moral challenges resulting from progress in genetic engineering. Yet, party competition in majoritarian democracies gives rise to a decision-making process that is markedly fixed on the present and systematically neglects the concerns of future generations. From a problem-solving point of view, an expansion of the representational basis of partisan politics would therefore be necessary in order to overcome the insufficient inclusion of such interests.

Institutionally two possibilities are conceivable: stronger cooperation at the parliamentary level itself and/or the provision of additional forms of consociationalism reaching beyond party competition.

The first alternative failed in Germany due to the deeply-rooted practice of competitive democracy. The main barrier stemmed from the dogma of a stable majority government. Due to the negative experience during the Weimar

Republic, neither the Scandinavian tradition of minority cabinets nor the occasional governance by changing majorities common in Southern European countries were able to become established in Germany. As a result, the stability of the government depended wholly on the development of the party system. The latter had to allow for the emergence of governments according to the pattern of a "minimum-winning-coalition" faced with an opposition of a similar size.

The development of a five-party system following German reunification removed the foundation for this previous governmental model. On the one hand, up to 2002, the post-communist PDS remained too weak at the national level to exert influence on the creation of governing coalitions. On the other hand, their percentage of the vote in 1994, 1998, and 2002 made it difficult for a coalition to be formed—which was ultimately only possible due to the institutional phenomenon of "supplemental seats in parliament" or *Überhangsmandate*. A similar development occurred on the state level where between 1990 and 2005 the diverging government format (Grand Coalitions and minority cabinets) accounted for one fifth of all cases.

After the early national parliamentary elections in 2005, the time had come: Because neither the incumbent "Red-Green" (SPD/Green Party) coalition nor the moderate-conservative bloc received a majority vote, the decision was reached to form a Grand Coalition for the first time since 1966. Some reasons included the strong growth of the post-communist PDS, which formed a new left-wing electoral alliance with the SPD-break-off group WASG and as a result expanded its terrain in western Germany. Although this process was foreseeable, the outcome of the election caught the entire political class unprepared. The discussions on election night gave the impression that anything would be possible: from an SPD-Green-FDP (red-green-yellow), or CDU-Green-FDP (black-green-yellow) three-party coalition to minority cabinets and even the Israeli model of rotating premierships. Until then all of these combinations had unambiguously been taboos or were denounced as the "downfall of the parliamentary system." The electoral result thus represented a profound turning point for the functioning of German parliamentarianism. The situation forced the parties to be more flexible in coalition negotiations, which could also signal the transition to a more cooperative and less competition-oriented style of governance. As regards its position on the Lijphart scale, Germany might therefore shift closer towards the consensual democratic systems.

If this change does not succeed or if the party system redevelops into a dualistic structure, there still remains the possibility of curbing competition through other consociational forms. For example, the introduction of direct democratic elements is conceivable. The debate on this issue in the Federal

Republic of Germany is, however, still overshadowed by legacies from the past. It would be wise if Germany were to look beyond its national border and consider the experiences which other countries have had with direct democratic practices. A sober empirical survey shows that the advantages and the risks of direct democracy are often portrayed incorrectly or in an exaggerated way. Mechanisms of direct democracy are not in themselves the cause of good or bad policies, nor do they automatically promote specific political interests or increase people's willingness to take a more active role in politics. For sure, disempowering parliament and parties alike, and letting the people govern instead, is not a solution for the problems of the political system. Instead, the key lies in the intermediary institutions which should fulfill their representative function more thoroughly. According to Claus Offe, the real significance of direct democracy is:

> That it is available [for use only in exceptional circumstances] as an alternative tool of political participation by the people. If this were the case, political elites would, in an optimal situation, be keen to justify and explicate their legislative decisions and shortcomings so accurately that they can be sure to avoid unpleasant surprises as experienced in the event of the Danish Europe-Referendum. Inversely, the bare presence of forms of direct democratic participation could help the people overcome the impression—caused by cynicism or mere convenience, but at any rate exploitable by populism—of being at the mercy of political elites. Their beneficial effect would thus in any case not lie in the actual use, but rather in the mere existence of direct democratic provisions. Hence, this instrument must be restored in a manner which neither welcomes its frivolous use nor erects deterringly high hurdles. (Offe 1992: 139–40)

Critics of direct democracy argue that it undermines the duality of majoritarian democracy inherent in the German parliamentary system. In extreme cases it could result in the opposition making use of direct democratic instruments to practically overthrow a bill passed or planned by the government. In itself this statement may be correct. Yet, the real question is how this statement should be assessed. The analysis offered here suggests that precisely the combination of the two system features could be beneficial. Assuming that direct democracy fulfills its preventive function, the governing majority is compelled to at least implicitly consider the views of the minority in their decisions. Direct democratic mechanisms thus by nature have a *consensual* effect in that they promote the more encompassing consideration of interests. Their implications on the parliamentary decision-making system thus bear resemblance to those of a presidential system or of a minority government, only that in direct democracy the pressure towards compromise occurs from the outside and is constructed beyond the actual parliamentary sphere.

The combination of strong competition-oriented politics and equally strong constitutional interlocking politics leads to government institutions in the Federal Republic of Germany which do not complement but instead obstruct each other. Forms of direct democratic participation could counteract this. Their introduction would have to unhinge the direct democratic trends from the electoral sphere and *shift* them in the consensual area of the political system. As a result, they could build a protective shield against populist temptations which are inherent in party competition. Political competition would nevertheless retain its electoral function. Indeed, disposing of an incompetent or corrupt government ("throwing the scoundrels out") would have to remain possible. In order to improve governance and policy formulation, however, the dogma of majority democracy would have to be moderated and the focus of democratization shifted to consensual decision-making mechanisms which would also have to be strengthened in their responsiveness. Today, due to the current state of the political system politics do not need less, but—in doubt— more consensus. Ultimately, it needs a well-organized consensus that does not burden the decision-making system. The current institutional configuration of the German political system cannot adequately meet these demands.

NOTES

1. This also holds true for practices of direct democracy which otherwise frequently have a delaying effect on the decision-making process.
2. In the case of other laws, the *Bundesrat* only has a suspensive veto right.

REFERENCES

Abromeit, Heidrun (1992): *Der verkappte Einheitsstaat.* Opladen: Leske and Budrich.
—— (1995): "Volkssouveränität, Parlamentssouveränität, Verfassungssouveränität. Drei Realmodelle der Legitimation staatlichen Handelns." *Politische Vierteljahresschrift 36*: 49–66.
Arnim, Hans Herbert von (2000): *Vom schönen Schein der Demokratie. Politik ohne Verantwortung—am Volk vorbei.* Munich: Droemer.
Benz, Arthur (1998): "Postparlamentarische Demokratie? Demokratische Legitimation im kooperativen Staat," in: Greven, Michael Th., ed.: *Demokratie—eine Kultur des Westens?* Opladen: Leske and Budrich, pp. 201–22.
—— (2000): "Anmerkung zur Diskussion über Verhandlungsdemokratien," in: Holtmann, Everhard, and Voelzkow, Helmut, eds.: *Zwischen Wettbewerbs—und Verhandlungsdemokratie.* Wiesbaden: Westdeutscher Verlag, pp. 201–22.

Beyme, Klaus von (1997): *Der Gesetzgeber. Der Bundestag als Entscheidungszentrum.* Wiesbaden: Westdeutscher Verlag.

Böckenförde, Ernst Wolfgang (1980): "Sozialer Bundesstaat und parlamentarische Demokratie. Zum Verhältnis von Parlamentarismus und Föderalismus unter den Bedingungen des Sozialstaats," in: Jekewitz, Jürgen, Melzer, Michael, and Zeh, Wolfgang, eds.: *Politik als gelebte Verfassung.* Wiesbaden: Westdeutscher Verlag, pp. 182–99.

Bolleyer, Nicole (2001): "Minderheitsparlamentarismus—eine akteursorientierte Erweiterung der Parlamentarismus-Präsidentialismus-Typologie." *Zeitschrift für Politikwissenschaft* 11, no. 4: 1519–46.

Blumenthal, Julia von (2001): *Amtsträger in der Parteiendemokratie.* Wiesbaden: Westdeutscher Verlag.

—— (2003): "Auswanderung aus den Verfassungsinstitutionen. Konsensrunden und Kommissionen." *Aus Politik und Zeitgeschichte* B43/2003: 9–15.

Canovan, Margaret (2002): "Taking Politics to the People. Populism and the Identity of Democracy," in: Mény, Yves, and Surel, Yves, eds.: *Democracies and the Populist Challenge.* Houndmills/New York: Palgrave Macmillan, pp. 81–98.

Czada, Roland (2000): "Konkordanz, Korporatismus und Politikverflechtung. Dimensionen der Verhandlungsdemokratie," in: Holtmann, Everhard, and Voelzkow, Helmut, eds.: *Zwischen Wettbewerbs- und Verhandlungsdemokratie.* Wiesbaden: Westdeutscher Verlag, pp. 23–49.

Czerwick, Erwin (1999): "Verhandlungsdemokratie—ein Politikstil zur Überwindung von Politikblockaden." *Zeitschrift für Politikwissenschaft* 9, no. 2: 415–38.

Dahrendorf, Ralf (2002): *Die Krise der Demokratie. Ein Gespräch mit Antonio Polito.* Munich: C. H. Beck.

Darnstädt, Thomas (2004): *Die Konsensfalle. Wie das Grundgesetz Reformen blockiert.* Stuttgart: DVA & Spiegel.

Decker, Frank (2003): "Der gute und der schlechte Populismus." *Berliner Republik* 5, no. 3: 66–73.

—— (2004a): *Der neue Rechtspopulismus.* Opladen: Leske and Budrich.

—— (2004b): "Konturen des 'neuen' Föderalismus aus Expertensicht: Eine Zwischenbilanz der Arbeit der Kommission zur Modernisierung der bundesstaatlichen Ordnung." *Zeitschrift für Parlamentsfragen* 35, no. 3: 540–58.

—— (2004c): *Föderalismus an der Wegscheide? Optionen und Perspektiven einer Reform der bundesstaatlichen Ordnung.* Wiesbaden: VS Verlag für Sozialwissenschaften.

—— (2004d): "Die Regierungssysteme in den Ländern." in: Decker, Frank, ed.: *Föderalismus an der Wegscheide? Optionen und Perspektiven einer Reform der bundesstaatlichen Ordnung.* Wiesbaden: VS Verlag für Sozialwissenschaften, pp. 188–99.

Decker, Frank, and Blumenthal, Julia von (2002): "Die bundespolitische Durchdringung der Landtagswahlen. Eine empirische Analyse von 1970 bis 2001." *Zeitschrift für Parlamentsfragen* 33, no. 1: 144–65.

Dörner, Andreas (2001): *Politainment. Politik in der medialen Erlebnisgesellschaft.* Frankfurt M.: Suhrkamp.

Elgie, Robert ed. (2001): *Divided Government in Comparative Perspective.* Oxford/New York: Oxford University Press.

Hennis, Wilhelm (1999): *Auf dem Weg in den Parteienstaat. Aufsätze aus vier Jahrzehnten.* Stuttgart: Reclam.

Hough, Daniel, and Jeffrey, Charlie (2003): "Landtagswahlen: Bundestestwahlen oder Regionalwahlen." *Zeitschrift für Parlamentsfragen* 34, no. 1: 79–94.

Kielmansegg, Peter Graf (2003) "Zukunftsverweigerung." *Frankfurter Allgemeine Zeitung*, 23 May 2003.

Ismayr, Wolfgang (2003): *Der Deutsche Bundestag im politischen System der Bundesrepublik Deutschland. Ein Studienbuch.* Opladen: Leske and Budrich.

Lehmbruch, Gerhard (1998): *Parteienwettbewerb im Bundesstaat.* Stuttgart: Kohlhammer.

Lijphart, Arend (1999): *Patterns of Democracy. Government Forms and Performance in Thirty-Six Countries.* New Haven/London: Yale University Press.

Mair, Peter (2002): "Populist Democracy vs. Party Democracy," in: Mény, Yves, and Surel, Yves, eds.: *Democracies and the Populist Challenge.* Houndmills/New York: Palgrave Macmillan, pp. 81–98.

Neidhart, Leonhard (2002): "Ein Stachel in der Konkordanz." *Neue Züricher Zeitung*, 5 February 2002.

Offe, Claus (1992): "Wider scheinradikale Thesen. Die Verfassungspolitik auf der Suche nach dem 'Volkswillen,'" in: Hofmann, Gunter, and Perger, Werner A., eds.: *Die Kontroverse. Weizäckers Parteienkritik in der Diskussion.* Frankfurt M.: Eichborn, pp. 126–42.

Patzelt, Werner J., and Schirmer, Roland (1996): "Parlamentarismusgründung in den neuen Bundesländern." *Aus Politik und Zeitgeschichte* B27/1996: 20–28.

Pelinka, Anton (2003) "Koalitionen in Österreich. Keine westeuropäische Normalität," in: Kropp, Sabine, Schüttemeyer, Suzanne S., and Sturm, Roland, eds.: *Koalitionen und Koalitionshandel in West- und Osteuropa.* Wiesbaden: VS Verlag für Sozialwissenschaften, pp. 69–87.

Renzsch, Wolfgang, and Schieren, Stefan (1997): "Große Koalition oder Minderheitsregierung. Sachsen-Anhalt als Zukunftsmodell des parlamentarischen Regierungssystems in den neuen Bundesländern?" *Zeitschrift für Parlamentsfragen* 28, no. 3: 391–406.

Rudzio, Wolfgang (2003): "Koalitionen in Deutschland. Flexibilität informellen Regierens," in: Kropp, Sabine, Schüttemeyer, Suzanne S., and Sturm, Roland, eds.: *Koalitionen und Koalitionshandeln in West- und Osteuropa.* Opladen: Leske and Budrich, pp. 43–67.

Rutz, Michael (2003): "Der Konsensstaat." *Die politische Meinung*, no. 406: 35–39.

Scharpf, Fritz W. (1997): "Die Malaise der deutschen Politik." *Frankfurter Allgemeine Zeitung*, 5 June 1997.

Schieren, Stefan (2001): *Die Stille Revolution. Der Wandel der britischen Demokratie unter dem Einfluß der europäischen Integration.* Darmstadt: Wissenschaftliche Buchgesellschaft.

Schmidt, Manfred G. "Das politische Leistungsprofil der Demokratien," in: Greven, Michael Th., ed.: *Demokratie—eine Kultur des Westens?* Opladen: Leske and Budrich, pp. 181–99.

Schütt-Wetschky, Eberhard (1984): *Grundtypen parlamentarischer Demokratie. Klassisch-liberaler Typ und Gruppentyp. Unter besonderer Berücksichtigung der Kritik am "Fraktionszwang."* Freiburgi. Br./Munich: Alber.

Siaroff, Alan (1999): "Corporatism in 24 Industrial Countries. Meaning and Measurement." *European Journal of Political Research* 36, no. 2: 175–205.

Sturm, Roland, and Pehle, Heinrich (2001): *Das neue deutsche Regierungssystem. Die Europäisierung von Institutionen, Entscheidungsprozessen und Politikfeldern in der Bundesrepublik Deutschland.* Opladen: Leske and Budrich.

Tsebelis, George (1995): "Veto Players and Law Production in Parliamentary Democracies," in: Döring, Herbert, ed.: *Parliaments and Majority Rule in Western Europe.* Frankfurt M./New York: Campus, pp. 83–113.

Walter, Frank, and Dürr, Tobias (2000): *Die Heimatlosigkeit der Macht. Wie die Politik in Deutschland den Boden verlor.* Berlin: Alexander Fest.

Wilson, Graham. "The Westminster Model in Comparative Perspective," in: Budge, Ian, and McKay, David, eds.: *Developing Democracy.* London/Thousand Oaks/New Delhi: Sage, pp. 197–99.

Zohnhöfer, Reimut (1999): "Die große Steuerreform 1998–1999. Ein Lehrstück für Politikentwicklung bei Parteienwettbewerb im Bundesstaat." *Zeitschrift für Parlamentsfragen* 30, no. 2: 326–45.

6

From Corporatist Consensualism to the Politics of Commissions: German Welfare Reform and the Inefficiency of the Alliance for Jobs

Sven Jochem

Social Pacts, Employment Pacts or other varieties of strategic policy alliances are new forms of corporatist concertation which, as many have argued, have the capacity to avoid reform gridlock as well as to foster democratic legitimacy and societal consensus (cf. Hassel 2000, 2003; Molina and Rhodes 2002; Regini 2000; Rhodes 2001; Jochem and Siegel 2003). In 1998 the first Red-Green government in German history launched the *Bündnis für Arbeit, Ausbildung und Wettbewerbsfähigkeit* (Alliance for Jobs, Training and Competitiveness) as a means of a new politics of the centre (*Politik der neuen Mitte*). This tripartite reform agency at the national level was intended to serve as a major reform engine.[1]

This Alliance for Jobs was no success. Neither could it significantly improve the economic efficiency of the German model, nor could it serve as a driving force to modernize the German welfare state. As the involved parties of the Alliance for Jobs met for the first time after the 2002 federal elections—in which the Red-Green coalition had been reelected by a small margin—Chancellor Gerhard Schröder terminated the Alliance for Jobs without a final press release and without the (traditional) official dinner on 3 March 2003. Already before the termination of the Alliance for Jobs, the Red-Green government appointed a special commission for the reform of the labour market, the so-called *Hartz-Kommission*, and in November 2003, the government installed the *Rürup-Kommission*, which was supposed to develop reform proposals for the funding of German social insurance schemes. These commissions, together with the announcement of the *Agenda 2010* on 14 March of the same year, in which Chancellor Schröder—without prior consultation of major policy partners—sketched out far-reaching reform measures, signaled the "farewell" to tripartite reform politics and the start of a new governance strategy.

Against this background, the key objective of this chapter is to highlight a shift of emphasis in German politics from tripartite corporatist consensus politics to the politics of expert commissions. This shift may be interpreted as a reduction of democratic qualities in the name of efficiency gains in terms of policy making. This provides an opportunity for exploring whether, and to what extent, efficiency gains can really only be achieved at the expense of democratic qualities, or, whether and to what extent a reduction of democratic qualities really lead to improved efficiency. It is argued that the shift from tripartite concertation to the politics of commissions has reduced the legitimacy of reform politics. However, the efficiency of the politics of commissions is not necessarily superior to tripartite concertation. In taking the Alliance for Jobs as a case illustrating the government's departure from consensual tripartism, the question is not so much why the Alliance for Jobs failed, but instead, why the government evidently regarded it as an inappropriate tool of policy making.

In order to clarify the argument, the next section—reiterating some points which have been explored in more detail above (see chapters 1 and 2)— briefly discusses the urgency of welfare reform in Germany. Section three then, further pursuing the analysis of the previous chapter, illustrates the various obstacles to welfare reform and tripartite concertation in German politics. In section four the democratic quality and reform efficiency of the Alliance for Jobs is discussed. And in section five this analysis is extended to the politics of commissions since 2002. A brief review of the argument is offered in the concluding section.

THE URGENCY OF WELFARE REFORM

Having been praised two decades ago as a highly successful model of organized or coordinated capitalism (Katzenstein 1987), the German welfare state is now in crisis (Kitschelt and Streeck 2004). Since German unification at the latest, the economy is troubled by low growth rates and insufficient investment (see chapters 1 and 2). Open unemployment increased to ever higher levels. At the same time, however, it also has to be pointed out that the German economy is still, together with Japan, world champion in manufacturing. Despite the common trend observable in all advanced economies of the OECD that this specific sector of the economy is shrinking, Germany and Japan have currently the highest share of employment in the manufacturing industries. There is still a large number of successful export-oriented firms which contribute significantly to economic growth and which are still highly competitive in the international market.

The German economy is nevertheless embedded into the global trend towards the service industries (Iversen and Wren 1998). High open unemployment, low employment elasticity, especially in the service sector, and only medium labor force participation rates seem to be the core problems of the German model (Siegel and Jochem 2000). In contrast to the social democratic roads towards welfare capitalism, the employment share of the public service sector is small in Germany, and in contrast to the liberal antipodes of welfare capitalism, such as the UK, the private service sector is underdeveloped in Germany. Thus, employment opportunities, especially for women, are restricted. Suppressed wage differentials and the high share of social contribution rates in overall wage costs are commonly held responsible for this dissatisfying employment situation, especially in the low-wage service sectors (cf. Scharpf 2000, Siegel and Jochem 2000).

The economic inactivity of a major part of the population is in fact the legacy of the characteristic way in which political actors during the golden age of German social market economy (*Soziale Marktwirtschaft*) used to manage the economic crisis since the 1970s and, more specifically, of the role social security played in this political exchange. Since the 1970s, trade unions, employers, and different governments used "the Bismarckian welfare state as a functional equivalent to Keynesianism" (Streeck 2003: 5). Far reaching and intensively used early retirement schemes dampened the supply of labor and, as a consequence, curbed the number of open unemployment. This strategy was further expanded after German unification. The transfer of the west-German model to the new German *Länder* in the East (Lehmbruch 1991; Wiesenthal 2002) implied rapidly rising numbers of employees taking early retirement. As a consequence, social contribution rates increased from 35.6 percent in 1990 to 42.1 percent at the end of the Kohl era in 1998. After a marginal reduction to 41.0 percent in 2000 and 2001, the rise of health insurance contributions led to an increase of the overall social contribution rate in 2003 to 42.0 percent.[2]

These data, however, should not obscure the fact that since the early 1980s various welfare reforms have successfully been implemented. As I have demonstrated elsewhere (Jochem 2001; also see Siegel 2002), the German welfare state had been efficiently stabilized prior to German unification. Only the Netherlands were more effective in reducing social spending during that period. Additionally, several reforms of the social insurance schemes changed the profile and character of the German welfare state. Nevertheless, there remained a striking inability to overcome the "welfare without work" syndrome (Manow and Seils 2000). Hence, the urgency for welfare reform implied and still implies the necessity to combine social security reforms with reforms to the labor market. And against this background, the German public as well as government had placed exceptionally high hopes in the tripartite Alliance for Jobs, which was seen as a forum where the state and both labor market partners could negotiate crucial reform steps in both welfare spheres.

OBSTACLES TO WELFARE REFORM

Already in 1995, the Christian Democratic-Liberal government had responded to an initiative by the leading trade union *IG Metall* and tried to design welfare reforms in a tripartite reform agency. This was the first Alliance for Jobs. However, after electoral gains for the liberal FDP in three *Länder*-elections, the government terminated this concertation strategy. Although some first agreements had been achieved, the government demanded the trade unions to accept a reduction of the level of sick pay from 100 percent to 80 percent of the full wage, an increase of the retirement age for women to 65, and a retrenchment of the dismissal protection law. For the trade unions, especially the abolition of full sick pay, which had been introduced in 1956–1957 after fierce conflicts between the labor market partners, was not negotiable. As the government was not willing to compromise on this issue, trade unions left the Alliance for Jobs. In 1996, the government then introduced these measures in an encompassing reform package. In the following round of wage negotiations, however, trade unions were successful in defending the full rate of sick pay because large firms in the manufacturing industry, in particular, agreed to pay the 100 percent rate voluntarily and thereby undermined the government's policy and reform strategy. The fate of the first Alliance for Jobs shows how effective concertation is dependent on the pattern of party competition. Furthermore, it provides evidence of the self-steering capacity of the labor market partners.

While some employers and some influential economists question the usefulness of concertation and social partnerships (Berthold and Hank 1999), the German public showed a preference for cooperation between labor, capital, and the state. In 1997, only 38 percent of the German population stated that employers and trade unions should cooperate in a kind of partnership. Only two years later, however, in 1999, some 51 percent regarded *Sozialpartnerschaft* as a core ingredient of German politics. Looking at the longer period from 1952 and 1999, the share of the population explicitly in favor of cooperation went up from 66 percent to 72 percent, while support for a more radical approach of class struggle remained at 19 percent. What is remarkable, however, is that the population in East Germany is significantly less inclined to cross-class cooperation. In 1999, 34 percent of the population in the new *Länder* was in favor of an offensive class struggle and only 53 percent—in contrast to 72 percent in the West—recommended a cooperative strategy (Noelle-Neumann and Köcher 2002: 820).

This widespread appreciation of consensual concertation is mirrored by the corporatist tradition and the institutional structure of Germanys *negotiation democracy* (Czada 2003). Ever since the first legislation introduced under Bismarck (1881), the German welfare state has been shaped by the fragmented corporatist structure of social insurance programs. Interest organizations, and especially those from organized capital and labor, are densely incorporated into the administration of the various social insurance schemes, and they are also comprehensively integrated into policy deliberations. Nevertheless, this style of concertation is quite different from the pattern commonly found in the Nordic countries. In contrast to those, corporatist patterns in Germany are located at the meso-level of public policy making. Furthermore, the role of the government in concertation can best be described through the term "enabling state" (Streeck 1997: 38), i.e., a state that leaves leeway for self-governance of the social partners and does not interfere into their spheres. In order to clarify the institutional and power framework for concertation in the German negotiation democracy it is helpful to highlight five peculiarities of and requirements for efficient concertation in Germany:

First, top-level nationwide policy concertation between the associations and the federal government is the exception, rather than the norm. The most prominent example of nationwide economic concertation was the *Konzertierte Aktion* (1967–1977) which was widely regarded as unsuccessful. Not only was the large number of actors involved an obstacle to agreement, but this social pact proved ineffective in managing Germany's economic problems. As the Social Democratic-Liberal coalition government under Chancellor Helmut Schmidt switched to the principles of institutionalized monetarism (which the *Bundesbank* had already adopted in 1973–1974) and tried to restrict the further expansion of social security spending, the *Konzertierte Aktion* was doomed to failure (Schroeder 2001).

Second, German corporatism is segmented along the dividing lines of the social insurance state (Czada 2003; Jochem 2001). The institutionalization of dense networks in the health insurance schemes (Döhler and Manow 1997), the pension insurance schemes (Nullmeier and Rüb 1993), and unemployment insurance (Heinelt and Weck 1998) is well documented. All contributions emphasize that this segregation implies an encapsulation of policy-communities vis-à-vis outside actors as well as a delegation of steering capacities from the executive to these segmented networks. There is, therefore, certainly a *prima facie* case for trying to use nationwide concertation as a means to overcome this segmentation and facilitate package deals that transcend policy boundaries.

Third, public steering capacity is constrained by *Tarifautonomie*. One feature of this kind of wage bargaining is the very limited role of the government. Both sides, i.e., the trade unions and the employers' associations, regard free wage bargaining without state intervention as a precious good that is strictly defended. To include wage issues into national concertation, as it has been done in the most successful social pacts in Europe (Hassel 2003), is institutionally impossible in Germany. But even without state intervention, wage growth has always been moderated by the key role of the manufacturing industry, i.e., the economic sector that is most strongly oriented towards international markets and mostly interested in keeping wages at a level that does not threaten international competitiveness.

Fourth, the German state is characterized by horizontal power separation between the federal executive (and the majority of the *Bundestag*) on the one side and the *Bundesrat*, i.e., the Chamber of the German *Länder*, on the other side. German federalism is a pattern of cooperative federalism with an inbuilt "joint-decision trap" (Scharpf 1988). Especially in times of rival majorities in both chambers, i.e., a situation of divided government, the danger of policy gridlock increases for those laws for which consent of both chambers is required (see Frank Decker's analysis in chapter 5). In April 1991 the Christian-Democratic-Liberal coalition lost its stable majority in the *Bundesrat* and then always depended on the support of at least one neutral *Land*. From January 1996, after the victory of the SPD in Hesse, the SPD (together with the Green Party) could essentially block policy reforms in the *Bundesrat* because together the two parties had an absolute majority (Bauer 1998: 94–109). The new Red-Green government could rely on stable majorities in both chambers only until February 1999. After that, the federal government lost more and more secure votes in the *Bundesrat*. But of course, as Frank Decker correctly argues above (see chapter 5), it would be short-sighted to suggest that the constraints of divided government *automatically* imply reform gridlock. Empirical investigations show that even under such political circumstances reforms are possible (Bauer 1998; Wachendorfer-Schmidt 2003). And where reform policies have failed, this has in many cases not been due to the institutional setup of, and specific power distribution within, the German federal system, but to the effective influence from actors outside the government (Manow and Burkhart 2004).

Fifth, the organizations of both capital and labor had (and still have) severe problems with internal compliance and stabilizing organizational strength. Since unification, in particular, German trade unions have lost a large number of members. Despite the territorial expansion, the absolute membership figure was, in 2002, down to the level of 1980 (cf. Ebbinghaus 2003: 180). The financial losses led to widespread mergers in the trade union camp, the most prominent ones being the fusion of the *IG Chemie* and *IG Bergbau* (1992–1997) and the creation of the service trade union, *ver.di*, in 2001. The traditional dominant position of the *IG Metall* in welfare politics has been challenged by these developments. Factionalism in the employers' camp has increased steadily after German unification. Traditionally, the employers' camp has been divided between the BDA, which is the national association of employers' organizations responsible mainly for wage bargaining and social policy, and the BDI (Association of German Industry), which is the national confederation of trade associations. During the 1990s, open conflicts between BDA and BDI escalated. Additionally, more and more firms, especially in East Germany left the employers' associations thereby undermining collective wage bargaining (Schroeder 2003).

In a context characterized by these five major features of the institutional framework in Germany, policy deliberation between labor, capital, and the state is generally popular with the German public and—ignoring for the moment the issue of a certain East-West divide—the legitimacy of policy concertation is generally high. Because of policy segmentation, the traditional pattern of concertation in the German welfare state is encapsulated into distinctive policy fields. Therefore, from an institutional point of view, national reform concertation transcending policy boundaries could be a strategy enabling the actors to strike package deals and efficiently reform the labor market as well as the social insurance schemes. In practice, however, institutional constraints as well as the established patterns of party competition and power distribution have tended to complicate efficient national concertation. Against this background, the next section investigates how the Red-Green government tried to use concertation as a means of dissolving reform gridlock.

CONSENSUAL CONCERTATION: THE ALLIANCE FOR JOBS

In contrast to the first Alliance for Jobs, the Red-Green government institutionalized national tripartism very explicitly. In order to emphasize the importance of this tripartite body, the Alliance for Jobs was directly attached to the *Bundeskanzleramt* (Federal Chancellery) and was regarded as a central reform project of the chancellor. In addition to the chancellor himself and the leader of the *Bundeskanzleramt*, seven government ministers represented the side of government. From the side of the trade unions, the leader of the DGB (German Association of Trade Unions) and the leaders of three single trade unions (*IG Metall, IG BCE, ver.di*) joined the negotiations. The employers' side was represented by the leaders from *BDA* and *BDI* and by the leaders of employers' associations which represent mostly small businesses (*IHK, ZDH*). The organizational design of the Alliance for Jobs did not reflect the possibility of divided government in Germany. Neither representatives from the *Länder* nor from the major party in opposition, the CDU/CSU, were included.

Beyond the negotiations at the top level of the involved actors, the *Steuerungsgruppe* (steering-group) was expected to guarantee steady contact and flow of information between the representatives of the state, industry, and the unions. In the public debate, however, meetings at the elite level received most attention. During the lifespan of the Alliance for Jobs eight *Spitzengespräche* (top-level talks) were held and different measures were presented as the final outcome of each round of negotiations. At the beginning, some compromises were agreed regarding the training of younger employees and test projects for the creation of a low-wage sector in Germany were launched. Over time, however, results were presented ever less frequently and became increasingly symbolic in qualitative terms (Schroeder 2003; Siegel 2003).

In the first phase of the Red-Green government, several laws were (hastily) implemented, as the government aspired to fulfill the pledges made during the election campaign. As Uwe Jun outlines in more detail above (see chapter 2), this period lasted roughly until the autumn of 1999. But the government steadily suffered losses in public opinion surveys. One reason for this was the poor manner in which these measures were prepared and implemented: the public and especially the media evaluated these reforms as not professional (for a closer analysis see chapter 8) and lacking a clear reform strategy.

This early phase of the "Red-Green project" (Egle et al. 2003) produced, above all, mixed signals to the actors in the Alliance for Jobs. The employers were rather dissatisfied with the first reform measures of the Schröder government. Indeed, the new government reintroduced full sick pay which had been reduced by its predecessor and also reversed reforms to the pension system which had been introduced by the Kohl government in order to cushion the effect of demographic change on the public pension scheme. Furthermore, the government reinstalled the status quo ante in the field of employment protection law. And finally, it also reregulated low-level employment (*geringfügige Beschäftigung*) which was included into the social insurance schemes, and tried to restrict jobs where employees, while essentially working for a single employer, were doing so on a self-employed basis (cf. Blancke and Schmid 2003).

It is tempting to argue that the Red-Green government fulfilled the wish list of its electoral clientele, or more specifically, the wish list of the trade unions

(Fickinger 2001). Indeed, organizational links between the SPD and the trade union movement were intact and trade unions could successfully exploit their routes of access to the major party in government. This provided evidence that the Alliance for Jobs was *not* the major avenue of influence for interest groups. None of the major reforms during this first period had been negotiated in the tripartite talks. This major strategic mistake of the government reduced the reform efficiency of tripartism considerably (Eichhorst 2002).

The political constellations shaping the government's reform agenda changed in 1999. Already in February, the elections in Hesse brought a majority for the CDU and hence, the Red-Green government lost its majority in the *Bundesrat*. Once again, divided government then set the institutional frame for reform politics. Nevertheless, with the support of some neutral *Länder* in the *Bundesrat* (cf. Merkel 2003: 171–75), the government passed legislation for a tax reform, and it also agreed a pensions reform. The major objective of the latter was to achieve a reduction in the pensions contribution rate. An incremental reduction in the benefit level was agreed and, as a supplement, a capital-funded pension pillar (*Riesterrente*) was introduced that is state-subsidized for low-income groups. In fact, this introduction of a capital funded scheme can actually be seen as a paradigm shift in German pension politics (Hinrichs 2004; critically Nullmeier 2004).

Not least because much in these reform projects contradicted the SPD's election program, the government provoked protests from the unions as well as the opposition parties. Trade unions mainly criticized the reduction in benefit levels, and the shift towards private (capital funded) pensions was seen as undermining the principle that pensions are funded by equal contributions from employers and employees. The oppositional CDU/CSU rejected the policy proposal because they were in favor of large scale subsidies for low income wage earners to build up the *Riesterrente*. Furthermore, particularly against the background of the SPD's successful attempt in 2000 to split the Christian-Democratic *Länder*, the Conservative party leadership was keen to maintain a united position and rejected the proposal "for mainly tactical reasons" (Schludi 2001: 35).

To these critical responses both from the trade unions and the opposition parties, the Red-Green coalition reacted in several ways. Firstly, it split the reform package into two laws, with only one having to pass the *Bundesrat*. Secondly, the incumbent coalition called consensus negotiations with the Christian-Democratic Union. In these negotiations, the government made far-reaching concessions regarding the level of state subsidies for the *Riesterrente*. Thirdly, in order to appease the trade unions (as well as the left wing within the SPD's own ranks), the party leadership reviewed the originally intended reduction of benefit levels and decided that "collectively-agreed pension provision" should "take precedence over private provision (*Tarifvorbehalt*), thus giving the unions a voice in the area of fully funded supplementary old-age provision" (Schludi 2001: 36). In the final stage of the decision-making process, the government made further concessions to specific *Länder* (Berlin and Brandenburg), to the FDP and to some prominent dissenters in the SPD (treatment of home-ownership as old-age provision). However, even despite these far-reaching (and expensive) concessions, the reform proposal was rejected in the *Bundesrat*. In the end, negotiations in the Conciliation Committee induced some further marginal changes and eventually forged a reform consensus.

The Riester reform exemplifies that the efficiency of the Alliance for Jobs was already then undermined by the strategic choices of the Red-Green government (and especially the SPD). In order to manage divided government, the coalition negotiated with the opposition, and the interest groups lobbied the political parties in a more or less traditional way. This reform process bypassed the Alliance for Jobs systematically. Hence, the efficiency of the Alliance for Jobs was low because the government did not even try to deal with this major reform project within this tripartite framework. And as trade unions could veto the demand of the employers to integrate wage issues into the remit of the Alliance for Jobs, it soon became obvious (already in 2000) that the Alliance was no more than a form of symbolic politics. These strategic choices of the Red-Green government may well be interpreted as a missed opportunity in German welfare history (Eichhorst 2002).

THE POLITICS OF EXPERT COMMISSIONS

The scandal of incorrect accounts in the *Bundesanstalt für Arbeit*, i.e., the federal labor market agency, was an important catalyst for the government's shift towards a new strategy of governance. Not least in order to stem the decline of support for the Red-Green government in public opinion polls, Chancellor Gerhard Schröder established in March 2002 the *Kommission zur Reform der Bundesanstalt für Arbeit* (Commission for the Reform of the Federal Labor Market Agency) under the leadership of Peter Hartz, then member of the management board of *Volkswagen* and responsible for personnel affairs. This commission had the brief to evaluate the work of the *Bundesanstalt* and explore strategies for reducing open unemployment. The appointment of the Hartz Commission provided further evidence for the mainly symbolic character of Alliance for Jobs. From a formal point of view both commissions existed side-by-side without organizational connections, even though they had closely related briefs.

Only six months later, in November 2002 and immediately after the federal election, the government expanded this strategy and set up another commission which was explicitly given the task to devise and assess reform options for the social security schemes. This *Kommission für die Nachhaltigkeit in der Finanzierung der Sozialen Sicherungssysteme* (Commission for the Sustainable Financing of the Social Security Systems) was chaired by the economist Bert Rürup who had been a long-standing advisor of the Kohl government and had also worked for the Schröder administration.

Revealingly, neither of these two new bodies included the top representatives from the trade unions or the employers' organizations. Instead, the government selectively chose its own preferred representatives from capital and labor, and also invited a range of academic experts, mainly from the social sciences and jurisprudence, into the commissions. In fact, only two out of fifteen members of the Hartz Commission were from the trade unions, and only one representative could directly be linked to organized business (however, some representatives from major companies such as *Deutsche Bank* and *BASF* were included). These new commissions, as well as Chancellor Schröder's *Agenda 2010* which was presented in a statement of policy on 14 March 2003, mark a significant shift in the reform strategies and reform ambitions of the Red-Green government.

The Hartz Commission recommended to introduce far-reaching reforms ranging from a new service orientation of local job agencies to the introduction of new forms of self-employment (*Ich-AG*) and the recommendation to merge the unemployment assistance scheme with the social assistance scheme (which implied lower benefits for the long-term unemployed). The tenor of the measures was to reduce benefits, enhance the incentives for the unemployed to take up work, and to increase (rather than reduce as the Red-Green reforms in 1998–1999 had done) the possibilities for minor jobs. Chancellor Gerhard Schröder and the Red-Green government backed the Hartz recommendations and announced that these would be implemented immediately and without major changes.

In 2005, the most far-reaching reform proposal, the conflation of unemployment insurance and social assistance, came into force (*Hartz IV*). Up to the present, however, this has not had the desired effect on Germany's labor market and employment figures. Indeed, the opposite of what had been intended seems to have been achieved: while unemployment figures are still increasing (partly a statistical artifact, as former social assistance receivers are now fully included into unemployment statistics), the financial burden for the merged long-time unemployment insurance scheme (*ALG II*) is heavier than originally expected, a result that undermines the policy's original objective of overall cost containment.

The Rürup-Commission presented its policy recommendations in August 2003. In contrast to the Hartz Commission, its members had been unable to agree on a clear-cut reform package. While the evaluation of the status quo and the impact of the socioeconomic challenges had not been controversial, no consensus had been achieved about the future of the social insurance schemes. One major issue in the debate had been whether the pension age should be increased to sixty-seven years. A majority of the SPD parliamentary group originally opposed this suggestion. In the Grand Coalition that was formed after the elections of September 2005, however, the CDU/CSU as well as the SPD agreed to increase the retirement age incrementally, beginning in 2007, to the age of sixty-seven. Another critical issue in the commission was if the mode of financing should be altered significantly. Up to the present, a consensus on this important issue has not been achieved.

Only one month after the Rürup Commission, the CDU/CSU presented the results of its own commission, chaired by the former federal president Roman Herzog. The Herzog Commission took up several issues which had also been discussed in the Rürup Commission, but it presented different policy recommendations. However, these reform proposals were not backed by the Bavarian CSU. Horst Seehofer, the social policy expert of the CSU and former federal government Minister for Health, openly rejected the policy recommendations as socially imbalanced and not in line with the programmatic visions of a Christian Democratic Party.

Thus, the new politics of expert commissions reveals that these agencies differ from the Alliance for Jobs in several aspects. Firstly, these commissions are no longer in line with the established tripartite principle. Several experts from business and the scientific community, cautiously selected by the executive, dominate the framing of policy recommendations. Secondly, these commissions can be interpreted as instruments which the federal executive uses to frame policy reforms and to influence public debate (Dyson 2005; Trampusch 2005). They are not forums for policy deliberation between organized interests groups. With the recommendations of such commissions, the Red-Green government as well as the CDU tried to overcome intra-party resistance against specific welfare reforms. Thirdly, these commissions have been able to break up the encapsulation of segmented policy communities. In sum, the steering capacity of the federal executive was increased, the willingness to initiate reforms enhanced, and the influence of vested interests to a great extent bypassed.

CONCLUSION

Interest mediation in developed democracies includes the integration of organized interests into the policy-making process. From a comparative perspective it becomes visible how different patterns of interest mediation are one of the features by which different countries are distinct from each other. With the tradition of segmented corporatism Germany lies between the Nordic model of national concertation that goes beyond specific policy boundaries ("package deals") and the Anglo-Saxon model of fragmented and pluralist lobbyism. Empirical studies have suggested that national tripartite concertation between labor, capital, and the state may be more efficient than other modes of policy making because the actors can coordinate their actions and adapt them to the systemic requirements of the political economy. At the same time, such joined-up reform approaches may have more legitimacy than can be achieved by means of simple majority decisions (Lehmbruch 1984; Scharpf 1987).

From an institutional point of view, the second Alliance for Jobs could have been a reform agency with the capacity to break up segmented corporatism and negotiate reform policies that systematically link labor market reforms with reforms in the social security systems. Given that this kind of consensual policy making is highly appreciated by the German public, one might have expected that the Red-Green government would be more successful in using this mode of problem solving. It is has been argued that the declining internal cohesion of organized interest groups renders this form of policy making increasingly difficult (Trampusch 2005). In contrast to this assessment, however, the analysis in this chapter has demonstrated that political mistakes by the government undermined the efficiency of the Alliance for Jobs.

The institutional setup of the Alliance had not been designed to accommodate the possibility of divided government. The case of Finland for example shows that in order to be efficient, social pacts need to be supported by all competing parties. An efficient Alliance for Jobs would have required the integration of the CDU/CSU into the negotiations. Just before the official inauguration of the Grand Coalition in 2005, there were rumors that the Merkel government was intending to revive the Alliance for Jobs (SPIEGEL Online, 8 October 2005). Indeed, both the institutional conditions as well as the power constellations would now be more conducive to successful concertation than they have been in the recent past. But for a new Alliance for Jobs to be successful, the new executive would also have to make sure it avoids the mistakes of the Red-Green government: for tripartite agencies to work efficiently, all dimensions of the reform agenda need to be included into the negotiations and considerable pressure needs to be put on the negotiation partners to find viable compromises.

The politics of commissions in Germany has been efficient only in a specific sense. Firstly, the new commissions could overcome segmented corporatism in that they effectively perforated the encapsulated policy communities. New actors entered the policy space and the importance of traditional actors was reduced. Secondly, this governance style stimulated public debate. While the Alliance for Jobs did not manage to catalyze public deliberation on the objectives and means of welfare state reform, the Hartz, Rürup, or Herzog Commissions were much more successful in this respect. Thirdly, the commissions were efficient in that they helped to disarm—at least to some extent—dissenters within the governing parties. These three functions of the politics of commissions enhanced the steering capacity of the executive. But the German disease of "welfare without work" (Manow and Seils 2000) has not been cured through the politics of commissions. In order to break the vicious circle of German reform politics it may well be useful to connect the project of labor market reforms more systematically with the reform of the social security schemes, as well as the reform of the tax system (Nullmeier 2004).

Thus, the question of the efficiency of consensual tripartism and the politics of commissions remains undecided, yet the issue of their respective legitimacy is even more complex. On the one hand, tripartist concertation is highly appreciated by the German public. On the other hand, tripartism may be criticized as exclusive: insiders deliberate behind closed doors and exclude marginal interests or interests with low conflict potential (Habermas 1992). Indeed, both governance strategies have been criticized for undermining the sovereignty of parliament and other formal political institutions (Blumenthal 2003; see also chapters 7 and 12 in this volume).

The legitimacy of the politics of commissions is at first sight rather limited. More than anything, the commissions are instruments of the executive for managing intra-party politics and for influencing public debate in a way that suits the executive. But these commissions also inspired public debate, stimulated popular criticism and opened the way for more public deliberation. In fact they brought an intensity of public debate on welfare reform that is new for German politics. Nevertheless, from an analytical point of view a clear distinction has to be made between the formal legitimacy of these commissions and their more or less coincidental effects on public debate. As Matthew Flinders shows in some detail below (see chapter 7), they are in the end not deliberative reform forums and they tend to approach policy making in a technocratic manner that is systematically insulated from the political process which should ensure legitimacy in politics.

The Alliance for Jobs was ineffective because of political mistakes, but at the same time it was popular in the public eye and enjoyed a form of democratic legitimacy. The commissions, in contrast, have low legitimacy but some efficiency effects on the reform process. As the Finnish experience shows, it is thoroughly possible to combine the best of both worlds, i.e., to achieve efficient tripartite concertation at the national level. And as the political circumstances in

Germany are now conducive for such a reform pattern, it would be desirable that Angela Merkel and her Grand Coalition learn from the Finnish example.

NOTES

1. For the purposes of this chapter, I am using the term *Alliance for Jobs* for both the Red-Green *Bündnis für Arbeit* (1998–2003) as well as for the short-lived *Bündnis für Arbeit und Standortsicherung* (Alliance for Jobs and Germany as an Industrial Location) under Chancellor Helmut Kohl in 1995–1996.
2. Data taken from: www.sozialpolitik-aktuell.de/docs/2/tab/tabII6.pdf (4 January 2006).

REFERENCES

Bauer, Thomas (1998): *Der Vermittlungsausschuss. Politik zwischen Konkurrenz und Konsens*. Inaugural dissertation, University of Bremen.

Berthold, Norbert, and Hank, Rainer (1999): *Bündnis für Arbeit: Korporatismus statt Wettbewerb*. Tübingen: Mohr.

Blancke, Susanne, and Schmid, Josef (2003): "Bilanz der Bundesregierung Schröder in der Arbeitsmartkpolitik 1998–2002: Ansätze zu einer doppelten Wende," in: Egle, Christoph, Ostheim, Tobias, and Zohlnhöfer, Reimut, eds.: *Das rot-grüne Projekt. Eine Bilanz der Regierung Schröder 1998–2002*. Wiesbaden: Westdeutscher Verlag, pp. 215–38.

Blumenthal, Julia von (2003): "Auswanderung aus den Verfassungsinstitutionen. Kommissionen und Konsensrunden." *Aus Politik und Zeitgeschichte* B43/2003: 9–15.

Czada, Roland (2003): "Konzertierung in verhandlungsdemokratischen Politikstrukturen," in: Jochem, Sven, and Siegel, Nico A., eds.: *Konzertierung, Verhandlungsdemokratie und Reformpolitik im Wohlfahrtsstaat. Das Modell Deutschland im Vergleich*. Opladen: Leske and Budrich, pp. 35–69.

Döhler, Marian, and Manow, Philip (1997): *Strukturbildung von Politikfeldern*. Opladen: Leske and Budrich.

Dyson, Kenneth (2005): "Binding Hands as a Strategy for Economic Reform: Government by Commission." *German Politics* 14, no. 2: 224–47.

Ebbinghaus, Bernhard (2003): "Die Mitgliederentwicklung deutscher Gewerschaften im historischen und internationalen Vergleich," in: Schroeder, Wolfgang, and Wessels, Bernhard, eds.: *Die Gewerkschaften in Politik und Gesellschaft*. Weisbaden: Westdeutscher Verlag, pp. 147–203.

Eichhorst, Werner (2002): "Bündnis für Arbeit: Chancen vergeben?" *Sozialer Fortschritt* 51, no. 11: 274–78.

Egle, Christoph, Ostheim, Tobias, and Zohlnhöfer, Reimut, eds. (2003): *Das rot-grüne Projekt. Eine Bilanz der Regierung Schröder 1998–2002*. Wiesbaden: Westdeutscher Verlag.

Fickinger, Nico (2001): "In der Glaubwürdigkeitsfalle: Die Gewerkschaften fordern einen kräftigen Nachschlag." *Frankfurter Allgemeine Zeitung*, 29 December 2001: 1–2.

Habermas, Jürgen (1992): *Faktizität und Geltung. Beiträge zur Diskurstheorie des Rechts und des demokratischen Rechtsstaats*. Frankfurt M.: Suhrkamp.

Hassel, Anke (2000): "Bündnisse für Arbeit. Nationale Handlungsfähigkeit im europäischen Regimewettbewerb." *Politische Vierteljahresschrift* 41, no. 3: 498–524.

—— (2003): "Soziale Pakte: Konzertierung als Instrument zur Anpassung an die europäische Währungsintegration," in: Jochem, Sven, and Siegel, Nico A., eds.: *Konzertierung, Verhandlungsdemokratie und Reformpolitik im Wohlfahrtsstaat. Das Modell Deutschland im Vergleich*. Opladen: Leske + Budrich, pp. 70–104.

Heinelt, Hubert, and Weck, Michael (1998): *Arbeitsmarktpolitik. Vom Vereinigungskonsens zur Standortdebatte*. Opladen: Leske + Budrich.

Hinrichs, Karl (2004): "Alterssicherungspolitik in Deutschland: Zwischen Kontinuität und Paradigmenwechsel," in: Stykow, Petra, and Beyer, Jürgen, eds.: *Gesellschaft mit beschränkter Hoffnung*. Wiesbaden: VS Verlag für Sozialwissenschaften, pp. 266–86.

Iversen, Torben, and Wren, Anne (1998): "Equality, Employment, and Budgetary Restraint. The Trilemma of the Service Economy." *World Politics,* no. 50: 507–46.

Jochem, Sven (2001): "Reformpolitik im deutschen Sozialversicherungsstaat," in: Schmidt, Manfred G., ed.: *Wohlfahrtsstaatliche Politik: Institutionen, Prozess und Leistungsprofil*. Opladen: Leske and Budrich, pp. 193–226.

Jochem, Sven, and Siegel, Nico A., eds. (2003): *Konzertierung, Verhandlungsdemokratie und Reformpolitik im Wohlfahrtsstaat. Das Modell Deutschland im Vergleich*. Opladen: Leske and Budrich.

Katzenstein, Peter J. (1987): *Policy and Politics in West Germany: The Growth of a Semi-Sovereign State*. Philadelphia: Temple University Press.

Kitschelt, Herbert, and Streeck, Wolfgang (2004): *Germany. Beyond the Stable State*. London: Frank Cass.

Lehmbruch, Gerhard (1984): "Concertation and the Structure of Corporatist Networks," in: Goldthorpe, John, ed.: *Order and Conflict in Contemporary Capitalism*. Oxford/New York: Oxford University Press, pp. 60–80.

—— (1991): "Die deutsche Vereinigung: Strukturen und Strategien." *Politische Vierteljahresschrift* 32, no. 4: 585–604.

Manow, Philip, and Burkhart, Simone (2004): *Legislative Autolimitation under Divided Government. Evidence from the German Case, 1976–2002*. MPIfG Discussion Paper 04/11, Cologne: MPIfG.

Manow, Philip, and Seils, Eric (2000): "Adjusting badly: The German welfare state, structural change, and the Open economy," in: Scharpf, Fritz W., and Schmidt, Vivien A., eds.: *Welfare and Work in the Open Economy, Vol. II: Diverse Responses to Common Challenges*. Oxford/New York: Oxford University Press, 2000, pp. 264–307.

Merkel, Wolfgang (2003): "Institutionen und Reformpolitik: Drei Fallstudien zur Vetospieler-Theorie," in: Egle, Christoph, Ostheim, Tobias, and Zohlnhöfer, Reimut, eds.: *Das rot-grüne Projekt. Eine Bilanz der Regierung Schröder 1998–2002*. Wiesbaden: Westdeutscher Verlag, pp. 163–90.

Molina, Oscar, and Rhodes, Martin (2002): "Corporatism: The Past, Present, and Future of a Concept." *Annual Review of Political Science* 5: 305–31.

Noelle-Neumann, Elisabeth, and Köcher, Renate, eds. (2002): *Allensbacher Jahrbuch der Demoskopie. 1998–2002*. Munich: Saur.

Nullmeier, Frank (2004): *Soziale Gerechtigkeit und Wettbewerbsfähigkeit*. Oldenburg: Oldenburger Universitätsreden.

Nullmeier, Frank, and Rüb, Friedbert W. (1993): *Die Transformation der Sozialpolitik. Vom Sozialstaat zum Sicherungsstaat*. Frankfurt M./New York: Campus.

Regini, Marino (2000): "Between de-regulation and social pacts. The responses of European economies to Globalisation." *Politics & Society* 28: 5–33.

Rhodes, Martin (2001): "The Political Economy of Social Pacts," in: Pierson, Paul, ed.: *The New Politics of the Welfare State*. Oxford/New York: Oxford University Press, pp. 165–94.

Scharpf, Fritz W. (1987): *Sozialdemokratische Krisenpolitik*. Frankfurt M./New York: Campus.

—— (1988): "The Joint Decision Trap. Lessons from German Federalism and European Integration." *Public Administration* 66, no. 3: 239–78.

—— (2000): "Economic Changes, Vulnerabilities, and Instiutional Capabilities," in: Scharpf, Fritz W., and Schmidt, Vivien A., eds.: *Welfare and Work in the Open Economy. From Vulnerability to Competitiveness*. Oxford/New York: Oxford University Press, pp. 21–124.

Schludi, Martin (2001): "The Politics of Pensions in European Social Insurance Countries." MPIfG Duscussion Paper 01/11. Cologne: MPIfG.

Schroeder, Wolfgang (2001): "Konzertierte Aktion und Bündnis für Arbeit: Zwei Varianten des deutschen Korporatismus," in: Zimmer, Annette, and Wessels, Bernhard, eds.: *Verbände und Demokratie in Deutschland*. Opladen: Leske and Budrich, pp. 29–54.

—— (2003): "Modell Deutschland und das Bündnis für Arbeit," in: Jochem, Sven, and Siegel, Nico A., eds.: *Konzertierung, Verhandlungsdemokratie und Reformpolitik im Wohlfahrtsstaat. Das Modell Deutschland im Vergleich*. Opladen: Leske and Budrich, pp. 107–47.

Siegel, Nico A. (2002): *Baustelle Sozialpolitik. Konsolidierung und Rückbau im internationalen Vergleich*. Frankfurt M./New York: Campus.

—— (2003): "Assessing the Effects of Social Pacts—With a Special Focus on the German Case." Paper Presented at the 6 Conference of the European Sociological Association. Murcia (Spain), 23–26 September 2003.

Siegel, Nico A., and Jochem, Sven (2000): "Der Sozialstaat als Beschäftigungsbremse? Deutschlands steiniger Weg in die Dienstleistungsgesellschaft," in: Czada, Roland, and Wollmann, Hellmut, eds.: *Von der Bonner zur Berliner Republik. 10 Jahre*

Deutsche Einheit. Leviathan Sonderheft 19/1999. Opladen: Westdeutscher Verlag, pp. 539–66.

SPIEGEL Online (2005): "Merkel plant neues Bündnis für Arbeit," 8 Oktober 2005, www.spiegel.de/politik/deutschland/0,1518,378702,00.html

Streeck, Wolfgang (1997): "German Capitalism: Does it Exist? Can it Survive?" in: Crouch, Colin, and Streeck, Wolfgang, eds.: *Political Economy of Modern Capitalism.* London/Thousand Oaks/New Dehli: Sage, pp. 33–54.

—— (2003): "From State Weakness as Strength to State Weakness as Weakness: Welfare Corporatism and the Private Use of the Public Interest." MPIfG Working Paper 03/2. Cologne: MPIfG.

Trampusch, Christine (2005): "Sozialpolitik in Post-Hartz Germany." Manuscript. Cologne: MPIfG, 2005.

Wachendorfer-Schmidt, Ute (2003): *Politikverflechtung im vereinigten Deutschland.* Wiesbaden: Westdeutscher Verlag.

Wiesenthal, Helmut (2002): "German Unification and the 'German Model.' An Adventure of Radical Institutional Conservatism." Paper presented at the Workshop *Germany Beyond the Stable State: A House United Cannot Stand?* Cologne: Max-Planck-Institut für Gesellschaftsforschung, 11–12 October 2002.

7

Efficiency versus Accountability?: Modernizing Governance and Democratic Renewal in Britain, 1997–2005

Matthew Flinders

This book explores the controversies and tensions surrounding the agendas of social, economic, and political modernization in Britain and Germany. The question whether a tension exists between the dual ambitions of *economic efficiency* and *democratic renewal* forms the spine or central focus of this collection. This chapter examines developments in Britain in relation to the deployment of an increasingly diverse array of public-private partnerships (P3s) since the election of New Labour in May 1997. Public-private partnerships have been a key strategy of the Blair government for increasing economic efficiency. At the same time Blair has introduced a raft of constitutional reforms with the ambition of achieving democratic renewal. In essence, the period since 1997 offers a rich case study through which questions regarding *trade-offs, balances, limits, dilemmas,* and *paradoxes* (Pollitt and Bouckaert 2000: 149–71) between economic efficiency and democratic renewal can be examined, not least because a strong case can be made that the New Labour government has, for a number of reasons, shifted their emphasis from the latter to the former.

This chapter is divided into three sections. The first section is largely conceptual: it examines the notion of trade-offs and *rejects* the common assumption that certain concepts (i.e., accountability and efficiency) exist in a zero-sum game in which an increase in one automatically leads to a concomitant reduction in the other.[1] This is not to say that such a relational change cannot occur but it does suggest a more sophisticated and nuanced approach, which accepts that certain tools of governance (in certain contexts) may be able to deliver increases in both criteria (i.e., a positive-sum game). The second section grounds this conceptual position through a discussion of two empirical case studies that examine particular kinds of P3 in Britain: the private finance initiative (PFI) and public interest companies (PICs). These case studies provide a gateway through which common assumptions regarding trade-offs and conceptual tensions can be further explored. The final section explores the value of Okun's seminal text of 1975 *Equality and Efficiency: The Big Trade-Off* and particularly his "leaky bucket" experiment. This, it is argued, provides a macro-level framework for understanding some of the problems and key themes arising from the case studies not just in terms of empirical modeling and relationships but also in terms of the epistemological and methodological challenges faced by scholars and public servants who seek to improve their grasp of the *potential* trade-offs that may form an aspect of both economic and democratic reforms. The next section examines and challenges the whole notion of conceptual trade-offs.

CONCEPTUAL ANALYSIS: HARMONY OR FRICTION?

There is a common assumption in the wider literature on societal modernization that certain key concepts are incompatible, and therefore exist in a pendulum-like zero-sum relationship. It is in this vein that Mulgan argues that "some aspects of accountability are inevitably reduced under contracting out" because "contracting out, at best involves a trade-off between efficiency and accountability. Denials of such a trade-off are fallacious rhetoric" (Mulgan 1997: 106). Similar exchanges are generally posited in relation to, for example, independence versus control, public service ethos versus private sector values, and freedom of information versus commercial confidentiality (see Smith and Hague 1971; Oughton 1995). In all these cases an implicit and frequently explicit preconception exists that you cannot have more of one without less of the other, to put it simply. It is in this vein that Hood and Jackson emphasized the way in which certain administrative principles frequently come in diametrically opposed pairs, with advantages and disadvantages trading off as one moves from one polar principle to its opposite (Hood and Jackson 1991). The simple argument of this section is that although such fixed ideas may reflect the experience of certain reform initiatives and be perennial themes within the public management literature it is vital to keep an open mind as to the possibility of forging relationships, institutions, and processes that actually deliver improvements in the levels of certain concepts or goals that were previously judged to be incompatible.

This is not to suggest that bureaucratic or democratic reforms are not replete with intrinsic limits or dilemmas (Perrow 1972). Politics, in terms of the efficiency of the bureaucratic structure or the degree of democratic support and engagement, cannot *solve* social problems due to the fact that vaunted *problems* and *solutions* are themselves highly political and socially constructed entities. Through the management of finite resources (e.g., political capital (public trust) and financial capital (tax derived public finance)) politicians must generally adopt a broadly utilitarian approach based around "satisficing"—obtaining an outcome that is broadly accepted and good enough—rather than optimization because in the real world there are simply too many multiple and competing objectives, societal demands, and value conflicts (Simon 1957). This, in itself, is linked to the fact that the whole notion of the *public interest* is somewhat limited in practical utility by the simple fact that *the public* is not a homogenous entity but a highly diverse social grouping in which diagnoses and reform prescriptions are contested. The meaning of common concepts such as accountability, efficiency, and democratic renewal are therefore in themselves "essentially contested" (Gallie 1956: 167–98). And yet the simple acceptance of the innate complexity of many of the concepts which form central pillars of the modernization discourse arguably undermines the idea that certain goals or objectives can be placed as opposing forces on a simple axis.

The comparative research of Chistopher Pollitt and Geert Bouckaert (2000) on public management reform supports this argument. They reviewed the wider literature to derive a list of ten *candidate contradictions* (see table 7.1) and concluded in the majority of cases that, although a rationale could be constructed for why such viewpoints had become common, little evidence existed that the dualisms were by definition inherently incompatible. Even in the small number of cases where Pollitt and Bouckaert did suggest that an intrinsic contradiction existed their position is somewhat contentious. For example, they suggested that an "obvious and inescapable contradiction" existed between the objectives of "motivating staff and promoting cultural change," on the one hand, and "weakening tenure and downsizing," on the other (Pollit and Bouckaert 2000: 155). However, an expert in public economics with neoliberal leanings, such as William Niskanen, might contest this position by arguing that the notion of incompatibility rests on the specific meaning ascribed to *motivating staff* and *promoting cultural change* (Niskanen 1996). At a very basic and highly contentious level increasing insecurity combined with reducing the workforce may well motivate staff and engender a change in cultural values as employees become aware that if they do not work harder and achieve "more bang for each buck"—to use Osborne and Gaebler's (1993) phrase—they may lose their job.

Whether one agrees with the specific conclusions of Pollitt and Bouckaert in relation to each specific "candidate contradiction" is somewhat irrelevant in relation to the specific focus of this chapter; the great value of their work is that it urges a more cautious discourse in relation to potential trade-offs that is sympathetic to agency, context, and structure. In terms of context, they

Table 7.1.   Potentially Incompatible Policy Objectives—Candidate Contradictions

Contradiction	Conclusion
1. *Increase political control of the bureaucracy/free managers to manage/empower service consumers.*	In a perfect world these would be more or less compatible. In the real world there is frequently a trade-off between one or more of the three corners.
2. *Promote flexibility and innovation/increase citizen trust and therefore governmental legitimacy.*	There is no fundamental contradiction here. However, there are specific contexts in which politicians and/or managers are obliged to trade-off between . . . innovation and values such as stability, predictability, continuity, and trust.
3. *Prioritize fiscal savings/give priority to improving performance.*	There is no general contradiction; much depends on the specific circumstances.
4. *"Responsibilize" government/reduce the range of tasks government is involved with.*	There is no necessary or general contradiction here.
5. *Motivate staff and promote cultural change/weaken tenure and downsize.*	This appears to be the most obvious and inescapable contradiction.
6. *Reduce burden of internal scrutiny and associated paperwork/sharpen management accountability.*	This seems to be principally a question of balance.
7. *Create more single-purpose agencies/improve policy and program coordination.*	We suggest there is an underlying trade-off here. It may be sharp or gentle, depending on the context.
8. *Decentralize management authority/improve program coordination.*	There is some evidence of a trade-off between these desiderata.
9. *Increase effectiveness/sharpen managerial accountability.*	Whilst this does not appear to be a contradiction, there does seem to be some tension between these two objectives, and there is evidence that the balance is hard to hold.
10. *Improve quality/cut costs.*	This is a relationship that depends heavily on the context and, in particular, whether cost cuts can be achieved through the exploitation of spare capacity and/or technological advances.

highlight a "nested paradox" in that far-reaching efficiency reforms are most likely to be introduced in countries that are already the most efficient and effective in service delivery. However, the impact of these reforms is frequently negative because there is no, or very little, spare capacity to be pruned. Moreover, like human beings, all state structures need to carry a little fat in order to deliver responsiveness and flexibility in times of unexpected demand. The context-dependent paradox is therefore that "in jurisdictions which are already super-efficient there is no 'fat' left to cut, and enforced economies are bound to carve into the bone of real services" (Pollitt and Bouckaert 2000: 160).

To recap, in *some* situations improvements in relation to one specific concept or ambition will be traded against a decline in relation to another—*but not in all situations.* Moreover, whether a certain concept—accountability for example—has been traded (zero-sum) or actually increased (positive-sum) while striving to increase economic efficiency depends on the understanding and values of certain stakeholders. The debate in the mid-1990s between

William Waldegrave and John Stewart, for example, over whether public accountability had increased or decreased as a consequence of public service reforms implemented during the previous fifteen years was based upon diametrically opposed understandings of the concept (see Waldegrave 1993; Stewart 1994). Pollitt and Bouckaert also usefully advocate greater precision in relation to vocabulary and seek to explicate the subtle yet critical differences between key terms; three of which will be used in this chapter—*trade-off*, *dilemma*, and *paradox*.

A *trade-off* is portrayed as a classic zero-sum game and is defined as a situation where having more than one desideratum, or lessening one problem, inevitably diminishes some other wished for quality, or increases a different problem. Alternatively, a *dilemma* is a defined as a lose-lose situation in that it is a form of trade-off in which the situation remains negative whichever option is chosen. A *paradox* is something that appears at first glance to be incompatible, oxymoronic, or false but may in fact contain some kind of logic or truth (Wright 1997: 7–13). Since 1997, for instance, the concept of *earned autonomy* has provided an underpinning principle for public sector reforms in Britain in relation to education, local government, and health care while the notion of *constrained discretion* has formed a central plank of New Labour's economic management strategy (Brown 1999, 2000; Balls 1998; Glyn and Wood 2001). At a very basic level earned autonomy and constrained discretion appear incongruous or contradictory terms. Indeed, the Conservative Party noted:

> The concept of "earned autonomy" is, by any standards, a nonsense. The phrase itself is an oxymoron. If you are autonomous you cannot have earned it from a higher authority. And in practice the policy of earned autonomy is being implemented a rather arbitrary and centralising way. (The Conservative Party, Press Release, 5 June 2003)

However, if one explores the practical application of these terms the possibility of positive-sum games becomes apparent, or at the very least the basic assumption of simple trade-offs is rejected. The 2002 Education Act, for example, made provision for the *earned autonomy scheme* in which schools meeting specified performance and leadership criteria would be rewarded with additional freedoms and flexibilities in the areas of teachers' pay and conditions and concerning the national curriculum on an indefinite basis, provided the school continues to meet the qualifying criteria. Health authorities, hospitals, local authorities, police forces, and other public bodies now operate within a similar environment. So although the concept of earned autonomy has the intuitive feel of a paradox it contains a certain coherence or rationality when examined in detail. Indeed, the concept of earned autonomy has evolved as a tool or relationship through which ministers have increasingly sought to harmonize apparently conflicting goals, most clearly delegation versus control, autonomy versus accountability (Cabinet Office, 5 December 2003). The idea of earned autonomy (and practical procedures and frameworks that underpin it) therefore provides a neat case study of a core executive seeking to *fill in* the *hollowing out* in a way that delivers a win-win situation or positive-sum game (Rhodes 1994; Holliday 2000; Taylor 2000).

Finally, the notion of trade-offs and balances in the context of societal modernization (be it in relation to the state structures or democratic frameworks) needs to be located within an appreciation of the public's perception of whether certain dilemmas or paradoxes exist irrespective of their actual empirical existence. Whether institutional or procedural relationships can be designed and implemented that avoid zero-sum games is in many ways irrelevant unless the public *believes* and *perceives* that certain benefits or goals are being delivered. This has been a key issue for the Labour government in Britain since 2001. During the 2001–2005 Parliament the government made significant real-term increases in public spending, particularly in relation to education and health, and although various National Audit Office and Audit Commission reports suggested that frontline services were improving as a result of this additional funding public opinion surveys suggested that the public did not *perceive* that services were improving.

Raising the experience of New Labour in Britain since their election in May 1997 is apt for two reasons. First, the whole notion of *New* Labour is explicitly constructed on a rejection of the traditional binary distinction between *left* and *right*. For Tony Blair and the other candidates of the New Labour project the aim has been to reject such coarse ideological distinctions and instead unite and marry together certain themes and threads from a range of positions. The social democracy—encapsulated in the notion of the *Third Way*—of the Labour government attempts, therefore, to eschew both ideological dogma and the binary divide between the public sector and private sector that had, to some extent, polarized debates up to the general election of 1997 (Giddens 1998). As Broadbent, Gray and Jackson note,

> [t]his "Third Way" rejects both the neo-liberal thrust of the previous Conservative Government's reliance on the market and the centralized planning and delivery associated with traditional social democracy. In its place it posits an approach that is grounded in the notion of partnership. (Broadbent et al. 2003: 136)

The notion of partnerships links with the second reason why an analysis of New Labour in Britain is pertinent to the wider themes and core thrust of this book: a major shift can be detected between the government's first term (1997–2001) and its second term (2001–2005). This shift was epitomized by an emphasis on economic efficiency, value for money and delivery during the government's second term—*What matters is what works!*—over the importance of democratic renewal, openness, and participation which had provided the hallmarks of the first term. The reasons for this shift in direction are complex. The Labour government's decision to stay within the spending limits of the previous Conservative government between 1997–1999 severely restricted developments in the social and economic sphere which had the knock-on effect of reducing the usual pressure on the parliamentary timetable thereby facilitating the passage of a large amount of legislation on constitutional reform. However, there has also been a more subtle but no less significant shift in the executive mentality since 2001; a shift in which ministers believe that the public is more interested in economic efficiency (high-quality public services delivered through an efficient governance framework without tax increases) than abstract democratic principles such as accountability, participation, public service ethos, civic empowerment, and openness. The next section explores this shift in emphasis and reflects upon some of the conceptual issues raised above by examining two case studies: the private finance initiative and public interest companies.

P3s AND NEW LABOUR

New Labour came into power in 1997 with the intention of reinvigorating British democracy through far-reaching constitutional reforms (see Lewis Baston's analysis in chapter 4) while also injecting the expertise and vaunted efficiencies of private sector management techniques into the state structure. The challenge faced by the government centered on reconciling and balancing potentially, but not inherently, incompatible values and goals (for example, efficiency and accountability, private sector values, and the public sector ethos). The notion of *partnership* provided the rhetorical and conceptual tool through which these values could be yoked together in a positive sum manner. Despite misgivings among large sections of the parliamentary Labour Party and open opposition from many public sector unions, who saw partnerships as a euphemism for privatization *through the back door*, the government pressed ahead with P3s as a central aspect of its modernization agenda. The then Secretary of State for Health, Alan Milburn, noted:

> Let me say at the outset that partnerships between the public and private sector are a cornerstone of the Government's modernisation programme for Britain. They are central to our drive to modernise our key public services. Such partnerships are here and they are here to stay. (Milburn 2001)

The notion of partnership is constructed on the idea that it is possible for capital projects and public services to be delivered by the private sector under contract with the state. *Private* in this sense incorporates a range of governance mechanisms including for-profit companies, not-for-profit companies, and, strategic/voluntary partnerships. The government prioritized outputs and outcomes over process in response to a belief that the public was no longer interested in who provided services but simply that they were delivered to a specified standard and at an appropriate cost. When launching the General Election Manifesto in May 2001 the prime minister emphasized that there should be "no barriers, no dogma, no vested interests that stand in the way of delivering the best services" (Brown 2003).

In this environment the areas of state activity that have been opened up to private sector involvement have been rapidly expanded (including education, prisons, clinical care) to the point where questions have been asked regarding whether a residual core of the state actually exists where the profit-motive should be permanently excluded. The varieties of P3s employed by the Labour government since 1997 provide a critical case through which to explore some of the tensions and trade-offs in relation to economic efficiency and democratic empowerment. In essence, some forms of P3 appear to have failed to reconcile increased efficiency with democratic accountability and openness and can therefore be seen as a zero-sum game or a trade-off in Pollitt and Bouckaert's vocabulary. There is an extensive scholarly and practitioner literature that suggests that the vaunted efficiency gains have not actually been delivered which leads to a dilemma or lose-lose situation (Flinders 2005a: 543–67). However, other forms of P3 do appear to have at least the potential to deliver both economic efficiency and democratic empowerment although questions exist regarding the degree to which the public actually wants to be "empowered" and play a more active socio-political role (see Blühdorn's discussion of "postdemocracy" in chapter 12). The next two subsections offer case studies giving an example of both of these forms of P3. Private Finance Initiative (PFI) projects, it is suggested, provide an example of a trade-off in which certain democratic values or precepts have been traded in for highly questionable efficiency gains whereas the model of the Public Interest Company, however, may have the capacity to deliver a win-win situation. The next subsection examines the PFI.

The Private Finance Initiative

The PFI was originally launched by Conservative ministers in 1992 and has been vigorously promoted by the Labour government since 1997. Under this scheme the government will form a partnership in which a private sector company finances, builds, and in many cases even manages a facility (school, hospital, prison, etc.) in return for a long-term (25 years or more) contract in which the government commits the state to pay an annual fee for the use of the facility. PFI contracts vary significantly in terms of size and scope; from £100,000 for small information technology facilities to large projects such as the £4 billion contract for the Channel Tunnel Rail Link. A total of 563 PFI contracts reached financial close by 4 April 2003, with a total capital value of £35.5 billion. Over £32.1 billion of the total has been signed since 1997. PFI therefore plays a limited—around 12 percent—but increasingly significant part in public sector capital investment. The theoretical benefit for the government is that the private sector delivers a facility and service at a lower price than could have been provided by conventional state procurement methods while at the same time transferring risk on to the private sector.

Two questions therefore arise which go to the heart of both this chapter and the broader themes of this book. First, are these economic benefits actually delivered in practice? Second, how have PFI projects affected traditional democratic frameworks and relationships? Taken together, the answers to these questions may shed light on whether a trade-off (more of one but less of another) or dilemma (less of both) exists.

In 2000 the then Chief Secretary to the Treasury, Andrew Smith, insisted that the PFI promises "more essential services to higher standard than otherwise would have been the case" and yet in terms of economic efficiency and risk transfer the evidence is far from conclusive (Pollock et al. 2001; Pollock et al. 2002; Shaoul 2005; Shaoul and Edwards 2006). Although a HMT commissioned report in 2000, based upon a limited number of contracts, estimated general efficiency savings of around 17 percent for PFI projects, more detailed research suggests that the PFI delivers increased efficiency in some policy areas, for example building and managing prisons and constructing roads but not in sectors such as hospitals (Dunnigan and Pollock 2003; Gaffney and Pollock 1999; Gaffney et al. 1999) and schools (Edwards and Shaoul 2003; Ball et al. 2001). Moreover, it has become clear that the PFI is not suitable for all policy areas, for example in July 2003 the government announced that the PFI route would no longer be followed for large IT projects.

In terms of risk transfer there is also reason to suggest that the PFI is not delivering. The vaunted transfer of risk to the private sector is arguably potentially hollow, as the government cannot allow essential public services, such as schools, hospitals, and prisons to fail, especially when these services are under great pressure and extra capacity is urgently needed (Shaw 2004; National Audit Office 2001; Gaffney et al. 1999). Shaoul notes:

> Far from transferring risk to the private sector, PPP/PFI transfers the risk to the Government, workforce and the public as users and tax payers [. . .] the

concept of risk transfer in the context of essential services is fundamentally flawed. (Shaoul 2003: 193)

In a large number of PFI projects the government has been forced to re-allocate extra financial resources after the initial contract has been signed despite the fact that this negates the notion of risk-transfer that is a central legitimating foundation of this tool of governance. The House of Commons' Public Accounts Committee has therefore criticized the government because

[d]epartments are too willing to bail out PFI contractors who get into trouble. Contractors should expect to lose out when things go wrong just as they expect to be rewarded when projects are successful. The taxpayer must not be expected to pick up the tab when things go wrong. (Report from the Public Accounts Committee, Session 2002–2003: paragraph 5)

In terms of economic efficiency, therefore, there is little evidence that the PFI actually delivers more efficient services or transfers risk to the private sector. However, there is evidence to support the argument that PFI projects have undermined or eviscerated established frameworks of representative democracy. This argument is based around concerns regarding institutional complexity, openness, and accountability.

Smith refers to PFI projects as a "bastard form of organization" because they are neither public nor private and yet their role, powers, and finances are ultimately derived from the public estate (Smith 2003: 580–96). The existence of numerous PFI projects has therefore exacerbated the institutional complexity of the British State and created questions about where responsibility now lies for the delivery of essential public services. This complexity is exacerbated by the fact that frequently secondary quasi-autonomous organizations are created to oversee and regulate the activity of these partnerships. For example, a new independent body called the Office of the Public Private Partnership Arbiter will decide upon disputes regarding the various contracts for the London Underground.

The obvious consequence of this complexity is that channels and lines of accountability become more opaque. The creation of multifaceted networks also facilitates what Hood has called "blame games" in which ministers and contractors seek to deflect responsibility for certain issues or adopt sophisticated blame management strategies (Hood 2002a: 15–37). The great value of the convention of individual ministerial responsibility is that it provides great clarity and a public focus when things go wrong. Elected politicians, therefore, provide a focus or lightning rod through which societal anguish or concern can be expressed and earthed. It may not be rational or fair to hold one individual to account, especially given the existence of increasingly complex institutional terrains and complex networks, but the fact that a political system provides focal points may be incredibly important in broader democratic terms (Ellis 1994). However, reconciling partnership or network governance strategies with a clear line of accountability between the governors and the governed is difficult (Goldsmith and Eggers 2004).

This is not purely due to an increase in the number of linkages and potential veto points but also relates to the changing nature of information. The need for actors to safeguard their market position introduces a barrier to the distribution and sharing of information. It has been suggested that the current framework for PFI projects in Britain fails to adequately balance the democratic demands of transparency and openness against the private sector's insistence that a large amount of information should be withheld under the "commercial confidentiality" exemption (IPPR 2004). The number of parliamentary questions that are not answered on the grounds that the information requested is commercially confidential has increasingly angered members of Parliament (Brazier et al. 2005). Moreover, the political empowerment offered to British citizens by the 1998 Freedom of Information Act is restricted through the existence of a *commercial confidentiality* exemption clause.

The nature of information is not solely affected by the need for private actors to protect their market position but it is also more widely altered by the changing capacity of the state vis-à-vis information and skills. The shifting boundaries of the British state are leading not just to institutional fragmentation in terms of structures but also in terms of knowledge as the growth in P3s, while designed to deliver increased *institutional* capacity, risks undermining the *intellectual* capacity of the state in terms of its institutional history and epistemic potential as the delegation of tasks risks *de-skilling* the remainder of the public sector in certain areas and fields, thereby creating information asymmetries that weaken its bargaining position and reducing its holistic knowledge base (for an extended discussion see Flinders 2005b). Developments in the sphere of P3s therefore need to be aware of two potential trade-offs: first, between transparency and commercial confidentiality; and secondly, between creating pools of specialist knowledge, on the one hand, while also safeguarding the benefits of that knowledge for the benefit of the many rather than the few.

A final democratic consideration that could be interpreted as trade-off against higher levels of economic efficiency relates to policy flexibility and democratic choice. PFI projects represent a *buy now, pay later* scheme—with contracts usually being signed for twenty-five to thirty years—which raises the possibility that the flexibility of future governments or local authorities may well be substantially constrained by the need to service significant contractual repayments entered into by previous governments. As the proportion of total investment made up by PFI projects increases, "more and more of the budget will be committed, leaving less and less to the discretion of the public agencies and reducing flexibility" (Pollock et al. 2001: 14). Moreover, should there be a need to reduce public spending in the future the existence of legally binding contractual obligations with the private sector will force non-PFI expenditure to carry proportionately deeper cuts. The issue of the policy flexibility of future government also feeds back into the issue of accountability as a change in political control, at the local or national level, may create a critical tension if the incoming political executive does not share the values and import enshrined in the partnership contract. "This is a recipe for confused accountability, the emergence of a blame culture between different public bodies, and public disenchantment" (IPPR 2002: 235).

In terms of a discussion of trade-offs, balances, dilemmas, and paradoxes the PFI initiative in Britain appears not to be a trade-off in terms of more economic efficiency in return for a reduction in certain democratic criteria but a dilemma because although the scheme has clearly undermined or diluted certain established democratic relationships it appears not to have generated the broad efficiency gains promised by the epistemic community that has promoted the scheme and continues to do so. More specifically, efficiency gains are delivered in certain specific sectors and the policy therefore needs to be better targeted. And yet the existence of such a dilemma is surprising in the light of New Labour's rhetorical commitment to evidence-based policy making and the constant ministerial emphasis on phrases (bordering on mantra) such as "it's delivery that matters," "results not rhetoric," and "what matters is what works" (Sanderson 2003: 331–45). Indeed, after an exhaustive review of the evidence Shaw concludes: "The case of the PFI casts a rather different light on the Third Way, since self-evidently it does not work" (Shaw 2004: 77).

The core argument of this chapter is that the whole notion of trade-offs in the context of economic efficiency and democratic empowerment is incredibly complex and that assumptions should not be made regarding the incompatibility of certain goals. The existence of trade-offs, paradoxes, and dilemmas are context specific and rely heavily on the design and nature of relationships and institutional frameworks. So although the PFI initiative may represent a form of P3 that creates a dilemma this does not mean that other forms of partnership cannot be designed and implemented to achieve a different set of results. This leads on to the second case study of this chapter, the Public Interest Company.

Public Interest Companies

Although drawing upon long-standing notions of mutualism and left-wing advocacy of cooperative models PICs represent a relatively recent addition to the P3 landscape in Britain. PICs became a notable feature of the modernization agenda during the 2001–2005 Parliament in Britain as the Labour government sought to develop new mechanisms through which the vaunted efficiencies and skills of the private sector could be harnessed to the public sector but in a way that protected certain features of the existing system. Examples of PICs in Britain include Network Rail, National Air Traffic Services, Welsh Water, and the 32 hospitals that have, as of July 2005, been granted *foundation* status (Maltby 2003a, 2003b). PICs have three core characteristics: they do not have shareholders (if they do they are restricted in terms of profits); they deliver a public service; and, they are legally independent of government (Birchall 2002: 181–213). The benefit of PICs over PFI projects is that they are suitable where a clear purchaser-provider split cannot be delineated due to the complexity of the function and the need to protect the public interest. Shareholder membership, driven by the profit motive, is replaced by stakeholder membership in order to harness certain specialisms and dilute the profit motive. The important aspect of this form of P3 is that it has been explicitly designed to balance both the demand for greater economic efficiency while also introducing new democratic arenas and forms of direct accountability with the users of the organization. The governance of foundation trust hospitals (FTHs) provides a timely example of this attempt to reconcile potentially conflictual aims while also demonstrating some of the negative unintended consequences of such a reform and secondary trade-offs.

FTHs were established under the Health and Social Care (Community Health and Standards) Act 2003. Although they remain fully or largely funded by the state they enjoy significant levels of autonomy and can borrow money from the private sector (subject to the approval of the Independent Regulator of NHS Foundation Trusts). FTHs are also able to subcontract clinical services to commercial companies, trade in NHS and non-NHS services, generate income from private patients and also form joint ventures with private companies, such as those currently bidding to provide diagnostic and treatment centers to the NHS. The specific rationale for trust status is that FTHs will: embrace private sector management strategies and tools; tailor their services to the needs of their locality and user base; enjoy greater flexibility in relation to services delivered, borrowing, and asset disposal; stimulate innovation by removing dense top-down governance structures; while also offering their staff higher rewards in recognition of providing enhanced levels of performance. These specific justifications fit into a broader New Labour logic based around increasing choice and diversity, injecting contestability or a "greater plurality of providers" into the public sector, and moving away from centrally directed modes of governance and "one size fits all" models of public provision (Milburn 2001).

However, although the progressive governance enthusiasts within the Labour government may espouse *diversity* and *choice* as positive goals this view has not been shared by a wide range of scholars and social commentators.[2] Indeed, the government was subject to a number of significant backbench rebellions (leading to a number of concessions) as the Health and Social Care Bill made its way through Parliament (Cowley and Stewart 2005).

The policy of creating FTHs is clearly based upon a new public management inspired approach to increasing economic efficiency and standards within the public sector (Dunleavy and Hood 1994; Hood 1991). Indeed the sole statutory general duty of FTHs is to operate "effectively, efficiently and economically" (Pollock et al. 2005: 982–85). However this emphasis on economic efficiency is balanced by the need to introduce new forms of civic engagement and democratic accountability (i.e., democratic empowerment) through locally elected board members. The initial plans for FTHs drawn up by the Department of Health in 2002 stated that they would introduce a new form of social ownership where health services are owned by and accountable to local people rather than government. The final legislation therefore provided for the direct election of foundation hospital governors by *members* of the trust (a resident of the area served by the hospital or a patient receiving specialized care) who must register with the hospital in order to be entitled to vote. The precise composition of board members varies from trust to trust and although a number of governors are nominated the majority must be elected. Although staff elect a number of governors, the public and patients must elect the majority.[3]

As Klein notes "the rhetoric of ownership by and accountability to local people assumes that local people do indeed want to be involved in running the NHS" (Klein 2004: 1332) and yet the results from the first round of elections to foundation trusts suggested that this was a misplaced assumption. Bradford Teaching Hospital NHS Trust had aimed to achieve a membership of ten percent of the local population but in the March 2004 board elections only 541 local people (less than 1 percent of the local population) voted. Possibly more surprising was that this disinterest permeated into staff elections as well (ibid.). The most recent round of elections to FTHs (1 April 2005) reveal similarly low levels of local participation as although the levels of registered members returning their ballot papers had generally increased (averaging around 30 percent across the six elections held in this round), the number of members as a proportion of the total potential electorate remained very low at around 5 percent (around five thousand registered members in constituencies of approximately one hundred thousand people).

It is quite possible that the levels of both registered members and electoral turnout will grow as FTHs become more established and build up relationships with their local constituencies. However, the initial rounds of elections to FTHs do at the very least raise questions about the degree to which civic participation should be a central goal of the modernization agenda. Or, alternatively, if civic participation is to be an ambition of the modernization agenda should there be a minimum threshold for either member registration or turnout? Neither the Independent Regulator for NHS Foundation Trusts nor the Secretary of State for Health has been willing to determine the exact level at which an acceptable degree of local participation has been achieved (Klein and Day 2005). Indeed, the member registration and turnout figures could be used to support the contention that the public is not interested or has little time for active engagement but would prefer the emphasis to be on effective and efficient service provision. The low turnout figures may also reflect a general political apathy and cynicism about politics in general and the hospital governing boards in particular. It may also reflect a rational preference among the public to influence the major policy issues of the day rather than become embroiled in the minutiae and technical intricacies of day-to-day delivery.

The critical aspect of FTHs is that they have been explicitly designed to deliver to two intuitively opposed goals—increased delegation leading to increased efficiency and improved levels of accountability in order to enhance democratic engagement. The Labour government has allocated unprecedented levels of funding the NHS since 2001 and a result of this is that it is difficult, or at least too early, to separate the economic effects of introducing FTHs from the impact of the increased financial resources. However, the lack of local participation in the first waves of elections to foundation hospitals in 2004 and 2005 adds a new dimension to discussions about the notion of trade-offs. In this case despite the fact that the government has to ensure that state modernization does not come at the cost of reduced levels of democratic engagement or accountability the public appears resistant to taking advantage of the opportunities offered (see Blühdorn's discussion of the *postdemocratic* Zeitgeist in chapter 12). This issue will be further discussed in the conclusion; however the debate surrounding the creation of FTHs has also generated questions concerning three other potential trade-offs or dilemmas.

The first of these revolves around the potential tension between public participation and professional knowledge. Questions surround the degree to which public representatives on governing boards or *Members' Councils*, as they have been labeled in some areas, have the necessary management of medical knowledge to make rational decisions on the governance of multimillion pound hospitals (Second Report of the Health Committee, Session 2002–2003). This information asymmetry between the public representatives, on one side, and the nominated members and staff representatives, on the other, clearly presents the potential for the Board of Governors to become a sham or rubber stamp for medical and managerial decisions taken by the Board of Management/Directors elsewhere, particularly in light of the weak statutory powers of the Board of Governors vis-à-vis the Board of Management/Directors (Mohan 2003; Klein and Day 2005).[4] So the whole notion of democratic empowerment in relation to certain essential public services is somewhat circumscribed by issues surrounding who is in the best position to make public interest decisions and where power lies within the internal governance framework.

The second potential trade-off that still has to be explicitly or adequately addressed by New Labour ministers concerns how to reconcile equity and choice in the context of foundation hospitals. Foundation trusts are still formally part of a NHS that is based upon the principle of universality—equal care for equal need—and yet the emphasis with the foundation trust model on independence, variability (coupled with autonomous service delivery) and breaking down certain national frameworks and procedures appears somewhat incongruous. Critics of the foundation hospital scheme suggest that it will lead to a *balkanization* of the NHS in which the notion of universal services and standards is replaced by high variations in service levels and provision, and a movement of talented or specialized staff towards a "premier league" of foundation hospitals.

The equity and equality issue is not restricted to issues of geographical locality but also relates to the nature of illness and the cost of care. The fact that foundation hospitals are expected to operate like market actors and will be able to retain surpluses risks creating a situation of *cream skimming* in which they focus on providing care to patients who are less likely to require long-term post-treatment care. It is in this vein that Pollock noted: "Markets undermine universality by limiting the public sector's ability to pool the costs of expensive patients and areas and spread them across the whole of society" (Pollock et al. 2001: 10).

This notion of *balkanization*, or fragmentation, facilitates the identification of a third potential trade-off or tension arising from the creation of foundation hospitals—the existence of *fragmegration*. The Labour government appears to be creating an increasingly fragmented governance structure in which networks contain a greater number of actors with legally entrenched levels of independence and autonomy through the creation of P3s and yet at the very same time it is seeking to move towards *joined-up* or *holistic* governance (Kavanagh and Richards: 2001: 1–18). The notion of *fragmegration*, a term coined by James Rosenau in the context of multilevel governance, therefore suggests the existence of trends that, although not being by definition incompatible, do create difficult challenges and demand new mechanisms or tools through which coexistent centrifugal and centripetal pressures can be managed (Rosenau 2004; see Flinders 2002).

The brief reviews of the PFI and PICs above display a number of similarities (e.g., the creation of secondary quasi-autonomous public bodies to regulate these forms of P3, issues surrounding how to balance openness and accountability with commercial confidentiality) but they also provide empirical substance to conceptual debates regarding trade-offs, paradoxes, and dilemmas. Both case studies demonstrate the existence of complex choices, bargaining, and exchanges but each in their own way demonstrates how oversimplistic assumptions about the existence of zero-sum trade-offs are something of a blunt instrument in the context of modern governance. Whereas the evidence might seem to suggest that the PFI project is actually a *dilemma* (lose-lose situation) rather than a *trade-off* (more of one goal for less of another) the example of foundation hospitals (formally PICs) suggests that modernization reforms can seek to enhance both economic efficiency and democratic participation and accountability but whether both goals are realized are dependent upon a complex web of variables that are largely independent of the specific reform itself (i.e., wider public apathy and popular disengagement with the political process and its institutions).

Both examples demonstrate that the measurement and understanding of certain base concepts such as *efficiency* and *accountability* are highly contested. These conceptual debates operate across a number of structural and temporal dimensions (see chapter 3 in this volume). The efficiency of a PIC may be higher from a narrow organization point of view if outputs increase while inputs diminish or remain constant. But this efficiency is somewhat shallow if the quality of the outputs decreases, or the outputs do not lead to the desired societal outcomes. Moreover, organizational efficiencies may well be offset against broader structural inefficiencies created by the increased fragmentation and the greater transaction costs involved in policing, steering, and *joining-up* numerous actors (Hood et al. 1999). Likewise, the PFI may be an efficient option for a government from a short-term point of view in light of the fact that it allows politicians to deliver increased capacity (hospitals, prisons, libraries, etc.) without increasing borrowing, raising taxes, or cutting spending elsewhere. However, from a long-term view the scheme is arguably highly inefficient, as the cost of the contract over the full term will far exceed the basic cost of the facilities several times over (Flinders 2005a).

The next concluding section aims to reintroduce the findings of this case study section to the broader debate on economic efficiency and democratic empowerment. It does this by seeking to utilize the work of Arthur Okun on equality and efficiency to offer a macro-level socioeconomic framework that may tease out and disentangle some of the more precise concerns and assumptions about trade-offs.

EQUALITY AND EFFICIENCY: THE BIG TRADE-OFF?

In line with the vast majority of advanced liberal democracies, Britain has in recent years moved further towards a convergence of the public and private sectors (Bovaird 2004: 199–215). This has involved not only adapting or adopting private sector methods and techniques but also increasing the direct participation of the private sector in the provision of services previously thought to be *core* public services (for a discussion see Barrett 2000). This process appears to be accelerating in Britain as the government faces increased pressure to deliver higher levels of public service but within finite resource boundaries. In this context the rhetoric of *diversity and choice* seeks to veil and soften the introduction of forms of governance that have major implications not just for the economic efficiency of the bureaucracy but also for the nature and functioning of British democracy.

And it is at this point that the central axis or crux of debates surrounding trade-offs, dilemmas, and paradoxes in relation to economic efficiency and democratic empowerment starts to become apparent. The foundational value-orientation of the public and private sectors contrasts sharply to the point where the question of fundamental compatibility becomes understandable. Moreover, democratic rights and powers are established on the basis of equality whereas in the private sector inequality is seen as a positive force in that it stimulates action and prevents free-riders (individuals who may attempt to benefit from a social good without contributing to the cost) (Pasour 1981: 453–64). This basic foundational clash formed the backbone of Arthur Okun's seminal text *Equality and Efficiency: The Big Trade-Off* (Okun 1975). In this Okun argued that the nature of modern democracy was established on the basis of equal and universally distributed rights and yet the economy relied upon market-determined incomes that generated inequalities among citizens that were designed to serve as incentives—rewards and penalties—to promote efficiency in the use of resources. The resulting mixture of equal rights but unequal incomes created a tension between the political principles of democracy and the economic principles of capitalism. Okun notes:

> At many points along the way, society confronts choices that offer somewhat more equality at the expense of [economic] efficiency or somewhat more efficiency at the expense of [democratic] equality. (Okun 1975: foreword p.vii)

Therefore, at the heart of modern capitalist democracy lay, in Okun's mind, a paradox or double standard in that the system professed and pursued an egalitarian political and social system while simultaneously promoting an economic system that created gaping disparities in well-being.

The sum of this situation was that society faced a trade-off between equality and efficiency.

The public sector evolved during the nineteenth and twentieth centuries in Britain and Germany due to the explicit societal acceptance that certain public goods and services should be universally available, enmeshed within certain nonmarket values (equity, accountability, transparency, etc.), and free from the profit motive. There was a commitment to the fact that certain services should be seen as basic rights that could not therefore be bought and sold. Democratic equality displayed as universal services provision according to need and free at the point of delivery, formed a protection or buffer zone against the market domination that was likely to occur if everything could be traded. Public sector rules, procedures, national frameworks—the bureaucracy—were seen as the supporting mechanisms through which universalism and equality could be ensured. Public accountability processes and mechanisms were equally accepted as being paramount despite the fact that they added greater transaction costs and imbued the bureaucracy with a risk-averse and arguably inflexible culture. The underlying principles of the public sector therefore generated genuine costs but these were viewed as costs worth bearing in the name of democracy and equality. "Society refuses" in Okun's words "to turn itself into a giant vending machine that delivers anything and everything in return for the proper number of coins" (ibid.: 13).

Although Okun rejects the idea that democratic equality and economic efficiency are inherently incompatible he does concede that the prospects for achieving these goals simultaneously are limited and that frequently society is forced to trade off one for the other. However, any sacrifice of either equality or efficiency has to be justified in terms of delivering more of the other. The problem for policy-makers and politicians, as displayed to a greater or lesser extent by the above case studies, is that gauging in advance how much a specific reform will add to efficiency or detract from equality is difficult, if not impossible. In order to understand and measure the nature of trade-offs Okun proposed a hypothetical framework—the leaky bucket experiment—through which attitudes to trade-offs can be assessed and evaluated. The leaky budget experiment emphasizes transaction-costs and the point at which these undermine the value of a policy. A redistributive tax policy, for example, may attempt to levy an added tax revenue of ten thousand euros a year from the wealthiest 5 percent of the population in order to increase the state benefits of the lowest income families (making up 20 percent of the population) by twenty-five hundred euros a year. However, as Okun writes "the money must be carried from the rich to the poor in a leaky bucket [. . .]. Some of it will simply disappear in transit, so the poor will not receive all the money that is taken from the rich" (ibid. 1975: 91). The question then becomes how much *leakage* you accept before the policy is rejected as inefficient.

Although Arthur Okun was an economist by training and profession his thesis of the equality of democracy and the inequality of modern capitalist economies (leading to a trade-off between efficiency and equality) provides a useful macro-level framework within which to locate and understand the use of PPPs in Britain under Labour. Like a great number of advanced liberal democracies, the Labour government is seeking to solve this *big trade-off* problem through the introduction of new forms of governance based around partnerships with the private sector. There has been, and continues to be, a detailed search for a *third way* in which the purported efficiencies of the market can be harnessed by the public sector but without undermining equality of access or democratic accountability. The question then becomes one of measuring and understanding the notion of "efficiency" in the public sector while also applying Okun's leaky-bucket experiment.

The major difference between PFI projects and PICs is that the former appears to involve far-higher transaction costs due to the fact that significant economic resources (i.e., profits) are taken out of the public sector and distributed to private shareholders. The total efficiencies accruing from the PFI are not therefore ploughed back into supporting other elements of the public sector—"What leaks out [. . .] is the water needed to irrigate the next crop" (ibid.: 92). The issue then becomes one of degree. Given that the PFI occasions certain democratic costs what proportion of economic savings can the private sector partner expect before the contract becomes counter-efficient? Should society accept a leak of 25, 50, or 75 percent? Taken another way, what price should society place on certain democratic principles? Using Okun's leaky bucket framework it is possible to suggest that the PFI is in certain policy areas arguably so leaky as to render the policy futile (Pollock 2004). The "big trade-off" has delivered very little in economic terms while carrying significant democratic costs. Conversely, PICs seem to offer a form of P3 that carries far-lower transaction costs (because efficiency savings do not drain away as private profits) while also seeking to engender democratic empowerment. Whether the public decide to take advantage of these new political arenas and conduits raises wider questions about the nature of British democracy, and the state of democracy more generally. Such questions are beyond the scope of this chapter but are dealt with elsewhere in this volume (see chapter 12).

It is, however, worth reemphasizing that during New Labour's second term in government (2001–2005) there was a clear feeling among ministers that they had spent too much time and energy on constitutional reform issues, for which the public gave them little political recognition or gratitude, and too little time on reform of the public sector (Morrison 2001). This led to a sharp shift in focus away from constitutional reform and democratic empowerment to increasing economic efficiency through the use of market mechanisms. It is also important to appreciate that the use of P3s and other forms of private sector involvement is located in a broader agenda that aims to cultivate greater social responsibility while also readjusting public expectations about the capacity of the state (Blair 2005). User fees (toll roads, congestion charges), top-up fees (universities), vouchers (childcare), and penalties (missed medical appointments) are all market-style mechanisms that not only fit within the rubric of "diversity and choice" but they also dovetail with New Labour's attempts to foster greater individual social responsibility within an explicit recognition of the limits of the state's capacity.

This chapter has examined the nature of trade-offs, paradoxes, tensions, and dilemmas in the context of economic efficiency and democratic empowerment by examining two forms of P3 and the experience in Britain. Analyses of this kind are likely to become more significant as experiments with P3s develop into something of a worldwide phenomenon (Ghobadian et al. 2004). Although published three decades ago the work of Arthur Okun arguably provides a rich framework through which issues of trade-offs and compatibilities can be better understood. Of particular significance was his plea to politicians and political scientists to take seriously the possible consequences (cynicism, radicalism, and alienation) of the wider perception that the blurring of the distinction between the public and private sectors was compromising certain cherished democratic rights and principles. Politicians in Britain might be well advised to take note of this warning.

NOTES

1. Guy Peters similarly argues that the existence of pure and absolute contradictions is somewhat rare and many prima facie contradictions are actually questions of finding the appropriate balance rather than simple choosing between incompatible alternatives. See Guy Peters (1998).

2. See www.progressive-governance.net.

3. For a detailed discussion of the governance of FTHs see Klein and Day (2005).

4. In this context also see Blühdorn's model of *simulative democracy* outlined in chapter 12.

REFERENCES

Ball, Rob, Heafy, Maryanne, and King, David (2001): "The Private Finance Initiative: A Good Deal for the Public Purse or a Drain on Future Generations." *Policy & Politics* 29, no. 1: 95–108.

Balls, Ed (1998): "Open Macroeconomics in an Open Economy." *Scottish Journal of Political Economy* 45, no. 2: 113–32.

Barrett, Pat (2000): "Balancing Accountability and Efficiency in a More Competitive Public Sector Environment." Address to Government in Excellence Summit, Singapore. *Australian Journal of Public Administration* 59, no. 3: 59–71.

Birchall, Johnston (2002): "Mutual, Non-profit or Public Interest Company?" *Annals of Public and Co-operative Economics* 73, no. 2: 181–213.

Blair, Tony (2005): "Common Sense Culture Not Compensation Culture." Speech to the Institute of Public Policy Research, 26 May 2005.

Bovaird, Tony (2004): "Public-Private Partnerships: From Contested Concepts to Prevalent Practice." *International Review of Administrative Sciences* 70, no. 2: 199–215.

Brazier, Alex, Flinders, Matthew, and McHugh, Declan (2005): *New Politics, New Parliament?* London: Hansard Society.

Broadbent, Jane, Gray, Andrew, and Jackson, Peter M. (2003): "Public-Private Partnerships." *Public Money and Management* 23, no. 3: 136.

Brown, Gordon (1999): *Mais Lecture: the Conditions for Full Employment*, 19 October 1999.

—— (2000): *Lecture to the Royal Economic Society*, 13 July 2000.

—— (2003): "A Modern Agenda for Prosperity and Social Reform." Speech to the Social Market Foundation at the Cass Business School London, 3 February 2003.

Cabinet Office (2003): "Earned Autonomy—Two Tier Treatment or the Key to Empowerment." Reforming for Customers Seminar Series #3, 5 December 2003.

Conservative Party (2003): Press Release, 5 June 2003.

Cowley, Philip, and Stewart, Mark (2005): *Dissension Amongst the Parliamentary Labour Party*. Nottingham: University of Nottingham.

Dunleavy, Patrick, and Hood, Christopher (1994): "From Old Public Administration to New Public Management." *Public Money and Management* 14, no. 3: 9–17.

Dunnigan, Matthew G., and Pollock, Allyson M. (2003): "Downsizing of Acute Inpatient Beds Associated with Private Finance Initiative: Scotland's Case Study." *British Medical Journal* 326, no. 7395: 905–908.

Edwards, Pamela, and Shaoul, Jean (2003): "Controlling the PFI Process in Schools." *Policy & Politics* 31, no. 3: 371–85.

Ellis, Richard J. (1994): *Presidential Lightning Rods*. Lawrence: University of Kansas.

Flinders, Matthew (2002): "Governance in Whitehall." *Public Administration* 80, no. 1: 51–75.

—— (2005a): "The Politics of Public-Private Partnerships." *British Journal of Politics and International Relations* 7, no. 2: 543–67.

—— (2005b): "The Boundaries of the State," in: Hay, Colin, Marsh, David, and Lister, Michael, eds.: *The State*. London/New York: Palgrave Macmillan, pp. 225–48.

Gaffney, Declan, and Pollock, Allyson M. (1999): "Pump-Priming the PFI: Why Are Privately Financed Hospital Schemes being Subsidized?" *Public Money and Management* 17, no. 3: 55–62.

Gaffney, Declan, Pollock, Allyson M., Price, David, and Shaoul, Jean (1999): "The Private Finance Initiative: PFI in the NHS: Is There an Economic Case?" *British Medical Journal* 319, no. 7202 : 116–19.

Gallie, William B. (1956): "Essentially Contested Concepts." *Proceeding of the Aristotelian Society* 56: 167–98.

Ghobadian, Abby, O'Regan, Nicholas, Gallear, David, and Viney, Howard (2004): *Public-Private Partnerships*. London/New York: Palgrave Macmillan.

Giddens, Anthony (1998): *The Third Way*. Cambridge: Polity.

Glyn, Andrew, and Wood, Stewart (2001): "Economic Policy Under New Labour: How Social Democratic is the Blair Government?" *Political Quarterly* 72, no. 1: 50–66.

Goldsmith, Stephen, and Eggers, William D. (2004): *Governing by Network*. Washington D.C.: The Brookings Institute.

Greve, Carsten, and Hodge, Graeme (2005): *The Challenge of Public-Private Partnerships. Learning from International Experience*. Chelterham/Northhampton/ Camberley: Edward Elgar.

Health Committee (2003): *HC 395 Foundation Trusts*. Second Report of the Health Committee, Session 2002–2003, London: HMSO.

Holliday, Ian (2000): "Is the British State Hollowing Out?" *Political Quarterly* 71, no. 2: 167–77.

Hood, Christopher (1991): "A Public Management for all Seasons?" *Public Administration* 69, no. 2: 3–19.

—— (2002a): "The Risk Game and the Blame Game." *Government and Opposition* 37, no. 1: 15–37.

—— (2002b) "Managing Risk and Managing Blame: a Political Science Approach," in: Weale, Albert, ed.: *Risk, Democratic Citizenship and Public Policy*. Oxford/New York: Oxford University Press/British Academy Press, pp. 73–84.

Hood, Christopher, James, Oliver, Jones, George, Scott, Colin, and Travers, Tony (1999): *Regulation Inside Government*. Oxford/New York: Oxford University Press.

Hood, Christopher, and Jackson, Michael (1991): *Administrative Argument*. Aldershot: Dartmouth.

IPPR (2002): *Building Better Partnerships*. London: IPPR.

—— (2004): *Opening It Up: Accountability and Partnerships*. London: IPPR.

Kavanagh, Dennis, and Richards, Steve (2001): "Departmentalism and Joined-Up Government: Back to the Future?" *Parliamentary Affairs* 54, no. 1: 1–18.

Klein, Rudolph (2004): "The First Wave of NHS Foundation Trusts." *British Medical Journal* 328, no. 7430: 13–32.

Klein, Rudolph, and Day, Patricia (2005): *The Governance of Foundation Trusts*, London: Nuffield Trust.

Maltby, Paul (2003a): "Public Interest Companies: Fad or Permanent Fixture?" *New Economy* 10, no.1: 21–27.

—— (2003b): *In the Public Interest? Assessing the Potential of Public Interest Companies.* London: IPPR.

Milburn, Alan (2001): "Reforming Public Services: Reconciling Equity with Choice." Speech to the Fabian Society, 25 October 2001.

Mohan, John (2003): *Reconciling Equity and Choice? Foundation Hospitals and the Future of the NHS.* London: Catalyst.

Morrison, John (2001): *Reforming Britain.* London: Reuteurs.

Mulgan, Richard (1997): "Contracting Out and Accountability." *Australian Journal of Public Administration* 56, no 4: 106–16.

National Audit Office (2001): *Managing the Relationship to Secure a Successful Partnership.* London: NAO.

Niskanen, William (1996): *Bureaucracy and Public Economics.* Cheltenham/Northhampton/Camberley: Edward Elgar.

Okun, Arthur (1975) *Equality and Efficiency: The Big Trade-Off.* Brookings Institution.

Osborne, David, and Gaebler, Ted (1993): *Reinventing Government.* London: Plume.

Oughton, John (1995): "Accountability versus Control—Rust never Sleeps." *Public Sector* 17, no. 3: 2–6.

Pasour, Ernest C. jr. (1981): "The Free Rider as a Basis for Government Intervention." *Journal of Libertarian Studies* 5, no. 4: 453–64.

Perrow, Charles (1972): *Complex Organisations.* Glenview: Foreman.

Peters, Guy (1998): "What Works? The Antiphons of Administrative Reform," in: Peters, Guy, and Savoie, Donald, eds.: *Taking Stock: Assessing Public Sector Reforms.* Montreal: McGill-Queen's University Press, pp. 78–108.

Pollitt, Christopher, and Bouckaert, Geert (2000): *Public Management Reform: A Comparative Analysis.* Oxford/New York: Oxford University Press.

Pollock, Allyson M. (2001): "Privateers on the March." *The Guardian,* 11 December 2001.

—— (2004): *NHS Plc.* London/New York: Verso.

Pollock, Allyson M., Shaoul, Jean, Rowland, David, and Player, Stewart (2001): *Public Services and the Private Sector.* London: Catalyst.

Pollock, Allyson M., Shaoul, Jean, and Vickers, Neil (2002): "Private Finance and Value for Money in NHS Hospitals: A Policy in Search of a Rationale?" *British Medical Journal* 324, no. 7347: 1205–1209.

Pollock, Allyson M., Price, David, Talbot-Smith, Alison, and Mohan, John (2005): "NHS and the Health and Social Care Bill: End of Bevan's Vision?" *British Medical Journal* 327, no. 7421: 982–85.

Public Accounts Committee (2003): *HC 764. Delivering Better Value for Money from the Private Finance Initiative.* Report from the Public Accounts Committee, Session 2002–2003, London: HMSO.

Rhodes, Rod (1994): "The Hollowing Out of the State." *Political Quarterly* 65, no. 2: 138–51.

Rosenau, James N. (2004): "Huge Demand, Over-Supply: Governance in an Emerging Epoch," in: Bache, Ian, and Flinders, Matthew, eds.: *Multi-Level Governance*. Oxford/New York: Oxford University Press, pp. 31–49.

Simon, Herbert (1957): *Models of Man, Social and Rational*. London: Wiley.

Sanderson, Ian (2003): "Is It 'What Works' that Matters? Evaluation and Evidence-based Policy-making." *Research Papers in Education* 18, no. 4: 331–45.

Shaoul, Jean (2003): "A Financial Analysis of the National Air Traffic Services PPP." *Public Money & Management* 23, no. 3: 185–94.

Shaoul, Jean (2005): "A Critical Financial Analysis of the PFI." *Critical Perspectives on Accounting* (forthcoming).

Shaoul, Jean, and Edwards, Pam (2006):"The PFI: Financing the NHS Hospitals or the Private Sector?" *British Medical Journal* (forthcoming).

Shaw, Eric (2004): "What Matters is What Works: the Third Way and the Private Finance Initiative," in: Hale, Sarah, Leggett, Will, and Martell, Luke, eds.: *The Third Way and Beyond*. Manchester: Manchester University Press, pp. 64–82.

Smith, Brian, and Hague, Douglas (1971): *The Dilemma of Accountability in Modern Government: Independence versus Control*. Houndmills/New York: Palgrave Macmillan.

Smith, Lord (2003): "Something Old, Something New. . ." *Parliamentary Affairs* 56, no. 4: 580–96.

Stewart, John (1994): "Reply to Waldegrave," in: Flynn, Norman, ed.: *Change in the Civil Service*. CIPFA Reader. London: Public Finance Foundation, pp. 33–55.

Taylor, Andrew (2000): "Hollowing Out or Filling In?" *British Journal of Politics and International Relations* 2, no. 1: 46–71.

Waldegrave, William (1993): *The Reality of Reform and Accountability in Today's Public Service*. London: Public Finance Foundation.

Wright, Vincent (1997): "The Paradoxes of Administrative Reform," in: Kickert, Walter, ed.: *Public Management and Administrative Reform in Western Europe*. Cheltenham/Northhampton/Camberley: Edward Elgar, pp. 7–13.

8

Efficiency in Political Communication and Public Management: A Comparative Analysis of New Labour and the SPD

Uwe Jun

The increased role of the media in publicizing political achievements has led to the parties' own information services being substituted by a communication set-up centering on the media (e.g., Jun 2004, Kamps 2006). The quickest way to reach the highest number of voters is via the mass media, which have come to be people's main sources of political information. Indirect information conveyed by the mass media has to a large extent replaced direct forms of political communication. Even direct forms of communication aim at setting up indirect communication through the media. The dominance of the mass media in the field of political communication, and the loosening connection between political parties and large sectors of society, have rendered the political parties' ability to communicate more important than ever in implementing reforms which are acceptable to the electorate. In media democracies this is defined in terms of the opportunities to use the mass media as a platform from which to present their political personalities and their projected reforms. The mass media supply parties with the public forum required for their own legitimation and the necessary acceptance of the voters; they provide the assembled systemic components of a society with a public face and thus the potential to reach huge numbers of people.

Since the mass media are practically the only remaining way open to political parties to express themselves and exert an influence on public opinion it is not surprising that political parties are actively, and increasingly, choosing to "go public." Mazzoleni and Schulz note that the last decade was one characterized *inter alia* by a huge growth in the media's role in political life: "The process of mediatization of political actors, political events, and political discourse is a major trend in political systems of the 1990s" (Mazzoleni and Schulz 1999: 249; see also Kuhn 1997). This process has even accelerated in recent years. From the political actors' perspective this increase in the media's influence on politics undoubtedly meant that the publicizing of political achievements is dependent on media systems and the latter's selection criteria, and that politics is much more influenced by interaction with the media than it was in the past. Faced with the challenge of an evolving mass media and the growing need to attract the attention of the electorate, political parties have little choice but to make the communications departments within their own organizations and the communiqués themselves more professional, to draw up modern communications strategies, and to outsource the work of publicizing their activity. Since they have little control over the forms of media coverage and the ways in which the media report a given issue, parties have come to deploy professionally elaborated strategic plans, as well as their own internal information and publicity systems, in an attempt to counter the power of the media and determine the political issues of the moment.

This professional elaboration and planning of communication procedures has become a major factor of influence in the strategic thinking and actions of political parties. Political reform programs and communication strategies are drawn up more and more as one single unit. The substance of reform and its portrayal in the various channels of communication are seen as going hand-in-hand within the political process as a whole (see Pfetsch 1995; Radunski 1980: 7; Tenscher 2003). In this way, communication strategy—in the sense of the strategic communication of a reform content, political processes, and their management by political actors—represents a single entity of constituent units.

As regards the *professionalization* of political information provision as a whole, this term refers to the delineation of competences, specializations, and skills in the area of detailed and specific instruments, goals, tasks, and means of political communication together with any corresponding action being planned to address specific tasks. The professionalization of structures is at once necessary for and a consequence of the work of communication experts. As much as political communication becomes more professional, as much does its orientation toward the media become more rigid. This chapter highlights how much emphasis is placed on strategic communication in order for reform policies to succeed. Furthermore, the chapter investigates in how far the SPD and the Labour Party have professionalized their communication processes in order to be in accordance with the demands of the media democracy and to ensure the success of their reform agendas in the media. For this, a short overview of the change in the relationship between politics and the media since the 1990s is needed. This will help to distinguish and categorize the communication strategies of both parties which aim to respond to this changing relationship. In this context, the question shall be pursued in how far the pressure for efficiency and professionalization of communication undermine the model of the democratic membership party.

THE PROFESSIONALIZATION OF
COMMUNICATION STRATEGIES AND REFORM POLICY

Political parties endeavor to utilize the media as a way of presenting an image of themselves and are at pains to influence the timing of the coverage and the way in which the topics are reported to the public. That is, they come to strategic decisions on how they might significantly influence the way in which political realities are presented by the media. It is also important for a party to obtain maximum exposure, to control which topics are rated as political issues in the media and among politicians in general—or at least to exert an influence on the selection of issues that is beneficial to itself—and to create a favorable image for its own program of reforms (Pfetsch and Schmitt-Beck 1994: 234). A positive self-generated image should go hand-in-hand with a favorable image generated from outside.

Political communication strategies can thus be seen as the parties' serious attempts to use political actors to design their own publicity, portraying their own positions in such a way as to achieve maximum acceptance and legitimization and assert themselves successfully in competition with political rivals. The strategies are designed to attract the voters' attention, to create positive images of a party's stance on political issues, and to control, or at least influence, the topics which are discussed in the political arena. They are an attempt to use communication tools to demonstrate competence; they include the ability to implement symbolic policy and paint a pseudo reality, and an attempt to influence the nature of media portrayals in advance.

The following are considered important factors in communication strategies: image construction, management of events and issues, portrayal and presentation of content and candidates, deployment of those instruments, issues and formats appropriate to specific target groups, and the creation of an identity discrete from that of political competitors. Communication strategies are supposed to create and extend the capacity to communicate, which is *the* most important factor in building competence within a party (Raschke 2001: 29). This study probes deeper into the communication strategies of political parties, i.e., it assumes that political parties, despite the limitations of their abilities in the area of political communication, are capable of a certain amount of long-term planning and do not consider themselves forever trapped into crossing bridges when they come to them. In a study of the communication strategies of political parties, four aspects, in particular, are worth closer analysis: the contextual framework (that is, the structure of the party and its relationship to the media), the strategic objectives, the methods utilized as well as methods considered, and the effectiveness of the methods utilized.

If in a media democracy a communication strategy is to be successfully implemented, political parties are compelled to anticipate the tools, instruments, and content of media processing mechanisms and to follow the presentation routines of the mass media. It is undisputable that political parties have succeeded in meeting this latter imperative; they have come up with communication strategies that respond to the dominance of the media logic in the area of political communication (Klingemann and Voltmer 1998: 399; see also the different contributions in Lawson and Poguntke 2004 and in Lilleker and Lees-Marshment 2005). Planting the image of a party as trustworthy, credible, competent, and honest into the minds of voters is a long process that eventually pays off by dint of the constant repetition of unchanging messages.

A successful communications strategy (see figure 8.1) distinguishes itself by a number of factors:

- the creation of a positive image;
- the ability to set the agenda in public debates and in media coverage;
- the removal from the political agenda of issues which are not advantageous to the party concerned;
- the successful placement of candidates;
- the dominant position as definer and interpreter of political issues (hegemony of definition/interpretation);
- successful negative campaigning aimed at reducing the competence and attractiveness of rivals in the party system.

To ignore these factors and to concentrate solely on decision-based politics with an unsophisticated system of explaining problems to the voters is generally considered disadvantageous for political actors in competition with others: "Laying out a realistic blueprint for addressing tough problems is

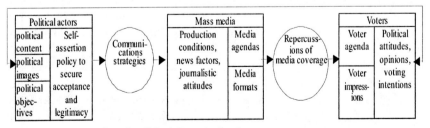

Figure 8.1. Strategies of Political Communication

perceived as political suicide" (Buchanan 2001: 367). At the same time, communication has to take into account the important aspect of credibility and to generate trust in politics and gain the necessary legitimation.

On the other hand, strategic communication can clearly be developed in an easier way based on coherent and goal-oriented political projects. The individual steps of a reform, if they are to be successful, need a combination of contents and orientation towards a certain goal. The communication strategy has to set out information on, and the rationale of, the reform process. Furthermore, it has to choose instruments in order to connect reform policies and communication strategies with regard to content, and to point out the meaning (i.e., the purpose and goal) of reforms to citizens. (See table 8.1.) From the perspective of communication, reform politics can be presented as a four-stage process:

- Planning and detailed development of the reform's contents
- Communication of contents and goals of the reform
- Political realization and implementation
- Evaluation and possible adjustments

The development of communication strategies affects all stages, yet only at the second stage it is in the foreground.

The combined effects of the pressure on politicians to react (felt by all political actors operating within the context of a media agenda centering on the news element), the pressure on the media to respond to events, the ever shortening lifespan of news items and the increasingly fickle electorate, render it essential for political actors to follow carefully designed strategies. This is particularly true in an environment where the competition for media and voter awareness—and eventually votes—is tough. Especially those sectors of the electorate which are not particularly interested in, or informed about, politics

Table 8.1. Model for Planning and Communicating Reforms

Planing and Implementing Reforms	Communicating Reforms
Ascertainment/Making inquiries about the present conditions (analysis of the given situation)	Emphasizing the deficiencies of the present situation and pointing to the inevitability of actions (setting problem definitions and interpretations)
Proclamation of the reform goals and process of putting them in concrete form with the inclusion of the constellation of power and the opportunities of profiling	Trying to dominate the agenda-setting process; defining the main concepts—basic mediation of the reform concept, including the expectations and ideas of the specific groups which are at the core in order to generate acceptance
Consideration of the practical means and tools of the reform with the inclusion of internal and external influences	Enhancing the orientation of the reform program, increasing persuasion of the necessity of the reform program, emphasizing the expected positive results
Implementation through formal decisions and permanent evaluation of the implementation process (effective use of resources)	Making clear immediate success, showing flexibility, placing solidity, coherence and acceptance in the foreground

can be reached by means of symbolic policies and strategies that appeal to personalities and emotions. If they want to be successful parties also have to bring about a convergence of the political agenda with the media agenda in order to create an impression of consistency. And providing that a high level of consonance exists within the media regarding the solution of a particular problem, successful communication can also lead to the electorate or rival political parties altering their ideological positions.

POLITICS AND THE MEDIA: A CHANGING INTERRELATIONSHIP

The interrelation between politics, the media, and the public in modern democracy is very complex and has become more complex during the last twenty-five years. Because of their organizational structure, political parties today reach a continually declining segment of the electorate via formal channels of their organizations (see also the empirical results of Poguntke 2000). Social ties have decreased noticeably and the possibilities for political parties to exert influence on their environment by means of personal communication have deteriorated considerably. Mass media have become the main source of political information for almost all social groups in western democracies. If the mass media choose not to take notice of an issue or event it has virtually not taken place for the public. As a consequence, the forms of organization-centered party communication (communication within and by the party) have to a large extent become superseded by media-oriented forms of presentation (Wiesendahl 1998: 447). Political parties use the mass media to present their programmatic agendas and candidates, a process which has gathered speed in the past 15 to 20 years. Mass media are offering the necessary public forum for legitimation in the eyes of the voters. To large parties which seek to recruit voters from almost all social groups, they offer the advantage of a wide reach. This is particularly the case with television as the main medium for political communication. Three important aspects which need to be addressed are the professionalization of communication strategies, the dominant position within the mass media of television, and the emergence of new (e.g., electronic) forms of communication:

Professionalization

The struggle for attention in the media has become a political necessity for political parties. Because the media have enormously expanded in recent years they penetrate almost all social sectors of society and continue to absorb an ever-increasing share of the time and attention of the public—the media have become an ever-present fact of life. Without mass media it is no longer possible to mold public opinion, simply because it is the media that determine public awareness of political actors and their daily actions. Political actors are therefore forced to adopt the logic of the media, and political actors and political processes alike, so to speak, have become "media-infected" (Sarcinelli 2000: 24; see also Sarcinelli 1998; Meyer 2001). The creation of a political public, informed and molded by the media, and the improvement of communication competencies by parties have become a central part of politics, especially in the realm of party competition. A consequence of these developments is that there needs to be close cooperation or a symbiosis between parties and the media: Politicians and parties are sources of information and the media are a provider of publicity. Politicians and the media are so intertwined because both sides need each other in order to reach one of their primary goals: to reach a broad public and to disseminate information, attitudes, and opinions. Each has its respective objective: the media want to get higher ratings and increased advertising revenues, the parties want a higher percentage of the voting electorate or more attention paid to their policy conceptions. The dependence of politicians and parties on the media has led to the professionalization of political communication as political leaders devote resources and expertise to influence the agenda-setting process and to manipulate the outcome of media reports and news. For this purpose, political parties increasingly engage the services of external PR-consultants, marketing specialists, and other experts for persuasive communication. In fact, party managers have become increasingly aware of the need to communicate with the electorate not just during the election campaign. Hence they are moving towards institutionalizing the cultivation and maintenance of public approval. The invasion of publicity experts who know how to tailor the parties' message to the voters' concerns and opinions is not just a Greek chorus. Their influence within parties has come to be recognized as significant. In comparison to twenty years ago, there are not only larger numbers of them, but the party leadership takes their advice infinitely more seriously (cf. Quinn 2005; Heffernan 1999; Jun 2004; Swanson and Mancini 1996). Quite often, the political decisions taken by parties have come to betray a "media logic," with visual events staged for television, scheduling reoriented to media deadlines, and the promotion of telegenic candidates to the forefront. Parties have in demonstrable ways adopted media priorities. As they adopt media priorities, they improve their chances of structuring the media's coverage of politics (agenda setting) and of constructing a favorable image. These gains, moreover, exist in a zero-sum relationship with the opponents' gains; in other words, the better the party plays the media game, the more of the agenda it gains, directly at the expense of rival parties. Frequent and favorable exposure on television news is an important goal of parties virtually everywhere (Swanson and Mancini 1996: 267). Parties address television journalists as the most important means of communication with the voters.

Parties and even single politicians work in tandem with research institutes and professional firms to wage long-term, media-oriented campaigns to win voters over to "their" agenda. Parties increasingly employ professional communication and marketing advisers to help them prepare their national-level parliamentary candidates to be successful media performers, particularly on television. This professionalization of political communication results in parties devoting more money, time, and energy than ever before to media relations, opinion polling, and marketing strategies, not only at election time. The professionalization of their communication departments, the improvement of their communication performance, and the design of modern communication strategies are also responses by the political parties to the most recent challenges of social change (individualization, pluralization of lifestyles, shift of focus concerning values) and the changes of the media. These responses are inevitable for parties which want to either become or remain powerful political forces in a highly complex and differentiated media world: "Modern parties have been forced to adapt, with greater or lesser success, to the new communications environment if they are to survive unscathed" (Norris et al. 1999: 41). To sum up: Media collaboration in modern publicity and policy-making processes is at the very heart of modern democracy. Media institutions and the media logic become indissolubly linked to democratic politics. What we know is, increasingly, what the media choose to tell us, with the result that political communication is increasingly media communication. It should not be surprising that political actors desire to affect that choice. To put it in the words of Susan Hayward: "Parliamentarism is out, live broadcast democracy is in" (Hayward 1990: 27).

Television as Dominant Media Actor

Television is the public's main source of political information and the most trusted one as well. Television changes the way politics is perceived: to an increasing extent television forms the link between the citizens and their representatives. It is worth taking a moment to consider how the nature of television as a medium shapes this citizen-representative link. Firstly, television emphasizes the importance of single politicians; the medium's shortcuts therefore result in a personalization of politics. Individual politicians no longer need the services of a party apparatus to aggregate the support of diverse groups. They can now do the job themselves with well-prepared and well-performed "sound bites." Television, for formal and structural reasons, favors covering an individual person rather than complex issues or complex organizations such as parties. Television reporting, by nature, seeks to simplify complex ideas, prefers confrontation over compromise, and places a heavy emphasis on "the horse race" in politics, especially during election campaigns. The recent shift in Europe towards privatized and commercial TV stations adds its own spin to the choices made about values, formats, and the "entertainment factor." The public broadcasting services have in turn adopted much from the commercial style of reporting instead of maintaining a vigorous alternative. There is little reason to hope that this development may be reversed. Politicians and parties, who want to get elected or to pressure their opponent(s) in public, need television because it reaches large and heterogeneous audiences, rather than just those who have a special interest in politics. Citizens are reduced to spectators, their participation limited to deciding which politician makes a better impression on television. The impression, in turn, depends on images which politicians or parties themselves construct. Perception is everything. The best image includes, not surprisingly, trustworthiness, competence, an ability to manage political problems, and a high probability of keeping promises. A pleasant appearance, good rhetorical skills, and social competence help a lot to build up a positive image. Former White House speech writer and media consultant David Gergen has summed up this "image-politics": "What sort of a person a politician actually is and what he actually does are not really important. What is important is the perceived image of what he is and what he does. Politics is not about objective reality, but virtual reality" (Gergen, quoted in Kelly 1993: 64).

New Modes of Communication

Beyond television, new forms of communication like the Internet, e-mail, or satellite broadcasting are leading to a worldwide provision with information which tends to break the bounds of the nation-state. Further developments cannot be definitely predicted even among experts. But whatever its future shapes, the possibility of interactive communication is a big challenge for parties and politicians. New technological advances will have special significance when they make it possible for individual citizens to bypass the mass media and get reliable information directly. The results are clearly noticeable: clusters of information recipients are becoming more fragmented; inner-organizational communication processes will have to be strengthened which bears the danger of a separation from the outside with the technology's inherent potentials for reciprocal communication remaining underused. Nevertheless, especially poorly or loosely organized political groups are increasingly using the new possibilities of communication, for example for information, mobilization, communication about forms of activities, or fund-raising. Within the established political parties, communicative inner-party network structures have been constructed; direct mailing and other forms of direct addressing have clearly gained ground and will shape the image of the party as perceived from the outside even more strongly in the future. At the same time, a professionalization of the established political actors concerning innovative technologies has started that could strengthen the already portrayed top-down communication more and could lead to gains in efficiency also in this case and area. Particularly in the case of established parties—this is not applicable to more informally organized groups—the ways which the new media are used have been determined more strongly by considerations of efficiency than participation.

THE SPD'S COMMUNICATION STRATEGY

Modernization and Professionalization of Election Campaigning

The SPD has not ignored this general development of political parties. On the contrary, professionalization and personalization, the application of the latest media-suited methods of mass communication has become an integral part of the SPD since the election campaign of 1998 (e.g., Jun 2004; Lees 2005). The 1998 election campaign shall be considered as the starting point of the SPD's communication modernization and will therefore be briefly discussed here.

With its election campaign center, called *Kampa*, the SPD in 1998 established a service center outside the party headquarters which closely cooperated with professional specialists from the areas of advertising, marketing, multimedia, event organization, and public opinion polling. Crucially, these forms of cooperation with professional agencies and public opinion poll institutes continued even after the election campaign in order to ensure the expansion of effective and modern management and communication structures within the SPD. To the party's secretary (*Bundesgeschäftsführer*), at that time Matthias Machnig, this direction of future party activities, which was increasingly pursued in the second half of the 1990s, is no longer reversible. In his view, logically consistent forms of media presentation were supposed to be given at least the same priority as programmatic work. This was a bold proposal for a party which has conceived of itself as an essentially program-oriented party for over one hundred years. Medium to long-term campaign planning, expansion of the professionalization of the organization, campaign forms and communication lines, personalization as a strategic element of positive image creation, and a strengthening of Federal Chancellor Schröder, an increased use of symbols for the dissemination of ideas and values—these were all central elements of the SPD's communication strategy (cf. Machnig 2001: 131). The coverage of issues perceived as deciding factors in elections can be added to this. To the SPD this meant to demonstrate competency in those areas of politics, and mainly with regard to those issues, which were at the top of the agenda in media reporting. But in order to also be the subject of media reporting and not only its object, it was necessary for the SPD to try and concentrate communication and external presentation of content on "winner issues" (Machnig 1999: 29). In order to achieve this, the party also relied on emotion, simplification, symbols, state-of-the-art visual forms of presentation as well as marketing and advertising rules. In Machnig's words: "Political communication has to take into account the aesthetic rules of the media if it wants to achieve the goal of conveying security, reliability, and hope." (ibid.: 130). According to Machnig, it is necessary that the advertising measures of parties should match the standards of commercial advertising.

A clear image uniformity of presentation and a unified message—all present in the 1998 election campaign—appear to be important prerequisites for the successful implementation of communication strategies. However, what proved decisive was the fact that in the SPD's executive committee, principal issues, and operational decisions were coordinated and directed with the extra-parliamentary party, the parliamentary group, and state governments. This strengthening of the party leadership in the political process follows research findings that party leaders should, in order to successfully adapt to dynamically changing framework conditions, have a relatively high degree of autonomy in order to be able to make strategic adaptations to changes in the voter market. This implies that especially in large parties the relevant leadership is more voter-oriented than other party segments such as activists and individual members. If political parties such as the SPD are regarded as "loosely coupled anarchies" (Lösche and Walter 1992) characterized by organizational variety and a relatively large amount of autonomy of individual organizational parts, their actions quite frequently run counter to systematic or efficient action. Top-down models of party organization, in contrast, seem to be more suited to develop and ensure adequate strategies for parties to succeed against their competitors in media democracies. But since these do not satisfy the organizational variety of large modern parties, a greater degree of autonomy for party leaders in strategic and programmatic issues seems to offer a way forward to achieve organizational efficiency without negating participation claims which are mainly asserted at lower party levels. The introduction of intra-party plebiscitary elements can fulfill this function at the federal level. The party model, described by Machnig as a *network party* (*Netzwerkpartei*) (see in greater detail Machnig 2000; Machnig 2001), is by no means hesitant to respond to claims for more participation, thereby approaching the notion of political parties as "centralized election campaign organizations" (Mair, Müller, and Plasser 1999: 392) or *professionalized voter parties*. Machnig makes his argument by placing professionalization in the forefront and simultaneously combining party leadership loosely with networks which are effective in the social sphere. The term which seems most appropriate here is that of the *professionalized media communication party*. In each of these models, the party leadership retains a comparably large maneuvering space for the development of strategies.

However, in order to permanently secure these structures it is insufficient to implement them in an ad hoc and informal manner, they have to be permanently anchored in the organization by means of reforms. Accordingly, appropriate measures were initiated by former SPD secretary-general Müntefering by intra-party reforms under the slogan "democracy needs party" and by the SPD's vice party leader Beck under the title "modern membership party." In both concepts the SPD wants to combine more offers to participate within the party organization with the professionalization of organizational structures and the party headquarter. Müntefering, as party leader, had then set up a planning, coordinating, and managing team called *election campaign management* at the party's headquarters that was supposed to coordinate all the SPD's communication-related strategic planning and to take part in its implementation.

Despite Professionalization: Deficiencies in Government Communication

The poor communication of government policy during Schröder's second term is not in accordance with the SPD's professional election campaigns since 1998, as many observers have noted. Although the Schröder administration initiated and implemented the comprehensive modernization and professionalization of governmental communication and simultaneously introduced a marketing approach (see Pfetsch 2004; Ruhenstroth-Bauer 2004), it had after 2002 only limited success with portraying its reform policy in the public space. Despite the concentration of communication strategies (which allowed to place special emphasis on certain topics), efforts to center the organizational structures in the federal press office, and the employment of state-of-the-art technology and instruments, there were still major obstacles such as institutional resistance and strategic problems with the preparation of the communication of the reform. Especially the Hartz reforms (see chapters 2 and 9 in this volume) have been poorly explained—as regards the causal context as well as the expected results— to both the public and the party's membership (see Eichhorst and Zimmermann 2005: 17).

Government communication in Germany can be seen as fragmented and decentralized, with each department and each coalition party as well as party faction producing its own communication services. This autonomously pursued public relations work impedes the role of the government's spokesperson at the federal press office as the center of government communication. In this context it has to be pointed out that party- and government-communication in Germany bring forth various actors: Ruling parties set themselves up as a multitude of actors (e.g., parliamentary party, member party, governmental actors), and tensions can arise between the parties' interests and the actual government machinery. The communication structure between the ruling party and the government is very complex and it varies depending on forum, form, content, and addressee. Party and government are in a continual and reflexive relationship towards each other and towards other actors, externally as well as internally (Kamps 2006: 128 ff.). The attempt to achieve an integrated government communication strategy has to consider the whole government machinery as well as the ruling parties involved. This has to happen with regard to its strategic considerations and its opportunities for action, if the program- and solution-finding shall appear to be coherent. Otherwise conflicts in information processing and its communication to the outside often arise from this diversity. With this structure, the demand for strategic coordination of communication increases, especially concerning general reform plans such as *Agenda 2010*. Here a great number of actors with their individual, diverse, sometimes conflicting interests in the reform process were involved on the side of the government parties. This led to ambiguities and ambivalence and stood in the way of inner party unity and a consistent communicative appearance. In order to be able to efficiently communicate such a complex reform plan a thorough, extensive specification of goals and a clear interpretation of possible consequences is needed. Both did not exist to a sufficient extent within the SPD and the governmental apparatus. Fischer talks about a lack of "normative policy management" (Fischer 2005: 143);Sell calls it "strategic visionlessness" (Sell 2005: 308). For a long time, the media suitability of the reform approach had been neglected in the general strategic plan. This reduced public acceptance of the reform project which, in turn, created negative repercussions concerning the consideration of the practical means and tools of the reform. Only in the course of the process, the chancellor and the federal press office intensified their efforts of coordination and adjusted their communications management to the complexity of the task. However, they failed to get across their idea of the reform goals and the direction of their policy, and they did not manage to convey the necessity of the reform process as leaving no alternative. Although the then government spokesman, Anda, demanded at that time an integrated overall strategic plan, and although the departments were advised to always integrate issues of communication into the process of decision-making, i.e., to harmonize the requirements of presentation with decision-making in terms of content (Meckel and Kamps 2006: 69), there was still a lack of the strategic integration and coordination. But as an explanation for the SPD's temporary major loss of popularity and their defeats in the regional elections which eventually led to early general elections in 2005, reference to deficits in communication is insufficient. It does not take into account the serious credibility problem nor the inner party conflicts.

The successful implementation of a communication strategy depends on the realistic and detailed overall planning of the contents and the clear definition of longer-term goals at the policy level. The SPD as the governing party did not take enough time for these tasks. Apart from that, not enough attention had been paid to spelling out and integrating different phases within the communication strategy, and there were inconsistencies as regards the contents of the represented concepts as well as the material decisions. This consistency, however, is a main precondition both for efficient reform management and agenda setting. In the reform process of *Agenda 2010*, the SPD did not succeed to a sufficient extent in creating a positive image and in retaining control of the way in which the reform was understood and debated in the public sphere. Furthermore, adding to the failure were the different expectations of politicians and journalists: While the government had hoped for support from the media concerning the implementation of the reforms, large parts of the media put their primary interest in the visual portrayal of policy results in the foreground and barely considered the procedural side of the process, nor did they help to clarify the contents and consequences of the reforms. Especially in the case of the Hartz IV reforms this has frequently led to disinformation and misconceptions.

PROFESSIONAL: NEW LABOUR'S COMMUNICATION TECHNIQUES

Professionalizing and Modernizing the Communication

New Labour's communication strategy can be described as extremely professional. The latest marketing and PR techniques are not only being used in the party's communication strategy, but are also a central pillar of the party's image. The professional communications management is regarded as the main feature of the Blair administration along with the centralization of power and the remolding of decision-making structures to become more informal (see Becker 2005a; Wring 2005b, Jun 2004). A glance back over the last sixteen years reveals a marked transformation within the party as a result of the modernization of its communication strategy: The influence exerted by marketing experts and researchers, and an outlook acknowledging the importance of communicative strategy were already being acknowledged as important in Kinnock's time, but have become a central preoccupation of the Party under Blair: "It is Blair's leadership that is most closely associated with the new era in communications" (Quinn 2005: 166). Both factors are instrumental in identifying the processes by which affairs are organized and decisions are arrived at.

One consequence of this is that party image has become a key aspect of New Labour policy. The party leadership is at pains to influence the portrayal of the party by outsiders, and party image has a crucial effect on the decision-making process. Labour's response to the challenges posed by the evolution of the media, and to the increasingly powerful influence that the media has, in its portrayal of Labour, on public opinion and the party's electoral fortunes, has been highly professional, complex, and cost-effective. The image presented to the media has become part of the daily political routine for New Labour and the Blair government. Thinking of communication strategy is ranked at least as high in importance as the formulation and implementation of policy: "Policy formation is itself a news event" (Heffernan 1999: 63). Policies and the issues that give rise to them are determined to a large extent by how they can be portrayed and presented to the public. They are coordinated and implemented according to how they impact on the party image. In order to set the agendas itself and frame them in favorable contexts, New Labour has been trying to apply, wherever possible, proactive image strategies. Labour Party spin doctors, mostly members of the government's Strategic Communication Unit (SCU), are keen to make the Party the subject of its own issues and policies rather than merely the object of media coverage. Particularly since Labour took power in 1997, they have tirelessly tried to place issues and news items in the media, give them a positive allure, and thereby have some direct measure of influence on the media's reporting of events. The election campaign, which began a full three years before the 1997 general election, continued almost without a break after the election. Being in government meant sustaining a never-ending tour of the electorate to rally and maintain acceptance for their policies (Jun 2002a).

Heffernan is of the opinion that Labour was even out to gain control of the media and their coverage of events: "Labour's principal objective is to limit the autonomy of the media and blunt their critical faculties in relation to their reportage of themselves" (Heffernan 1999: 52). This entails, among other things, constantly initiating events and news items, continually using the media's own logic and working to their own production imperatives, orienting itself

excessively to news situations that can change unexpectedly, adopting an offensive communication policy and endeavoring to use spin to control the agenda of
the mass media and the contextual framework in which that agenda is pursued.
It also entails submitting its own policy to constant evaluation by means of quantitative and qualitative opinion polls. Feedback from voters became an integral
part of the party's decision-making process (Wring 2005a: 102). The biggest
change to take place in the party's communication strategy was the sophisticated
use of qualitative research, in particular focus groups (cf. Quinn 2005; Scammell
2001). Competition among parties at this level amounts to competition for the
attention of the media, for hegemony in the voter-relevant areas, for media readiness to take up the images of credibility and competence produced for them. The
evening news, the chat show, the leading article, and the front page photo have
long since supplanted the local club in terms of their significance in the hurly-
burly of party political existence (Webb 2000: 154). This is not only the case during electioneering; it is true across the board and shapes the day-to-day dealing
of all parties. Paul Webb notes: "Indeed it is abundantly clear that the major
British Parties have evolved into highly professional, market-oriented organizations which are geared to the needs of virtually permanent campaigning" (ibid.:
156). Labour has been quicker than the Conservatives to spearhead this development. For many commentators it represents the "prototype of a modern party
professionally geared to securing the support of the electorate" (ibid.: 1999: 66)
or "a Bonapartist precedent in party politics" (Hörnle 2000: 374). It has a leader
who is adept in handling the media and writes more columns for the Sun than he
gives speeches in the House of Commons (Scammell 2000: 182). Lees-Marshment sees Labour as the prime example of a market-oriented party turning more
and more towards marketing strategies (Lees-Marshment 2001: 181ff.). The result has been an unprecedented drive to center political affairs on the party leadership and the person of the prime minister, to personalize issues, and to conceive and implement policy as part of a permanent, self-imposed electioneering
campaign originating in Downing Street 10. The strategic communication is
mainly focused on the prime minister (Painter 2005: 215). Within the party, this
form of strategic communication not only causes the centering of competences
and the orientation towards campaigns, but it also implies a considerable weakening of the active membership which in permanent election campaigning is not
a major resource. This leads to apathy and to some extent withdrawal from the
party (see Quinn 2005; Seyd and Whiteley 2004).

"Over Spin"?

"Spin" is not simply perceived as inevitable by the Blair administration to
survive in media democracies, nor is it just an integrated part of Labour

policy, but it is actually a central element of governmental practice. The question arises however: have the Blair Government and the Labour Party gone too far in their excessive preoccupation with the media that has even extended to direct attempts to manipulate media coverage (Becker 2001: 273; Stanyer 2004)? Not the professional communication management as such, but the extent and the fixation on media influence are at the center of such criticism. There are already self-critical voices within the party that New Labour, skilful though it may be in dealing with the media, might have been overly liberal in its employment of "spin." At any rate, the media have not accepted these attempts to curb their autonomy without responding; the increased negativity of their coverage reflects a political cynicism that has partially transmitted itself onto the electorate. Already during the conservatives' administration many journalists displayed distancing and cynical reactions to professionalization and to the increasing attempts of manipulation (see Newton 2000). At the beginning of their first term in office the Labour administration tried to counter this trend, but over the years the Blair administration got into major trouble. "Over spin" tends to work against the creation of a positive image. For long-standing governmental parties credibility problems arise because the normal course of governance with its long-winded processes of decision- and policy-making cannot always be shaped in terms of the own reform goals, even if Labour themselves had worked them out. Ambivalences and inconsistencies can hardly be avoided when being a party in government.

The Labour government's declining popularity rates, disillusionment, and decreasing credibility scores are at any rate consequences that can, albeit only partially, be traced back to the phenomenon of "over spin." The mood in Britain has clearly changed by all means to the disadvantage of Labour and Blair (see Becker 2005b). The events accompanying the *Hutton inquiry* to resolve the *Kelly affair* made clear that there is a fine line between professional media management and media manipulation, and the Blair administration has drawn the conclusion from this not to overstretch the structure of professional strategy-setting which remains, nevertheless, indispensable in media democracies (see more in detail Voltmer and Stamper 2006). Strategically the major change has been the replacement of a political appointee by a senior civil servant who is overall in charge of coordinating government media operations. Alastair Campbell's successor David Hill is responsible only for party political communication to "provide the political perspective on behalf of the Prime Minister and assist cabinet ministers with the political context for departmental communications" (Stanyer 2004: 432). Again during the election campaign in 2005, there was "less spontaneous contact between the leaders and the voters than in previous elections. Rallies and visits were staged before invited audiences and, more than ever, were geared to generating favourable pictures for press and television" (Butler and Kavanagh 2005: 181). In many cases professional staff at the center directed local operations. Public opinion data collected through social research were still used to tame the party to the leadership's will concerning the election manifesto and the presentation (e.g., Lilleker 2005: 576f.; Butler and Kavanagh 2005: 195). Blair appeared in an "unprecedented range of media formats" (Wring 2005b: 723), even if his ratings were significantly worse compared to 1997 and 2001 (Kellner 2005) he was again the leading figure in a candidate-centered campaign, despite Gordon Brown's higher approval ratings. These new developments, however, are not intended to replace the mass media-oriented communication strategy, but instead to complement it.

Also the party leadership has not stayed inactive with regard to the party members' diminishing mobilization and willingness to participate in activities. The Labour Party has recently responded to this by developing new strategic forms. It is advocating a new form of communication for the future, the so-called *Participatory Campaigning*, which is designed to offer more participation for party members and sympathizers in the areas of information dissemination and political activity (Becker 2003). Not control, but trust are to be in the foreground of the activities: "bottom-up, not top-down, local not national, interactive, not one-sided, individual connection not mass communication, communication through word of mouth not mass technology" (Gould in Becker 2005b: 780). Once again, however, these new tools are to be employed not instead of, but in addition to the mass media-oriented communication strategy.

CONCLUSION:
LABOUR MORE PROFESSIONALIZED THAN THE SPD

With a view to the goal of responsible government, i.e., a form of governance that is concerned with a balancing of interests, that involves public opinion, wants to create a consensus, and that does not rely on formal procedures of ruling, the media clearly gains in relevance. Public communication is constantly engaged in investigating what is worthy of support and what has to be rejected; it constantly explores if there are chances for the implementation and acceptance of reforms or if there are none (Kamps 2006: 124). Gerhard Schröder as well as Tony Blair centrally worked this increasing importance into their style of governance, but implemented it in different ways. Differences can be discerned in the way the British government organizes its communication: A central position in the area of the government's media and PR work is held by the SCU which is responsible for drafting a communication strategy for the entire government. The SCU also processes all government documents, compiles the annual governmental report, writes all the newspaper articles published in Blair's name and all his speeches. It is also responsible for the government's Internet page. The press office, and in particular the SCU, takes over seamlessly from the communications department that operated at the Labour Party Headquarters until 1997. It is responsible for all coordination at the center, the incorporation of key news from the ministries into a unified communication strategy, the organization of information channels and the vast majority of contacts with the media and public events, and the utilization of all media formats. Franklin summarizes the Labour government's process of centralizing communications management concisely: "Blair's government is controlling the flow of political communications by and about the government to a degree which is unprecedented in the UK in peacetime" (Franklin 2001: 141). All communiqués are coordinated from the prime minister's press office. The instruments of news management are now also a matter for ministerial attention. The personalization and centralization of political culture complements the media-oriented agenda setting of the Blair government. The conclusion can be drawn that the communication strategy of reform policy in Britain was much more efficient than in Germany and that the concept of integrated communication management has been realized.

In comparison to this, the communications strategy of the Red-Green coalition government in Germany was more fragmented and decentralized: each department and the two coalition parties with their respective parliamentary factions delivered statements largely independent of each other and were differently active in the field of PR, which rendered the role of the government spokesperson in the Federal Press Office a very difficult one. There were often conflicts in the processing and dissemination of information. Such a system puts heavier demands on the strategic coordination of communication, especially when a comprehensive package of reforms is at stake, as it was the case with *Agenda 2010*. Here the diverse and sometimes conflicting inputs and interests of a large number of actors from the government's ranks came to bear on the reform process, which resulted in ambiguities and ambivalence, and was an impediment to presenting an appearance of internal unity. Only when the process was well under way did the federal and the chancellor's press offices intensify their coordination. Only then they began to address the complexity of the task of managing communications. But they remained unable to determine the objectives and direction of their governance in accordance with their preferences, and they remained unsuccessful in trying to get across to the electorate that there was no alternative to pushing the reform process. Hence a comparison of SPD and Labour reveals differences in the way reforms are planned, carried out, and communicated to the outside. Particularly outside the phases of election campaigning, the SPD was clearly less efficient and successful regarding the implementation of its communication strategy. The SPD has not adopted a coherent communication strategy with regard to its policies and delivery.

Governing will be even more dependent on communication in the future. Therefore, the ability to control is linked to the party's and government's ability to communicate externally and internally in a coherent and strategically planned manner. If the two social democratic parties want to retain power for the long run, their social democratic identity has to be combined with a professional system of communications management. If both dimensions are thought out and planned in concert, success should be forthcoming. Both parties have tackled the key issues regarding their future: an all-encompassing education system, reformation of the social security systems as a way of preserving the welfare state, the expansion of the liberal constitutional state (particularly regarding immigration policy), a policy designed to safeguard and create jobs, and the creation of an efficient public sector are all issues that confer a potentially successful image on a modern social democracy. Efficiency in political communication without too much spin, enough room for participation inside and outside the party, and a clear identity are promising success for a reform-oriented social democracy in Britain and Germany. The example of Great Britain teaches that the improvement of communicative efficiency alone does not generate wider public support for the reform policy. At the same time, this chapter has shown that efficiency and professionalization of political communication, due to the central importance of the media logic, strengthen the respective leadership, partially undermine inner-party democracy and evoke inner-party as well as outer-party opposition. The Labour Party as well as the SPD have tried to prioritize efficiency of the communication of reforms to inner-party processes of discussion and with that, have caused considerable apathy at the party base (Lilleker 2005: 573). Due to the imperatives emerging from the media logic, government parties are faced with a dilemma: On the one hand they need to secure efficient management and the coherence of the reform plan; on the other hand, however, they need to secure legitimacy for their reform policy, which calls for inner-party as well as outer-party discussion processes. A strategic element modeled after the rules of political marketing, which comprises an almost exclusive orientation towards the voter, runs the risk of giving away the concept of the member party. Neither the Labour Party nor the SPD seem to be ready for this at present. A central fact which both parties have to consider in their strategic planning is that credibility and trust have, according to all available evidence, become more important in recent years for a successful communication strategy both in the electoral market and in the relationship with journalists and the media at large. The issue of credibility and trust has contributed as much to Schröder's loss of office as to Blair's loss of popularity and, in due course, retirement from office. The new SPD party leader Kurt Beck is trying to take this on board and promises to build up confidence and to stand for credibility. Gordon Brown, as Blair's likely successor, should follow this example in order to reestablish what is missing for Tony Blair at present. Trust, not only strategically understood, seems to be emerging as the central theme of political communication and reform policies for the years to come. With this the wheel turns: in the long run only the close combination of (reform) policies and professional communication strategies can guarantee success for governing parties at elections.

REFERENCES

Becker, Bernd (2001): "New Labour auf Dritten Wegen. Tony Blairs Politikvermark-tung—und was die SPD daraus lernte," in: Althaus, Marco, ed.: *Kampagne! Neue Strategien für Wahlkampf, PR und Lobbying*. Münster: LIT, pp. 258–75.

—— (2003): "Labour: Ende der totalen Kampagne," in: Althaus, Marco, and Cecere, Vito, eds.: *Kampagne! 2. Neue Strategien für Wahlkampf, PR und Lobbying*. Münster: LIT, pp. 50–68.

—— (2005a): "Machterhalt und Zukunftsgestaltung: Elemente erfolgreicher politischer Steuerung in Großbritannien." *Zeitschrift für Parlamentsfragen* 36, no. 2: 301–11.

—— (2005b): "How to campaign against a lack of faith. Britischer Unter-hauswahlkampf 2005." *Zeitschrift für Politikwissenschaft* 15, no. 3: 765–91.

Bogumil, Jörg, and Schmid, Josef (2001): *Politik in Organisationen. Organisations-theoretische Ansätze und praxisbezogene Anwendungsbeispiele.* Opladen: Leske and Budrich.

Buchanan, Bruce I. (2001): "Mediated Electoral Democracy: Campaigns, Incentives, and Reform," in: Bennett, Lance W., and Entman, Robert M., eds.: *Mediated Politics. Communication in the Future of Democracy.* Cambridge: Cambridge University Press, pp. 362–79.

Busch, Andreas, and Manow, Philip (2001): "The SPD and the Neue Mitte in Germany," in: White, Stuart, ed.: *New Labour. The Progressive Future?* Houndmills/New York: Palgrave Macmillan, pp. 175–89.

Butler, David, and Kavanagh, Dennis (2005): *The British General Election of 2005,* Houndmills: Palgrave-MacMillan.

Crozier, Michel, and Friedberg, Erhard (1979): *Macht und Organisation. Die Zwänge kollektiven Handelns.* Königstein/Ts.: Athenäum.

Eichhorst, Werner, Zimmerman, Klaus F. (2005): "Eine wirtschaftspolitische Bilanz der rot-grünen Bundesregierung." *Aud Politik und Zeitgeschichte* B 43, 11–17.

Fischer, Sebastian (2005): *Gerhard Schröder und die SPD. Das Management des programmatischen Wandels als Machtfaktor*. München: Forschungsgruppe Deutschland.

Franklin, Bob (2001): "The Hand of History: New Labour, News Management and Governance," in: Ludlam, Steve, and Smith, Martin J., eds.: *New Labour in Government*. Houndmills/New York: Palgrave Macmillan, pp. 130–44.

Habermas, Jürgen (1965): *Strukturwandel der Öffentlichkeit. Untersuchungen zu einer Kategorie der bürgerlichen Gesellschaft*. Darmstadt: Luchterhand.

Hayward, Susan (1990): "French Politicians and Political Communication," in: Alastair Cole, ed.: French Political Parties in Transition, Aldershot: Dartmouth, pp. 25–41.

Heffernan, Richard (1999): "Media Management: Labour's Political Communications Strategy," in: Taylor, Gerald R., ed.: *The Impact of New Labour*. Houndmills/New York: Palgrave Macmillan, pp. 50–67.

—— (2003): "Prime Ministerial predominance? Core executive politics in the UK." *British Journal of Politics and International Relations* 5, no. 3: 347–72.

Hitzler, Ronald and Maurizio Andreas Cavaliere (2005): "Die Quadratur des Kreises. Parteien zwischen medialen und partizipativen Ansprüchen," in: Haubner, Dominik, Mezger, Erika, and Schwengel, Hermann, eds.: *Agendasetting und Reformpolitik. Strategische Kommunikation zwischen verschiedenen politischen Welten*. Marburg: Metropolis, pp. 201–27.

Hörnle, Micha (2000): "What's Left? Die SPD und die British Labour Party in der Opposition." Frankfurt/Main: Peter Lang.

Jun, Uwe (2002a): "Politische Parteien und Kommunikation in Großbritannien. Labour Party und Konservative als professionalisierte Medienkommunikationsparteien?" in: Aleman, Ulrich von, and Marschall, Stefan, eds. *Parteien in der Mediendemokratie*. Wiesbaden: Westdeutscher Verlag, pp. 278–309.

—— (2002b): "Professionalisiert, medialisiert und etatisiert. Zur Lage der deutschen Großparteien am Beginn des 21. Jahrhunders." *Zeitschrift für Parlamentsfragen* 33, no. 4: 770–89.

—— (2004): *Der Wandel von Parteien in der Mediendemokratie. SPD und Labour Party im Vergleich*. Frankfurt/Main/New York: Campus.

Kamps, Klaus (2006): "Regierung, Partei, Medien. Meinungsfindung in der Mediengesellschaft," in: Kamps, Klaus, and Nieland, Jörg-Uwe, eds.: *Regieren und Kommunikation, Meinungsbildung, Entscheidungsfindung, Kommunikationsmanagement*. Köln: Herbert von Halem Verlag, pp. 110–38.

Kavanagh, Dennis, and Seldon, Anthony (1999): *The Powers behind the Prime Minister. The Hidden Influence of Number 10*. London: Harper Collins.

Kellner, Peter (2005): "Clearing the Fog: What really happened in the 2005 Election Campaign." The Political Quarterly, no. 3: 323–32.

Klingemann, Hans-Dieter, and Voltmer, Katrin (1998): "Politische Kommunikation als Wahlkampfkommunikation," in: Jarren, Otfried, Sarcinelli, Ulrich, and Saxen, Ulrich, eds.: *Politische Kommunikation in der demokratischen Gesellschaft*. Wiesbaden: Westdeutscher Verlag, pp. 395–405.

Kuhn, Raymond (1997): "The Media and Politics," in: Rhodes, Martin, Heywood, Paul, and Wright, Vincent, eds.: *Developments in West European Politics*. Houndmills/New York: Palgrave Macmillan, pp. 263–80.

Lawson, Kay, and Poguntke, Thomas, eds. (2004): *How Parties Respond to Voters: Interest Aggregation Revisited*. London: Routledge.

Lees, Charles (2005): "Political Marketing in Germany: The case of the Social Democratic Party," in: Lilleker, Darren G., and Lees-Marsment, Jennifer, eds. (2005): *Political Marketing. A Comparative Perspective*. Manchester: Manchester University Press, pp. 114–31.

Lees-Marshment, Jennifer (2001): *Political Marketing and British Political Parties. The Party's just Begun*. Manchester: Manchester University Press.

Lilleker, Darren G. (2005): "The Impact of Political Marketing on Internal Party Democracy." *Parliamantary Affairs* 58, 570–84

Lilleker, Darren G., and Lees-Marsment, Jennifer, eds. (2005): *Political Marketing. A Comparative Perspective*. Manchester: Manchester University Press.

Lösche, Peter, and Walter, Franz (1992): *Die SPD. Klassenpartei, Volkspartei, Quotenpartei*. Darmstadt: Wissenschaftliche Buchgesellschaft.

Machnig, Matthias (1999): "Die Kampa als SPD-Wahlkampfzentrale der Bundestagswahl '98." *Forschungsjournal Neue Soziale Bewegungen* 12, no. 3: 20–39.

―― (2000): "Auf dem Weg zur Netzwerkpartei." *Die Neue Gesellschaft/Frankfurter Hefte* 47, no. 11: 654–60.

―― (2001): "Vom Tanker zur Flotte, Die SPD als Volkspartei und Mitgliederpartei von morgen," in: Machig, Matthias, and Bartels, Peter, eds.: *Der rasende Tanker, Analysen und Konzepte zur Modernisierung der sozialdemokratischen Organisation*. Göttingen: Steidl, pp. 101–17.

Mair, Peter, Müller, Wolfgang C., and Plasser, Fritz (1999): "Die Antworten der Parteien auf Veränderungen in den Wählermärkten in Westeuropa," in: Mair, Peter, Müller, Wolfgang C., and Plasser, Fritz, eds.: *Parteien auf komplexen Wählermärkten, Reaktionsstrategien politischer Parteien in Westeuropa*. Wien: Signum, pp. 391–401.

Mandelson, Peter (2002): *The Blair Revolution Revisited*. London: Politico.

Mazzoleni, Gianpietro, and Schulz, Winfried (1999): "'Mediatization' of Politics: A Challenge for Democracy?" *Political Communication* 16, no. 3: 247–61.

Meckel, Miriam, and Kamps, Klaus (2006): "Regierungskommunikation und Marketing. Differenzen und Schnittstellen," in: Kamps, Klaus, and Nieland, Jörg-Uwe, eds.: *Regieren und Kommunikation, Meinungsbildung, Entscheidungsfindung, Kommunikationsmanagement*. Köln: Herbert von Halem Verlag, pp. 54–72.

Meyer, Thomas (2001): *Mediokratie. Die Kolonisierung der Politik durch die Medien*. Frankfurt/Main: Suhrkamp.

Neuwerth, Lars (2001): *Strategisches Handeln in Wahlkampfsituationen. Der Bundestagswahlkampf 1998*. Hamburg: Dr. Kovac.

Newton, Kenneth (2000): "Versagt Politisches Marketing?" in: Niedermayer, Oskar, and Westle, Bettina, eds.: *Demokratie und Partizipation*. Wiesbaden: Westdeutscher Verlag, pp. 177–91.

Norris, Pippa, Curtis, John, Sanders, David, Scammell, Margaret, and Semetko, Holli (1999): *On Message. Communicating the Campaign*. London/Thousand Oaks/New Delhi: Sage.

Painter, Anthony (2005): "New Labour: Der Aufbau eines 'progressiven Konsenses,'" in: Schmid, Josef, and Zolleis, Udo, eds.: *Zwischen Anarchie und Strategie. Der*

Erfolg von Parteiorganisation. Wiesbaden: VS Verlag für Sozialwissenschaften, pp. 207–17.

Pfetsch, Barbara (1995): "Chancen und Risiken der medialen Politikvermittlung. Strategien der Öffentlichkeitsarbeit bei politischen Sachfragen," in: Armingeon, Klaus, and Blum, Roger, eds.: *Das öffentliche Theater, Politik und Medien in der Demokratie.* Bern: Paul Haupt, pp. 65–93.

——— (2003): *Politische Kommunikationskultur. Politische Sprecher und Journalisten in der Bundesrepublik und den USA im Vergleich.* Wiesbaden: Westdeutscher Verlag.

——— (2004): "Regierung als Markenprodukt. Moderne Regierungskommunikation auf dem Prüfstand," in: Sarcinelli, Ulrich, and Tenscher, Jens, eds.: *Machtdarstellung und Darstellungsmacht. Beiträge zu Theorie und Praxis moderner Politikvermittlung.* Baden-Baden: Nomos, pp. 23–32.

Pfetsch, Barbara, and Schmitt-Beck, Rüdiger (1994): "Amerikanisierung von Wahlkämpfen? Kommunikationsstrategien und Massenmedien im politischen Mobilisierungsprozeß," in: Jäkel, Michael, and Winterhoff-Spurk, Peter, eds.: *Politik und Medien. Analysen zur Entwicklung der politischen Kommunikation.* Berlin: Vistas, pp. 231–52.

Poguntke, Thomas. (2000): *Parteiorganisation im Wandel. Gesellschaftliche Verankerung und organisatorische Anpassung im europäischen Vergleich.* Wiesbaden: Westdeutscher Verlag.

Quinn, Thomas (2005): *Modernising the Labour Party. Organisational Change since 1983.* Houndmills/New York: Palgrave Macmillan.

Radunski, Peter (1980): *Wahlkämpfe. Moderne Wahlkampfführung als politische Kommunikation.* München: Olzog.

Raschke, Joachim (2001): *Die Zukunft der Grünen.* Frankfurt/Main/New York: Campus.

——— (2002): "Politische Strategie. Überlegungen zu einem politischen und politologischen Konzept," in: Nullmeier, Frank, and Saretzki, Thomas, eds.: *Jenseits des Regierungsalltags. Strategiefähigkeit politischer Parteien.* Frankfurt/Main/New York: Campus, pp. 207–41.

Riegger, Volker (2006): "*Können Kampagnen Reformen retten? Integrierte Informationskampagnen in der regierungsamtlichen Politikvermittlung,*" Unpublished Paper.

Römmele, Andrea (2002): "Konvergenzen durch professionalisierte Wahlkampfkommunikation? Parteien auf dem Prüfstand," in: Alemann, Ulrich von, and Marschall, Stefan, eds. *Parteien in der Mediendemokratie.* Wiesbaden: Westdeutscher Verlag, pp. 328–46.

Ruhenstroth-Bauer, Peter (2004): "Moderne Regierungskommunikation. Aktuelle Konzepte, Strategien und Vorhaben des Presse- und Informationsamtes der Bundesregierung," in: Sarcinelli, Ulrich, and Tenscher, Jens, eds.: *Machtdarstellung und Darstellungsmacht. Beiträge zu Theorie und Praxis moderner Politikvermittlung.* Baden-Baden: Nomos, pp. 33–47.

Sarcinelli, Ulrich (1998): "Parteien- und Politikvermittlung: Von der Parteien-zur Mediendemokratie?" in: Sarcinelli, Ulrich, ed.: *Politikvermittlung und Demokratie in der Mediengesellschaft.* Wiesbaden: Westdeutscher Verlag, pp. 273–96.

—— (2000): "Politikvermittlung und Wahlen—Sonderfall oder Normalität des politischen Prozesses? Essayistische Anmerkungen and Anregungen für die Forschung," in: Bohrmann, Hans, Jarren, Otfried, Melischek, Gabriele, and Seethaler, Josef, eds.: *Wahlen und Politikvermittlung durch Massenmedien*. Wiesbaden: Westdeutscher Verlag, pp. 19–30.

—— (2005): *Politische Kommunikation in Deutschland. Zur Politikvermittlung im demokratischen System*. Wiesbaden: Westdeutscher Verlag.

Scammell, Margaret (2000): "New Media, New Politics," in: Dunleavy, Patrick, Gamble, Andrew, Holliday, Ian, and Peele, Gillian, eds.: *Developments in British Politics 6*. New York: St. Martin's Press, pp. 169–84.

—— (2001): "The Media and Media Management," in: Seldon, Anthony, ed.: *The Blair Effect*. London: Little, Brown and Company, pp. 509–33.

Sell, Stefan (2005): "Vom Vermittlungsskandal der Bundesanstalt für Arbeit zu Hartz IV: Tiefen und Untiefen rot-grüner Arbeitsmarktpolitik in einer Mediengesellschaft," in: Haubner, Dominik, Mezger, Erika, and Schwengel, Hermann, eds.: *Agendasetting und Reformpolitik. Strategische Kommunikation zwischen verschiedenen politischen Welten*. Marburg: Metropolis, pp. 285–310.

Seyd, Patrick, and Whiteley, Paul (2004): "From Disaster to Landslide: The Case of the British Labour Party," in: Lawson, Kay, and Poguntke, Thomas, eds.: *How Political Parties respond. Interest Aggregation revisited*. London/New York: Routledge, pp. 41–60.

Stanyer, James (2004): "Politics and the Media: A Crisis of Trust?" *Parliamentary Affairs* 57, no. 2: 420–34.

Stöss, Richard, and Niedermayer, Oskar (2000): "Zwischen Anpassung und Profilierung: Die SPD an der Schwelle zum neuen Jahrhundert." *Aus Politik und Zeitgeschichte* B5/2000: 3–11.

Strohmeier, Gerd (2004): *Politik und Massenmedien. Eine Einführung*. Baden-Baden: Nomos.

Swanson, David L., and Mancini, Paolo (1996): "Patterns of Modern Electoral Campaigning and Their Consequences," in: Swanson, David L., and Manicini, Paolo, eds.: *Politics, Media, and Modern Democracy. An International Study of Innovations in Electoral Campaigning and Their Consequences*. Westport: Praeger, pp. 247–76.

Tenscher, Jens (2003): *Professionalisierung der Politikvermittlung? Politikvermittlungsexperten im Spannungsfeld von Politik und Massenmedien*. Wiesbaden: Westdeutscher Verlag.

Voltmer, Katrin, and Stamper, Judith (2006): "Die innenpolitische Sprengkraft von Massenvernichtungswaffen. Zum Verhältnis von Regierung und öffentlichen Rundfunk in Großbritannien," in: Kamps, Klaus, and Nieland, Jörg-Uwe, eds.: *Regieren und Kommunikation, Meinungsbildung, Entscheidungsfindung, Kommunikationsmanagement*. Köln: Herbert von Halem Verlag, pp. 285–304.

Walter, Franz (2000): "Vom Betriebsrat der Nation zum Kanzlerwahlverein? Die SPD," in: Pickel, Gert, Walz, Dieter, and Brunner, Wolfram, eds.: *Deutschland nach den Wahlen. Befunde zur Bundestagswahl und zur Zukunft des deutschen Parteiensystems*. Opladen: Leske + Budrich, pp. 227.252.

—— (2002): "Stillgelegt und ausgebrannt. Die SPD als Kanzlerpartei." *Vorgänge* 41, no. 1: 8–14.

Webb, Paul (1999): "Die Reaktion der britischen Parteien auf die Erosion der Wählerloyalitäten," in: Mair, Peter, Müller, Wolfgang C., and Plasser, Fritz, eds.: *Parteien auf komplexen Wählermärkten. Reaktionsstrategien politischer Parteien in Westeuropa.* Wien: Signum, pp. 31–70.

—— (2000): "Political Parties: Adapting to the Electoral Market," in: Dunleavy, Patrick, Gamble, Andrew, Holliday, Ian, and Peele, Gillian, eds.: *Developments in British Politics 6.* New York: St. Martin's Press, pp. 151–68.

Wiesendahl, Elmar (1998): "Parteienkommunikation," in: Jarren, Otfried, Sarcinelli, Ulrich, and Saxer, Ulrich, eds.: *Politische Kommunikation in der demokratischen Gesellschaft.* Wiesbaden: Westdeutscher Verlag, pp. 442–49.

—— (2002): "Die Strategie(un)fähigkeit politischer Parteien," in: Nullmeier, Frank, and Saretzki, Thomas, eds.: *Jenseits des Regierungsalltags. Strategiefähigkeit politischer Parteien.* Frankfurt/Main/New York: Campus, pp. 187–206.

Wring, Dominic (2005a): *The Politics of Marketing of the Labour Party.* Houndmills/New York: Palgrave Macmillan.

—— (2005b): "The Labour Campaign." *Parliamentary Affairs* 58: 712–24.

Zohlnhöfer, Reimut (2004): Die Wirtschaftspolitik der rot-grünen Koalition: Ende des Reformstaus?" *Zeitschrift für Politikwissenschaft* 14: 381–402.

ACTORS

9

Efficiency versus Party Democracy? Political Parties and Societal Modernization in Germany

Elmar Wiesendahl

Parties belong to the key political actors in the process of societal modernization. There are, of course, other collective actors, but parties are the only ones that are able to connect the *policy* and the *politics* of societal reform. They are involved in both problem solving and in handling political conflict. They have to be successful in reconciling contradictory expectations and competing interests, even when they are not very well prepared for the job (Bartolini and Mair 2001: 330–36). In managing the process of modernization they firstly have to articulate, represent, and protect the interests of their party members, voters, allied interest groups, and civil organizations. Secondly, they have to lead the process of policy making by formulating policy programs, deciding on them, and eventually implementing them. Last but not least, they have to link the party state with civil society by generating visions, engaging and convincing the public, and by explaining why and how specific objectives should be accomplished. They have to communicate with the people and channel controversial debates regarding alternative paths of societal modernization. In short they have to try to make politics meaningful.

Rather than maximizing their own goals, parties have to deal with conflicts between multiple goals and interests, and they have to find an optimal balance between competing functions (Strøm and Müller 1999). Most obviously, they are seeking votes and offices. In order to win elections they have to build coalitions and organize voter majorities. This means that they have to respond to the needs and demands of a heterogeneous electorate and to cooperate with interest groups and other allies. To attract party members, supporters and the electorate in general, party programs and policy proposals try to express and represent the voters' preferences. But in trying to win votes parties compete with others for public attention and public support. And once in office, they have to react to societal and economic problems which have to be solved by the state. Not only are parties able to control public administration and to mobilize rare state subsidies, parties in parliament and government are generally the only actors who are held responsible for effective policy making and problem solving. It is obvious that when having to decide about unpopular but essentially important policy issues, parties may be forced to act against their own interest of vote-maximization.

In the recent academic debate, the capabilities of parties as strategic modernizers and agents of change tend to be either overestimated or they are shown in a too pessimistic light. Adopting a perspective that focuses on structures, several political scientists have drawn attention to the many constraints and barriers which make Germany a problematic case of reform deficiency and reform gridlock. They have highlighted the gap between comprehensive reform requirements and the country's ability to agree and implement reforms (Benz 2003: 33). This perspective captures parts of the truth, yet for a more encompassing assessment, not only the influence of structures but also reform actors, their intentions and their actual behavior need to be examined more closely. The actor perspective investigates the available room for maneuver and how political actors actually make use of it. Research into parties as reform actors has to combine structure and actor perspectives without overlooking the factor of human behavior. So, the important academic issue of German reform gridlock would be better discussed taking into account reform restrictions or the inability to achieve structural reforms.

Parties are not deterministically controlled by exogenous pressures for societal reform. They can choose between adopting ambitious reform strategies and keeping a low profile in reform politics. It is easy to demand that political parties ought to offer strategic visions for the future, but it is much less easy to devise such visions (Franz and Immerfall 2003: 4). It is not immediately obvious what kind of normative yardstick or quality standards should be applied when evaluating party strategies and party strategy building. Strategy making requires long-term thinking and the identification of specific objectives which are to be realized through incremental action (Wiesendahl 2000a: 189). To act strategically means to be able to intervene into social and economic developments and to take control of the reform process. In practice, however, parties have to operate in a competitive, ambiguous, turbulent, and mostly unfriendly environment. They can no longer be certain of their members, supporters, and voters, nor of affiliated interest groups, societal associations, or the mass media. Under conditions of uncertainty and turbulence parties are vulnerable but they are keen to avoid risks. Usually they do not make full use of the strategic capacities and opportunities available to them.

Either because they prefer to be cautious or because they lack strategic imagination, party elites do not normally develop grand strategies or master plans. Instead they focus on their day-to-day business which they tend to conduct without any strategic vision. In short, party politicians follow the logic of incrementalism and muddling through (Walter and Dürr 2000: 8).

It may be questioned to what extent this commonly presented picture accurately reflects the contemporary situation. Established party policies and party strategies face new dramatic challenges. And it is doubtful if experiences and methods proven in the past can be transferred into the future. Prior to the *Bundestag* elections in September 2002 it was striking how little the parties in Germany engaged themselves in the process of societal modernization. But in 2003 parties obviously took the reform initiative. This chapter will analyze how seriously the German parties are committed to playing the role of strategic modernizers. The objective is to find out to what extent, in conditions of limited external structures of opportunity and limited inner-party action capabilities, parties are ready and able to adopt strategic reform agendas. It is, obviously, not possible to investigate all dimensions of societal modernization. Therefore the analysis is limited to the present process of welfare state reform. At first the changed circumstances are outlined, which have forced the parties to reform the labour market and the health and pension system. Secondly the factors which the parties have to take into account when developing plans and strategies for modernization of the welfare state will be analyzed. Following this, the strategic approaches of the Schröder government and the opposition parties are assessed by measuring them against their opportunities for action. Finally, some generalizations are made about the reform strategies of the parties in relation to the conflicting goals of more efficiency and party democracy in Germany.

PRESSURES FOR SOCIAL REFORM
AND RESPONSES BY POLITICAL PARTIES

Following reunification in 1990, Germany went through a critical period of societal and economic transition into an uncertain future. There were, and still are, several developments to which Germany has to adapt because the country has lost its ability to maintain the level of wealth and welfare to which its citizens have become used. Prominent factors are, in particular, the globalization of the world economy, the financial costs of German unity, and decreasing rates of economic growth. Furthermore, the process of societal aging has far-reaching implications. These trends are interconnected and their consequences are further aggravated by the still rising unemployment rate, high wage costs, increasing expenditure for welfare benefits, growing tax rates, decreasing spending power of those who are in gainful employment, and excessive budget deficits and public debts. These factors dramatically changed the circumstances of economic and social life in Germany. They put political decision makers under considerable pressure to devise appropriate policy responses.

As a precondition, however, for successful social reform and innovative strategies of problem solving, it was necessary to review the established ways in which the problems to be addressed were framed and articulated (Wiesenthal 2003: 38). Established problem perceptions and beliefs about the most appropriate course of action had been shaped in the comparatively quiet period prior to reunification. In the present context societal elites in Germany seem to be moving towards a new consensus regarding their views and assumptions about social reform. Leading representatives of the economic, political, and administrative sectors agree on the necessity of radical cuts in social benefits and a comprehensive deregulation of the labor market (Hübner 2003: 19). This agreement provides evidence that a reform policy consensus is emerging among the leading groups in Germany, yet this does not include elites from the trade unions, churches, and social sciences. The decline of elite support for the old-style welfare state is not new but actually goes back to the 1970s (Roller 1992: 198). In the middle of the 1990s, party elites in Germany had diverse views about the most appropriate way of reducing state responsibility for social security (Kaina 2002: 232–36). Since then, however, polarization among the political elite regarding welfare reform has decreased. The necessity of reducing welfare benefits and deregulating the labor market is no longer contested because economic experts insist that those social policy reforms are essential if economic growth is to be promoted. Not least because the print media in Germany are themselves affected by a long-lasting economic crisis, media elites have an interest in promoting social reform policies which might facilitate new growth.

It is evident that the wave of market-oriented neoliberal thought has hit the policy arena and has influenced the ways in which the political class frames and articulates societal problems. The substantial impact of neoliberal ideas may be explained by the lack of attractive neokeynesian economic ideas and alternative sociological or philosophical theories of societal modernization and social reform. Those who are still defending the traditional welfare state have lost ground both in the elite debate as well as in public appreciation. They no longer occupy the centre of the debate. Fighting from a defensive minority position, they are no longer able to respond effectively to mainstream attacks on the idea of the inclusive *social state* and to the critics of social policies. This has led to a narrowing of the elite debate which is increasingly restricted to the exchange of purely economic or fiscal views and policy proposals. The fundamental role of the welfare state as a mechanism of social integration, and the link between the welfare state and modern social democracy are neglected.

Political parties are challenged by these fundamental changes in economic and societal circumstances as well as by public anxieties caused by them. They can no longer respond in the ways in which they used to do because they have lost the *road map* that in the past guided them towards electoral success: Practices of redistributing economic growth and expanding state provision of welfare benefits used to function as a substitute for other forms of mobilizing party support. The major parties' catchall strategy was underpinned by the ideology of welfare handouts. The expansion of the welfare state has been regarded as the collective voter interest and used as the tool for coalition-building. For a long time party competition followed the logic of welfare expansion (Rieger 2002: 12). This logic, however, does not have a solid economic foundation. For this reason there can be no doubt that the social democratic policy model which idealizes social equality, the equal distribution of social costs, and a strong welfare state has reached its limits (Schroeder 2001: 251).

In the wake of comprehensive changes in the electoral market (Mair and Müller 2000), there are now strong demands that both the economic crisis as well as the financial crisis of the welfare state are addressed in an effective manner. Being exposed to these new pressures parties have to change their ways, but they are confronted with a choice between Scylla and Charybdis: They can either try to please the electorate by avoiding unpopular policy measures, in which case they will be held responsible for ever mounting economic and social problems. Or alternatively, they can try to gain support by adopting a proactive role in modernization politics, in which case they will have to abandon the established politics of welfare presents and thereby frustrate voter interests. A central point for understanding Germany's reform problems is that the political parties are themselves a major cause and part of the social spending crisis which they are now supposed to resolve. Any serious attempt by the parties to reduce public expenditure for pensions, health, and unemployment benefits implies that they undermine the basis of their own electoral support. And the risks inherent to the role of the ambitious and active modernizer are further increased by the fact that parties cannot predict the complex consequences and impacts of social policy decision making (Offe 2003: 807–17). The expectation that social reform proposals will actually achieve new economic growth and stabilize the systems of welfare services rests on vague conjectures with prospects of success still being a matter of gross speculation. However if the governing parties fail to take effective action, this too increases the risk of painful electoral losses. Indeed, wait-and-see approaches may well bear even larger risks than taking the reform initiative.

It is against the background of these uncomfortable circumstances, that the political parties in Germany moved towards a modernizer approach. Between the summer of 2002 and the middle of 2005 reforms to the labor market, the health care system, and the pension scheme were agreed and implemented by the Red-Green government which would previously have been unthinkable. As a matter of fact, these reforms were more drastic than anything implemented over the past five decades. As chapters 2 and 6 in this volume discuss in more detail, the reform package was developed in line with the Hartz Commission's proposals of August 2002 and Chancellor Schröder's *Agenda 2010* that was announced in March 2003. But the reform package also reflects the input of the CDU and CSU, which successfully exerted influence via the *Bundesrat* and its Mediation Committee (also see chapter 5).

The core elements of the labor market reform include new requirements for the unemployed to accept any (legal) job that may be offered to them, a shortening of the period during which they are eligible for unemployment benefits, a loosening of employment protection rules, and the consolidation of long-term unemployment and social assistance benefits into a single new unemployment benefit. Reforms to the health care system imply that patients with statutory health insurance now have to pay a quarterly medical consultation fee and fully cover the cost of dentures and occupational sick pay. And as regards the pensions system, early retirement schemes have been curbed, and the level of state pensions has been reduced.

At closer consideration, however, most of the proposals that have been made and implemented are measures of short-term crisis management and attempts to repair costly policy mistakes that had been made earlier. The main objective of the welfare state reform programs has been to reduce wage costs and to ease the employers' burden of social security contributions. By reducing previously granted social benefits and by reviewing both employment protection laws and charges and taxes imposed on businesses, the government has tried to promote economic growth and increase Germany's international competitiveness. Moreover, the reform measures are hoped to attract foreign investment and prevent the relocation of enterprises abroad. As regards the reform objectives, there is broad agreement not only between the former partners of the Red-Green coalition, but this also extends to the Conservatives (CDU/CSU) and the Liberal Democrats (FDP), both of which differ only marginally in terms of their neoliberal, supply side–oriented reform ideas.

The combined strategy of, on the one hand, easing the burdens for businesses and deregulating the labor market, and on the other, imposing heavier burdens on employees (e.g., moves towards private pension provision, reduction of social benefits, longer working hours without additional pay) is presented by the parties' leading politicians as the only possible solution. However, these neoliberal reform policies do not take into account that in Germany a major cause of week economic growth is actually the declining spending power of employees and, as a result, a depressed domestic consumer market. In addition to this, economic growth is, obviously, also hampered by the still enormous transfer cost caused by German unification. First and foremost, the social reforms of the Red-Green government have affected the traditional social-democratic clientele. For the majority of those traditionally voting Conservative (CDU/CSU), in contrast, and in particular for the clientele of the FDP, the reform measures have not had a detrimental impact or have actually implied a change for the better. Interestingly, the interests of the self-employed and suppliers of goods and services in the health sector, which are particularly protected by the FDP and the CDU/CSU, have not been touched by the reforms.

Trying to give an overall assessment of the policy suggestions which are currently on the social reform agenda, one might note that all of these measures have been designed to counter the short-term financial problems facing the social insurance systems. Cost-saving measures are supposed to reduce social expenditure and stabilize the level of social insurance contributions. The reform measures are not aimed at dismantling the welfare state and its supporting pillars (Tálos 2004: 231). This approach of social cost-saving policy goes back to the 1970s (Gerlinger 2003: 6–13). Current social policy reform is determined neither by any grand reform design nor any master plan solution. On the whole, the parties have opted for hastily implemented measures of short-term crisis management. But the parties have so far avoided addressing the fundamental problems of restructuring the public systems of social security. Major efforts are required to reform the very foundations of the welfare system and to map out an inspiring vision for the modernization of German society. It will probably not be long before the competing parties are forced to adopt much more ambitious reform policies, not least because of the mounting problems caused by ongoing demographic shifts.

THE FRAME OF REFERENCE FOR
STRATEGIC REFORM BEHAVIOR OF PARTIES

In order to be successful in the role of strategic reform actors, political parties need to be aware of, and take into account, a range of factors which determine their room for maneuver. For reasons of simplicity the following examination will discuss only the most important ones of these factors, and it will differentiate between internal and external factors.

PUBLIC SECURITY PREFERENCES AS STRATEGIC BARRIERS

In the model of ideal party democracy, policy making means to transfer public preferences into policy decisions. This ideal model assumes a principal-agent relationship. The electorate as principal generates interest and preferences, and parties as agents try to match and represent voter preferences and translate them into political decisions. The most difficult strategic challenge for political parties is to be sensitive about public concerns relating to social security and protection and to handle tensions which emerge when established arrangements for social security and protection need to be changed.

It is therefore no surprise that at least declaratory commitment to the widely shared principle and value of social justice figures prominently in current agendas of welfare reform. In Germany, the welfare state and public investment into social security enjoy overwhelming support. Social security is one of the most value-laden terms in Germany (Rieger 2002: 5). Seventy-one percent of the population want to live in a country that is committed to social security and would reject a system that demands and rewards the individualization and privatization of social risks (Piel 2003). Sixty-seven percent of the public support the statement: "Social justice means that all people enjoy equal conditions of life" (Piper 2003: 22). Also, social justice is generally regarded as a political term, located at the center of the social question. The handling of social justice issues is seen as embedded into the long-standing fight against societal inequality and into the historical class struggle that has always centered on reducing the gap between the rich and the poor. For the German public, the issue of social justice is closely associated with proactive state intervention trying to increase social equality by redistributing wealth and protecting social justice achievements (Kersting 2000). For this reason, almost all Germans have positive feelings about the *social state* which is considerably more than the welfare state (Andreß et al. 2002: 122–23). The social state consensus in Germany is built on the assumption that the state is capable of and actively engaged in protecting its citizens against the risks of age, ill health, and unemployment (ibid.: 152–53, 154–55). These collective social benefits are understood as social property rights guaranteed by the state. German citizens generally agree to the high levels of public social spending and they are generally opposed to welfare cuts (Roller 1992: 110, 187, 199).

After 120 years of state responsibility for public welfare and social security, there is no societal basis or historical tradition for any influential philosophy of individual self-reliance. And none of the parties or leading politicians in Germany have a convincing vision for possible ways in which public opinion on how to deal with the social question could be changed. This societal consensus on the social state has so far not been affected by the elite-dominated debates about welfare reform which have been mentioned above. While most of the leading groups argue for less state, more market, more deregulation, less social spending, and more emphasis on economic competitiveness,[1] most of the people want to maintain the welfare state and secure social achievements. They prefer the socialization of the costs of social protection and are concerned about scenarios of lower levels of public security provision and higher levels of individual responsibility and social inequality. East Germans, in particular, expect the state to actively support them (Lippl and Wegner 2004: 271f., 278) and address social injustices which are perceived to be more severe in the new *Länder* than in those of the old west.

In Germany, the overwhelmingly negative public sentiments about a fundamental reform of the social state do leave room for more positive attitudes towards specific reform measures. But the key point is that the public in Germany is predominantly skeptical and not willing to support large-scale social reforms. A majority of people are convinced that social reform policies will most likely create new injustice and social inequalities. One in two Germans believes Germany is moving towards higher levels of social injustice (Rieger 2002: 4–5). Eighty-four percent are of the opinion that the recent reforms to the health system are socially imbalanced (STERN 32/2003: 104). For Christoph Böhr, former vice-chairman of the CDU, there is a simple explanation for such anxieties and for public resistance against welfare reforms. For most citizens each reform proposal means "that at the end of the process there will be some winners and many losers" (Böhr 2003: 2). And Böhr goes on: "Whilst public expenditure on the social state is decreasing, the financial burdens for individuals are increasing," and then "suddenly a big majority see themselves as the exploited losers of the cost cutting cycles" (ibid.).

At closer analysis, public attitudes about the reform of the social state display fundamental contradictions. The great majority of Germans believe that their country is currently experiencing a profound crisis (Piel 2005:35). And most of them tend to have pessimistic views concerning the future stability of the social security systems. For example, 89 percent of the public believe that pensions are not secure beyond the short term (Köcher 2002: 5). Opinion surveys reveal that most Germans are concerned about the imminent collapse of their health, pension, and employment insurances (Piel 2003: 29). This is one reason why 81 percent of Germans are in favor of a fundamental reform of the insurance systems covering the risks of old age (Schöppner 2003a: 31). Seventy-eight percent do not believe that the political efforts undertaken to stabilize the health care system are sufficient (Emnid 2003a: 26). At the same time, however, two thirds of the population believe that the recent reforms to the health system are unreasonable (Institut für Demoskopie Allensbach 2003). Overall, the reform policies agreed and implemented between 2002 and 2005 did not have any support in the electorate. In the sense that the current social reform agenda does not mirror public preferences, none of the major parties can be said to be responsive to public opinion. Therefore, principal-agent theory does, evidently, not provide a suitable framework for the analysis of welfare reform policy.

PUBLIC DISTRUST
AND THE UNCERTAINTY OF PARTY POLITICIANS

The tension between the reality of social reform policies and the social security preferences of the public would be more bearable if political decision makers were perceived as genuine representatives of the people who can be trusted when dealing with social and economic modernization. This, however, is not how policy makers are seen. Party elites do not spend much effort on communicating and explaining their reform proposals to the public. The more party politicians fail in connecting their social reform agenda to legitimate goals and inspiring visions for a better future, the more do they leave the public alone in their attempt to make sense of modernization and find orientation for the way to go. Prior to the Bundestag election of 2002 there had been no indication of the dramatic change of policy which the SPD was planning. In fact the election platforms had remained silent about the problems. Therefore, the voters were unprepared for the reform measures which were initiated after the elections and which were taking the electorate by surprise. The objectives of these reform ideas appealed to only small sections of the public, and the expected outcomes of the reform measures were not described accurately. With regard to the labor market and social security reforms, for example, the SPD members were told by Olaf Scholz, secretary general of the SPD, that these were inevitable "if we want to save and modernize the welfare state as a whole" (Scholz 2003: 3). He declared: "If we do not act now, we can be certain that the social security systems will collapse or be swept away by the forces of the market" (ibid.). Franz Müntefering, chairman of the SPD's parliamentary group and later SPD party leader, claimed that the suggested reform packages would "make the welfare state in Germany sustainable in substance and make prosperity possible in our country today, tomorrow and the day after tomorrow" (Müntefering 2003: 17).

Essentially, the policies of welfare retrenchment are presented and justified as inescapable necessities with no alternatives. The emphasis is put on purely economic arguments while the concerns and interests of the voters and their fear of losing social benefits are not taken seriously. For this eloquent silence of the political class there is no plausible explanation or justification. It confirms suspicions held by the public that the responsible politicians either do not know where their party is heading or that they pursue reform goals which they do not want to reveal to the public. This negatively affects the strategic environment of the parties because there are no reserves of loyalty or confidence left in the electorate which policy makers could tap when planning to implement unpopular reform measures. There is no doubt that parties and party politicians operate in an environment of distrust and lack of support. For whatever reason, the relationship between the electorate and the parties has come under considerable stress. After the golden age of strong ties and high emotional commitments between society and party system in the 1970s (Wiesendahl 2002b), this relationship has persistently deteriorated and there is no indication that it might once again improve (Wiesendahl 1998). Faith in the parties has decreased dramatically. In 2003 only eight percent of Germans trusted the parties (Schöppner 2003b: 2). A survey conducted in the summer of 2005 put the figure at one out of ten (Noelle 2005: 5). Starting in the 1980s, parties have lost large numbers of members. The ability of the parties to mobilize and integrate voters diminished. Public dissatisfaction with the behavior and performance of the parties increased in the 1990s and throughout that decade *Parteiverdrossenheit* (disaffection with political parties) was one of the key terms dominating public debate as well as political science in Germany. Yet parties have not only lost public trust, but also voters, members, and organizational capacities. The reputation of party politicians has deteriorated, too. At the beginning of the new decade, 89 percent of the public believed that politicians were not in touch with the problems of the country (Schöppner 2003b: 2), and a majority of the people associated the work of politicians with lies and deception (Noelle-Neumann and Köcher 2002: 206). And there is no indication that this situation might improve. According to a poll conducted by the opinion research institute FORSA in July 2005 (STERN 20/2005: 17), 84 percent of the Germans believed that the parties would not stick to their political programs after the elections.

The most worrying feature of the dominant public mood is the lack of confidence in the efficiency and effectiveness of the present social reform policies. Two years after the launch of *Agenda 2010*, eight out of ten Germans doubt that the politicians will be able to handle the problems (Piel 2005: 35). Most of the voters were equally distrustful of the reform proposals presented by the CDU/CSU. Yet public dissatisfaction with the program of reform focused primarily on the SPD as the main governing party. Even though the reform laws had factually been adopted by an informal grand coalition of SPD and CDU/CSU, the opposition parties left Schröder and his government with the task to implement the unpopular reform decisions and defend them against an upset public. As a result, public protests and the voters' resentment were focused solely on Schröder and the SPD, while the opposition parties maintained a low profile and enjoyed high popularity ratings. The governing party, however, had to pay a high price. Irrespective of the policy area, the reform proposals of SPD government lacked public support. This is hardly astonishing because most of their loyal party supporters expect high social state spending (Andreß et al. 2002: 150). With regard to public opinion the SPD suffered a disastrous decline in acceptance in the reform year 2003. Public dissatisfaction with the performance of the Red-Green government rose from 57 to 88 percent between September 2002 and November 2003 (Hank and Höfinghoff 2003: 42). For the SPD, the survey results were particularly disastrous. Confidence that the party would care for social justice fell from 52 to 33 percent between September 2002 and October 2003. Moreover, 71 percent subscribed to the view that the reforms promoted the interests of industry but not those of common citizens (Tagesschau.de 2003: 1–2). Also more than 70 percent believed that the SPD has no clear strategy or plan for achieving the recovery of Germany (Emnid: 2003: 1b).

The voters' dissatisfaction with the SPD was reflected in the party's dramatic loss of popularity and various massive election defeats. At the end of 2002, polls already showed that the approval for the reelected Schröder government fell from 38 percent to approximately 30 percent and then plummeted further to the disastrous level of 24 percent (TNS Infratest) after the first six months of 2003. The fact that Schröder stepped down as SPD leader at the beginning of March 2004 did not really improve the negative mood among the people. Quite the contrary: Following the implementation of health reform policies at the beginning of 2004, the SPD's popularity decreased once more and fell to a low of 23 percent. Afterwards, public approval increased temporarily until the turn of the year 2004–2005, when the SPD reached 33 percent. However, the enforcement of the Hartz IV reform on 1 January 2005 and an increase (partially statistics related) of the official unemployment rate to five million unemployed people led to another downswing in which the SPD's popularity fell to a level of about 27 percent. The electoral consequences of this sustained disapproval were blatantly evident. Since the miserable start of the Schröder's second term in September 2002 and his *Agenda 2010* speech in March 2003, the SPD had to face severe electoral defeats in each of the subsequent eleven state elections. The average loss in these elections was 6.9 percent. As a result, Germany's political map turned completely black (Conservative) in summer 2005. While the CDU/CSU had the parliamentary majority in eleven federal states, there were only five *Bun-*

desländer, where the SPD still had a majority which is large enough to form a government. After being defeated in Lower Saxony, the SPD on 22 May 2005 also lost the psychologically important social democratic core state of North Rhine-Westphalia to the CDU. After this, there was no Red-Green coalition left at *Länder*-level.

The parties alone have to take the main responsibility for the anxiety and anger among the electorate. They glaringly failed to explain the reforms which they initiated. The impression arises that the parties do not inform the citizens about the course of the journey because they are most uncertain themselves as to the destination of the reform trajectory. Perhaps this uncertainty explains the strikingly low level of *emotional intelligence* displayed by the ruling elites, i.e., their inability to deal sensitively with the feelings and worries of the socially vulnerable sections of the population in Germany.

POLICY REFORM CAPACITIES OF PARTIES AND THE LOGIC OF PARTY COMPETITION

There are some essential prerequisites for the development of successful strategic policy reform agendas. First of all, parties should present themselves as united actors. In practice, however, parties organize actor multiplicity and are misunderstood as behaving as a unitary actor (Wiesendahl 1999). Another organizational deficiency concerns the lack of far-reaching strategy building. Some limited guidance from party leaders and top organizers cannot substitute for a properly developed strategic center (Raschke 2001: 25) at the top of German parties. Party elites are not qualified and trained to think and act strategically. Perhaps political communication experts and campaign professionals in the parties' headquarters possess special strategic skills, but they are not normally part of the parties' major committees.

The task to generate reform policy goals and implementation plans demands capacities and efforts which differ sharply from the routine efforts of day-to-day trial and error and incremental politics. To deal with societal modernization means to leave behind the preference for security and the patterns of well-known tactics which the political actors are accustomed to. The strategic challenge for party elites is to place the emphasis on securing Germany's future and not on selfish and short-term measures which might bring electoral advantages. If they want to be genuine reformers, party politicians must define fairly long term policy goals for the modernization and renewal of German society and the country's economy. In order to achieve significant social and economic change, they must be willing to insist on sacrifices made by the public and perhaps by their own party, and they need to support strategic allies. An additional effort is expected from them: in the short term, difficult periods and uncomfortable decisions are to be demanded from the party, and for some individuals it may even be necessary to accept the end of their political carrier. The politics of strategic reform policy is concerned with risk assessment because circumstances out of the ordinary have to be handled by extraordinary decisions. Strategy building cannot be made to work unless it reaches beyond optimal vote seeking, office seeking, and policy seeking (Strøm and Müller 1999: 5–13).

In practice, the decision whether to join forces with the proponents of specific reform policies or to take the side of the opponents depends on how interested the individual is to stabilize or remove the power structure of the party. These power-gaining interests are most relevant when looking at the pattern of inter-party competition. The logic of party competition in Germany does not offer any incentives to focus on devising the most efficient policy proposals and problem solutions. Instead, the ineradicable priority is to compete for votes in a volatile electoral market. This seduces party strategists into playing the game in an obstructive way, i.e., by blocking the rivals' opportunities for voter mobilization. Within this framework of party competition, the primary objective is to discredit the policy proposals and reform intentions of the opposite parties and to deny the opponents the opportunity to do the right thing. This self-destructive inclination towards unfair party competition becomes particularly pronounced if the policy emphasis shifts from the distribution of wealth to the delivery of social cuts and unpopular measures to reduce established social privileges. Governing parties are no longer in a position to satisfy voter preferences because, instead, they have to reduce social benefits and hope that a one-sided imposition of disadvantages may promote economic growth. Parties have to shift from a policy of redistribution to a policy of reducing social spending. The further progress in social policy reform is determined by the distribution of risks and incentives in the struggle for votes which centers on attempts to attack and reduce the chances of governing parties to generate and implement social reform programs.

PARTY MANIFESTOS AS SCOPE FOR POLICY REFORM MANEUVER

Basic party programs which are updated only in larger time intervals cannot guide day-to-day political action. They do not stimulate efforts to link fundamental party positions with swiftly changing demands of societal modernization. Indeed they are not at the forefront but in the background of day-to-day policy debates. In comparison to long-term programmatic documents, electoral party platforms are in some respects more precise, but in general they are written in a way that doesn't determine policy making. Much freedom is left for party officials once the party is in the office (Volkens 1989: 139–42). Nevertheless, party manifestos are not useless; they are important for the party itself. First of all they describe the beliefs, principles, and goals the party is fighting for. These normative proposals are the source for the party's corporate identity and its members' organizational commitment and role identification. Indeed, party platforms are a cornerstone for party democracy and responsible party government (Wiesendahl 2003). They enable voters to choose between different policy alternatives in elections and to hold party representatives in parliament and government accountable. Beyond this, however, the usefulness of party manifestos for policy change is limited. Most of the ideological views and basic policy orientations do not reflect short term policy challenges or future developments. This is because the basic party programs of the German parties have normally been written a long time ago and have, since then, lost contact with reality—which has changed—and with new issues on the current public policy agenda. So, debates on the basic party program do in general not influence the future and have lost contact with the actual stream of events (Siller 2002: 11–12). Usually party program policy lines and inner-party debates are decoupled from the policy agenda setting process that deals with daily decisions at parliamentary and governmental level. The loosely connected levels of internal policy talk and external political action will, however, collapse if the party in office suddenly changes the party's policy course. In such cases, there is an obvious discrepancy between the new reform suggestions and the basic party positions formulated in long-term programmatic manifestos.

This was the case in Germany when in 2003 the SPD launched the reform policy process of *Agenda 2010*. Following the implementation of this new reform agenda, the party needs to shorten the distance between its new policy proposals and basic party program. Program renewal, however, is a very complicated and long-winded process. Firstly, it absorbs much energy and time as well as capacities for conflict-handling. Considering efficiency, there is the evident danger that meanwhile the policy cycle determined by the flow of changing problems will move on to new issues. By the time that party manifesto reforms are finally completed and approved by the decision of the party congress, many of the new programmatic proposals will have lost contact with the changed reality and with the changed policy agenda. So basic party programs normally fail to provide guidance for political problem solving. They cannot offer precise policy solutions corresponding to the flow of emergent problems. Secondly, program adaptation to new policy challenges is limited by the program conservatism of the party's rank and file who fear the loss of established party beliefs and principles. Many party activists are committed to policy purity and closely watch over the unity of party principles. Therefore modifying crucial party positions would cause inner party conflicts and division between ideological party wings. Another point of inner party conflict is that the party's membership is expected to support measures of program adaptation to radical policy changes which have been agreed, at their own discretion, by central party officials and party politicians holding public offices. For the three established parties in Germany, there is still much work to do: In the CDU Angela Merkel initiated a debate on programmatic reform in 2000, but there has been little progress so far (Bösch 2002: 71). The *Wiesbadener Grundsätze* which the FDP produced in 1997 are limited to some rather general neoliberal proposals. And as regards the SPD, the party's internal process of manifesto renewal has come to a halt because of the unresolved ideological conflicts related to the values of social justice and social equality (Egle and Henkes 2003: 71, 84–87). Only the German Greens have completed their process of program reform. In 2002 they adopted a new written party manifesto. Some of the policy proposals of the program are quite precise and in touch with the issues which have been placed on the current social policy reform agenda (ibid.: 104ff.).

The developments in party platform work over the past one hundred years may be captured by distinguishing three different phases. During the first of these, party manifestos have been written in ideological terms (*Weltanschauung*) and they described visions for changing society as a whole. Those programs have been understood to guide the political actions of party leaders and members and to unite them with party supporters, integrating all of them into a social movement. After World War II, parties reformulated their manifestos with the primary goal of vote maximization. Being transformed from mass integration parties to catchall parties, manifestos lost their sharp ideological profile and were moderated by offering voters social benefits and state subsidies for better living standards. In this phase of "end of ideology," platforms lost their strong ties to the party principles and placed more emphasis on voter preferences and special group interests. Programs have changed from guiding lines for party policy action to instruments of vote-winning. In current times of postindustrial transformation and the rise of the globalized information society, party manifestos are changing for a third time. Now, challenged by critical societal and economic disruptions, party policy is directed by party leaders in public office and goes its own way that is less in line with and committed to basic party principles and programmatic positions. In the third phase, party manifestos follow and legitimize party government and not vice versa. This loss of party platforms for the governmental parties' policy actions is perhaps the starting point of an era beyond party democracy with a cartel party regime.

PROBLEMS OF PARTY DISCIPLINE
AND MEMBERSHIP SUPPORT FOR REFORM ACTIONS

Parties as a whole are not very well prepared to act as reform agents. To speak of *the party* means to overlook the different levels and wings within this special kind of voluntary organization. Party researchers divide the whole body of parties into the party in public office, the party's central office, and the party at the grassroots level (Katz and Mair 1993). Each of these organizational parts follows its own logic. The party in office and the party on the ground have separate frames of reference for their world views and problem perceptions. The parties' public office holders are directly influenced by reform pressures; whilst the activists and lower officials of the party at the grassroots level are somewhat more isolated from and insensitive to societal winds of change. What parties in parliament and in government have to do is often not the same as what parties outside the state believe should be done. The world of policy makers and governmental actors is different. The demands for connecting social and economic problems with adequate political problem solving are very different from the demands of party members who expect ideas for dealing with problems and who want to discuss policy projects. These differences need to be considered when parties deal with policy reforms.

Party leaders should take into account that party activists are loyal and motivated party soldiers only as long as the chief commander and party officers match the feelings and values of the troops (Wiesendahl 2000a: 200–202). Party activists want to know what they are fighting for and the goals and principles they believe in should be the guidelines for the policy course of the party. Sixty-four percent of the SPD party members wanted the party to stand for their principles and not simply to be an instrument for obtaining and retaining government control. Attempts to change the minds and attitudes of party members in Germany concerning social reform proposals is limited by the fact that most of them were politicized and recruited by the parties in the golden age of welfare state expansion back in the 1970s. Several party members and especially those who are members of parliament in Germany are employed in the public sector and the welfare state bureaucracy and have a self-interest in maintaining welfare activities by the state (Best et al. 2000: 173).

The logic of party identity is one of the most deeply rooted barriers against reform policy. It is very difficult to bridge the gap between the demand for problem solving and the demand for the expression of the party's identity. Parties at the grassroots level observe new courses of policy initiated by government with concern because they want to save the beliefs and ideals of the party. If, however, responses to new realities have to be designed on the basis of outdated *Weltanschauung*, this may imply that parties cannot move. The changed policy line of the SPD as represented by the *Agenda 2010* attacks party principles which, for the whole period after the Godesberg party reform in 1959, have integrated all ideological wings and levels of the party. The concept of social justice, in particular, that is laid down in the 1989 political program of the SPD—which is still in force—aims for the continued realization of socially fair burden sharing. The measures of *Agenda 2010* contrast sharply with this political goal. Indeed the social democratic concept of social justice is completely inappropriate as a legitimizing basis for *Agenda 2010* (Meyer 2005: 183f). The debate within the SPD was influenced by the party at the grassroots level and did not support the pragmatic way in which the Schröder government was dealing with the necessity of reforms. Instead it assessed whether the government's reform policy proposals corresponded to the principles of the party. Both wings of the party, the party in government and the party on the ground, spoke different languages. One side was trying to manage practical policy problems whereas the other side was talking about saving party principles and the party identity. Party activists were not open-minded about a review of the party identity, required to legitimize reform programs by government or party elites. Instead, these policy suggestions were viewed as ill-designed and unjust. Six out of ten members of the SPD thought that the reform policies promoted by their own government were not socially balanced.

As the inner party conflict of the SPD indicates, party members regard the destruction of a party's corporate identity with the disposal of party ideals such as *democratic socialism* or *social justice* and *equality* as unacceptable. In the summer of 2003, most of the tensions within the SPD were caused by the top-down fashion in which the party leadership acted. SPD party members felt deprived of their identity when the party's secretary general, Olaf Scholz, tried to eliminate those terms and substitute them by terms taken from the vocabulary of the opponent liberal and conservative parties. The reformists at the head of the SPD and in the government were pessimistic as to their ability to convince the grassroot members that they should follow the social policy reform course. The small group of SPD reform advocates did initially not include the party outside parliament into the reform process. This tactic failed miserably because of major protest from party members. The party executive only changed course when party rebels initiated a membership survey trying to mobilize the party on the ground against the new party line. At that point the party leadership agreed to hold a party conference on 4 June 2003. In the run up to this event, meetings organized by the party leaders and the chancellor were held at the lower party level in order to explain the reform agenda and exert influence on the inner party discussion.

Party members were invited to discuss the implications of *Agenda 2010*, but not to decide on its content. This was underlined by Chancellor Schröder's threat that he would resign from office if the party did not follow his line of reform. He and other leading advocates of the party made little effort to engage into debate with the grass roots of the party about the major policy change by the governmental wing of the party. Schröder urged the party not to allow that the SPD be excluded from governing for a period that might last a full decade (Schröder 2003: 50). The manner in which he was dealing with his own party had no precedence in the post war history of the SPD. The result of the vote taken at the party conference on 4 June 2003 and at the party congress on 18–19 November 2003 demonstrates that the strategy was successful. But this success came at a high price. Many party members were frustrated and disappointed about having been excluded from the decision-making process of *Agenda 2010*. They felt degraded and humiliated by Chancellor Schröder and his advisory group who had devised a policy course which they did not agree with. Quite soon Schröder, who was increasingly estranged from the party's grass roots, resigned from the office of party leader and was, at the beginning of March 2004, succeeded by Franz Müntefering. The party was relieved but even under the new leadership it did not come to terms with the chancellor's reform policies. Schröder never obtained his party members' support for his *Agenda 2010*. But more than 150.000 members left the party between 2002 and 2005. The left wing within the party has lost any incentive and motivation for helping to mobilize public support for a policy of welfare modernization that they perceive as unjust. And with this assessment, the SPD party members do not stand alone; they represent the views and attitudes of the majority of German society.

STRATEGIC CONSEQUENCES FOR PARTIES AS REFORM ACTORS

In their entirety, political parties are not capable of acting as efficient unitary reform actors. Only party elites and top politicians in public office can take the role of agents of change and reform promoters (Raschke 2001: 25). This small party elite has some freedom to act. However, whatever their reform intentions and proposals might be, they have to consider several barriers and opposing groups attempting to decelerate their program of change. Implementing a reform project as large as the reduction of state benefits and the imposition of cuts into the established privileges of certain social groups is by no means an easy undertaking that may well entail political risks and trigger major conflicts. When trying to cross the minefield of reform politics, parties have to take several restricting factors into account which are external to the party. There is the pessimistic mood of the public; negative sentiments of frustrated supporters; allied interests groups which get upset about particular details; the decline of enthusiasm for political parties in general; painful electoral defeats in midterm elections; and the ever-present efforts of political competitors who try to stir up negative feelings in the public and to block the wheels of the reform process which the governing parties want to keep going. Another important external factor is, furthermore, the mass press, influential sectors of which are engaging in a cynical double-edged campaign. On the one hand, these daily papers call for radical reform policies and criticize the political class for their incrementalism. On the other hand, they join forces with the reform opponents and stir up public opinion and negatively influence the voters' opinions on political decisions. As regards inner party reform barriers, key factors to be reckoned with are the restricting power of the party's ideological heritage and the potential resistance of party activists. Beyond this, the time and energy that need to be invested into convincing the party's rank and file of the advantages of a suggested policy program play an important role in the strategy building.

Under these circumstances it is unwise to delegate consensus formation and decision making on social reform policies to self-regulating committees of trade unionists and representatives of the employers' organizations, even if such committees, as in the case of the "Alliance for Jobs" (*Bündnis für Arbeit*) are chaired by the chancellor or top ministers. The example of the Alliance for Jobs provides evidence that this moderation and consensus building strategy is doomed to failure. It would not have been possible to convince the public and the electorate that the reform program was indeed necessary and in the interest of securing Germany's future. It is, however, not unrealistic to suggest that adequate efforts could change the public's preferences and attitudes concerning social security issues. Yet, no party in Germany possesses any well-reasoned and convincing vision and strategy that might encourage people to cover their social insurance needs by private means. This is the main reason why party elites did not put much effort into explaining and legitimizing the new social reform agenda and into advertising it to their own electorate.

The first requirement for a successful reform strategy is the formation of an efficient advocacy coalition at the parliamentary and governmental level of policy making. Secondly, the positions of power and sources of influence controlled by potential opponent groups need to be identified and cut off. Most prominent among these, the long-established social security network, represented by leading trade unionists and the workers' associations of both major parties, has been one of the most influential groups in Germany fighting in defense of the social state (Trampusch 2004). Therefore, at the beginning of his second term in office, Schröder disbanded the ministry of employment and social order, which had traditionally been the policy domain of the social policy network in Germany. The department of employment was integrated into the ministry of economics, which was led by minister Wolfgang Clement, a well-known advocate of social policy reform. The department of social order became part of the new ministry of health and social security. Ulla Schmidt, another proven reform advocate, took control of the new ministry—and actually retained this position in Angela Merkel's new Grand Coalition. Schmidt has only weak ties to the old social security establishment which gradually lost its power base in government.

Following his reelection, Schröder himself, supported by only a small group of reform advisers and loyal followers in government, parliament, and party, decided to adopt a different reform strategy. His new approach was based on the logic of dealing with social reform policy against the rationale of short-term vote-winning and interest group integration. The strategic reform operation was inaugurated by his *Agenda 2010* speech in the Bundestag on 14 March 2003. Going public in this way implied explicitly abandoning the populist advertising mode of politics which had been a characteristic feature of his first term in office. Realistically Schröder had to assume that in this case the majority of the electorate would object to his reform agenda. He could not rely on the support of most of the activists and grassroot members of his own party. His speech therefore initiated a new style of leadership. Schröder signaled his willingness to decide single-handedly how to change social security and employment policy in Germany. Everyone else had been excluded from the decision-making process leading to *Agenda 2010* and was forced to agree and follow. Schröder's new strategic reform line represented an attack on the long-standing traditional consensus culture of public debate and political decision making in Germany. Rather abruptly, the public had to face the chancellor as a self-appointed reformer. Schröder adopted the role of a man who acts on his own accord and presents his ideas of policy reform as nonnegotiable. On 17 March 2003 he declared that the only thing left to be done "is policy implementation and not debate" (Süddeutsche Zeitung, 18 March 2003). Looking ahead to the SPD party congress, he stated: "the party has to agree with the policy of the Chancellor [. . .] or not" (Hamburger Abendblatt, 15 April 2003).

Clearly, one central element of the new strategy was Schröder's changed style of leadership. His preferred style during the first term in office has been described as presidential leadership (Helms 2001: 1512–13). The new style he adopted in 2003 is better described as executive-authoritative leadership. This style reestablished government by hierarchy and exclusive leadership by the head of the government. With this new strategy Schröder was aiming to convey the image of the strategic man of action (Lösche 2003: 160–63). He abandoned the long-lasting and time-wasting procedures of party democracy. He had broken with the cooperative pattern of interest group bargaining and compromising. He had left the arena of multi-step parliamentary political decision making. Instead of institutionalized reform engineering, he now adopted the role of the authoritative decision maker who stands by his decisions. The signals this gave to the opposition parties were that the chancellor was no longer prepared to take on board all kinds of considerations and that he was determined to show leadership. One tactical move designed to limit and undermine the obstruction strategies of the opposition via the public and the *Bundesrat* was to merge a whole range of policy change proposals into one giant reform bill. Another component of the reform strategy was to integrate the reform decision and implementation process. In doing so the efforts of changing a central field of the German policy agenda were supposed to come to fruition by the end of 2003. The integration of the reform process by high-speed time management was intended to reduce the scope of action for the CDU/CSU opposition. So, the price paid in policy trade-offs for the acceptance of most of Schröder's reform bill by the Christian Democrats was time-limited and restricted to the *Bundesrat*'s compromise decision making. The acceleration of the reform process was supported by public opinion because the voters wanted the long-lasting reform debate to be stopped and followed by decisive action (Ehrlich 2003).

At first, Schröder's daring proposals inspired the opposition elites to come up with their own reform ideas which, eventually, were even more radical than the *Agenda 2010*. CDU leader Angela Merkel took the first step with her keynote address "Quo vadis Deutschland" which she delivered on 1 October 2003 in Berlin. Her rival candidate from the CSU, Bavarian minister president Edmund Stoiber, used a policy statement of 6 November 2003 to announce a "paradigmatic" change in welfare state policy. The reform euphoria was reflected in a strategy paper by the CDU leadership regarding the privatization of the health care system. The party adopted the paper at its party convention held in early December 2003 in Leipzig. The most radical approach, however, was presented by the FDP on its party conference in June 2004. The Liberals took the stance that the "welfare state itself" should be given up and replaced by a purely market-oriented approach. However, CDU leadership called for radical reforms only as long as the party achieved clear victories in regional elections in which the SPD alone was electorally punished for the reforms. The situation changed in the autumn of 2004, when the CDU's results in *Länder* elections in Eastern Germany slumped. Eventually, the reform euphoria displayed by the CDU elite vanished completely when, at the beginning of 2005, the Bavarian CSU's resistance against Merkel's radical health care reform plans put an end to the party's popularity high. In their programme for the early elections on 18 September 2005, the CDU/CSU were again honest enough to speak out for tax increases, further social cuts, and measures to deregulate the labour market. The FDP suggested system-changing reform measures in its electoral program which were warmly welcomed by the entrepreneurs' associations.

CONCLUSION

When the last part of Schröder's health reform became effective in July 2005, the reform process in Germany came to a preliminary halt. The rise in health costs had—at least temporarily—been stopped. However, the reforms of the labor market have not produced the desired cost-saving effects or an improved employment rate. Quite the contrary, the unemployment rate has risen to a record high. It will take more time until the reorganization of the job placement system (Hartz IV) and the merging of unemployment and welfare benefits (implemented since the beginning of 2005) yield the desired positive effects. It is too early to accurately assess the effectiveness of Schröder's modernization process. The process has successfully been kicked off, but there are some problematic aspects and unpleasant effects to be noted. On the one hand, societal modernization has to be accomplished and the indicators of crisis cannot be ignored. The expensive German welfare state must be reformed. Unquestionably, the reform policy has to improve systemic efficiency. On the other hand, the project of societal modernization in Germany is not coupled with that of party democracy. The limiting circumstances and widespread resistance to policies aiming at social state reform are so powerful that reform advocates have to resort to top-down strategies presenting the public and institutional political actors with fait accompli. There is no place for any bottom-up change management, i.e., for discussing or legitimizing the modernization process in the broader public. Party leaders and the political class invariably fail in convincing the public and offering visions of a better future that is worth fighting for.

One elementary part of Schröder's new reform strategy was to decrease substantive participation and increase the scope for influencing opposing actors in the power play of reform politics. Representatives of interest groups, ordinary party members, and actors of the active strata of society are not welcome to participate in or influence the modernization process. They are expected to simply support it. Parties outside government and parliament do not take part in decision making for social policy reform and in programmatic activities of societal modernization. Top-down reform politics, however, undermine the morals and the compliance of many party loyalists. At the membership level, parties have been weakened. Once the modernization process has been completed—if such a stage can ever be reached—the principal-agent relationship between parties and the electorate must be renewed and reactivated. Even more problematic is the social justice gap created by the reforms. For instance it was not until the election campaign of summer 2005 that the Schröder government demanded sacrifices from the wealthier people in Germany in the form of a reintroduced wealth tax or increased inheritance tax. With benefit cuts being imposed on the less wealthy people only, the voters got the impression that the chancellor spared and even favored entrepreneurs and wealthier people while the proverbial hard-working man on the street had to bear the brunt of the reform burden. As a result many traditionally social democratic voters no longer believed that the Schröder government represented their basic interests.

With the Schröder reforms coming close to the neoliberal ideas of the center-right opposition parties, the gap between the policies pursued by the parties and the demands for social protection by the lower social classes, in particular, was growing and finally led to a wave of protests in the spring of 2004. In this situation, the chancellor had to deliver a strategic coup. After on 22 May 2005 the SPD had lost the elections in North Rhine-Westphalia, he therefore announced early elections in order to have a plebiscitary vote on his reform agenda. However, the chancellor's hasty reaction turned out to be a miscalculation as it opened a window of opportunity for the traditional left: A far-left faction of dissident Social Democrats (*Wahlalternative soziale Gerechtigkeit—WASG*) joined forces with the PDS and formed the "Left Party." They promised to give the losers of the social reforms a voice in parliament. For the role of political parties as reform actors, the result of the early elections in September 2005 may be seen as a writing on the wall: With 8.7 percent of the vote, the Left Party successfully established itself in the party spectrum and caused a fragmentation of the left in the German party system. Schröder's Red-Green reform government secured only 42.4 percent of the vote (a loss of 4.7 percent) and was voted out of office. Losing 4.2 percent, the SPD had to pay a much higher price than the Greens. However, the opposition parties CDU/CSU and FDP also failed to win a combined majority. Together, they obtained only 45.0 percent of the vote, and the CDU/CSU which only shortly before the elections had been predicted a possible absolute majority, came out with a miserable 35.2 percent which was 3.3 percent below their 2002 result. What the elections demonstrated is that no party can win the majority of votes by promoting socially imbalanced reforms of the welfare state and suggesting a deregulation of the labor market. Political parties clearly have to learn the lesson that they need to balance their efforts for economic modernization with the demand for social justice. In the future it is imperative for them to pursue the required increase in efficiency on the basis of genuine commitment to party democracy.

NOTE

1. This is why Chancellor Schröder could be certain that his *Agenda 2010* would be fully supported by the political, administrative and economic elites in Germany.

REFERENCES

Andreß, Hans-Jürgen, Heien, Thorsten, and Hofacker, Dirk (2002): *Wozu brauchen wir noch den Sozialstaat? Der deutsche Sozialstaat im Urteil seiner Bürger.* Wiesbaden: Westdeutscher Verlag.

Bartolini, Stefano, and Mair, Peter (2001): "Challenges to Contemporary Political Parties," in: Diamond, Larry, and Gunther, Richard, eds.: *Political Parties and Democracy.* Baltimore/London: John Hopkins University Press, pp. 327–43.

Benz, Arthur (2003): "Reformpromotoren oder Reformblockierer? Die Rolle der Parteien im Bundesstaat." *Aus Politik und Zeitgeschichte* B29-30/2003: 32–38.

Best, Heinrich, Hausmann, Christopher, and Schmitt, Karl (2000): "Challenges, Failures, and Final Success: The winding Path of German Parliamentary Leadership Groups towards a Structurally Integrated Elite 1848–1999," in: Best, Heinrich, and Cotta, Maurizio, eds.: *Parliamentary Representatives in Europe 1848–2000. Legislative Recruitment and Careers in Eleven European Countries.* Oxford/New York: Oxford University Press, pp. 138–73.

Böhr, Christoph (2003): "Verlierer und Gewinner." *Frankfurter Allgemeine Sonntagszeitung*, 20 July 2003: 2.

Bösch, Frank (2002): *Macht und Machtverlust. Die Geschichte der CDU.* München: Deutsche Verlags-Anstalt.

Egle, Christoph, and Henkes, Christian (2003): "Später Sieg der Modernisierer über die Traditionalisten? Die Programmdebatte in der SPD," in: Egle, Christoph, Ostheim, Tobias, and Zohlnhöfer, Reimut, eds.: *Das rot-grüne Projekt. Eine Bilanz der Regierung Schröder 1998–2003.* Wiesbaden: Westdeutscher Verlag, pp. 67–92.

Ehrlich, Peter (2003): "Die Bürger wollen Reformen—aber die Richtung passt ihnen nicht." *Financial Times Deutschland*, 28 March 2003: 18.

Emnid (2003a): "Befragung zur Gesundheitsreform." *Umfrage & Analyse* 7-8/2003: 26.

——— (2003b): "Schnelle und umfassende versus langsame und schrittweise Durchführung notwendiger Reform." *Umfrage & Analyse* 3-4/2003: 16.

Franz, Peter, and Immerfall, Stefan (2003): "Zeitlupenland Deutschland? Zum Vollzugsdefizit wirtschaftspolitischer Reformen." *Aus Politik und Zeitgeschichte* B18-19/2003: 3–8.

Gerlinger, Thomas. "Rot-grüne Gesundheitspolitik 1998–2003." *Aus Politik und Zeit-geschichte* B33-34/2003: 6–13.

Hank, Rainer, and Höfinghoff, Tim (2003): "Wer wird Reformer des Jahres?" *Frank-furter Allgemeine Sonntagszeitung*, 16 November 2003: 42–43.

Helms, Ludger (2001): "Gerhard Schröder und die Entwicklung der deutschen Kan-zlerschaft." *Zeitschrift für Politikwissenschaft* 11, no. 4: 1497–1517.

Hoidn-Borchers, Andreas, Rittgerott, Mathias, Schneider, Kerstin, Schmitz, Stefan, Schmitz, Werner, Wedemeyer, Georg, Weitz, Regina, and Witzel, Holger (2003): ". . . dann muss der Kanzler weg!" *Stern* 18/2003: 57–60.

Hoidn-Borchers, Andreas, and Wolf-Doettinchem, Lorenz (2003): "So denkt die SPD wirklich, Herr Schröder." *Stern* 47/2003: 53–58.

Hübner, Rainer (2003): "Aufbruchsignal. Capital-Elite-Panel." *Capital* 15/2003: 18–21.

Institut für Demoskopie Allensbach (2003): "Vorschläge zur Reform des Gesund-heitssystems." *Allensbacher berichte* 20/2003: 1–4.

Kaina, Viktoria (2002): *Elitenvertrauen und Demokratie.* Wiesbaden: Westdeutscher Verlag.

Katz, Richard S., and Mair, Peter (1993): "The Evolution of Party Organization in Eu-rope. The Three Faces of Party Organization." *The American Review of Politics* 14: 593–617. Special Issue: Parties in an Age of Change.

Kersting, Wolfgang, ed. (2000): *Politische Philosophie des Sozialstaats.* Weilerwist: Velbruck Wissenschaft.

Köcher, Renate (2002): "Politik als Risikofaktor." *Frankfurter Allgemeine Zeitung,* 18 December 2002: 5.

Lippl, Bodo, and Wegener, Bernd (2004): "Soziale Gerechtigkeit in West- und Ost-deutschland." *Gesellschaft—Wirtschaft—Politik* 53, no. 2: 261–80.

Lösche, Peter (2003): "Bundeskanzler—Superman? Wie die Medien die politische Wirklichkeit auf den Kopf stellen." *Universita* 58, no. 480: 160–72.

Mair, Peter, Müller, Wolfgang C., and Plasser, Fritz, eds. (1999): *Parteien auf kom-plexen Wählermärkten. Reaktionsstrategien politischer Parteien in Westeuropa.* Wien: Signum.

Meyer, Thomas (2005): "Die Agenda 2010 und die soziale Gerechtigkeit." *Politische Vierteljahresschrift* 46, no. 1: 181–90.

Müntefering, Franz (2003): "Rede im Deutschen Bundestag." *Das Parlament,* 20 No-vember 2003: 17.

Noelle, Elisabeth (2005): "Vertrauen ist besser." *Frankfurter Allgemeine Zeitung,* 2 July 2005: 5.

Noelle-Neumann, Elisabeth, and Köcher, Renate, eds. (2002): *Allensbacher Jahrbuch der Demoskopie. 1998–2002.* München: Knaur.

n-tv (2003): "Die aktuellen Emnid-Umfragen im Auftrag von n-tv." *TNS EMNID Pressinformationen,* 4. October 2003: 1.

Offe, Claus (2003): "Perspektivloses Zappeln. Oder: Politik mit der Agenda 2010." *Blätter für deutsche und internationale Politik* 48, no. 7: 807–17.

Piel, Edgar (2003a): "Sicher ist sicher." *Frankfurter Allgemeine Sonntagszeitung,* 7 September 2003, S. 29.

—— (2003b): "Sicherung defekt." *Frankfurter Allgemeine Sonntagszeitung*, 15 June 2003: 29.

—— (2005): "Ohne Vertrauen." *Frankfurter Allgemeine Sonntagszeitung*, 18 September 2005: 35.

Piper, Nikolaus (2003): "Gleiche Chancen und Leistungsanreize." *Süddeutsche Zeitung*,16 October 2003: 22.

Raschke, Joachim (2001): *Die Zukunft der Grünen. So kann man nicht regieren.* Frankfurt/Main/New York: Campus.

Rieger, Elmar (2002): "Die sozialpolitische Gegenreformation. Eine kritische Analyse der Wirtschafts- und Sozialpolitik seit 1998." *Aus Politik und Zeitgeschichte* B46-47/2002: 3–12.

Roller, Edeltraud (1992): *Einstellungen der Bürger zum Wohlfahrtsstaat der Bundesrepublik Deutschland.* Wiesbaden: Westdeutscher Verlag.

Scholz, Olaf (2003): "Editorial." *Vorwärts* 42, no. 5: 3.

Schöppner, Klaus Peter (2003a): "Eins ist sicher: die Rentenreform." *Umfrage & Analyse* 1/2003: 31–32.

—— (2003b): "Mehrheit der Bürger will Reformen." *Die Welt*, 30 July 2003: 2.

Schröder, Gerhard (2003): "Spiegel-Gespräch." *Spiegel* 17/2003: 50.

Schroeder, Wolfgang (2001): "Ursprünge und Unterschiede sozialdemokratischer Reformstrategien. Großbritannien, Frankreich und Deutschland im Vergleich," in: Schroeder, Wolfgang, ed.: *Neue Balance zwischen Markt und Staat?* Schwalbach: Wochenschau Verlag, pp. 251–75.

Siller, Peter (2002): "Neue Grundsätzlichkeit. Auf der Suche nach der verlorenen Programmatik," in: Siller, Peter, and Pitz, Gerhard, eds.: *Zukunft der Programmpartei. Politik zwischen Programmatik und Pragmatik.* Baden-Baden: Nomos, pp. 11–30.

STERN (2003): "Das kommt auf die Patienten zu." 32/2003: 100–105.

Strøm Kaare, and Müller, Wolfgang C. (1999): "Political Parties and Hard Choices," in: Müller, Wolfgang C, and Strøm, Kaare, eds.: *Policy, Office or Votes? How Political Parties in Western Europe make hard Decisions.* Cambridge: Cambridge University Press, pp. 1–35.

Tagesschau.de (2003): "Soziale Gerechtigkeit." Deutschland Trend Infratest dimap, 4 April 2003.

Tálos, Emmerich (2004): "Umbau des Sozialstaates? Österreich und Deutschland im Vergleich." *Politische Vierteljahresschrift* 45, no. 4: 213–36.

Thissen, Torsten (2003): "'Entscheider' unterstützen Reformen." *Die Welt*, 10 July 2003: 2.

Trampusch, Christine (2004): "Von Verbänden zu Parteien. Der Elitenwechsel in der Sozialpolitik." *Zeitschrift für Parlamentsfragen* 35, no. 4: 646–66.

Volkens, Andrea ((1989): "Parteiprogrammatik und Einstellungen politischer Eliten: Konsens- und Konfliktstrukturen in Wahlprogrammen," in: Herzog, Dietrich, and Wessels, Bernhard, eds.: *Konfliktpotentiale und Konsensstrategien. Beiträge zur politischen Soziologie der Bundesrepublik.* Wiesbaden: Westdeutscher Verlag, pp. 116–44.

Walter, Franz, and Dürr, Tobias (2000): *Die Heimatlosigkeit der Macht. Wie die Politik in Deutschland ihren Boden verlor.* Berlin: Alexander Fest Verlag.

Wiesendahl, Elmar (1998): "The Present State and Future Prospects of the German Volksparteien." *German Politics* 7, no. 2: 151–75.

—— (1999): "Changing Party Organisations in Germany: How to Deal with Uncertainty and Organised Anarchy." *German Politics* 8, no. 2: 108–25.

—— (2000a): "Die Strategie(un)fähigkeit politischer Parteien," in: Nullmeier, Frank, and Saretzki, Thomas, eds.: *Jenseits des Regierungsalltags. Strategiefähigkeit politischer Parteien.* Frankfurt/Main/New York: Campus, pp. 187–206.

—— (2002b): "Überhitzung und Abkühlung: Parteien und Gesellschaft im Zeitenwechsel der siebziger und achtziger Jahre," in: Schildt, Axel, and Vogel, Barbara, eds.: *Auf dem Weg zur Parteiendemokratie. Beiträge zum deutschen Parteiensystem 1848–1989.* Hamburg: Ergebnisse Verlag, pp. 138–69.

—— (2003): "Parteiendemokratie in der Krise, oder: Das Ende der Mitgliederparteien," in: Glaab, Manuela, ed.: *Impulse für eine neue Parteiendemokratie.* München: CAP, pp. 17–36.

Wiesenthal, Helmuth (2003): "Beyond Incrementalism—Sozialpolitische Basisinnovationen im Lichte der politiktheoretischen Skepsis," in: Mayntz, Renate, and Streeck, Wolfgang, eds.: *Die Reformierbarkeit der Demokratie. Innovation und Blockaden.* Frankfurt/Main/New York: Campus, pp. 31–70.

German Trade Unions: Partners for Reform or Trapped in Nested Games?

Josef Schmid and Christian Steffen

German trade unions are currently in trouble. Even though in comparison to Britain they still are mighty actors in terms of organization and effect, this is of little consolation. They currently live on the substance of past successes that were achieved under significantly more favorable framework conditions. However, those conditions cannot be reproduced today. The crisis that is frequently diagnosed can be described by a whole set of indicators: decrease in membership figures, deficits in representation, the partial erosion of existing instruments of regulation, and diminishing political influence. These indicators go along with the difficult search for room for maneuver under changed economic, political, and social conditions. Old certainties and established patterns of action have partially vanished without clear alternatives having developed yet. The expression "navigating without a compass" comes to mind.

The institutional embedding of the DGB (*Deutscher Gewerkschaftsbund*, German Trade Union Association) Unions into the political economy of the Federal Republic contributed considerably to their strengthening, yet in times of change this requires adaptation in many interrelated fields of action and arenas.[1] German trade unions are many things at the same time: Instrument of the safety of real wages, agency for the setting of collective standards, reinsurance against employer arbitrariness, expert pool for labor relations, supervisor of conflict and conciliation processes, and projection screen for sociopolitical interests (Wiesenthal and Clasen 2003: 21). Similar to the situation in Great Britain, the relationship with the former natural partner in the political arena, the Social Democrats (SPD), has to be described as severely strained—at least since the point when the SPD took governing responsibility. Additionally the unions' public image has reached a historical low point which causes concerns for the unions because their image as a force of block-ade and an organized preserver of privileges provides the breeding ground for critical discourses which reach beyond the critique of the material policies of the unions such as the call for wage increases, and question central elements of the whole system of industrial relations portraying the need for compre-hensive structural reform.

In this article we have three main objectives: (1) to identify the changes of context and environment which the unions are confronted with, (2) to discuss the concrete organizational and programmatic challenges stemming from this, and (3) to describe the strategic options available to the unions and the inherent strategic dilemmas. The actor-centered perspective taken here is probably the best way to explain the problems of German unions. Borrowing from Scharpf's actor-centered institutionalism (1997) and Tsebelis' theory of nested games (1990) we try to show that an appropriate understanding of the current malaise of the DGB unions can be achieved only from a holistic per-spective that considers all areas of activity rather than focusing on only one specific problem. Such a holistic perspective reveals that seemingly "simple" problem-solving strategies which have been suggested to the unions, not least by academic observers, are often completely inadequate or unrealistic.[2]

"NESTED GAMES"—OR THE RATIONALITY OF THE IRRATIONAL

The starting point of Tsebelis' approach (1990) is the apparent tension be-tween the seemingly irrational behavior of individual or collective actors, and the assumption that these actors must, nevertheless, be seen as adopting a ra-tional choice approach. Tsebelis (1990: 119ff.) illustrates his theses for the ex-planation of apparently irrational behavior using various examples, such as the question why British labor delegates refuse to renominate members of parliament for new elections, even if they have good electoral chances. In such cases, labor activists have referred to these MP's lack of radicalism, and risked the loss of the mandate or even supported liberal or conservative can-didates instead. Following Tsebelis, this behavior of actors needs closer analysis because simply describing these activists as "fanatics, lunatics, and extremists" is of little help and the premise of rationality ought to be main-tained. Tsebelis explains this behavior that initially appears as irrational—if one sees parties as office seeking—by pointing to the fact that the game de-scribed (candidate nomination at the local level) has to be seen in relation to other (power) games at the local or regional party level, as well as to games between the local or regional and the national party levels. All (nested) games considered, what at first sight might appear as political suicide turns out to be an attempt of the lower party ranks, firstly, to discipline candidates and, secondly, to signal to the party leadership what kind of political positioning is desired. Therefore, this behavior can be interpreted as perfectly rational.

Tsebelis analyzes situations in which participants in specific negotiations choose a course of action that—seen from an outside perspective—falls short of what a strict application of rational choice would suggest. He attributes this finding to two causes: Firstly, the participants often do not "play" in one, but several "nested" games at the same time; and secondly, the observer (or, the public) does not take this into consideration, and makes judgments with regard to only one game failing to pay attention to the "nested" situation (limited focus). Tsebelis conceptualizes the games as separate, but stresses the interdependence between them. It can be assumed that, on the one hand, negotiations in other arenas are always subconsciously considered, and that the results obtained have concrete consequences for negotiations in other arenas or games. The latter entails that—depending on specific context conditions—it is often hardly possible (or rational) to aim at maximum success in arena A (however defined) if this implies a degradation of the result in arena B. This "trade-off" means that, under certain conditions, the sum of all individual decisions made appears to be suboptimal. However it is just as conceivable that under more favorable conditions a positive-sum game develops in a sense that the results in arena A have positive effects on the results in arena B, illustrating a possible spectrum between a virtuous and a vicious circle.

A common reproach towards the trade unions is that they are neither capable of solving their organizational problems nor manage to constructively support the necessary structural reforms in social policy and labor relations. However, this perception is misleading in two ways: First, it would imply a quasi "context-free" negotiation arena, thus underestimating the complexity and interdependence of decision-making processes and, reversely, overestimating the actual room for maneuver. Second, it would constrain its evaluation of outcomes to singular isolated areas instead of viewing the output as a product of a nested decision-making process touching various arenas. This process takes place in the ambivalent context of social responsibility and specific organizational interests.

Applying game theory to this case involves the problem that the players are conceived as uniform entities, an assumption that holds true only in rare cases. Scharpf defines a player as an individual or a group capable of making a rational choice between several alternatives (strategy); a game exists if the "outcome" also depends on the strategy of other players (Scharpf 1997: 2ff.). As regards the behavior of trade unions much points into the direction of the participants (particularly the trade unions themselves, but also the employers

and the government) being everything but homogeneous players. Strategy selection is in itself already a laborious bargaining process. Therefore it appears
necessary to supplement the game-theoretical perspective with a micro-
political approach. The "games" of the trade unions are not only "nested," but
they are accompanied by intense inner-organizational conflicts.[3] But which
"games" do the unions actually play?

Owing to their multi-goal orientation, German unions are—concerning
material policy—particularly active in three arenas:

(1) In the field of labor relations and tariff policy as an economic actor;
(2) in the field of general and work-related social policy, the latter both by
    institutional integration[4] and by political lobbying[5]; and
(3) in the field of organizational development (especially member acquisi-
    tion), which is both the precondition for, and product of, successful
    union politics.

The further analysis will therefore focus on the question how German trade
unions acted in these arenas at different points in time, in how far socioeconomic conditions supported or constrained successful "playing," which
"increasing returns" and negative externalities occur(red) in the interplay of
the arenas, and why since the 1990s the unions have had difficulties with replacing their incremental "muddling through" by a coherent policy. A closer
analysis of the role of the trade unions in the political economy of the Federal
Republic of Germany must take a historical approach, because in each phase
of its existence, the system of labor relations (and thus the role and function
of the trade unions) not only corresponded with specific context conditions,
but was also by and large reproduced by them. Table 10.1 distinguishes five
different phases in the development of German industrial relations and outlines some basic features of each phase. Our analysis emphasizes the role and
function of unions in a differentiated institutional network. It understands
unions as "embedded institutions" which shape their (institutional) environment (economical and political) and are at the same time shaped by it.

THE ROLE OF THE TRADE UNIONS IN THE
POLITICAL ECONOMY OF THE FEDERAL REPUBLIC OF GERMANY

Looking Back to Golden Days

After the end of World War II the trade unions were rather quick to find their
role in the new political and economic system. One lesson they had learned
from the interwar years, and especially from the bitter experience of collec-

Table 10.1. Industrial Relations in Germany—Phases Since 1949

Phase	Governmental Impact	Trade-Unions	Employers' Associations	Collective Bargaining System	Classification
1949–1955	- framework legislation for industrial relations	- fast increment of members - offensive politics	- fast increment of members	- inordinate system	**trial-phase**
1956–1966	- defensive stabilization of industrial relations	- stagnation in number of members - positive wage-drift	- growing union density	- dominance of association top-level	**golden age I**
1967–1977	- trade-union supportive reform of the Works Council Constitution Act - social pact	- active wage-and new formation policy - growing union density	- number of members at high level	- regionally centralized conflict cooperation	**golden age II**
1978–1989	- employer supportive change of the AFG 116 (Arbeitsförderungs gesetz, law for promoting employment)	- ability to manage conflict situations testified (1978 and 1984) - policy of reduction of working hours	- declining capability of obligation	- realignment of industrial relations	**conversion-phase I**
1990–	- "Vereinigungskorp oratismus" (reunification-corporatism) - reduction of wage continuation	- declining union density - Alliance for Jobs (1995–2001) - strike defeat in Eastern Germany (2003)	- declining union density and number of members	- oscillation between cooperative and conflict-oriented crisis policy - strengthening of the company level	**conversion-phase II**

Source: Wolfgang Schroeder 2000 (slightly modified)

tive impotence during the collapse of the Weimar Republic (Schönhoven 2003: 50), was that they had to overcome internal conflicts about the strategic course to take. Despite the initial socialist rhetoric of the socialization of the means of production, a pragmatic cooperative strategy was generally accepted relatively soon. The historical circumstances in Germany proved favorable to a "historic compromise" between labor, capital, and politics. Common sense suggested—not least against the background of East-West competition—that general acceptance of the "new" system could be promoted through the development of strong welfare services and the introduction of democratic elements into the economic system. Put differently, the trade unions accepted that the national economy was based on privately owned means of production, while capital should make concessions in welfare and labor rights and participation (especially codetermination). Taking a labor movement perspective, Schneider therefore describes the period from

1950–1965 as the combination of "social progress and political defeat" (Schneider 2000: 270).

In a context of rapid economic growth, a specific economic system, structure, and institutional order developed which was retrospectively described with the term "German model" (Kitschelt and Streeck 2003: 3). Following Streeck's analysis (Streeck 1999), this model rests on high world market integration of the national economy, a considerable measure of national market regulation, a high general wage level, and low wage inequality. In addition there are continuity warranties in the form of contribution-based social insurance systems aiming at status guarantees, and privileges for the social partners, such as participation rights and quasi-political functions. The function of the German trade unions in the German economic system may be summarized as follows:

> [I]n regard to their market and cartel functions all German trade unions saw it as their main task to conduct—in antagonistic cooperation—wage bargaining with the employers and the employers' associations that resulted in settlements which considered industry-specific competition demands, supported economic rationalization and innovation, and which turned macro-economic necessities like low inflation, high growth rates and international competitiveness into their own aims. This micro- and meso-corporatism was supported by the institutional embedding of the unions in the area of corporate governance, constitutionally secured by collective bargaining autonomy written down in Article 9 of the Basic Law, the existence of sectoral collective agreements as well as the increasing legalization of the industrial relations. (Esser 2003: 77)

The state (or more specifically, the government) benefited from this arrangement, since the stable contract and bargaining relations between labor and capital brought about economic stability, labor peace, and calculability, fostering overall specific as well as diffuse support.[6] Over two decades a productive combination of three factors evolved: the innovative application of advanced technology (in the secondary sector) across the country, the development of high worker skills (fostered by the dual system of work training), and an egalitarian wage distribution on a comparatively high level (see Schroeder and Weinert 1999). The latter pushed and legitimated the application of modern and capital-intensive production techniques, which again resulted in a leading position for Germany. This combination turned out to be so successful that until the beginning of the 1990s, Germany had a top position in added value per capita (per employee). As far as incremental innovation in high technology is concerned (especially in the secondary sector), the country was highly competitive, and to some extent it still is.

However, the economic success cannot be attributed exclusively to the labor market parties and the institutional structure of the German economy. To a large part it was also the product of a favorable worldwide economic situation. The end of World War II marked the beginning of a phase of growth and prosperity (*Korea Boom*) that gathered momentum, inter alia, from the massive demand and need for reconstruction, the Fordist mode of production, a homogeneous industrial class, the low degree of (financial) economic internationalization, comparatively high state autonomy in regulation, and a favorable demographic structure in comparison to today. On the basis of these conditions—and embedded into the framework of an expansive welfare state—a virtuous circle developed that consisted of increases in productivity, rising wages, buoyant consumer demand, rising company profits and investment, growing productivity, and so forth. In this economic system, a kind of "universalization" of the workers' interests came about from which the unions derived their extensive claim on representation and influence. Given the circumstances outlined above, this was not problematic. Due to the comparatively homogeneous occupation structure, and the favorable economic situation, the unions did not strive for particular, but universal aims, and by and large the policy devised for the members coincided with general societal aims. The importance of these exceptionally favorable conditions for the three arenas of union acting highlighted above may be summarized as follows:

(1) In the area of labor relations and collective wage policy, the institutional structures developed along with the rights and privileges of the labor market parties involved. The overall structure of labor relations proved to be an efficient cornerstone of the German model insofar as, together with a rising degree of institutionalization (or rule observance), the efficiency or economic performance of the system could be boosted at first.[7]
(2) In the arena of general social politics, the situation of economic growth and a favorable demographic structure enabled the incremental extension of the existing social security system. This secured privileges and was financed by contributions. It is evident that the unions did not resist this, especially as social politics increasingly took over complementary functions such as reducing the labor force or stabilizing the labor market.
(3) In the arena of organizational problems, there was at that stage no need for finding solutions because there had not been any problem. Membership figures increased—which was probably not so much a sign of the need for protection, but indicative of the homogeneous working population increasingly participating in the rising national income. Strategic debates and differences were suspended by organizational

success or they fell victim to a kind of "Keep going!" (*Weiter so!*) mentality.

The Slow End of the Golden Era and the Shock of Unification

Towards the beginning of the 1970s, the German Model showed its first cracks as the phenomenon of increased unemployment appeared, yet they could be managed politically—at least at the beginning. Among the causes of the crisis was the rise of the oil price, the partial transformation from an industrial economy to a service-oriented society, along with the differentiation of working lives (erosion of the blue-collar working class), and rising international interdependence accompanied by intensified global competition (globalization). In this setting the question arose whether the positive virtuous circle, due to a changed economic and social basic environment, might be destroyed between the pressures of union action and economic performance (Esser 2003: 79).

Taking a look at the critical and stabilizing elements it can be concluded that the economic system of the Federal Republic has taken an exceptional position in international comparison because the economic capacity rests to a large extent on the efficiency of the secondary sector (mechanical engineering, vehicle construction, steel and electrical industry, chemistry). The high share of workers in this sector and the success in global markets (high export quota) are indicators of this comparative success. Imbedded in an institution structure that according to the *Varieties of Capitalism* approach was described as a "coordinated market economy" (also called Rhineland capitalism) (Hall and Soskice 2001), economic success was based on incremental product innovation.[8] This development took advantage of the strengths of coordinated capitalism using its long-term perspective and added, due to the overall positive performance, to its legitimacy.

To put it crudely, it was possible to sell "superior," and thus in the sense of yield increasing, "more expensive" products on international markets, which again opened up scope for real wage increases. In order to remain competitive, despite the increased pressure, a company policy of rationalization and productivity improvement was carried out that successively lowered the need for labor—partly supported or at least tolerated by the unions. Some serious decisions were made by the labor market parties to face the pressure of the so-called "whip of productivity." First the unions (IG Metall) tried to spread the volume of work on more employees by vigorously promoting and finally imposing a weekly working time of thirty-five hours.[9]

Furthermore, a certain practice was introduced which Streeck (2003) described appropriately as "welfare corporatism." Over a long time social politics functioned as a kind of lubricant, which provided crucial support to the German model: Social and labor market policy were used as an instrument to reduce the overall size of the workforce. A social policy that was basically family policy motivated, along with the so-called "bread winner model" (separate taxation for man and wife, coinsurance of family members, poorly developed systems of child care etc.; cf. Sainsbury 1999), reduced the number of women in the labor market and led to a low labor force participation rate of women. Furthermore, since the 1970s, social and labor market policy were used increasingly to facilitate the early retirement of older employees, especially from the traditional mining, steel, and building industries, without loss in personal income. A look at the figures illustrates this trend: In 1970 the activity rate of the older male employees (aged fifty-five to sixty-five) was still 80.1 percent; by 1995 this figure had dropped to 52.7 percent (OECD 1997)—a decrease that is drastic even in a cross-European comparison (Mares 2001: 208).

Resources offered by the BA (*Bundesanstalt für Arbeit*, Federal Office for Employment) for passive and active labor policy were used to mitigate the effects of economic structural crises and fiscal bottlenecks of the federal budget and in the mandatory health insurance (Trampusch 2003: 7). The widening gap between shrinking and expanding sectors of the economy seemed to call for intervention; the overall favorable economic (and also demographic) situation generated the necessary resources, and the trade unions had the necessary channels of influence to exert pressure on the parties and the ministerial bureaucracy (committee for work and economics). In order to socially cushion processes of structural change, work councils and corporate management developed "intelligent" solutions to externalize the costs of inevitable employment restructuring. Initially all parties involved benefited from this practice: The trade unions could defend a generally high wage level despite the industrial reserve army and increasingly severe economic problems; the employers could speed up the process of structural change (and rejuvenate their staff) while avoiding major social conflicts (see Mares 2001: 208–209); and the state could reduce the problem of unemployment and thereby relieve the national budget (rising wages lead to rising income through the unemployment insurance). In slightly simplified terms the broad interest coalition between the state and the labor market actors led to a successive increase of nonwage labor costs (negative effects on employment). Practices such as early retirement schemes, active labor market policies, and structural adjustment measures culminated in a massive increase in expenses that skyrocketed again after unification and its economic consequences (Simonis 1998).

After 1989 the BA needed subsidies of 1.93 billion DM and a contribution rate of 4.3 percent of the earnings, the latter rose to 6.5 percent in 1993, and the Federal Republic had to settle a deficit of 24.4 billion DM. Between 1989 and 1993 the BA's expenses had tripled (from 40 billion to 110 billion DM), with Eastern Germany receiving 46 percent of this. As regards public employment schemes, about five hundred thousand people from East Germany participated in further vocational training measures, four hundred thousand took part in active labor market schemes, three hundred seventy thousand received compensation for having to work short shifts, and eight hundred thousand retired early or received a retirement bonus and finally retired early (BT Drucksache 12/7130: 29).

When in 1993 unemployment increased in West Germany, too, the costs increased at an even higher rate. Rising expenses and income losses became so heavy a burden on the federal budget that a continuation of these politics became economically unviable and increasingly triggered unwanted secondary effects such as the further rise of unemployment because of excessive non-wage costs (e.g., Scharpf 2000), rising interest rates, and falling investment into education and research. Accordingly the interest coalition outlined above showed first cracks. With the transfer of the law for promoting employment (*Arbeitsförderungsgesetz*) into the SGB III (*Sozialgesetzbuch* III, social security statutes) a whole range of further instruments for active labor market politics was created. At the same time, however, various reforms to the law on part-time work for elderly people (1996, 1999, and 2000) as well as the pension reform of 2001 provided evidence of a gradual departure from the old path (see Trampusch 2003: 24, 2004). The newly introduced *Tarifvorbehalt* (collective agreement reservation) shifted responsibility back to the social partners insofar as the reduction in retirement pay (in cases of early retirement) nowadays has to be compensated for by collective wage agreements put down in agreements on part-time employment of the elderly and pension schemes. In the meantime, especially medium-sized companies (which have limited opportunities for cutting or passing on costs) are complaining about high nonwage costs, and break out of the employers' alliance. The state is obliged to reduce the budget (deficit), not least because of the European stability pact, and the unions had to realize that the policy of reducing labor force has become so cost intensive that even their regular clientele is threatened by secondary effects.

Until today central elements of the German model are in place and effective, however costs for maintaining the status quo have risen substantially. While in the secondary sector large enterprises which are strong in exports continue to cope well with the existing institutional structure, small and medium-sized companies as well as enterprises in new branches like the Internet economy are increasingly under cost pressure (Menez and Steffen 2005). Additionally, the group of those who benefit from the model has be-

Table 10.2.   Changes in Basic (Macro-) Economic Data in Germany 1970–2002

	1970	1980	1991	2002
Unemployment rate in %	0.7%	3.8%	7.3%	10.8%
Share of public debts of GDP in %	38.8	30.9	39.7	58.1
Gross domestic product per resident at prices of 1995 in €	14.800	19.100	24.300* 21.400**	24.100
Contributions to social insurance in %	26.5	32.4	35.8 (1990)	41.3
Social expenses in % of GDP	25.1	30.6	28.5	32.1 (2001)
Employees in thousand	26.817	27.948	31.360* 40.126**	32.549* 40.550**

Source: Federal Office for Statistics

*   former West Germany
**   unified Germany

come a shrinking part of the economy that will decline even further in relative importance (regarding effects for employment) in line with structural changes and continuing improvements in productivity. As has been outlined in more detail earlier in this volume (e.g., chapters 1 and 2), growing competition in the world markets and high cost pressure, higher labor costs, debts as a result of unification,[10] and mass unemployment have in recent years reached a critical level. In many areas further adaptations will be necessary that will change—and already have changed—central cornerstones of the German model. Table 10.2 summarizes the development of some key indicators of social and economic development from the early 1970s to the early 2000s.

CHANGE IN FRAMEWORK CONDITIONS AND CHALLENGES FOR THE UNIONS

Organizational Challenges

Müller-Jentsch writes that (German) unions are only capable of acting if, firstly, they have the ability to recruit new members, secondly, can manage to aggregate their members' interests and, thirdly, can oblige them to act on behalf of the organization (Müller-Jentsch 1997: 119–37). A look at the empirical findings reveals that from the unions' perspective there is reason for concern in all three dimensions. The most obvious sign of organizational problems is the steady decline of membership figures which, notwithstanding a short-lived increase in the wake of unification, has been ongoing since the beginning of the 1990s. While in 1980, the joint membership of all DGB unions had added up to a total of 7.8 million, and the figure had gone up to 11.8 million shortly after unification (1991), by 2002 membership was down below the level of 1980 (7.7 million). It is sometimes asserted that the German unions, because they are strongly embedded into the institutionalized system of labor relations, are less dependent on high membership numbers (Heery 2003). From a strictly comparative perspective this may actually be true, but it should not be overinterpreted. The failed strike by the IG Metall in the new German *Länder* (in the spring of 2003) provided evidence that in case of a weak member base the potential for mobilization is insufficient and "system relevant refusal" cannot materialize.[11] In addition, a loss in members automatically means a loss in revenue. Even though the German unions are still relatively affluent as far as assets are concerned, they are currently running structural deficits because in many cases fixed costs are eroding the substance. The service sector union ver.di seems to be in a particularly critical situation: The combination of an inflated body of functionaries (due to the merger), protection against dismissal until 2007, and the loss of about two hundred fifty thousand members since 2001 alone, turn out to be a heavy burden. Figure 10.1 illustrates the membership decline over the decade to 2002.

Figure 10.1.   Unionization of the German Workforce (DGB, DBB, DBG)

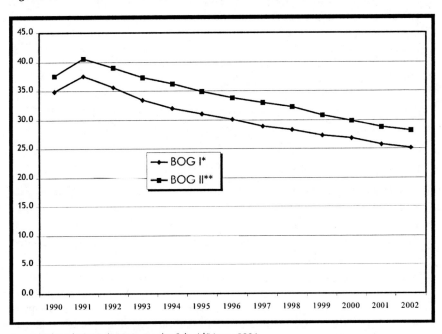

Source: Schroeder/Weßels 2003; see also Schmid/Menez 2004.
 *BOG I: Union members in employment.
**BOG II: Union members including those without employment.

It seems important, however, not to discuss diminishing membership figures simply as an empirical phenomenon or in regard to the impact they have on the overall functioning of the organization, but to understand the underlying causes of this obvious lack of attractiveness. These are a profound crisis in the areas of representation, acceptance, and legitimacy. Hassel and Leif (2002) make a point that the development of the IG Metall membership by and large runs parallel to the overall size of the (shrinking) sector, but they go on to say that there is still much reason for concern. The overall number of retired members within the German unions is steadily rising (2002: IG Metall 20 percent, ver.di 17 percent); the average IG Metall member is already fifty-two years of age. While 40 percent of all people employed in the metal industry are union members, this figure drops to 15 percent for the white-collar employees, primarily in large companies. The percentage of younger members has dropped by 50 percent over the last ten years. Today only 5 percent of the union members are under twenty-five, which seems particularly problematic for recruitment as it is much more difficult to encourage people to join at a later stage of their working life. In summary, the average IG Metall union member is rather old, male, and a blue-collar worker in a large company doing business in a sector that is shrinking in terms of personnel employed. Table 10.3 provides an overview of the membership of the DGB's unions.

The middle- and long-term implications of this are evident. Whatever the reason may be, the unions have obviously not managed to open up to new labor market segments. Possible explanations could be a lack of appropriate recruitment strategies, short-term cost-benefit calculations, or simply complacency. However, despite the fact that the increase in so-called *precarious jobs* and the perceived decline of social protection should provide favorable

Table 10.3. Membership of DGB Unions 2002

	IG BAU	IG BCE	GEW	IG Metall	NGG	Gew. der Polizei	TRANSNET	ver.di	DGB-totally
Workers total	439.046	654.814	0	2.187.829	189.344	8.022	70.539	853.062	4.402.656
Employees total	48.844	178.879	95.570	456.144	56.006	20.171	39.450	1.553.729	2.448.793
Civil servants total	1.912	0	122.637	0	0	156.714	38.132	229.495	548.890
youth total	51.637	60.988	40.357	218.256	23.196	34.849	15.481	142.303	587.067
male total	423.434	673.609	84.576	2.150.527	147.524	152.285	236.427	1.384.235	5.252.617
female total	66.368	160.084	180.108	493.446	97.826	32.622	60.944	1.355.888	2.447.286
Altogether	489.802	833.693	264.684	2.643.973	245.350	184.907	297.371	2.740.123	7.699.903
in %	6.4	10.8	3.4	34.3	3.2	2.4	3.9	35,6	100

Source: Deutscher Gewerkschaftsbund, www.dgb.de

conditions for unionization, the times when people joined the unions almost automatically are long passed. In the words of Streeck the "patrons" are an endangered species (Streeck 1987).

The organizational dilemma sketched by Wiesenthal (1993) quite accurately describes the difficulties the unions have to confront in the face of pluralization of work life and life styles. The ostensible dilemma between recruitment, representation, and effectiveness is at the center of intense debates within the trade unions themselves. In principle everybody agrees that the unions have to open up towards new groups of workers and employees. However, when it comes to assessing the strategic value of concrete measures, this broad consensus begins to crumble. Especially the IG Metall turns out to be rather conservative. The primary focus of the organization remains on the blue-collar worker in the West German metal industry which has always been their core constituency. From the internal logic this seems rational in the sense that a forced opening towards new groups implies uncertainties about prospects of success, costs, and especially trade-offs. Opening up to new groups would probably demand just those policy compromises which would not be in the interest of the core constituency or that may even threaten their privileged position.[12] The IG Metall for example could not bring itself to demand a minimum wage in its area of responsibility. While this would improve incomes in some areas (e.g., call centers), it is feared that the new minimum wage would be misused by employers as the basis for wage dumping. From a more theoretical perspective it seems indeed highly problematic to synthesize the heterogeneous demands of a pluralized labor world into concrete programs and to implement them. Unions do not only have to operate in a context of decreasing scope for the allocation of benefits, but as Streeck puts it: "The times of all standardized solutions for standardized problems are over" (Streeck 1987: 477). Unions in almost all other European countries—with the exception of the Scandinavian countries where very strong institutional organizational incentives exist—are facing similar problems. A blue print solution does not seem to suggest itself despite the fact that unions in Great Britain and Italy, for example, managed to slightly increase their membership. Coming back to the Müller-Jentsch statement mentioned above, there are clear signs that the preconditions for effective action in all three dimensions—recruitment, interest aggregation, and the obligation to act—have deteriorated significantly, and there is good reason to believe that this trend will continue in the foreseeable future.

Challenged Labor Relations

Despite the fact that the German system of labor relations can by and large be characterized as being surprisingly resilient (Schroeder 2000: 391), some developments can be observed that point into the direction of a more or less "hidden" or incremental change. These can best be described with the terms of flexibilization and a shifting of decision making to the company level. At the same time a creeping erosion of existing regulatory mechanisms can be observed which takes the form of external erosion, since the overall scope of collective sectoral agreements is diminishing. Figure 10.2 illustrates the changes in the degree of organization for companies and employees in the old and the new *Länder*. The overall percentage of employees covered by collective bargaining stands at 63 percent in West Germany and 44 percent in East Germany. In the whole of Germany, about 60 percent of all employees are directly covered by a collective agreement. In addition to that, 16 percent of employees benefit indirectly (at least partially) from the regulations because their companies use the collective agreements as a guideline. This clearly demonstrates that collective bargaining still plays a dominating role in the (West) German wage settling system—despite premature reports on their demise (Kohaut and Schnabel 2003: 199; Rehder 2003: 18).

With regard to the shift of competences to the company level a study published in 2003 is instructive: it reveals a quantitative as well as qualitative growth of plant level management—management pacts that gain importance through the expansion of issues dealt with (see Rehder 2003). The local pacts are looking for integrated solutions for issues such as personnel policy, wage policy, the regulation of management relations, product organization, investment decisions, and the interpretation of company codetermination. They make full use of the existing legal maneuvering space and in some cases they actually go beyond the scope defined by the formal rules. This shift to the

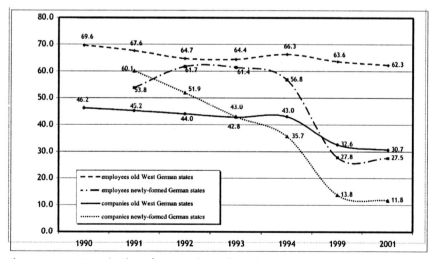

Figure 10.2. Organization of Companies and Employees in the Employers' Association Gesamtmetall

local level has its origin not only in the general management opposition towards collective agreements but rather reflects a (factual or perceived) need to adapt to changing circumstances more swiftly. Only recently Porsche announced record profit margins whereas in the same week Opel couldn't avert massive dismissals despite mass protests. The need for differentiation becomes more pressing as the economic performance of companies within the same sector may differ substantially.

As already indicated, one cannot speak of a disintegration of the existing structures. It seems more adequate to speak of institutional conversion or institutional overlapping. A possible interpretation concerning these developments is that new elements are added to the old outdated structures in such a way that already existing negotiation arenas experience an increase in scope and competences. Whereas questions concerning the allocation of working time have always been (co-)decided by the work councils, recently hard wage issues were included into their negotiation spectrum, sometimes even outside the already existing opening clauses. In this context, it cannot come as a surprise that in some instances this practice has led to conflicts between the union and a company against the will of the staff.[13] The strategic dilemma is not hard to see: The unions think in macro-economic categories and try to prevent any open breaches of the collective agreements in order to maintain their regulatory powers at the meso-level, whereas the employees' primary interest at the company level is, invariably, job security.

The failed IG Metall strike in the spring of 2003 in the new German *Länder* also reveals a growing rift between work councils and the union. Despite the fact that the union headquarters in Frankfurt offered different explanations, the failure was not due to interference by politics, but rather to deficits in mobilization at the plant level and fierce protests by several work council leaders in the important West German car industry. As the surveys of the Future Debate clearly indicate, IG Metall members do commonly not regard the reduction of working hours as a priority. The impact of the strike quickly reached the West German car industry which, due to new technologies in management and production (e.g., "just in sequence" and a low vertical range of manufacture), is very sensitive regarding supplier absence. Work council leaders and some union officials openly questioned the industrial action thereby showing a rift in the allegedly united union. Against the backdrop of high unemployment and increasing competition the necessity of high wage increases is hard to communicate and hard to achieve. In addition, the importance of wage (and social) politics as an instrument of competition has risen insofar as the common European currency increases transparency and comparability. All attempts by the European unions to develop a common guideline for their wage policy to avoid dumping at the expense of other economies can be described as a failure.[14] In summary, one has to come to the conclusion that the unions face considerable pressure to develop new instruments of collective bargaining. Changes in the social and economic environment are taken into account insofar as opening clauses in existing frameworks are increasingly used to take pressure off the system.

Socio-political Challenges

As shown in the discussion of the German model, the trade unions depend to some extent on the established social welfare institutions and the protection offered by them. The existing arrangements help them to maintain their position within the system and to have an impact on the formulation and implementation of concrete policy. Also, the welfare institutions alleviate the consequences of structural change, and thus reduce the pressure on the unions to take action.[15] However, the German trade unions do not pursue commonly shared social programs. Still, the normative overall concept of social justice and democratic participation remains their lens through which all attempts of welfare reform are seen and which determines the unions' ability and willingness to reach agreements. While the unions claim to be the "social conscience" of the country, it should not be surprising that they are, first and foremost, committed to the interests and demands of their core membership.

In the last few years conflicts over social policy reforms became more and more the subject of intense struggles between the unions and the government. Until the 1980s it seemed possible to find common solutions on the basis of win-win strategies. In the 1990s, in the face of structural budget deficits and negative externalities, conflicts intensified.[16] In fact, the unions themselves began to realize that the demographic developments, the economic weakness (together with high unemployment), and the costs of German unification renders reforms inevitable. However, the policy suggestions they are making are largely incompatible with the reform agendas discussed by the political parties and academics (see Engelen-Kefer and Wiesenhügel 2003). Closer analysis of their remedy for the German disease reveals to what extent the unions are sticking to their own principles: The high nonwage management costs are interpreted as being the result of a too narrow base of income, a lack of top-down redistribution, and, by implication, weak purchasing power. The expansive welfare state is seen as a competitive advantage, and all remaining problems such as the unfavorable demographic development, can supposedly be solved by fostering economic growth.

Crucially, the reform debate between the unions and the government lacks a shared perception of the problem which, in turn, makes agreeing to compromises rather difficult. The conflict between the DGB[17] and politics escalated when in March 2003 Chancellor Schröder presented his *Agenda 2010*, a policy proposal that included suggestions for several different fields of social and economic policy (see chapters 2, 6, and 9 in this volume). The trade unions, especially IG Metall and ver.di, almost instantly heavily criticized the program, and refused to discuss the matter. They publicly announced that they would stop the government's plans or even compensate them by higher wage demands. However, participation at central events of protest was disappointing for the unions. In response to this, the unions even cancelled their participation at some events, and it soon transpired that the unions' radical rhetoric had only created far-reaching expectations which could not be fulfilled. The unions had thus conveyed the public image of organized weakness.

So it is obvious that the unions are challenged in the area of social policy in many different ways. Table 10.4 summarizes key changes in the political and institutional environments which the German unions have to confront. The times when the production systems could be directed in a way as to generate rents for their members have come to an end. New answers to (different) social problems have to be developed and communicated. Possible starting points are to be found in the practical connection of wage politics and social politics, e.g., strengthening the qualitative dimension of collective agreements (qualification, innovation), improving the compatibility of work and child raising, working towards better security for people in precarious jobs, devising company-based retirement schemes, and developing offers for

Table 10.4.   Changes in the Unions' Political and Institutional Environment in Germany

	1960s–1980s	1990s
Federalism	cooperative federalism; 11 Länder; predictable relations	16 Länder; increasing involvement and interdependence of the levels (Beteiligungsföderalismus); (distribution) conflicts
Party system	Three relevant parties, moderate polarization, consensus on welfare state	Five relevant parties, growing polarization in matters of welfare policy
Economic structure	Adjustment of (life) circumstances; crisis management (structural change) within corporatist arrangements	Increasing heterogencity, huge prosperity gap; market-driven adaptation; regional marginalization
Bank and financing	House bank system; low importance of (international) financial markets	Erosion of house bank system, enforcing of investment banking; liberalization of financial markets; growing dependency on international markets (internationalization of property)
European Integration / Globalization	Low degree of integration and globalization; national state as central level of reference for relevant agents	State loss of autonomy and regulation; intensification of competition; communitarization of financial policy (ECB)
Variety of capitalism	Coordinated market economy (Hall/Soskice); Rhineland capitalism, German model	Significant tendency of erosion; partial rapprochement to Liberal Market Economy

the employment of elder workers. However, while this might be a way out of the (organizational) crises, it presupposes the willingness of the organization to reform and its capability to act.[18]

TRADE UNIONS ACTING UNDER COMPLEX CONDITIONS

It is obvious that the German trade unions can hardly be described as protagonists of far-reaching reform initiatives. One may regret this, but it shouldn't come as a surprise. Due to a bundle of reasons they have a hard time fulfilling the diverse expectations they are confronted with. Employers, politics, and academics publicly voice demands for low wage settlements, more flexible legal frameworks in the field of management relations, and cooperation regarding the large-scale welfare state restructuring. The common diagnosis that the unions refuse to cooperate reflects, in our view, the distorted outside perspective highlighted by Tsebelis that only refers to a singular aspect without giving appropriate consideration to the nested character of the games. Put differently, it is tacitly implied that the unions are acting in only one (isolated) arena, and there is no appropriate understanding of the multiple demands and wide-ranging potentials for disappointment. In addition to this, it is unrealistic to demand the unions to accept low wage settlements and welfare retrenchment, simply because massive trade-offs exist between the different policy arenas. This interplay of social policy, wage agreement, and plant politics was illustrated by the example of the early retirement policies, which were favorable for unions and employers. Finally, the maneuvering space of unions is constrained by problems at the organizational level.

In view of these challenges the current union strategy seems to be to "deny and defend." The risks of radical change seem to be feared greater than the imminent threats emerging from a long-term process of erosion. To point up those ideas, the following conclusions can be drawn for the different arenas:

(1) In the area of management relations and collective bargaining, the unions are faced with the great challenge of coping with the increasing heterogeneity of the economy. As the examples of Porsche and Opel showed, the performance even in one sector are divergent in a way that poses an obstacle to regulation at the meso-level. Thus, the unions face the choice of either allowing local bargaining and the differentiation of collective agreements, or to encourage the exit of companies from employers' associations. While the former entails the danger of losing long-term collective regulation capability, the latter would actually lead to the same effect by the loss of a bargaining partner. Furthermore,

given the context of mass unemployment and low growth rates, it is hard to implement real wage increases which, in turn, leads to disappointment of at least parts of the membership in prospering firms and sectors.

(2) In the area of general social politics, it is evident that a further expansion of social security currently cannot be financed. Indeed, it is much more realistic to expect further selective cuts in the system of social insurance. The financing by means of shared employers' and employee's contributions proves to be an obstacle to employment. This shows clearly that social politics should not be "misused" as a means to reducing the labor force. As a consequence, the unions are forced more than ever to justify their policy regarding the effects on the labor market.

(3) In the area of organizational problems, the unions are challenged in multiple ways. The question they have to answer is how, in the face of the challenges described, they can put together a coherent and attractive offer for their members that does justice to the heterogeneity of the environment without disintegrating into arbitrariness. Due to the diversity of challenges and the high level of uncertainty on the possible stages of reform, a reorientation of the unions' work has so far not been achieved. This is illustrated by the characteristic ambivalence between blockade and will to compromise.

The analysis of these challenges from a "nested games" perspective reveals the dilemma of the large DGB unions. While in the golden era win-win strategies could be achieved in all three arenas, the unions are now caught up in a vicious circle. Table 10.5 illustrates this by succinctly sketching and contrasting the starting points of the three "players," i.e., the trade unions, the employers, and the state.

For the trade unions we may note: Even if they were to achieve wage increases and the further extension of social welfare, they would probably have to pay for this success by forced exit as well as a tightening of the employment crisis. This would backfire on them, at the latest, when jobs within their competence were lost and their capability to regulate be restrained to shrinking sectors of the economy. On the other hand, it seems questionable how an attractive offer for the existing and potential members might be constructed on the basis of self-restraint regarding wage increases and active cooperation regarding cuts in the welfare state. Anyway, any such approach would demand at least a partial abandonment of traditional patterns of action, routines, and ideology. Against the background of the changes which have been dis-

Table 10.5. Dilemmas of Employers, the State, and Trade Unions

	Employers		Politics / State		Trade unions	
Starting point	∞	increasing competition pressure / domestic market / globalization	∞	Necessity for budget consolidation	∞	decreasing organizational degree / erosion of membership base
	∞	very heterogeneous profits and resulting different needs	∞	Shrinking margins for distribution	∞	shrinking margins for redistribution
	∞	conflicts of interests between large enterprises and SME	∞	Mass unemployment	∞	decreasing capability of regulation
	∞	unequal distribution of "costs" of the existing system of regulation	∞	Deficits in social security	∞	conflicts between and among DGB unions
	∞	decreasing degree of organization (very weak in the new Länder)	∞	Restricted capability to act, especially as a consequence of unification (large difference in prosperity between now 16 Länder)	∞	partial disintegration of old certainties and routines / no development of clear alternatives yet
	∞	Exit-Option	∞	European integration / globalization	∞	tensed relations to politics (loss of a common agenda)

cussed throughout this chapter, the only possible way forward for the unions is one that is, admittedly, still rather vague and in need of further development in line with the interests of existing and potential members: the unions have to go beyond the one-dimensional logic of redistribution and focus on areas such as job security, qualification, collective social politics, regulation of precarious jobs, and so forth. In all of this, it goes without saying that they always have to remain a kind of "counter-power."

Finally, the question of the unions' potential for blockading necessary reforms needs to be addressed. This question arises irrespective of the arguments which have been presented so far and of the thesis that in the present circumstances the unions have only a limited scope of action. It seems that the unions' blocking or even veto position is actually rather weak. This claim shall be substantiated, firstly, by a brief analysis of the unions' formal and informal veto points with special emphasis on the latest developments in the fields of social reforms policy and labor relations; and secondly, through a closer look at, and evaluation of, other possible veto points and veto players. Despite their overall privileged position in the political and economic system of the Federal Republic, the formal veto points of the unions are restricted to the field of collective bargaining, which is their very own field of action.

However, the potential for obstruction in bargaining, or even using obstruction as a means of extortion, is increasingly limited as excessive demands will fall back on the unions and cause unintended effects such as employers leaving employers' associations, the use of exit options, work force shedding, bankruptcies, conflicts between unions and work councils, and so forth. Union leaders (e.g., IG Metall chairman Peters) may announce that they will fight to compensate cuts in social services by achieving significant wage increases, but no matter how the aims of the unions' bargaining policy are defined, the fact of restricted room for maneuver cannot be denied.

With regard to social policy the unions simply lack the formal competencies to have things their way. The DGB takes part in many arenas of self-administration, however, only at regulated, lower administrative levels. A closer look at the Federal Agency for Employment can illustrate this point: The unions have their place in the newly founded board of directors and take part in the decision-making process at all levels concerning the arrangements of active labor market policy, but they are not able to determine the overall budget for such measures. Thus, it is conceivable that due to shrinking budgets and efficiency deficits, the resources for an active labor market policy will decrease in the medium term, which will also reduce the influence of self-administration. Despite the fact that out of 251 SPD parliamentarians 186 are union members, the traditionally close link between the unions and Social Democrats has been put under severe pressure, because the unions' policy is directed towards their own clientele, while the Social Democrats follow a course similar to that of Tony Blair's New Labour. The initial hope within the DGB that many problems concerning the unions' future would be resolved once the Kohl government was defeated turned out to be premature; the unions woke up in a different reality.

In conclusion one might say that due to unfavorable conditions the unions cannot really capitalize on their formal or informal rights and potentials to an extent that would justify describing them as a real veto power. This obviously leaves the question who, if not the unions, can be held accountable for Germany's lasting inability to implement comprehensive reforms. In search of a plausible explanation, it seems appropriate to place more emphasis on factors such as the intense party competition[19] and the German variant of cooperative federalism. In addition to these, clear resistance in the public to policies of welfare retrenchment is a third important factor. As various contributions to this volume have demonstrated, the majority of Germans are aware of the need for reforms, but enthusiasm cools down considerably if their own established privileges and entitlements are curtailed. The fact that Germany is an exception insofar as strong constitutional power sharing in the bicameral system coincides with influential associations (Czada 2003) is, of course, of importance, but as a primary explanation for reform gridlock, it assigns the unions a functional role which they cannot fulfill when the reform debates in politics are brought into the picture. Their radical rhetoric is, in this respect, more a sign of their own powerlessness or a means to combat uncertainty. Instead of blaming the unions, it might therefore be more promising to explore whether it is possible to engage them positively in the reform process by making use of their organizational resources and their know-how if, in return, they were granted additional rights that would secure their position and stabilize their organizations.

NOTES

1. Behrends et al. identified six strategic fields in which unions are active at the moment: (1) initiatives for acquiring members, (2) merger of unions and internal restructuring, (3) further development of industrial relations, (4) political participation, (5) alliances and joint action with social movements, and (6) extension of the international collaboration of unions (WSI Mitteilungen 9/2003). To this list one should add (7) day-to-day business, i.e., collective wage negotiations, company crisis management, etc., and (8) integration in the self-administration of the social insurance system.

2. In the following we will often refer to the IG Metall which is the union of the metalworking industry. Due to its strong position in the crucial metalworking and electrical industries it gained, at an early point of time, an unofficial leading position among the DGB unions. This manifested itself in the fact that wage agreements in these sectors had pioneering character for negotiations in other fields. This also helps to explain why the IG Metall has always considered macro-economic needs and performance when formulating its demands.

3. As we have demonstrated elsewhere (Schmid and Steffen 2004; Menez and Steffen 2005), the future debate of the IG Metall offers plenty of evidence of internal conflicts among the unions which could not be resolved in any lasting way.

4. Especially through the self-administration of the social insurances.

5. All major DGB unions maintain their own departments for social policy.

6. In this context, Katzenstein's ideas on the semi-sovereign state are instructive. Simply put, he argues that the relative weakness of the state leads to the formation of strong interests (especially trade unions and employers' associations). The latter relieve the state by acting on their own authority, and due to their de facto claim of representing the common interest, their behavior does not lead to the collision of sectoral interests and the common good (Katzenstein 1987).

7. Streeck regards 1969 as a turning point because the unions, pushed by their members, then adopted a more offensive allocation policy (Streeck 2003). However, even though it is correct that in the early 1970s wage increases of more than 10 percent were enforced (e.g., civil service), this did not imply any lasting departure from the wage-setting formula (growth and productivity) (Kädtler 2003).

8. In this context the house bank system should be mentioned as well as the interconnection of the economic elites in the so-called Deutschland AG, long-term cooperation between enterprises, the regulation of labor relations, etc. See also the "Varieties of Capitalism" debate by Hall and Soskice (2001).

9. However, the incremental reduction of overall working time per week was accompanied by a far-reaching flexibilization of working times, so that retrospectively it may be argued that the theoretically greater need of workforce was overcompensated by a "better fitting" use of labor.

10. The costs of unification cannot be overestimated in this context. For political reasons the immense costs could not be financed by tax increases; therefore, the adaptation of life conditions has been financed through the funds of social insurances and credits. The size of this challenge becomes clear if one just looks at the fact that the share of employees in the secondary sector fell from 50 percent to 20 percent only in three years—this equals the winding up of 50 years of industrialization (Wiesenthal 2003: 41).

11. The IG Metall correctly points out that in the ballot vote on possible industrial action more than 80 percent of its members voted for strike. However, these only represented about ten thousand of approximately one hundred twenty-five thousand workers in the metal and electrical industries between Leipzig and Dresden. The industrial action for the thirty-five-hour week thus turned into a traumatic experiences for the IG Metall which divided the workforce and led to dramatic scenarios of "strike breakers" having to sleep at the workplace, climb fences, etc.

12. The more specific interests are aggregated in order to gain relevance in the political system, the more does the position of the association move away from the ideal point of the single member. At the same time, an increasing number of members makes it more difficult to feed specific interests effectively into decision-making processes concerning society at large because they cannot be formulated as purposefully (Kittel et al. 2003: 83).

13. The example of the heating system producer Viessmann shows that the unions are in a conflict between their demand for regulation at the meso-level and the local needs or demands of the companies. When Viessmann's work council had agreed with the company on three additional working hours per week for free in order to avoid jobs being shifted into the cheaper Czech Republic, IG Metall filed suit at the industrial tribunals in Marburg and Frankfurt, arguing that the working time regulation of thirty-five hours fixed in the collective agreement had been violated.

14. Just recently the Dutch unions announced they would accept low wage increases (below a neutral range of distribution) in order to foster competitiveness and employment.

15. As regards self-administration, however, the continued extension of legislation in the field of social security has in recent years restrained their room for maneuver.

16. In this context, the distinction between expansion and cutback policies concerning the welfare state becomes relevant. The policies are based on completely different mechanisms and, in the latter case, lead to massive resistance by groups privileged by the status quo.

17. The chairman of the IG BCE, however, publicly stated that he supported the general line of the *Agenda 2010*; therefore, one cannot really speak of a coalition across all DGB unions.

18. We know from organizational sociology that the capability for organizational learning is restricted. Special challenges and innovative measures inside the organizations are required in order to overcome the cumbersomeness of organizational learning processes. Additionally, unions are "by nature" badly prepared for reform, because in protecting those dependent on wages against the dynamics of the market, their behavior is primarily reactive rather than proactive. On the one hand, this is charm of the trade unions, but it is also a factor that restricts their learning capacity (Müller-Jentsch 2003: 656).

19. In the past the unions could "exploit" party competition insofar that the oppositional alliance of SPD and DGB developed a considerable blockade potential. However, since Schröder's announcement that after any reelection the SPD would proceed with the reform agenda that was started by the Red-Green coalition, the unions are lacking a strategic political ally by means of which their influence can be raised to a higher level.

REFERENCES

Behrends, Martin, Hurd, Richard, and Waddington, Jeremy (2003): "Wege zur Transformation gewerkschaftlicher Organisationsstrukturen." *WSI Mitteilungen* 56, no. 9: 534–40.

Czada, Roland (2003): "Konzertierung in verhandlungsdemokratischen Politikstrukturen," in: Jochem, Sven, and Siegel, Nico A., eds.: *Konzertierung, Verhandlungsdemokratie und Reformpolitik im Wohlfahrtsstaat. Das Modell Deutschland im Vergleich*. Opladen: Leske and Budrich, pp. 35–74.

Deutscher Bundestag (1993): *Sozialbericht 2003*. Bundestags-Drucksache 12/7130.

Deutscher Gewerkschaftsbund, ed. (2003): "Mut zum Umsteuern. Für Wachstum, Beschäftigung und soziale Gerechtigkeit. Hintergrundpapier für die wirtschafts- und sozialpoliotische Reformagenda des DGB." 8 May 2003.

Döring, Diether, and Koch,Thomas (2003): "Gewerkschaften und soziale Sicherung," in: Schroeder, Wolfgang, and Weßels, Bernhard, eds.: *Die Gewerkschaften in Politik und Gesellschaft der Bundesrepublik Deutschland*. Wiesbaden: Westdeutscher Verlag, pp. 376–404.

Engelen-Kefer, Ursula, and Wiesenhügel, Klaus, eds. (2003): *Sozialstaat. Solidarisch, effizient, zukunftssicher. Alternativen zu den Vorschlägen der Rürup-Kommission*. Hamburg: VSA Verlag.

Esser, Josef (2003): "Funktion und Funktionswandel der Gewerkschaften in Deutschland," in: Schroeder, Wolfgang, and Wessels, Bernhard, eds.: *Die Gewerkschaften in Politik und Gesellschaft der Bundesrepublik Deutschland*. Wiesbaden: Westdeutscher Verlag, pp. 65–85.

Hall, Peter A., and Soskice, David (2001): *Varieties of Capitalism. The Institutional Foundations of Comparative Advantage*. Oxford/New York: Oxford University Press.

Hassel, Anke, and Leif, Thomas (2002): "Reformfähige Gewerkschaften. Zum Zukunftsprozess der IG Metall." *Gewerkschaftliche Monatshefte* no. 6: 288–304.

Heery, Edmund (2003): "Gewerkschaftliche Strategien gegen Mitgliederschwund." *WSI Mitteilungen* 56, no. 9: 522–27.

Kädtler, Jürgen (2003): "Tarifpolitik und tarifpolitisches System in der Bundesrepublik," in: Schroeder, Wolfgang, and Wessels, Bernhard, eds.: *Die Gewerkschaften in Politik und Gesellschaft der Bundesrepublik Deutschland.* Wiesbaden: Westdeutscher Verlag, pp. 344–75.

Katzenstein, Peter J. (1987): *Policy and Politics in West Germany. The Growth of a Semisovereign State.* Philadelphia: Temple University Press.

Kitschelt, Herbert, and Streeck, Wolfgang (2003): "From Stability to Stagnation. Germany at the Beginning of the Twenty-First Century." *West European Politics* 26, no. 4: 1–34.

Kittel, Bernhard, Obinger, Herbert, and Wagschal, Uwe, eds. (2003): *Politische Ökonomie: Demokratie und wirtschaftliche Leistungsfähigkeit.* Opladen: Leske + Budrich.

Kohaut, Susanne, and Schnabel, Claus (2003): "Zur Erosion des Flächentarifvertrags. Ausmaß, Einflussfaktoren und Gegenmaßnahmen." *Industrielle Beziehungen* 10, no. 2: 193–219.

Mares, Isabela (2001): "Firms and the Welfare State. When, Why and How Does Social Policy Matter to Employers?" in: Hall, Peter A., and Soskice, David, eds.: *Varieties of Capitalism. The Institutional Foundations of Comparative Advantage.* Oxford/New York: Oxford University Press, pp. 184–212.

Menez, Raphael, and Steffen, Christian (2005): "Gewerkschaften und soziale Innovationen. Die Zukunftsdebatte der IG-Metall unter der Perspektive organisationalen Lernens," in: Aderhold, Jens, and John, René, eds.: *Innovationen. Sozialwissenschaftliche Perspektiven.* Konstanz: UVK, pp. 131–48.

Menez, Raphael, Schmid, Josef, and Springer, Stephanie (2005): "Arbeitspolitik und industrielle Beziehungen. Begriffe und Veränderungstendenzen am Beispiel der Internetökonomie." *WeltTrends* 13, no. 47: 26–40.

Müller-Jentsch, Walther (1997): *Soziologie der industriellen Beziehungen.* Frankfurt/Main/New York: Campus.

——— (2003): "Gewerkschaften heute: Zwischen arbeitspolitischer Kompetenz und sozialer Gerechtigkeit." *Gewerkschaftliche Monatshefte* 54, no.10–11: 654–58.

Rehder, Britta (2003): "Betriebliche Bündnisse für Arbeit in Deutschland. Mitbestimmung und Flächentarif im Wandel." Frankfurt/Main/New York: Campus. Schriftenreihe des Max-Planck-Instituts für Gesellschaftsforschung Köln, no. 48.

Sainsbury, Diane (1999): *Gender and Welfare State Regimes.* Oxford: Oxford University Press.

Scharpf, Fritz W. (1997): *Games Real Actors Play. Actor. Centered Institutionalism in Policy Research.* Boulder/Oxford: Westview Press.

——— (2000): "The Viability of Advanced Welfare States in the International Economy: Vulnerabilities and Options." *Journal of European Public Policy* 2, no. 7: 190–228.

Schmid, Josef, and Menez, Raphael (2004): "Engagement in Berufsverbänden." in: Statistisches Bundesamt, ed.: *Datenreport 2004.* Bonn: Bundeszentrale für Politische Bildung, pp. 178–84.

Schmid, Josef, and Steffen, Christian (2004): "Evaluation der Zukunftsdebatte der IG Metall." Studie im Auftrag der IG Metall und der Hans-Böckler Stiftung. Unpublished Manuscript. Tübingen.

Schneider, Michael (2000): *Kleine Geschichte der Gewerkschaften.* Bonn: Bundeszentrale für politische Bildung.

Schönhoven, Klaus (2003): "Geschichte der deutschen Gewerkschaften. Phasen und Probleme," in: Schroeder, Wolfgang, and Wessels, Bernhard, eds.: *Die Gewerkschaften in Politik und Gesellschaft der Bundesrepublik Deutschland.* Wiesbaden: Westdeutscher Verlag, pp. 40–64.

Schroeder, Wolfgang (2000): *Das Modell Deutschland auf dem Prüfstand.* Wiesbaden: Westdeutscher Verlag.

Schroeder, Wolfgang, and Weinert, Rainer (1999): "Anmerkungen zum Wandel industrieller Beziehungen in Deutschland. Kontrollierte oder unkontrollierte Dezentralisierung?" *Zeitschrift für Politikwissenschaft* 28, no. 4: 1295–1317.

Schroeder, Wolfgang, and Wessels, Bernhard, eds. (2003): *Die Gewerkschaften in Politik und Gesellschaft der Bundesrepublik Deutschland.* Wiesbaden: Westdeutscher Verlag.

Simonis, Georg, ed. (1998): *Deutschland nach der Wende.* Opladen: Leske and Budrich.

Streeck, Wolfgang (1987): "Vielfalt und Interdependenz. Überlegungen zur Rolle von intermediären Organisationen in sich ändernden Umwelten." *Kölner Zeitschrift für Soziologie und Sozialpsychologie* 39, no. 3: 452–70.

—— (1999): *Korporatismus in Deutschland: zwischen Nationalstaat und Europäischer Union.* Frankfurt/Main/New York: Campus Verlag.

—— (2003): "From State Weakness as Strength to State Weakness as Weakness. Welfare Corporatism and the Private Use of the Public Interest." *MPIfG Working Paper* no. 3, Köln: MPIfG.

Trampusch, Christine (2003): "Ein Bündnis für die nachhaltige Finanzierung der Sozialversicherungssysteme. Interessenvermittlung in der bundesdeutschen Arbeitsmarkt- und Rentenpolitik." *MPIfG Discussion Paper* no. 1, Köln: MPIfG.

—— (2004): "Von Verbänden zu Parteien. Der Elitenwechsel in der Sozialpolitik." *MPIfG Discussion Paper* no. 3, Köln: MPIfG.

Tsebelis, George (1990): *Nested Games: Rational Choice in Comparative Politics.* Berkeley: University of California Press.

Wahlprogramm zur Bundestagswahl 2005 der FDP. http://files.liberale.de/fdp-wahlprogramm.pdf (28 December 2005).

Wahlprogramm zur Bundestagswahl 2005 von CDU/CSU. www.regierungsprogramm.cdu.de/download/regierungsprogramm-05-09-cducsu.pdf (28 December 2005).

Wiesenthal, Helmut (1993): "Akteurkompetenz im Organisationsdilemma. Grundprobleme strategisch ambitionierter Mitgliederverbände und zwei Techniken ihrer Überwindung." *Berliner Journal für Soziologie* 14, no. 1: 3–18.

—— (2003): "German Unification and 'Model Germany.' An Adventure in Institutional Conservatism." *West European Politics* 26, no. 7: 37–58.

Wiesenthal, Helmut, and Clasen, Ralf (2003): "Gewerkschaften in Politik und Gesellschaft. Von der Gestaltungsmacht zum Traditionswächter?" in: Schroeder, Wolfgang, and Wessels, Bernhard, eds.: *Die Gewerkschaften in Politik und Gesellschaft der Bundesrepublik Deutschland*. Wiesbaden: Westdeutscher Verlag, pp. 296–322.

WSI Mitteilungen 9/2003 "Mut zum Steuern. Für Wachstum, Beschäftigung und soziale Gerechtigkeit." Hintergrundpapier für die wirtschafts- und sozialpolitische Reformagenda des DGB, 8 May 2003, www.verdijugend-nsb.de/download/hintergrund/ 2003-05-8-Langfassung-ENDVERSION_DGB-Reformagenda.PDF (28 December 2005).

11

Participation, Innovation, and Efficiency: Social Movements and the New Genetics in Germany and the UK

Ian Welsh

This chapter situates German social movement activity in relation to issues of modernization and efficiency through a consideration of the emergent stakes associated with the "new genetics." It is argued that neoliberal globalization introduces significant issues for both the anatomy of "Big" science advances associated with the mapping of the human genome and social movement engagement with techno-science and associated social stakes. At the heart of this argument lies the increasing prominence of networks and network actors operating simultaneously at local, regional, national, and global levels in ways which increase complexity (Castells 1996, 1997; Urry 2003). The extensive canon of German theory relating to social movement engagement (Beck 1992; Habermas 1981; Marcuse 1964, 1968; Offe 1985) is set within the context of increasing participation within the "Alternative Globalization Movement" (Chesters and Welsh 2005, 2006; Welsh 2004). Analytically, it is suggested that the rise of network actors attenuates the utility of key approaches including the association of radicalism with margins (Marcuse 1964) and notions of "defensive" or "offensive" social movements (Habermas 1981). These systemic shifts in movement anatomy are intensified by the crosscutting nature of genomic science.

Biotechnology in the widest sense was identified as one of the critical areas for all industrialized societies during the 1970s (Bud 1993, 1995). The mapping of the human genome in 2000 foreshadowed efficiency issues as the publicly funded Human Genome Project and the private sector competed to complete the sequence. Initial confidence that mapping the genome would lead to cures for many fatal and chronic conditions reaffirmed the importance of competitive biotech sectors as components of knowledge economies. As such the efficient translation of "near market science" into product lines became a priority as agricultural genetics became a Europe-wide controversy. Implicitly and explicitly the threat of "red" (medical) genetics becoming contaminated by association with "green" (agricultural) genetics became a specter haunting political, regulatory, financial, and corporate players. Such fears were, if anything, intensified by the crosscutting nature of genomic science where animal genes can be tested within plant species and the boundaries between diagnostic and therapeutic techniques become blurred (Bowring, 2003). For Habermas the prospect of genetic enhancement techniques becoming available as individual free-market choices raises the prospect of a "neoliberal eugenics" (Habermas 2003: vii) requiring collective social engagement and, implicitly, social measures of efficiency.

The distinction between market efficiency and social efficiency is an evolving area which this volume codifies in important ways. In terms of this chapter key distinctions between neoliberal notions of efficiency and social efficiency are:

- Short Time Frames versus Long Time Frames
- Primary Focus on Individual Needs and Wants versus Collective Needs and Wants
- Public Involvement at Near Market Stage versus Public Involvement at R & D Stage

Given scientific uncertainty Habermas is arguing that serious engagement with "upstream" social concerns provides a firmer basis for development than the pursuit of short-term efficiency via commercialization. The idea that slower can be better, that public provision is central to market viability and that social contracts not flexible employment contracts secure efficiency represent significant themes articulated by a range of movement actors.

This chapter will elaborate each of the points introduced here demonstrating how multiple cultural and social framings of "efficiency" represent "hinges" articulating an emergent era of complex movement capacity building. This has major implications for established notions of social movement associated with national political opportunity structures and notions of efficiency based in economic, political, and business cycles.

SOCIAL MOVEMENTS AND GLOBAL NETWORKS

The status of the term "social movement" as a constructed and contested concept is a crucial starting point. The term "new social movement" which European social theory played a central role in establishing in the post-1968 era, intensifies and extends these stakes. In terms of German social movement Schmidt-Beck (1992) notes the dismissal of (new) social movements as "a myth" created through academic usage by Stöss (1984). Melucci also recognized the limitations of the term imposed by competing definitions, interpretations, and methodological modes of engagement but considered it futile to seek an alternative (Melucci, 1984, 1996). Weivorka has revisited these issues in an attempt to move beyond the concept of social movement. The notion of network movements (Chesters and Welsh 2006) underpinning this chapter is an attempt to refine the terms of engagement with the movement milieu.

A comprehensive review of German social movement theory is clearly beyond the scope of this chapter (see Schmidt-Beck 1992). The key issue relevant here can be presented thematically via the chronological consideration of important contributions by Marcuse, Habermas, and Offe. In *One Dimensional Man*, Marcuse (1964) argued for the centrality of marginal social actors as agents of social change, identifying groups central to the post-1968 "New Left" cultural Marxism. Following events in 1968 Marcuse (1968) placed renewed emphasis on such agency despite his earlier arguments about "repressive desublimation" appearing to reaffirm the potential for systemic social change to come about through marginal actors. Marcuse and other advocates of the "New Left" elevated cultural actors to a position of revolutionary agents of social change because of their marginality and capacity for critical reflection. This theoretical radicalism left the tensions between resistance, reform, or revolution unresolved as correspondence between Adorno, Horkheimer, and Marcuse over the student occupation of the "Frankfurt School" reveals (Adorno and Marcuse 1999).

This "ambivalence" is reflected in Habermas's output on new social movement actors from *Towards a Rational Society* onwards. This is reflected nowhere more clearly than in his short 1981 paper where he placed "the life world" at the center of movement activity dividing the movement milieu into "defensive" and "offensive" forms and identifying feminism as the sole offensive force. For present purposes the essential points are that the contemporary movement milieu is configured in a manner which means that marginality is no longer a *necessary* defining feature of social movement actors and a milieu where the either/or of defense or offense has been transcended. Network actors increasingly constitute a "radical flank" through crossover memberships that enable established movement actors to create room for engagement once the limits of their access to formal political opportunity structures are reached.

A consideration of Offe's impressive (1985) article on German new social movements reveals precisely how and why this is the case, laying the necessary groundwork for an appreciation of the place of cultural and social contestation within the contemporary milieu. This prescient paper was firmly based in an appreciation of the changing social structure of West Germany during the postwar era leading to confrontation between citizens and neocorporatist programs of techno-scientific modernization. Nuclear power was the most prominent example of such confrontation between corporatist technocracy and citizens and continues to mobilize massive expressions of social movement and public opposition in Germany.

Offe thus addressed social movement formation and engagement in terms of the cultural and political alignment of *emergent* social and cultural concerns and activities present within the prevailing fabric of West German society.[1] The rise of new social movements within West Germany was an urban phenomenon associated with growing middle-class activism among those in occupations "distant from the point of production." The development of Citizens Action Groups (CAGs) organized around "community" issues[2] contributed to the antinuclear movement and the emergence of *Die Grünen* as a formal political party. The important point for present purposes is Offe's argument that these new social movements represented an attempt to "selectively modernize" modernity's values. This position effectively transcends the "marginal or mainstream" and "defensive or offensive" dualisms of Marcuse and Habermas and prefigured Beck's notion of a "sub-politics" (Beck et al. 1994).[3] The attempt to achieve this selective modernization "exceeds the limits" of the established system reconfiguring it in a systemic fashion. Schmidt-Beck's (1992) argument that the consolidation of these social forces as both a formal political party and a vibrant range of new social movement actors constituting a permanent standing movement milieu with both formal representation and a "radical flank" is a tacit recognition of a durable systemic change. The growing sense of residual responsibility for the actions of elected representatives noted by Offe (1985) found expression through both formal political engagement and movement participation.

In the contemporary context this theoretical discourse is important because of the massive shift in the social structure of postunification German society, the rise of the knowledge economy, and pressures to introduce neoliberal modernization agendas in the spheres of science, technology, and wider social and public policy. There are supra-national political and policy pressures associated with the EU and higher order global institutions, such as the World Bank, International Monetary Fund, and G8 which increasingly shape national agendas. These global pressures, including deregulated markets and flexible labor strategies, have been accompanied by a growing emphasis on governance as an adjunct to both corporate responsibility and good government (Held et al. 1999; Baker 2006).

These global agendas impact upon German Social Movement Organizations (SMOs) and political parties which emerged from the CAGs of the 1970s and the international SMOs such as Greenpeace and Friends of the Earth which have been a substantive focus of academic work on NSMs. Work in these areas has focused upon the impact of such NSMs within prevailing political opportunity structures (POS), policy formation and outputs, and the formalization of "green knowledge" (Jamison 2001; Rucht 2003; Rudig 1990). Since at least the 1980s such work sat alongside other significant movement forms less easily formalized as unitary movements with clearly defined boundaries. Here, the peace and antinuclear movements were prime examples of diverse movements (Welsh 2000). Such diverse movements sit uneasily with definitions of social movement excluding coalitions and emphasizing the centrality of a collective identity (Diani 1992) having significant crossover memberships and political affiliations (Schmidt-Beck 1992; Welsh 2000). At a global level neoliberal ascendancy during the 1990s was accompanied by a new wave of grassroots activism emphasizing forms of self help and direct action (McKay 1996, 1998; Notes from Nowhere 2003) articulating issues of social and economic justice (Bullard 1990) on an increasingly global stage (Chesters and Welsh 2005, 2006).

This Meluccian "movement of movements" arguably embodies the selective modernization of modern values identified by Offe in 1985 but exists alongside less progressive movements such as the US Patriots (Castells 1997), the resurgence of neo-Nazi movements in Germany, and econationalist movements in the Former Soviet Union (FSU) and Eastern Europe (Tickle and Welsh 1998). This diversity of movement mobilizations empirically demonstrates the Janus-like nature of social movement underlining the point that the term does not inevitably denote progressive social change.

A central tension thus emerges between forms of social movement advocating centralized and often authoritarian positions, frequently associated with nationalist expressions, and those seeking to broaden and deepen democratic processes through the recognition of difference, the extension of inclusion; and increased citizen participation in the pursuit of social agendas. Within Europe and Germany ATTAC, a group originating in France through Le Monde Diplomatique, perhaps best represents this latter category (Waters 2004). ATTAC's advocacy of the Tobin tax on large financial transactions and a universal social wage are part of a program for social justice consolidated within the World Social Forum and the ESF. These networks also engage established "sub-political" (Beck et al. 1994) actors including NSMs, trades unions, and a diverse range of other established and emergent actors.

The importance of changes in social structure for the composition and anatomy of the movement milieu were emphasized towards the start of this chapter. One recent account relates the transformation of German social structure to widely accepted periods of public political engagement (Mayer and Hillmert 2003). This paper depicts a nation with a high degree of welfare security and the social reproduction of established class locations throughout the 1990s. The analysis, based on a range of macroeconomic factors, also reveals an increase in female educational and labor market activity levels; the continuation of extra-marital household and family forms; delayed entry into parenthood; an increase in people of pensionable age; and the existence of an indeterminate number of "globalization losers." Unification was, of course, the most significant single event making Germany more Protestant and atheist, more elderly (as a result of early retirement), more unequal in income distribution, and more dependent on the welfare state. At first glance there is nothing particularly remarkable about this in terms of political orientation and action. But growing female educational achievement and labor market participation in the context of short-term contracts combined with greater voter volatility resonate with UK experiences leading to decreases in formal political participation and increased public involvement with a wide range of civil society actors redolent of Tarrow's postulated social movement society.

This effectively leaves both formal political and social movement actors operating in an environment where coalition building and networking become central concerns. The resultant networks are symptomatic of the process of emergence associated with Meluccian "latency periods" during which collective stakes are negotiated and declared by apparently marginal actors (Chesters and Welsh 2005). This is the context within which the emergent politics of genomics is unfolding amidst the spectre of contamination from "green" genetics, which Jones and Salter characterize in particularly stark terms.

Although the body politic of human genetics and health may at present appear to be unaffected by the political virus which has so virulently attacked green biotechnology, it would be unwise to assume immunity (Salter and Jones 2002:337).

GENOMICS AND NEAR MARKET SCIENCE

The mapping of the human genome in 2000 raised the prospect of an extraordinarily diverse range of new genetic technologies with major implications for therapeutic, reproductive, diagnostic screening, and enhancement techniques. This diversity of applications is further compounded by the potential for multiple uses of any particular technological application. This diversity of overlapping applications and impacts renders genomic science a creator of assemblages which crosscut boundaries and categories central to established regulatory stances, public understandings, scientific disciplines, and critical campaigning stances (Irwin and Michael 2003). The risk potential of synergistic effects formalized by Beck (1992) in relation to the "natural" environment is extended to the composition of "human nature" itself (Habermas 2003). Throughout the 1990s biotech companies competed with dot.com companies in attracting significant amounts of venture capital as *The Biotech Century* (Rifkin 1998) approached. Within the EU, member states with a significant science base, including the UK and Germany, were potential beneficiaries of a new long wave of global technological progress and profit generation.

The linkages between modernization, progress, and efficiency with the biotechnology frontier were particularly prominent in the UK with Prime Minister Tony Blair acting as a prominent advocate of biotechnology despite significant expressions of concern, opposition, and *support* within the public sphere. This public ambivalence is a feature of both German and British publics and underpins the wide variance in opinion recorded in Eurobarometer polls. While there are some discernible divides in public opinion in both the UK and Germany, with higher degrees of skepticism over agricultural (green) applications compared to medical (red) techniques, ambivalence persists amidst the absence of any clear consensus on socially acceptable applications, regulatory structures, and degrees of upstream public influence. In the UK the recourse to direct action strategies, by road protestors, animal rights, peace and antiwar activists, have resulted in significant legal limitations upon rights of assembly and the covert use of state security services within the social movement milieu (Chesters and Welsh 2006: especially chapter 4). The efficient application of biotechnology thus impinges upon the role of "civil disobedience" seen as central to the effective social dynamics of representative democracies by Habermas (1985).

German press responses to the new genetics reflect this wider societal consternation as familiar boundaries and values become the subject of "parameter collapse" (Ardener 1989) as established meanings and orientations are confounded by scientific developments. German media coverage of the successful cloning of "Dolly the Sheep" illustrate this with *Der Spiegel* contrasting the lamb as symbol of "devout nativity" with the "lost innocence of science" while other sections of the German press used themes such as the "bestialization of science" and the "preliminary stage of Frankenstein labour creatures" (Einsiedel et al. 2002: 322; see also Bauer and Bonfadelli 2002). As scientific techniques introduce increasingly sophisticated interventions in human subjects and nascent humans, consternation and ambivalence have deepened as publics seek to define acceptable limits and boundaries (Kerr et

al. 1998). If anything, these concerns intensify in the face of commercial genetic diagnostic techniques purporting to identify individual predispositions
to pathological medical and lifestyle conditions.[4]

In summary biotechnology has been represented as the next great scientific
and technological revolution ushering in new cures and founding new industries while simultaneously calling into question established categories of
meaning relating to individual identity, kinship, and species being. The associated scientific knowledge and technical details are complex, heightening
debate about the ability of publics to understand and engage with the issues.
Notions of interest representation in this domain cannot be easily reduced to
knowledge stakes, however. Given that many of the applications of this
knowledge remain ill-defined it is difficult to identify the full range of associated social stakes, for example.

The assumption that individuals can be and are sufficiently informed to
formulate "interests" in the face of such open-ended commitments to techno-
scientific trajectories remains a fundamental problem confronted by interest
representation models linked to established political opportunity structures
(Wynne 1982). These concerns are intensified when the scientific knowledge
underpinning such commitments is developing rapidly, intensifying the importance of recognizing that scientific knowledge is the formalization of *uncertainty* and *contingency*. The premature commodification of such knowledge through near market science approaches risks launching products
underpinned by epistemologically questionable premises with weakly formalized social impacts. Such dilemmas typically impact upon movement
milieus as "latency periods" (Melucci 1989, 1996) during which movement
actors negotiate individual and collective stakes through active networking
(Diani 1992).[5] This is consistent with Habermas's call for social closure in the
face of indeterminate techno-science.

This call for a sustained and open-ended public debate on human genomic
applications draws upon the work of Jonas (1985), arguing that genomics represents an irreversible "intervention in a complex, self-regulating process,
leading to consequences which we cannot control" as genetic products "com-
mit something to the stream of evolution in which the producer himself is carried along" (Habermas 2003: 47). The current rate of progress in genetic engineering is seen as the main obstacle to such a debate as it "threatens to
steamroller [. . .] ethicopolitical opinion and will formation" (ibid.: 18). This,
combined with the potential for a neoliberal eugenics where "decisions would
be transferred, via markets governed by profit orientation and preferential demands, to the individual choice of parents and, on the whole, to the anarchic
whims of consumers and clients" (ibid.: 48) represents a threat to human
species being. While Habermas's arguments are pursued at a high level of

philosophical abstraction he also recognizes the importance of concrete sites of contestation and issue definition and it is here that emergent network actors become important.

Before discussing the significance of such network actors in the context of German and EU modernization agendas it is useful to summarize another key element in Habermas's argument. Habermas is clear that while medical and therapeutic uses of genomics are controversial ultimately it is the "upstream" issues of genetic enhancement that have to be engaged with in order to arrive at durable measures of social acceptability. Confronted by open-ended techno-scientific commitments that remain indeterminate such social and moral compacts represent the highest form of certainty available in developing genetic techniques.[6] Habermas thus presents a highly abstract argument advancing what is addressed here in terms of social efficiency within the network movement milieu. German and UK movement engagement with both green and red biotechnology thus assumes a position of analytical centrality and it is to this that we can now turn.

GREEN-RED BIOTECHNOLOGY MEETS GREEN-RED SUB-POLITICS

Purdue's work (2000) reveals the potency of small network actors in terms of their impacts upon formal political decision-making processes associated with green genetics within the EU. In terms of patent legislation and green genetics this qualitative engagement demonstrates the role of numerically small network actors utilizing "weak ties" (Granovetter 1973) with MEPs and more formalized "lobby" groups to frame issues and stakes within the EU's legislative process. Purdue also demonstrates the sophistication of such actors in terms of their "strategic positioning" (Blühdorn and Szarka 2004) decisions. Key network actors knew that a bad compromise would be easier to overturn within the EU conciliation process and left MEPs to their own devices before engaging in any significant lobbying. Their subsequent campaign included an emphasis on "The human gene issue" which mobilized "the churches and medical lobbies" which were crucial in the fall of the legislation in 1995 (Purdue 2000: 32). Another example of civil society actor influence, this time from engaged academic commentators, was the adoption of Levidow and Tait's definition of "precautionary" and "preventative" (Patterson 2000: 325).

Public sensitivity to biotech issues contributed to the formation of The European Group on Ethics (EGE) which plays a central role in addressing the complex stakes associated with the new genetics. While it has been argued that EGE have prioritized ethical issues associated with access to human genetic materials for research and development process (Welsh 2006), it also formalizes wider issues with implications for efficiency and social justice. Here, EGE argue that "science and technology must increase—and not decrease—freedom and choice for everyone." Further, EGE call on "this civilization to show more active generosity than nature and tradition show. This means that science and technology should strive to alleviate the suffering, inequality, injustice and discrimination that tradition and nature have brought out" (EGE 2000: 3–4).

In the early stages of engagement EGE declared difficulty in identifying relevant "stake holders." Despite this apparent lack of public engagement, work in the UK[7] rapidly identified a range of active groups, organizations, and individuals. These included patient and disability groups, increasingly regarded as Health Social Movements (Brown and Zavestoki 2004), as well as specialist campaigning groups such as Human Genetics Alert and Genewatch. Beyond these emergent actors established SMOs like Greenpeace and FOE were also increasing the attention given to red genetics following their active engagement with green domains. Ethnographic interviewing within these networks underlined the presence of both concerned citizens and concerned scientists attempting to make sense of collapsing boundaries. One particularly clear example can be seen in medical diagnostic techniques for known genetic conditions with disability groups framing this "advance" as a "threat" given the assumed linkage between a positive test result and termination.

In the UK the termination of a pregnancy on grounds of a "harelip" in 2004 further fuelled debate about the definition of a "viable/valuable" life and the place of diversity and difference within societies. The German and UK public spheres can thus both be regarded as ambivalent towards human genetic applications, particularly those lying "upstream" where the pace of technical innovation raising the prospect of "regulatory lag." Within this the stances of engaged groups within the movement milieu represent early formalizations of stakes which in many cases are informed by direct experience.[8] Such Anglo-German groups are actively networked beyond the confines of the EU.

German involvement in this is significant with Berlin serving as a network hub to a global gathering of ninety civil society activists representing seventy organizations from thirty countries in 2003.[9] Convened under the title *Within and Beyond the Limits to Human Nature: The Challenge of the New Human Genetic Technologies* by the Heinrich Böll Foundation in collaboration with the Institut Mensch, Ethik und Wissenschaft and the US Centre for Genetics and Society the meeting addressed themes reflecting Habermas's philosophical concerns. These included: balancing attention between future technologies introducing inheritable genetic modification and existing techniques enabling sex selection; linkages between reproductive genetic technologies and global health inequalities in terms of health related R & D priorities; and the importance of ensuring the representation of a wide range of civil society inputs in the face of expert dominated debates.[10]

That such a meeting took place demonstrates the presence, in microcosm, of the kind of discursive engagement by concrete actors envisaged by Habermas. In the era of Castells' *Network Society* such meetings are integrated within sets of nested networks. These constitute iterative processes which negotiate meaning and begin the process of negotiating and declaring collective stakes (Chesters and Welsh 2006). In the current context the 2003 Berlin meeting networked into the 2004 World Social Forum (WSF) in India and the WSF affiliated European Social Forum (ESF) meeting also held during 2004 in London. A process of cumulative network amplification commences within the "shadow realm" (Welsh 2002) outside formal channels of interest representation, governance initiatives, and consultative fora such as those convened by the EGE and bodies such as the Nuffield Council of Bioethics in the UK.

In this manner the network movement milieu engages with the temporally distant issues which tend to be subordinated to more immediate concerns within dominant discourses. As such these are niches of informed public engagement representing critical[11] sub-groups articulating what can be readily dismissed as minoritarian concerns. However, the sum of these minoritarian concerns embody in their specificity the components of the ethico-moral renegotiation of post-genomic species being sought by Habermas, making them important expressions of emergent social concerns. The extension of this process within the London ESF meeting reveals how such network extension and amplification take place and becomes articulated with concerns of efficiency.

Tangible German network connections to the London ESF include the involvement of *The International Network of Engineers and Scientists for Global Responsibility* (INES www.inesglobal.com), a workshop run by Reprokult (see www.reprokult.de) and more than eight hundred individual German pre-event affiliations. Within the London ESF science and technology policy was engaged within terms of systemic public influence over EU agendas and the implications of human genomics. While these were separate streams within a program including over one thousand sessions both addressed the implications of neoliberal measures of efficiency in the context of deregulated market relations (for an extended treatment see Welsh et al. 2005).

Werner Braun of the Max Planck Institute, a previous Director of INES, considered that "neoliberalism destroys society, cultures and nature," and argued that the "nucleus" of critical scientists from the 1968 generation must be transformed into the "critical mass" needed for a globally responsible science. Issues formalized included the corporate appropriation of university research agendas; insecure labor markets for the two million EU science work force; dominant military R & D agendas; and profit orientation. These themes were reflected by representatives of scientific and technical trade unions in terms of the impact of short-term employment contracts and relatively low postgraduate entry salaries. One female speaker illustrated these impacts through her decision to abandon a career in bench science for school teaching as this made her parental ambitions more credible. In her view neoliberal labor market conditions were undermining the stability and growth of the science base by neglecting the life cycle aspirations of scientists. A deepening of this trend would further jeopardize the social reproduction of the scientific labor force.

Speakers emphasized the centrality of scientific and technological innovation to social and economic change, the emancipatory role of science since the seventeenth century, and the traditional association between "neutral" scientific knowledge and progress. These themes were then juxtaposed with recent controversies (Chernobyl, BSE, GMOs, and infected blood supplies); the short-termism associated with private capitals' need to secure prompt returns on investment, and the "penetration" of both public and private domains by techno-scientific agendas. A progressive response required the "social control of science via scientific citizenship," an area requiring both "concepts" and the "tools" despite the plethora of "experiments" in this area (particularly those modeled on the Danish Consensus Conference). INES called for the coordination of initiatives by scientists across Europe to create a "network that can mobilize in physical space."

The EU's 6th Framework Programme was declared an "unaccountable" project "conceived by experts" intensifying the commodification of science by harnessing it to the economic and political goals of neoliberalism. In France an insecure and fragmented scientific workforce had lobbied for "legal rights" within the EU, a struggle in which stronger links to citizens through attention to wider issues was urgently needed. The resolution of these problems was seen as providing greater public control over science. Here, discussion revolved around issues of public representation within science policy formulation; the accountability of the policy process itself; the priorities expressed in existing EU science policy commitments, most notably the "science and society" program established during the EU funding of Framework 6 programme, and given increased prominence within the research priorities of Framework 7 (the Lisbon agenda). In general, the discussion was characterized by a determined attempt to work within the WSF leitmotif "Another World is Possible" and identify some specific policies that would be compatible with this aim. The outcome was a clear emphasis on locating EU science policy within a global context, addressing the "needs" of both the industrialized "north" and the "emergent" south. Three dominant themes coalesced within this:

- Promoting sustainable development to address immediate social needs by prioritizing locally defined stakes;
- Reform of labor market conditions within the EU science-base to reduce the influence of private funding coupled with an increase in citizen influence on policy agendas;
- The need for permanently constituted local feedback mechanisms to secure public input as an iterative phenomenon.

Significantly activist-orientated sessions convened by Reprokult, Genewatch, and other SMOs also identified the location of human genomic techniques within a neoliberal corporate ethos as a major concern. There was thus a significant degree of symmetry between established radical science, trade union and newer network movement actors within the ESF. Habermas considered that the era of techno-scientific corporatism was an attempt "to bring society under control in the same way as nature by reconstructing it according to the pattern of self-regulated systems of purposive-rational action and adaptive behaviour" (Habermas 1971: 117).[12] The contemporary movement milieu is engaging with a prevailing neoliberal axiomatic by reasserting the primacy of the social and models and measures of "efficiency" prioritizing life cycle rather than business cycle needs.

EFFICIENCY IS POSSIBLE

In the context of an aspirational EU-wide knowledge economy within which the science base plays a key role the systemic shifts outlined here have major implications. The EGE envisaged "a European civilization with a new kind of values involving a new concept of citizenship [. . .] a more direct and active participation of citizens in debate and public life" utilizing information technology to produce a participatory culture, "without which the building of Europe would be meaningless" (EGE 2000: 27). As detailed earlier this model of active citizenship was seen as running in parallel with the prioritization of citizens' human dignity over the appropriation of genetic material for biotechnology applications. Together these twin tracks underpin a form of citizenship consistent with European values antithetical to the dominant U.S. neoliberal prioritization of national economic interest and freedom over individual rights (Welsh et al. 2005).

Within the contemporary social structure of Germany the adoption of scientific, labor, and wider public policy stances consistent with a neoliberal approach to efficiency would further impinge upon both the biological and social "life worlds" of citizens. In this context the adoption of social movement repertoires of action by sections of the population not normally associated with forms of direct action, renders Tarrow's notion of the social movement society more tangible. Germany's long-standing consolidated movement milieu, the active presence of network movements, and the impact of neoliberal agendas on the life worlds of economically active young females combined with a growing retired population have the potential for widespread and diverse network actions. Such actions simultaneously defend old rights while militating for the establishment of new ones capable of delivering forms of efficiency consistent with the social ambitions expressed most formally through the EGE.

In terms of the realization of techno-scientific trajectories as product lines and established techniques the alignment of R & D agendas with citizens' aspirations and moral values would *contribute towards* greater public support for the science base. This kind of social efficiency would improve scientific, technical, and economic efficiency of a distinctly European form characterized by *planning* through dialogical exchange rather than top-down initiatives. Biotechnology applications have long term implications requiring an extended period of evaluation if the initial unknowns embedded in the multiple exchanges of *both* genetic material and meaning attached to bio-tech product and process are to be deciphered before products become widely dispersed through markets. To adopt such a stance *requires* a social efficiency approach subordinating shorter term economic measures of efficiency to secure longer term social, scientific, technical, and economic goods. German social movement actors pursuing such ends are now nested within European and global activist networks in an evolving process of hybridization which is transforming the movement milieu.

While governance initiatives, mainstreaming, and public consultation exercises have proliferated across the EU the impacts of such exercises upon "upstream" political and policy outputs remain opaque. Leaving aside the resultant issues of trust this dominant discourse of inclusion and consultation has not been translated into meaningful structures and provision. Prominent activists who are repeatedly called upon to participate in such events amidst their already pressing schedules speak openly of being "consulted to death" while organizers bemoan poor public uptake. In the UK, where flexible specialization has been driven through the economy, it is estimated that the adults of a dual income household have just two hours of free time per day (Carvel 2004). Given this intensity of socially necessary labor time public participation remains a chimera in the UK on purely pragmatic grounds.

Consultation can only be credible if the public has the time to appraise options, reflect, and come to a considered view. In the absence of structured provision, such as a social wage which would enable increased participation, then critical sub-groups articulate formalizations derived from situated experiences of specific life worlds. Such views resonate to varying degrees with wider publics increasingly prepared to adopt social movement repertoires of action. The criminalization of such acts and the extension of terrorism tropes to environmental and animal right activists impinges directly upon the role of "civil disobedience" seen as central to the effective social dynamics of representative democracies by Habermas (1985).

Failure to incorporate movement concerns of the 1970s within *state* provision have been linked to the rise of political violence in Germany (Elias 1996) and violence has become an increasingly prominent feature of contemporary German street mobilizations (Rucht 2003). The contemporary milieu differs in that state-centric corporatist techno-science has been significantly displaced by near market science approaches. In the UK this sunrise sector is defended by the use of the police and criminal justice system in the name of economic efficiency and competitiveness. The targeting of activist minorities assumes that the concerns being policed have no significant social base.[13] As this chapter has argued concerns over the neoliberal context within which genomic techniques are evolving are dispersed across a wide range of social locations. In a German and UK contest flexible labor markets represent one of the biggest threats to the science base with job security and remuneration levels encouraging migration to other occupations or countries.

The European Social Forum represents one example of a milieu within which a diverse range of civil society actors engage with issues spanning the spectrum of concerns confronting modern polities. The models of accountability evolving within this movement milieu features iterative cycles of consultation and feedback between the local, regional, national, georegional, and global levels. Such social negotiation may appear protracted and *inefficient* in the short term but in a paradoxical manner becomes more important given the centrality of the consumer in neoliberal market societies. This is a lesson which has been learned the hard way by sections of the agricultural bio-technology sector. An Iowa State University bio-tech researcher reflected that in the United States:

> The consumer is King. [. . .] It's risky to take a supply orientated concept and have that collide with a demand orientated system and that is literally what we are seeing here. Consumers are aware that the greatest change is occurring in the history—probably—of the human family on the globe in their foodstuffs and no processor, no seller of food products wants to ever be caught selling something the consumer does not want. (Seeds of Trouble Part 2, BBC, Radio 4 broadcast 14 January 2003)

Against this background German and EU wide movement milieu concerns over the upstream impacts of human genomics in terms of human biodiversity,

the appropriate use of the precautionary principle, and inter-generational concerns associated with sustainable development all involve longer term approaches to efficiency. One way to address public concerns over the financial
ability to access marketized genomic techniques would be the adoption of public sector provision. A public interest science base would also enhance the capacity to evaluate claims-making originating within the private sector.

In the wake of the French and Dutch "no" votes—widely interpreted as the
voice of globalization (i.e., neoliberal modernization) losers—the German
stance on modernization assumes a position of centrality in terms of the identity of Europe and the place of the EU within the global order (Manners and
Lucarelli 2006). The marginal outcome of Germany's federal elections in
2005 demonstrates the absence of a societal consensus on the "market efficiency" program advocated by Merkel during the election campaign.

The outcome of Germany's 2005 elections left both formal political parties
and actors within the movement milieu engaged in coalition and network
building to meet the changed circumstances. Enhanced mobility (Urry 2000)
and computer-mediated communications (Chesters and Welsh 2006) are
transforming the density of such network exchanges enabling more linkages
between the global, national, and local movement milieus. In Castells' terms:

> Networks constitute the new social morphology of our societies, and the diffu-
> sion of networking logic substantially modifies the operation and outcomes in
> processes of production, experience, power and culture. [. . .] This networking
> logic induces a social determination of a higher level than that of the specific so-
> cial interests expressed through the networks: the power of flows takes prece-
> dence over the flows of power. (Castells, 1996: 469)

The network movements engaging with techno-science and modernization
in Germany, the UK and the EU are bearers of a model of "social efficiency"
which speaks social justice, human dignity, and the long-term view to the
centers of power advocating short-term market efficiency. Given German
social structure "life world" issues will be central in the ongoing process of
mobilization.

NOTES

1. The key features here were of course a declining class of rural smallholders, a
growing middle class associated with public sector employment and a weakening proletariat as the shifts towards the service sector intensified.

2. These included "minor" environmental and urban quality of life issues such as
road safety and air purity.

3. Beck's sub-politics combines established actors such as trades unions, professional associations, trade associations, and new social movement actors to constitute a "bottom up" force for social change.

4. The sequencing of the human genome was portrayed as a means to identify and remedy the genetic cause of medical conditions providing a "map" to guide medical science. The precision implied by the cartographic metaphor is however illusory given the massive number of shared genes across species. Very few single gene conditions have in effect been identified as the expressive role of proteins (proteomics) has become recognized as increasingly important. Irrespective of this, commercial tests claimed to assess individuals' genetic predisposition to a range of lifestyle conditions, such as addictive behavioral patterns, are a growing market.

5. In previous iterations such as those associated with opposition to nuclear power the forging and maintenance of active alliances were outcomes from such latency periods with the US Clamshell and Abalone Alliance and the UK Torness Alliance being prime examples. The prominence of such alliances makes unitary definitions of social movement based on collective identity and the exclusion of alliances as movement actors increasingly problematic.

6. Habermas argues that without the wide-ranging (re)negotiation of a postgenomic species being there can be no human collectivity capable of moral judgment. Failure to achieve such a moral community will lead to the continued application of judgments of inferiority/superiority (between enhanced and non-enhanced humans and types of enhanced humans) and the "highly momentous distinction between life worth living and life not worth living *for others*" (Habermas 2003: 69).

7. CESAGen flagship project "The Emerging Politics of Human Genetic Technologies" www.cesagen.lancs.ac.uk/research/projects/newgentechs.htm.

8. The stakes formalized by such actors are informed by the experience of daily life which frequently involves having or living with someone with a "genetic" condition or having been genetically profiled. Methodologically data from such groups and individuals is qualitatively different from polling and focus group data based on representative sampling. For present purposes they are regarded as critical sub-groups in a manner analogous to critical sub-groups within environmental risk assessments.

9. Participants represented a wide range of international health equity networks such as: Citizens Health Initiative; Peoples Health Movement; feminist and women's health organizations including the Association for Women in Development (AWID); the Centre for Health Gender and Inequality; Reprokult; Disabled Peoples International; the International Centre for Bioethics Culture and Disability; NGOs from developing nations from Ghana (ABANTU); and Bolivia (FOBOMADE). Religious social justice activists included: the World Council of Churches and the US National Council of Churches. FOE and GENET were prominent environmental constituencies.

10. For further details see www.genetics-and-society.org/analysis/opposing/2003_berlin_report.html.

11. "Critical" is used here in the sense of critically important in a manner analogous to the use of the term within risk assessment where a particular group becomes a critical consideration in coming to a judgment due to their specific characteristics or lifestyle. In terms of radiation risks then age and diet constitute significant critical sub-groups.

12. Here, Habermas lists "genetic control or influence over the basic constitution of an individual" as one of the emergent examples of the control process (Habermas 1971: 117).

13. In the UK this is a questionable assumption given the involvement of individuals of pensionable age in animal rights protests from the 1990s onwards and certainly underestimates the degree of support for activist communities among those with too little free time for participation.

REFERENCES

Adorno, Theodor W., and Marcuse, Herbert (1999): "Correspondence on the German Student Movement." *New Left Review* 233/1999: 118–36.

Ardener, Edward (1989): "The Voice of Prophecy" in: Champman, Malcolm, ed: *The Voice of Prophecy and other Essays*. Oxford: Blackwell.

Baker, Susan (2006): *Sustainable Development*. London/New York: Routledge.

Bauer, Martin W., ed. (1995): *Resistance to New Technology: Nuclear Power, Information Technology and Biotechnology*. Cambridge: Cambridge University Press.

Bauer, Martin W., and Bonfadelli, Heinz (2002): "Controversy, media coverage and public knowledge," in: Bauer, Martin W., and Gaskell, Georg, eds.: *Biotechnology: The Making of a Global Controversy*. Cambridge: Cambridge University Press, pp. 149–75.

Bauer, Martin W., and Gaskell, George, eds. (2002): *Biotechnology: The Making of a Global Controversy*. Cambridge: Cambridge University Press.

Beck, Ulrich (1992): *Risk Society: Towards a New Modernity*. London/Thousand Oaks/New Delhi: Sage.

Beck, Ulrich, Giddens, Anthony, and Lash, Scott (1994): *Reflexive Modernisation*. Cambridge, Polity.

Blühdorn, Ingolfur, and Szarka, Joseph (2004): "Managing Strategic Positioning Choices: A Reappraisal of the Development Paths of the French and German Green Parties." *Journal of Contemporary European Studies* 12, no. 3: 303–19.

Bowring, Finn (2003): *Science, Seeds and Cyborgs: Biotechnology & The Appropriation of Life*. London/New York: Verso.

Brown, Phil, and Zavestoki, Stephen (2004): "Social Movements in Health: An Introduction," *Sociology of Health and Illness* 26, no. 6: 679–94.

Bud, Robert (1993): *The Uses of Life: a History of Biotechnology*. Cambridge: Cambridge University Press.

—— (1995): "In the engine of industry: regulators of biotechnology 1970–86," in: Bauer, Martin W., ed.: *Resistance to New Technology: Nuclear Power, Information Technology and Biotechnology*. Cambridge: Cambridge University Press, pp. 293–309.

Bullard, Robert D. (1990): *Dumping in Dixie: Race, Class and Environmental Quality*. Boulder Colorado: Westview Press.

Carvel, John (2004): "Couples spend just two hours together a day." *The Guardian*, 16 July 2004: 7.

Castells, Manuel (1996): *The Rise of the Network Society. Vol. 1 of The Information Age: Economy, Society and Culture*. Oxford: Blackwell.

—— (1997): *The Power of Identity. Vol. 2 of The Information Age: Economy, Society and Culture*. Oxford: Blackwell.

Chesters, Graeme C., and Welsh, Ian (2006): *Complexity & Social Movements: Multitudes on the Edge of Chaos*. London/New York: Routledge.

—— (2005): "Complexity and Social Movement: Process and Emergence in Planetary Action Systems." *Theory, Culture and Society* 25, no. 5: 187–211.

Diani, Mario (1992): "The Concept of Social Movement." *The Sociological Review* 40, no. 1: 1–25.

EGE (2000): *Citizens Rights and New Technologies: A European Challenge*. Report of the Charter on Fundamental Rights related to technological Innovation, 23 May 2000.

Einsiedel, Edna et al. (2002): "Brave new Sheep—the Clone called Dolly," in: Bauer, Martin W., and Gaskell, George, eds.: *Biotechnology: The Making of a Global Controversy*. Cambridge: Cambridge University Press, pp. 313–47.

Elias, Norbert (1996): *The Germans*. Cambridge: Polity.

Granovetter, Martin (1973): "The Strength of Weak Ties." *American Journal of Sociology* 78, no. 6: 1360–80.

Habermas, Jürgen (1971): *Towards a Rational Society*. London: Heinemann.

—— (1981): "New Social Movements." *Telos* 49/1981: 33–37.

—— (1985): "Civil Disobedience: The Litmus Test for the Democratic Constitutional State." *Berkeley Journal of Sociology* 30: 95–116.

—— (2003): *The Future of Human Nature*. Cambridge: Polity.

Held, David, McGrew, Anthony, Goldblatt, David, and Perraton, Jonathan (1999): *Global Transformations: Politics, Economics and Culture*. Cambridge: Polity.

Irwin, Alan, and Michael, Mike (2003): *Science, Social Theory and Public Knowledge*. Maidenhead: Open University Press.

Jamison, Andrew (2001): *The Making of Green Knowledge: Environmental Politics and Cultural Transformation*. Cambridge: Cambridge University Press.

Jonas, Hans (1985): *Technik, Medizin und Eugenik: Zur Praxis de Prinzips Verantwortung*. Frankfurt/Main: Suhrkamp.

Kepplinger, Hans M. (1995): "Individual and institutional Impacts upon Press Coverage of Sciences: the Case of Nuclear Power and Genetic Engineering in Germany," in: Bauer, Martin, ed.: *Resistance to New Technology: Nuclear Power, Information Technology and Biotechnology*. Cambridge: Cambridge University Press, pp. 357–77.

Kerr, Anne, Cunningham-Burly, Sara, and Amos, Amanda (1998): "Drawing the line: an analysis of Lay People's Discussions about the New Genetics." *Public Understanding of Science* 7, no. 2, 113–33.

Manners, Ian, and Lucarelli, Sonia, eds. (2006): *Values and Principles in EU Foreign Policy*. London/New York: Routledge.

Marcuse, Herbert (1964): *One Dimensional Man*. London: Abacus.

—— (1968): *An Essay on Liberation*. Harmondsworth: Penguin.

Mayer, Karl U., and Hillmert, Steffen (2003): "New Ways of Life or old Rigidities? Changes in Social Structure and Life Courses and their Political Impact." *West European Politics* 26, no. 4: 79–100.

McKay George (1996): *Senseless Acts of Beauty: Cultures of Resistance Since the Sixties.* London/New York: Verso.

—— (1998): *DiY Culture: Party & Protest in Nineties Britain.* London/New York: Verso.

Melucci, Alberto (1984): "An End to Social Movements?" *Social Science Information* 23, no. 3/4: 819–35.

—— (1985): "The Symbolic Challenge of Contemporary Movements." *Social Research* 52, no. 4: 789–815.

—— (1989): *Nomads of the Present.* London: Radius.

—— (1996): *Challenging Codes.* Cambridge: Cambridge University Press.

Notes from Nowhere (2003): *We Are Everywhere: the Irresistible Rise of Global Anticapitalism.* London/New York: Verso.

Offe, Claus (1985): "Challenging the Boundaries of Traditional Politics: The Contemporary Challenge of Social Movements." *Social Research* 52, no. 4: 817–68.

Patterson, Lee Ann (2000): "Biotechnology Policy: Regulating Risks and Risking Regulation," in: Wallace, Helen, and Wallace, William, eds.: *Policy Making in the EU.* Oxford/New York: Oxford University Press, pp. 317–43.

Purdue, Derrick A. (2000): *Anti-GenetiX: The Emergence of the Anti-GM Movement.* Aldershot: Ashgate.

Rifkin, Jeremy (1998): *The Biotech Century: How Genetic Commerce Will Change the World.* London: Phoenix.

Rucht, Dieter (2003): "The Changing Role of Political Protest Movements." *West European Politics* 26, no. 4: 153–76.

Rudig, Wolfgang (1990): *Anti-nuclear Movements.* Harlow: Longman.

Salter, Brian, and Mavis, Jones (2002): "Regulating Human Genetics: the Changing Politics of Biotechnology Governance in the European Union." *Health, Risk & Society* 4, no. 3: 325–40.

Schmidt-Beck, Rüdiger (1992): " A Myth Institutionalised: Theory and Research on New Social Movements in Germany," *European Journal of Political Research* no. 4: 357–83.

—— (2003). *Global Complexity.* London/New York: Routledge.

Stöss Richard (1984): "Vom Mythos der 'neuen sozialen Bewegungen': Neun Thesen und ein Exkurs zum Elend der NSB-Forschung," in: Falter, Jürgen W., Fenner, Christian, and Greven, Michael Th., eds.: *Politische Willensbildung und Interessenvermittlung.* Wiesbaden: Westdeutscher Verlag, pp. 548–65.

Tickle, Andrew, and Welsh, Ian, eds. (1998): *Environment and Society in Eastern Europe.* Harlow: Longman.

Urry, John (2000): *Sociology Beyond Societies: Mobilities for the Twenty-first Century.* London/New York: Routledge.

Waters, Sarah (2004): "Mobilising against Globalisation. Attac and the French Intellectuals." *West European Politics* 27, no. 5: 854–74.

Welsh, Ian (2000): *Mobilising Modernity: The Nuclear Moment.* London/New York: Routledge.

—— (2002): "Where do Movement Frames come from? Insights from S26 and global 'anti-capitalist' Mobilizations." *Proceedings 8th Alternative Futures and Popular Protest Conference. Volume 2.* Manchester: Metropolitan University Press, 2–4 April 2002.

—— (2004): "Network Movement in the Czech Republic: Perpetuating Prague." *Journal of European Area Studies* 12, No. 3: 321–37.

—— (2006): "Values, Science and the EU: Bio-technology & Transatlantic Relations, " in: Manners, Ian, and Luracelli, Sonia, eds.: *Peace and War: Values in EU Global Action.* London/New York: Routledge, pp. 59–76.

Welsh, Ian, Evans, Robert J., and Plows, Alexandra (2005): "Another Science for Another World?: Science and Genomics at the London European Social Forum." *Cardiff School of Social Sciences.* Working Paper Series, No. 70. Cardiff: Cardiff University Press.

Wynne, Brian (1982): *Rationality and Ritual: The Windscale Inquiry and Nuclear Decisions in Britain.* Chalfont St. Giles: BSHS.

PROSPECTS

12

The Third Transformation of Democracy: On the Efficient Management of Late-Modern Complexity

Ingolfur Blühdorn

Advanced modern societies are experiencing a transformation of their politics and style of policy making that can arguably be described as something like a *paradigm change*. The two countries which have been the focus of this volume, Germany and Britain, are not just modernizing their economic structures and social systems in order to adapt to the necessities of the increasingly globalized economy but they are, this chapter will suggest, caught up in a comprehensive transformation of late-modern democracy, and at the very center of this transformation are the notions of complexity and efficiency. The "continuous decline of effectiveness that undermines the confidence of citizens in the democratic regime" (Roller 2005: 1) has concerned political elites and academic observers for some time. In "nearly all advanced industrial democracies" and "by almost any measure, public confidence and trust in, and support for" the established structures of democracy "has eroded over the past generation" (Dalton 2004: 191). There is evidence suggesting that "adherence to the *norms* and *ideals* of the democratic process have apparently increased" (ibid.: 192; my emphases), but citizens are becoming ever more "sceptical towards politicians, political parties, and political institutions" (ibid.: 191) which are widely perceived as, to put it colloquially, *a waste of time*. Public debates about the "end of democracy" or even the "end of politics" (Baumann 1999; Gamble 2000; Furedi 2005), but also about the "reinvention" (Beck 1997) or "revival of politics" (Boggs 2000: 243ff.) indicate just how intensely the arrival of a turning point in democratic politics is being perceived.

It sometimes seems that in advanced democracies "voters want to run the show directly and are impatient with all forms of intermediaries between their opinions and public policy" (Dahrendorf 2000: 311; Dalton 2004). Nontraditional forms of political articulation such as consumer boycotts, single issue pressure groups, or direct action movements are actually on the rise (Cain et al. 2003). It has, therefore, been suggested that the "fundamental paradigm that dominates our politics is the shift from *representative* to *direct* democracy" (Dahrendorf 2000: 311; my emphasis). Referring to the realm of democratic *theory*, John Dryzek has boldly announced the "definite deliberative turn" (Dryzek 2000: v). Others have tried to capture the ongoing transformation of advanced democracies with terms such as *de-parliamentarization* and *post-parliamentary* democracy (e.g., Benz 1998; Blumenthal 2003; Decker in this volume). Debates on the *politics of delegation* (e.g., Thatcher and Stone Sweet 2002; Strøm et al. 2003; Flinders 2004a, 2004b; Jochem, and also Flinders, in this volume), the *presidentialization* of democracy (e.g., Poguntke and Webb 2005), and on the new *politics of leadership* (Körösényi 2005) are centering on very closely related phenomena. This also applies to the literature on *depoliticization* (e.g., Burnham 2001; Buller and Flinders 2005), the *politics of regulation* (e.g., Czada et al. 2003; Moran 2003), and the transition from the *politics of decisions* to that of *presentation* (Sarcinelli 2003; Jun in this volume). While these debates are all taking different perspectives and are focusing on different aspects, they are ultimately all concerned with exploring the ongoing transformation of democracy, and they all converge in the basic diagnosis that in the evolution of democratic politics "we have unmistakably arrived at the end of the parliamentary epoch" (Walter 2005: 57).[1]

To pull together some elements of these debates, to theorize the post-parliamentary and *post-representative* form of politics towards which the ongoing transformation is taking late-modern democracies, and to explore the central role of complexity and efficiency in this transformation are the objectives of this concluding chapter. With this agenda, the chapter opens the perspective well beyond the two countries whose politics of modernization have been investigated throughout this book. Key terms in the analysis that follows will be the *post-democratic revolution* and the *politics of simulation*, both of which have already come up earlier in this volume (chapter 3). The first of these, the post-democratic revolution (Blühdorn 2004a), is, I will argue, the motor that powers the ongoing transformation of democracy. The term aims to indicate that this transformation may be seen as the counterpart of the *participatory revolution* since the late 1960s (Blühdorn 2007a), and it implies that the experience of hyper-complexity, normative disorientation, and democratic sclerosis are important drivers of this ongoing paradigm shift. The second concept, the *politics of simulation*, refers to a theoretical framework for the conceptualization and interpretation of late-modern politics (Blühdorn 2002, 2003, 2004b, 2005, 2007b, 2007c). It suggests that the form of democracy that emerges beyond the phase of parliamentary democracy, and that is characteristic of the *late-modern condition*, is a mixture of democratic performance and uncompromising adherence to the *metaphysics of efficiency* (see chapter 3). Insofar as Britain has been described as a country with a particularly *post-democratic* political culture (Crouch 2004), while Germany's political culture has been very strongly reshaped by the participatory revolution and is, not least because of this, beset by problems of hyper-complexity and democratic sclerosis, the two countries remain important points of reference throughout this chapter. Yet, with its focus on the transformation of democracy and the efficient management of late-modern complexity this chapter is a journey into democratic theory in a much larger sense.

As was indicated above, much of the recent literature on the current transformation of democracy proceeds from the assumption that the vast majority of citizens in late-modern democracies are deeply committed to democratic ideals but have become what Klingemann (1999) calls *disappointed democrats*. Accordingly, the objective in this literature is to identify means by which contemporary institutionalized democracies may be moved closer towards the democratic ideal. It will be immediately evident that an analysis that is built upon the concepts of a post-democratic revolution and the politics of simulation will take a very different approach and pursue a much less normatively loaded agenda. This chapter begins by reviewing different ways in which the historical evolution of democracy and its most recent transformation have been conceptualized. In order to prepare the ground for the analysis of what I am calling the *post-democratic revolution*, I will then undertake a critical discussion of the way in which Colin Crouch (2004) has used the term post-democracy. Section three focuses on *depoliticization* and *delegation* which are, arguably, the core constitutive elements of the post-democratic revolution since the 1990s and the primary strategies late-modern societies have developed for the efficient management of their unprecedented complexity. Section four delves into the theory of the politics of simulation and develops the concept of *simulative democracy* which is contrasted, as a third historical form of democracy, with the models of direct and representative democracy. The concluding section focuses on the *performance of democracy*. It supplements the exploration of the performance of democracies in terms of their tangible outcomes (e.g., Roller 2005) by a discussion of democratic performance in the sense of the simulative regeneration of emancipatory-progressive values.

GREAT TRANSFORMATIONS

Robert Dahl has suggested that "the history of democracy can be viewed as consisting of three great transformations" (Dahl 1994: 25). The first of these was the one that led from pre-democratic societies to Athenian assembly democracy; the second one was the transition from Greek direct democracy to modern representative democracy in the nation-state; and the third one is the currently ongoing transformation from national representative democracy towards a third form of democracy whose contours are only gradually becoming visible. How may this third transformation be determined in temporal terms? What triggered this third transformation? What kind of qualitative transformation does it entail? For Dahl, the third transformation of democracy is associated with the era of globalization. As societal function systems and the life world experience of modern individuals are growing beyond the nation state, the internationalization of politics is a necessary and inescapable consequence. Size and complexity were the key factors which triggered the transition from city-state democracy towards nation-state democracy, and according to Dahl, these factors are now once again at the center of the shift towards a transnational or even global democracy: The Greek "city-state was made obsolete by the emergence of the large scale nation-state" (ibid.: 25), and the currently ongoing transformation is "something like the second transformation writ large on a world scale" (ibid.: 27). "Like the second transformation, then, the third is associated with a great increase in the scale of the political system" (ibid.: 28).

As regards the qualitative changes to democracy which come along with its third transformation, Dahl notes that at the levels of national and sub-national politics, the efficient management of ever-increasing societal differentiation and complexity "will require considerable delegation of power" (ibid.: 27) and reduce the scope for "effective citizen participation" (ibid.: 28). At the level of transnational politics, he warns, "the danger is that the third transformation will not lead to an extension of the democratic idea beyond the national state but to the victory in that domain of *de facto guardianship*" (ibid.: 33; my emphasis). Thus the history of democracy may firstly be described as the development from city-state democracy towards nation-state democracy and further towards an as yet unknown transnational or even global democracy. But beyond this it is, secondly, a process of qualitative transformation leading from *direct participation* via *parliamentary representation* towards *de facto guardianship*. In the course of its historical evolution, democracy seems to be incrementally moving away from the theoretical ideal of *rule of the people by the people*, and an increasing "democratic deficit" (ibid.: 23) emerges.

Dahl's analysis anticipates key elements which have been elaborated in much detail in the critical literature on corporate globalization, yet it seems at odds with the widely held view that advanced western democracies have actually become more open, participatory, transparent, and accountable than at any earlier stage. Mark Warren's assessment of the current transformation of democracy may be regarded as representative of this literature. In his article *A Second Transformation of Democracy?* Warren raises the question whether the currently ongoing changes really "so alter or complement the institutions of representative democracy that we are entitled to speak of a *second transformation of democracy*[2] leading to a *third* historical form" (Warren 2003: 224). He shares the view that "in the face of globalization, the decentering of the nation-state, complexity, and functional differentiation," representative democracy faces, "if not obsolescence, at least diminished importance" (ibid.). Yet he suggests that the notion of a second transformation is appropriate only if "democracies now function in ways that represent a *qualitative break* with the representative model" (ibid.; my emphasis). The pluralization of political arenas and conflict lines; the unprecedented opportunities for political articulation and participation; the ever-increasing skepticism of democratic publics towards their elected representatives; the high level of public information about political issues; and the rapid spread of experiments with elements of direct and deliberative democracy lead Warren to suggest that "something as dramatic as a second transformation of democracy" (ibid.: 246) has indeed occurred. He believes that recent decades have brought "only *moderate increases* in democracy in political venues closely tied to the representative electoral system," but "*dramatic increases* in those venues that supplement, complement, and compete with the representative system" (ibid. my emphasis). So he implies that a "third historical form" of democracy has actually emerged, but he remains rather vague how it may be conceptualized, how exactly it is categorically different from its representative predecessor, and in what respect this "third historical form" of democracy is categorically new.

Essentially, the transformation that Warren discusses is the one that has been initiated by the emancipatory social movements of the 1960s and 1970s. While in Dahl's model the second and third great transformations appear as moves *away from* the democratic ideal, Warren's second transformation is, in line with Dryzek's *deliberative turn*, clearly a move *towards* citizen empowerment and democratic self-rule. Warren is ambiguous whether this second transformation has actually been completed or whether it is still ongoing. But interestingly, he gives no indication that the changes which have occurred to western democracies since the collapse of their communist counterparts and since the emergence of the post-communist era of economic globalization may represent a further transformation. While Dahl regards these changes since the 1990s as the essence of his third transformation, Warren does not seem to believe that they represent a further "qualitative break" that leads beyond the "historical form of democracy" which the participatory revolution since the 1960s had brought about.

So, Dahl and Warren are both highlighting important dimensions of the ongoing third transformation of democracy, yet neither of their models offers a satisfactory conceptualization of the paradigm change that is the focus of this chapter. Dahl does not recognize the enormous significance of the participatory revolution which is undoubtedly a determining factor in this third transformation. Warren, in turn, fails to recognize that his *second* transformation is in fact only the predecessor of the *third* transformation which has been going on since the early 1990s. Warren not only neglects much debated phenomena such as increasing political cynicism and apathy, but he also does not recognize the significance of Dahl's point about *complexity, delegation*, and *guardianship*. This shift towards delegation and guardianship, however, is arguably the central dimension of the great transformation that is currently reshaping late-modern democracies. It has been explored in the bourgeoning literature on the politics of delegation, the media-related trend towards personalization, and the presidentialization of western democracies. But in a way that goes well beyond this literature, András Körösényi (2005) has interpreted this shift as indicative of a categorically new form of democracy that he calls *leader democracy*.

Like Warren, Dalton, and many others, Körösényi takes "the decline of political parties and parliaments in the last decades" (Körösényi 2005: 358) and "the crisis of representation" (ibid.: 368) as the starting point for his analysis. Yet in trying to identify the novel elements in contemporary democratic politics he looks into a direction that is exactly opposite to Warren's citizen empowerment. Reviving the Weberian-Schumpeterian model of *competitive elitism*, he points towards the delegation and concentration of power, and to the striking rehabilitation of leadership as the most striking political innovations of the past fifteen years. The rise of these phenomena most certainly represents a radical "qualitative break" from the principle of self-rule and DIY-politics that was promoted by the participatory revolution. Körösényi's primary empirical point of reference is Britain under Prime Minister Tony Blair whose political career and government is indeed widely associated with the explicit celebration and promotion of leadership. Yet, Körösényi suggests that the decline of traditional-style representation and the new appreciation of leadership are phenomena that have significance well beyond the UK. Indeed, even in Germany, which for historical reasons has in the past half century been deeply suspicious of any leader figures and centralization of political power, there has recently been a striking rehabilitation of the idea of leadership.[3]

Körösényi argues that in late-modern democracies there is a marked shift from *input* responsiveness and *input* legitimacy towards *output* responsiveness and *output* legitimacy. For contemporary electorates, he believes, *What matters is what works!* (Gordon Brown), and in order to make sure that things work, late-modern democracies have embraced the principle of leadership. In leader democracy, Körösényi suggests, citizens are assumed to be "less competent than politicians in deciding on specific policy issues" (ibid: 361). Political elites are therefore expected to take a lead and *get on with the job*, and electorates who "may be capable of giving some overall retrospective assessment of the achievement of the government" (ibid.), make use of the democratic elections in order to pass their verdict on their leaders' performance. The distinctive feature of leader democracies, Körösényi believes, is that the "political process is not generated by the political preferences of the electorate" but "by the aspirations and ambitions of politicians" (ibid: 364). Rather than identifying and accommodating electoral preferences, rival politicians are, supposedly, "trying to shape and produce the electoral preferences of the people themselves" (ibid.). Efficient political communication and the government's public relations machine are, according to Körösényi's analysis, the primary tools by which politicians are trying "to convince the public or rather to generate a public opinion that suits them" (ibid.: 365). In leader democracy, the political process works top-down rather than bottom-up. "The active players of politics are not the constituents but the politicians" and electorates are merely "*re*active" (ibid.: 364). In the political market, Körösényi suggests, "the emphasis is on the supply side," and a successful leader is "a political *entrepreneur* who does not cater to existing demands but creates new demand by supplying new policies" (ibid.: 367). The categorically new feature in advanced modern democracies is, therefore, that "representation means not *re*-presentation or the mirroring of something existing" but "*creation* of something which has not existed before" (ibid.: 375). The objective of leader democracy is not to provide "responsive government" but, if anything, to provide "responsible government" (ibid.: 378).

On the basis of Körösényi's model, the historical evolution of democracy can be described as moving from *direct democracy* via *representative democracy* towards *leader democracy*, or as the transformation of *participatory government* into *representative government* and further into *responsible government*. Körösényi's analysis seems to describe a political condition that is radically different from the one that Warren finds himself confronted with. While Warren regards *post-representative* democracy as more direct and more participatory than its predecessor, Körösényi's leader democracy could hardly be further away from the ideal of the demos ruling itself. Körösényi's model sheds an interesting light on Tony Blair's politics: Blair's public sector reform (see Flinders in this volume), his constitutional reforms (see Baston in this volume), and his ever more sophisticated management of public relations and political communication (see Jun in this volume) can all fruitfully be interpreted within Körösényi's framework. Indeed the model of leader democracy is a useful tool for the analysis of late-modern democracies well beyond Britain, and in particular, Körösényi offers a very perceptive analysis of the changing meaning and significance of *representation*.

Nevertheless, the model of leader democracy is, if taken on its own, clearly not a sufficient conceptualization of contemporary post-representative democracy.[4] For example, it does not account for the enormous influence which professional lobbies and organized interest groups have on political leaders. It does not acknowledge the tight restrictions that transnational economic actors—or systemic imperatives—impose on the leaders' supposedly "free mandate for leadership" (Körösényi 2005: 375). Also, Körösényi's model does not account for the enormous significance of opinion polling in contemporary swing-voter democracies. It does not recognize that in certain respects the democratic expectations of contemporary electorates are indeed getting more inflated, that there is a significant measure of grassroots direct action and bottom-up political interference, and that governments feel under considerable pressure to experiment with new methods of democratic involvement and direct participation. Beyond this, the concept of leadership is at least as closely connected to varieties of *irresponsible government*, such as populism, neoauthoritarianism, and *soft fascism* (Sennett 2004) as it is to Körösényi's notion of *responsible government*—which is, incidentally, a concept with very questionable normative overtones. And very importantly in the present context, Körösényi does not offer any explanation *why* the shift towards leader democracy is supposedly taking place. He neither takes up Dahl's point about complexity and efficiency, nor does he give any alternative reasons for this ongoing transformation.

Thus, Körösényi's model is just as reductionist as the ones discussed before, but it fully develops an important dimension of the ongoing great transformation that Warren ignores and that Dahl only touches upon. In different ways, Dahl's, Warren's, and Körösényi's models are all unsatisfactory, but their discussion has provided important clues about the temporal dimensions and constitutive elements of the great transformation which is the focus of this chapter, and it has revealed some distinctive features of the third historical form of democracy that is characteristic of late-modern societies. The tensions and indeed incompatibilities between the ways in which Dahl, Warren, and Körösényi conceptualize and assess this ongoing transformation highlight the extent to which their three *narratives* rely on simplification as a key strategy for *making sense* of a highly complex and unintelligible development. If it is possible to develop any more comprehensive conceptualization of the currently ongoing third transformation of democracy, this would have to integrate the seemingly incompatible perspectives and constitutive elements discussed so far. It would have to be a *meta-narrative* that can accommodate and explain these apparently conflicting narratives. The concept of the *post-democratic revolution* (Blühdorn 2004a, 2007a) is a stepping stone for the development of such a more comprehensive model. It corresponds to the neomaterialist *silent counter-revolution* and the *post-ecologist revolution* (Blühdorn 2002, 2004b), and it aims to capture a qualitative transformation of democracy that responds to both the social movements' participatory revolution and to the process of globalization. The concept will be further developed by taking a critical look at the way in which Colin Crouch has used the notion of post-democracy.

POST-DEMOCRACY AND THE REPRESSION OF THE EMANCIPATORY-PROGRESSIVE PROJECT

Colin Crouch's *Post-Democracy* warrants some discussion firstly because it contributes further to the analysis of democracy beyond the parliamentary-representative model, and secondly because it helps to identify pitfalls which an adequate conceptualization of the third transformation of democracy should seek to avoid. Like Dahl and Warren, Crouch, too, tries to capture the historical development of democracy with a three-stage model. In his version, a *pre-democratic* condition is followed by an extended *democratic moment* in which political elites come under pressure "to admit the voices of ordinary people into affairs of state" (Crouch 2004: 4), until in *post-democracy* "these voices [are] being squeezed out again, as the economically powerful continue to use their instruments of the influence while those of the *demos* become weakened" (ibid.: 5). Crouch suggests that European societies have had their "democratic moment" in the first few decades following World War II, and the phase of post-democracy emerged in the latter part of the century. According to Crouch's analysis the characteristic feature of post-democracy is that "virtually all the formal components of democracy survive" (ibid.: 22), but "citizens have been reduced to the role of manipulated, passive, rare participants" (ibid.: 21). Indeed, Crouch notes that "the forms of democracy" not only "remain fully in place," but are "today in some respects . . . actually strengthened" (ibid.: 6). Nevertheless, "politics and government are increasingly slipping back into the control of privileged elites in the manner characteristic of pre-democratic times" (ibid.). Post-democratic politics, Crouch believes, has "little interest in widespread citizen involvement or the role of organizations outside the business sector" (ibid.: 3). Citizens remain indispensable as the source of political legitimacy, but this can be obtained by "means of encouraging the maximum level of minimal participation" (ibid.: 112). Ritualized elections, consultation processes, and tightly managed exercises of public involvement fulfill this purpose, while "politics is really shaped in private by interaction between elected governments and elites that overwhelmingly represent business interests" (ibid.: 4).

Crouch believes "the idea of post-democracy helps us describe situations when boredom, frustration and disillusion have settled in after a democratic moment" (ibid.: 19). He suggests that "egalitarians cannot reverse the arrival of post-democracy" (ibid.: 12) because it is the result of an "inevitable entropy of democracy" (ibid.: 104). To some extent, "the growing complexity of issues" (ibid.: 9) is responsible for this inevitable entropy, and this complexity problem is aggravated by the fact that "democracy has simply not kept pace with capitalism's rush to the global" (ibid.: 29). Another explanatory factor, Crouch argues, is the decline of the industrial working class and its replacement by a highly fragmented service sector (ibid.: 53–57). Yet, "the fundamental change lying behind the advance of post-democracy" is, in Crouch's view, the "growing political power of *the firm*"(ibid.: 105; my emphasis). What he means by this is not just the much debated power of transnational corporations, but also the transformation of politicians into "shopkeepers" who, in order to stay in business, are "anxiously seeking to discover what their *customers* want" (ibid.: 21), and the transformation of political parties which privatize and delegate substantive politics to nonelected bodies, and then fully concentrate on cultivating their brand and marketing their image (ibid.: 101–103). Thus, for Crouch post-democracy is the condition where (a) democratic institutions and rituals are maintained, but (b) the demos has been largely disempowered, and where (c) party politics and political competition are more or less void of substantive content, while (d) the substance of political decisions is dictated by "the firm." Post-democratic politics, for Crouch, is neither *representative*, nor *participatory*, nor indeed *responsible*. On the contrary, the post-democratic fusion of populism and corporate dictates gives rise to highly irresponsible government.

In a number of respects Crouch's diagnoses are very close to those of Körösényi, and like the latter, Crouch presents Blair's Britain as his primary empirical evidence and illustration for his theory (ibid.: 5). He suggests that "the shift from Labour to New Labour can be read as the shift from a party suited to democratic politics to one prepared for post-democracy" (ibid.: 64). Like Körösényi, however, Crouch is keen to point out that his diagnosis is, *mutatis mutandis*, also applicable to other advanced democracies. A significant difference between the two models concerns the center of political power. While Körösényi and Crouch converge in their diagnosis of a radical shift of power away from the demos and towards elites which are at best symbolically accountable, their views of political leaders seem diametrically opposed to each other. Crouch's model leaves little space for Körösényi's "free mandate for leadership." Instead political elites are torn between their "anxieties about their relations with citizens" (ibid.: 21) and the categorical imperatives emerging from the global economic system and its powerful agents. Indeed this paradox between the politicians' obsession with opinion poll ratings and the increasing disempowerment of citizens is, in Crouch's view, a defining criterion of post-democracy: "One cannot call this kind of politics non- or anti-democratic" because relations with citizens are so important a factor for political elites, but it can also not be called democratic "because so many citizens have been reduced to the role of manipulated, passive" spectators of the political process (ibid.). Like Körösényi, Crouch sees the *management of public opinion* by means of the media-based public relations machine as the central tool that renders public disempowerment compatible with government dependence on public approval. But while Körösényi's model of responsible government places considerable emphasis on the substantive performance of political leaders which is measured and assessed at election time, a distinctive feature of Crouch's post-democracy is its reliance on rhetorical performance that is not backed up by the delivery of any substantive outcomes.

Crouch's analysis takes up all the major elements which are commonly rehearsed in post- and neo-Marxist critiques of corporate globalization; and while in a number of respects its social-theoretical foundations are appreciably more solid than in much of this literature, the major weaknesses of his analysis are indeed of a Marxian-modernist origin. Having stated that the changes that lead towards post-democracy "are so powerful and widespread that it is impossible to see any major reversal of them" (ibid.: 104), Crouch then proceeds to suggesting that "the time is ripe for a counterattack on the Anglo-American model" (ibid.: 107). He argues that "however far post-democracy advances, it is unlikely that it will exhaust the capacity for new social identities to form," and points out that the prospect of "mobilizing new identities" is what "gives egalitarian democrats their main hope for the future" (ibid.: 116). The flexibilized, fragmented, and politically excluded "bottom third of the working population," in particular, is at the center of Crouch's hopes, and he believes that in the "purely market-oriented societies to which we are moving," "a potential radical and democratic agenda remains unused" as long as no political party takes up their "cause" (ibid.: 66–67). In line with the bulk of the anti-globalization literature, Crouch is confident that eventually "a massive escalation of truly disruptive actions" will put "global capital" under sufficient pressure "to bring its representatives to the bargaining table" (ibid.: 123).

As Crouch correctly states, what he is outlining in this part of his argument are his *hopes* rather than insights derived from descriptive-explanatory social science and social theory. Given that "the growth of the firm" has not only re-shaped political parties and competition, but has also comprehensively re-molded the very structure of late-modern identity and identity formation (see chapter 3 in this volume), any implicit suggestions that democracy which has "not kept pace with capitalism's rush to the global" still can—or would even wish to—catch up seem highly questionable. The problem is not simply that, as Crouch himself indicates, the neglected *cause* of the post-industrial service proletariat is in fact so differentiated, fragmented, and volatile that, from a sociological point of view, any coordinated and sustained mobilization is virtually inconceivable,[5] but ironically, one might even say that (at least *inside* of the late-modern universe) there *is no cause* at all that might be represented. In the late-modern context where identity construction is a highly individualized project pursued, first and foremost, by means of ever accelerated product choices and acts of consumption, the capacity to form social identities which are not only distinct from the market but could also be mobilized against it is rapidly disappearing. At Crouch's hypothetical bargaining table the mobilized consumer proletariat would undoubtedly voice a wide range of concerns, but their key messages for the representatives of global capital—complementing the middle class demand for higher returns of their direct and indirect investments—may well be the battle cry that rules at the bargain table: *Geiz ist geil!* and *Billig will ich!*[6] Rather than challenging the principles of global consumer capitalism such messages would provide them with something like democratic legitimacy.

Crouch's narrative of the "massive escalation of truly disruptive actions" is based on the Marxist dichotomy of labor and capital, or the post-Marxist tension between the system and the individual. In the late-modern condition, however, the Marxian category of *alienation* is rapidly losing its sociological foundation. There is little evidence of any serious desire to remove what the old progressive left used to portray as *false consciousness*. Social movements which would genuinely threaten the established political-economic system are nowhere in sight. However, the bulk of sociological and political analysis remains deeply indebted to the pervasive tradition of idealist-humanist thought. In Crouch's model this is more immediately evident than in the ones discussed before, but at closer consideration this is also applicable to Dahl, Warren, and Körösényi. Despite all their differences, Crouch's narrative of *truly disruptive actions*, Dahl's narrative of the expanding *democratic deficit*,

Warren's narrative of *progressive citizen empowerment*, and Körösényi's narrative of leadership and *responsible government* are all united in their firm reliance on deeply modernist assumptions and normative frameworks of analysis. Essentially, none of them really captures the ongoing great transformation, but first and foremost, they are all fighting the old emancipatory and progressive battle. In line with Beck (1992; 1997) and Giddens (1990; 1991) they are hoping for a *second modernity*. Even where their tentative explorations of the post-representative or post-democratic condition do not swiftly metamorphose into open campaigns for a *neodemocratic* turn, their key concepts such as the *democratic deficit* or *responsible government* still reproduce the fundamentally modernist beliefs about the autonomous individual as the central category of sociological and political analysis, of democratic ideals towards which existing democracies are—or ought to be—progressing, and about a common good which, beyond the limitations of *participatory* and *representative* government, may still be pursued through *responsible* government.

Ultimately, Dahl, Warren, Körösényi, and Crouch all produce *societal self-descriptions* which, intentionally or not, provide reassurance that the modernist values and belief systems are still in place (Blühdorn 2007c). None of them really captures the state of politics that emerges *beyond* this framework. They all assume that the progressive emancipatory project is essentially still operational, even though it may suffer repression and require reactivation. This is most graphically illustrated by Crouch who claims that the evolution from *pre-democracy* through the *democratic moment* to *post-democracy* follows the line of a "parabola" (2004: 5), but then remains firmly within a model that believes in a fixed ideal of democracy which is incrementally realized through cyclical phases of mobilization, demobilization, and remobilization. Morally and politically, these campaigns are highly commendable. Yet from the perspective of social and political theory, a post-democratic era that genuinely deserves this name only starts beyond the abdication of this supposedly unchanging democratic ideal, beyond this cyclical movement, and beyond the exhaustion of the motor that powers the emancipatory-progressive project. At this point any reminders that "the market is not capable of being an absolute principle, a categorical imperative, since it is a means for achieving ends and not an end in itself" (ibid.: 84), or that "the apparent efficiency gains" achieved by contemporary agendas of modernization "can become quite illusory" and "may even be a loss of real effectiveness" (ibid.: 87) will be received with a complete lack of understanding.

Sociological and political analyses which aim to capture this condition will have to abandon normative guiding questions such as the ones for "the balance of improved efficiency against distorted goals" (Crouch 2004: 110), how we may "move the democratic process closer towards its theoretical ideal" (Dalton 2004: 203), or how we may "reverse" the "distortions" of post-democracy (Crouch 2004: 104). Instead, questions such as *What are the distinctive characteristics and specific problems of the post-democratic condition?* and *How do late-modern democracies manage these challenges?* will have to move into the center of attention. For such analyses, the concept of post-democracy will be unsatisfactory because, like all conceptualizations relying on the prefix "post," it fails to capture the distinctive features of the new phase that is said to be emerging. It determines this "third historical form" only in the terms of the one that it supersedes. While the notion of the *post-democratic revolution*, if used in conjunction with that of the *participatory revolution*, is a helpful label for the ongoing *process* of the third transformation, a more powerful concept needs to be found in order to describe the new form of politics that this transformation is bringing about.

DEPOLITICIZATION AND THE *EXHAUSTION* OF THE EMANCIPATORY-PROGRESSIVE PROJECT

In contrast to narratives of the *suppression* of the emancipatory-progressive project which may, however, be reinstated and revitalized, the argument that is explored here is that the ongoing third transformation of democracy may have to be understood as the *exhaustion* of the emancipatory-progressive project which implies that any reinstatement of earlier democratic ideals or revitalization of earlier democratic agendas will not easily be possible, nor in fact desired. This exhaustion, or at least radical transformation, of the modernist-emancipatory agenda is what the concept of the *post-democratic revolution* aims to capture and it is, therefore, clearly distinct from the way in which Crouch uses the concept of post-democracy. Phenomena such as the *deparliamentarization* and *presidentialization* of advanced democracies (Benz 1998; Poguntke and Webb 2005; Decker in this volume), Körösényi's shift towards leadership and responsible government, the proliferation of nonparliamentary advisory, regulatory, and auditing bodies (e.g., Power 1997; Moran 2003), the advance of *political marketing* (e.g., Lees-Marshment 2001; O'shaughnessy and Henneberg 2002), or Crouch's shift from substantive politics to the politics of presentation and communication (also see Sarcinelli 2003 and Jun in this volume) may all be interpreted as indicators of the exhaustion or at least radical transformation of the emancipatory-democratic agenda. Arguably, they can all be summarized under the conceptual umbrella of *depoliticization* which is at the very center of the post-democratic revolution.

The implications and significance of depoliticization are best explored by contrasting it with the concept of politicization. The three dimensions of politicization are, firstly, the politicization of *issues*, secondly the politicization of *people*, and thirdly the politicization of social organizations and *institutions*. The first of these dimensions implies that previously nonnegotiable issues become negotiable and decidable, i.e., these issues are dragged from nonpolitical spheres such as religion, tradition, nature, or intangible political authorities into the arenas of public contestation and scrutiny, where value pluralism gives rise to alternative scenarios, and where decisions have to be justified and democratically legitimated. The politicization of *people* implies that citizens or groups of citizens who have previously been uninterested in politics and excluded from it become engaged in political debates and turn into political actors. And the politicization of social organizations and *institutions* is the process in which previously nonpolitical organizations, such as nature conservation societies, sports clubs, youth centers, universities, or even courts of justice embrace and more or less openly promote specific political agendas.[7] In the most general sense, politicization is the realization that established social norms, social practices, and social relations are contingent rather than sacrosanct, that things could also be different, and that citizens, individually and collectively, have political agency by means of which alternatives can be explored and implemented. This recognition that *things could also be different* has always been the igniting spark of emancipatory-progressive movements, and politicization has always been their key strategy.

Against this background, depoliticization can be described as a process in which previously political issues, people, and social institutions are becoming less political or nonpolitical. As regards political *issues*, their depoliticization implies that they are relocated from the arenas of democratic contestation and decision into arenas which are governed by—at least supposedly— unambiguous and nonnegotiable codes rather than contestable social values. Economic markets, scientific laboratories, regulatory bodies, courts of justice, or international regimes are prominent examples of such supposedly apolitical arenas, and interest rates, education standards, health provision, or environmental quality are just a few examples of issues which have recently been transferred towards them. The depoliticization of *people*, secondly, implies that citizens which had previously been interested and engaged in public affairs withdraw from political arenas and retreat into the nonpolitical pursuit of their personal affairs and well-being.[8] Widespread disengagement from political organizations and activities, the delegation of political interests to (semi-) professional agents (single issue groups, lobbies), the spread of political cynicism and apathy, and the focus on individualized activities of entertainment, consumption, and wellness may be seen as evidence for the depoliticization of citizens in advanced modern democracies. The depoliticization of *social organizations* and institutions, thirdly, implies that bodies ranging from environmental organizations and alternative self-help groups to building societies and retail cooperatives shed their ideological commitments and political agendas and focus on their *core business*. Deideologization, professionalization, pragmatism, managerial best practice, and the pursuit of efficiency gains are the principles that guide this transformation of social institutions. Ironically, this process even affects political parties which are keen to avoid association with any ideological orientations, but want to be perceived as pragmatic managers of public interests and professional contractors for the political job that needs to be done.

In some of the recent literature, the phenomenon of depoliticization has been defined and discussed in a much narrower way. Rather than as a conceptual umbrella for a wide range of practices and tendencies which in the present analysis are all interpreted as indicators of the ongoing third transformation of democracy, this literature understands depoliticization primarily as a form of "statecraft" and a "strategy of governing" (Burnham 2001; Buller and Flinders 2005). Like the *politics of delegation*[9] (e.g., Thatcher and Stone Sweet 2002; Strøm et al. 2003) it has been analyzed first and foremost as a "novel code of polity management" (Buller and Flinders 2005: 529) that has been employed in a particularly skillful manner by the British government under Tony Blair. A common criticism of practices of depoliticization and delegation is that they merely *veil* the essentially political character of political decisions and deprive democratic electorates of their right to deliberate and decide upon the affected issues (Burnham 2001; Buller and Flinders 2005). Conceptualizations of depoliticization and delegation along these lines capture an important dimension of these phenomena, yet they are, arguably, rather reductionist and on the whole not conducive to an adequate understanding of the exceptional significance of these practices for the ongoing transformation of democracy. Depoliticization and delegation are much more than just elements of statecraft, strategies of government, means of "ideological mobilization" (Burnham 2001: 129), or "control mechanism[s], enhancing central government management while off-loading difficult issues" (ibid.: 140) and "responsibility for unpopular policies" (ibid.: 137). They are insufficiently understood if they are explained, as Burnham does, primarily as a response to accelerated economic globalization since the collapse of the bipolar world order or, as Buller and Flinders do, as the result of "domestic factors" such as the "institutional duality between the industrial and the political" (Buller and Flinders 2005: 540). Instead, depoliticization and delegation should, arguably, be regarded as phenomena which are relevant at all levels of advanced modern society (Boggs 2000: 25–40), and as the key elements of the post-democratic revolution that transforms not only late-modern politics, but late-modern society as a whole—and indeed the notion of modernity itself.

What the wide range of practices which may be summarized under the conceptual umbrella of depoliticization have in common is that they all serve the purpose of reducing the complexity and increasing the efficiency of societal systems and processes. The objective of all of them is to reduce the potential for conflicts, to accelerate decision-making processes, and to increase the effectiveness of policy delivery. In the most general sense, depoliticization means *taking the politics out* of issues, people, and institutions, and in each case this implies a dramatic reduction of complexity which is achieved by cutting the number of potential veto players and veto points and reducing the number of alternative perspectives and scenarios which have to be considered. Depoliticization bears the potential for considerable efficiency gains because it simplifies issues and allows people and institutions to *focus on their core business*, however that may be defined, optimize the use of their issue specific expertise, and *get on with the job*. Strategies of depoliticization are thus geared towards a central problem of late-modern societies: Unprecedented normative pluralism and structural complexity belong to their key characteristics and severely reduce their ability to address their major problems ranging from economic growth and environmental protection to social justice and international security. In late-modern society's *political economy of uncertainty* (Baumann 1999: 173–75) the efficient management of this complexity is *the* central challenge that has to be confronted at every level of society, from the individual management of comparatively mundane life world decisions—what Giddens (1991) calls *life politics*—to the management of highly complex scientific and technological issues by national and transnational governments. Whether or not practices of depoliticization *can actually deliver* on the objectives of complexity reduction and efficiency gains is a secondary question that is difficult to assess but that does not need to bother us here. More relevant in the present context is that they *promise* to achieve these objectives, that they offer at least *short-term* relief from the problems of complexity, and thereby respond to problems and concerns which in the late-modern societies are pervasive. In a condition where complexity-induced sclerosis and paralysis are a permanent threat, but where decisions still have to be taken, practices of depoliticization help to facilitate decision making, reduce anxiety, and reestablish some measure of certainty. They may well be unable to genuinely *resolve* the problems of hyper-complexity and low efficiency, but they still provide assistance with the *management* of late-modern complexity.

In the sense that the problems of normative and institutional hyper-complexity have been, if not originally generated then at least severely aggravated by the participatory revolution; and in the sense that depoliticization and delegation are the exact opposite of the core demands promoted by the participatory revolution, the post-democratic revolution may appear as a reactionary *counter-movement* against the participatory revolution since the 1960s. Curiously, however, strategies of depoliticization and delegation pursue objectives which are surprisingly similar to those of which the participatory revolution believed that they could be achieved only by means of politicization, the disempowerment of established authorities, and the shift of decision making and executive power towards the democratic grass roots. These objectives were

- to protect the public good against *systemic irrationalities* (e.g., political, administrative, economic, scientific-technological);
- to protect the public good from *sectional interests* and the irrationality of short term fashions, populisms, or media generated moods;
- to manage highly complex technologies and risks responsibly, and generally improve the quality, legitimacy, and implementability of policy decisions;
- to replace political short-termism by a long-term societal perspective; and
- to protect minority identities.

Overall the participatory revolution aimed to create space and provide the necessary power and tools for the realization, articulation, and experience of diversified individual and collective identities and the implementation of the public good. The notion of comprehensive *social efficiency* (see chapter 3) summarizes these objectives. However, the strategies favored by the participatory revolution, i.e., the strategies of politicization and grassroots empowerment did not deliver. Or, more precisely, they did deliver in that they created unprecedented space for the differentiation of value preferences and life styles, but they were a failure firstly in that they led into a condition of normative disorientation and democratic sclerosis, and secondly in that they obstructed rather than facilitated economic growth and the efficient provision with consumer goods which—in the face of changing patterns of identity construction—became increasingly central to the project of identity construction. Hence, the strategies of politicization and grassroots empowerment had to be reviewed and supplemented by strategies which can firstly remedy the unexpected and undesirable side effects of the participatory revolution and secondly deliver on those expectations which the latter has failed to deliver.

Strategies of depoliticization and the delegation of issues, decisions, and responsibilities to supposedly nonpartisan, professional, independent, and objective mechanisms, agencies and authorities are expected to achieve exactly this. They are expected to deliver on two equally important fronts: to reduce *normative* complexity and give relief from the condition of normative disorientation; and to reduce *systemic* complexity, i.e., the complexity of social organizations and processes which reduces their efficiency. Both of these bear significant emancipatory potentials.

In this context it is worth calling to mind that politicization and the shift of power towards the demos have actually never been regarded as intrinsic values, but they have always merely been means for the realization, expression, and experience of the modernist ideal of the autonomous Self (see chapter 3). In the late-modern condition, however, notions of the Self and patterns of Self-construction, Self-expression, and Self-experience have changed. More than anything, Self-construction, Self-expression, and Self-experience have become a matter of product choices and acts of consumption (e.g., Du Gay 1996; Baumann 2000, 2005). And this late-modern form of Self-construction, Self-expression, and Self-experience is no longer pursued most effectively through the strategies favored by the participatory revolution. Indeed, to the extent that these strategies obstruct economic growth and the availability of a wide range of affordable consumer options, they have actually become counterproductive, and strategies of depoliticization and delegation now appear as far more effective. So in the sense that the key strategies of the post-democratic revolution are still geared towards the same purposes as the strategies of the participatory revolution—Self-construction, Self-expression, and Self-experience—the post-democratic revolution is not a *countermovement* to the participatory revolution, but it actually *continues* its agenda. Therefore, the claim of the British Secretary of State for Constitutional Affairs, Lord Falconer, that the "depoliticization of key decision-making" and policy delivery "is a vital element in bringing power closer to the people" (Falconer 2003) is not entirely a piece of cynical rhetoric, but it contains at least some element of truth.

Thus the transformation of democracy that is, according to this analysis, propelled by a post-democratic revolution in response to the social movements' participatory revolution may be said to entail a shift of emphasis from *politicization* to *depoliticization*, from *DIY-politics* to the *politics of delegation*, from *extra-parliamentary opposition* to *post-parliamentary government*, from *public discourse* to *public management*, from *democratic deliberation* and representation to *post-democratic leadership*, from the *idealist notion* of individual and collective identity to the late-modern individualized *consumer* identity, from *hyper-complexity* to *manufactured simplicity*, and from *social*

Table 12.1. Distinctive Features of the Participatory versus the Post-democratic Revolutions

Participatory Revolution	Post-democratic Revolution
politicization	depoliticization
grassroots demand for decision-making power	delegation to nonpolitical authorities
grassroots demand for executive power (DIY)	delegation to service providers, agents, professionals
grassroots demand for control and scrutiny	delegation to auditors and regulators
extra-parliamentary politics in civil society	extra-parliamentary politics in depoliticized bodies
decentralization of decision making and provision	centralization of managerial powers and subcontracting, outsourcing of provision
civil society as the seedbed of radical alternatives	civil society as a resource for efficiency gains
democratic deliberation	postdemocratic leadership
substantive value-based contestation	formal rule-based managerialism
bottom-up representation	top-down persuasion / communication
bottom-up activism	top-down activation
input legitimacy	output legitimacy
idealist autonomous Self	late-modern consumer profile
social efficiency	economic efficiency
differentiation, pluralization	complexity reduction

efficiency to *economic efficiency*. Table 12.1 further expands this tentative list of distinctive features. Rather than claiming to be in any respect exhaustive, the illustration merely aims to capture some key characteristics that have emerged from the discussion so far.

As regards the driving forces that power the ongoing transformation of democracy, most of the existing literature has placed the emphasis either on the globalizing economic system and its demands for competitiveness, innovation, and expansion, or on the political system which is under pressure to provide favorable conditions for economic growth, which lacks the financial and other resources to comply with rising public expectations, and which has to generate electoral support and reproduce its basis of legitimacy. These are, undoubtedly, important explanatory factors, but they need to be supplemented by a closer analysis of the changing needs and expectations of late-modern individuals and, more specifically, of their desire for complexity reduction and efficiency gains. It is, therefore, worth reiterating the point that in late-modern societies, hyper-complexity has become a major problem. In a way that had not been anticipated by the participatory revolution, the differentiation, fragmentation and ephemeralization of identities, values, interests, and political actors have rendered democratic processes slow and cumbersome. At the same time, the complexity of the social, economic, environmental, scientific, or security issues which the political system is expected to handle has increased so dramatically that they outstretch the capabilities of democratic procedures. While late-modern individuals are fully occupied trying to manage their ever-increasing opportunities, risks, and responsibilities, they expect scientific, political, and administrative elites, now reconceptualized as *public service providers*, to offer *leadership* and secure the efficient management of societal affairs. While consumption-oriented patterns of identity construction fuel the demand for effective and efficient policy delivery, foster the desire to maximize earning capacity and spending power, and up-value the logic of competitiveness and accumulation vis-à-vis the logic of cooperation and redistribution, the ethos of the new *service society* nurtures public frustration with problems of democratic tardiness, with politicians who fail to deliver on their promises, and with policies decisions which bear the marks of a democratic compromise. All this is radically incompatible with the visions and beliefs which the social movements had sought to promote. In all this, however, two points are important to note: firstly, nothing has been said about whether the strategies of complexity reduction and efficiency gains can really deliver what is expected from them; and secondly, it would be entirely inappropriate to suggest that the post-democratic revolution has put a halt to and superseded the participatory revolution.

THE SIMULTANEITY OF OPPOSITES: THE *POLITICS OF SIMULATION*

The analysis of depoliticization and the post-democratic revolution reveals a number of distinctive features of the emerging third historical form of democracy, but for an appropriate understanding of this new state of democracy, further discussion of the relationship between the participatory and the post-democratic revolution is essential. It has been noted that the post-democratic revolution is not simply a countermovement reversing the participatory revolution but, at least in a sense, it continues its agenda. In fact, the post-democratic revolution which is currently reshaping western democracies must not be understood as the historical *successor* of the social movements'-participatory revolution, but as *coexisting* with it. The proliferation of local direct action groups and transnational social movement networks (e.g., Diani and McAdam 2003; Carter 2005) provide plenty of evidence that while the post-democratic revolution is pursuing its efficiency-oriented agenda of depoliticization and delegation, the participatory revolution, with its agenda of politicization and grassroots empowerment, is still going on as well. Indeed, the simultaneity of these two movements is a distinctive—and most confusing—feature of the emerging third historical form of democracy. Depoliticization does not *replace* politicization, but *supplements* it. In fact, in late-modern societies the objective is to retain—and further develop—what the participatory revolution has achieved in terms of democratic rights and expectations, but at the same time to reduce normative and organizational complexity and thereby achieve higher levels of systemic efficiency.

These objectives are *complementary* in the sense that they are both geared towards the emancipatory goals of Self-construction, Self-expression and Self-experience. But they are *contradictory* in the sense that they pursue two different and incompatible notions of the Self: the idealist *subject* and the late-modern *consumer*. While the participatory revolution is committed to the idealist notion of *autonomy*, the post-democratic revolution centers on the notion of *efficiency*, which in late-modern society is understood almost exclusively in terms of *economic* efficiency (see chapter 3). The modernist idea of autonomy is compatible with this late-modern understanding of efficiency if, and to the extent that, it is itself interpreted in economic terms, i.e., as free choice from a wide range of consumer options provided by the market. Indeed, this is the very understanding of autonomy that is much trumpeted by contemporary politicians and economic entrepreneurs, and it is much appreciated by voters and consumers. However, unless it is supplemented by other interpretations, this is an unacceptably narrow form of autonomy. For this reason, the participatory revolution needs to continue alongside its post-democratic counterpart. Their simultaneity represents the attempt to have the best of both worlds: *autonomy* in the *idealist* sense, and *efficiency* in the *late-modern* sense. Put differently, it is the attempt to elevate the late-modern *consumer profile* into the status of an *idealist subject*.

This simultaneous pursuit of *modernist* autonomy (participatory revolution) and *late-modern* efficiency (post-democratic revolution) is desirable, indeed necessary, not only because late-modern individuals, while they are happily immersing themselves into the consumer culture, still like to perceive of themselves as *subjects* which are clearly distinct from and autonomous vis-à-vis the market. Beyond this, there is a further respect in which the modernist notion of the autonomous subject remains indispensable even though it might have abdicated both as an ideal of self-construction and as a category of sociological analysis: Both the system of democratic politics and the system of consumer capitalism come under severe threats of *self-referentiality* unless the belief in the modernist autonomous Self can be stabilized. The former vitally depends on the autonomous citizen from which it derives its legitimacy and whose interests and values it supposedly represents; and the latter vitally depends on the autonomous customer whose interests and needs it supposedly serves and whose demand supposedly justifies the price. For these reasons, the agendas of politicization and depoliticization, i.e., the participatory revolution and the post-democratic revolution, have to be pursued at the same time. This is equally essential for the late-modern individual, the political system, and the economic system. For its own stabilization, late-modern society must secure the simultaneity of incompatibles. And the strategies which it has developed for this purpose may be described as practices of *simulation* (Blühdorn 2002, 2003, 2004b, 2005, 2007b, 2007c).

The concept of simulation refers to a range of societal practices that provide reassurance that in late-modern society the constitutive elements of traditional modernity are still in place, while at the same time providing space for the emancipation and liberation from their restrictive implications and undesirable side effects. Practices of simulation rely on *signs* which do not (no longer) relate to any substantive *referents*. In fact, simulation substitutes the *sign* for the *signified*, and presents the visibility of the former as evidence for the reality of the latter. Practices of simulation pursue the production of societal self-descriptions in which late-modern society portrays itself in the colors of traditional modernity. They are the societal *performance*, the *performative regeneration*, of modernist values and ideas which have become exhausted but which, nevertheless, remain an indispensable resource. Simulation allows for the simultaneity of incompatibles; it helps to avoid trade-offs between, and facilitates the maximization of, mutually exclusive goals. Put colloquially, practices of simulation allow late-modern society *to have its cake and eat it*. Thus, the distinctive feature of late-modern democracy is, strictly speaking, not really the simultaneity of the participatory revolution and the post-democratic revolution, i.e., the simultaneity of politicization and depoliticization, but the *performance* or the *simulation* of this simultaneity. For this reason, the emerging third historical form of democracy may suitably be referred to as *simulative democracy*, and the historical evolution of democracy can now be conceptualized as the transformation from *direct democracy* via *representative democracy* to *simulative democracy*.

The distinctive element in the contemporary third historical form of democracy, i.e., the feature that marks its difference from representative democracy and justifies the talk of a categorically new phase of democracy are not the phenomena of depoliticization and delegation which have been described above as the core elements of the post-democratic revolution. Instead, this distinctive feature is the element of *simulation* which responds to the demise of *representation*. The identification of this distinctive feature renders is possible to describe the third historical form of democracy not just, as Crouch does, in retrospective and negative terms as post-democracy, but in positive terms as simulative democracy. What emerges is simulation, what it supersedes is representation. In a condition where individual and collective identity are rapidly being permeated by, and losing their autonomy vis-à-vis, the market; in a condition where, furthermore, differentiation, flexibilization, and ephemeralization are not just *liquidizing* (Bauman 2000, 2005) but actually *evaporating* any stable individual and social identities, the idea of representation becomes increasingly problematic because, to put it drastically, there is nothing there to be represented. Of course there is a wide range of concerns, values, interests, and demands. But these are highly diversified, inconsistent and volatile. They do not emerge from and cannot be (re)presented as the expression of any tangible identity. In this condition, the model of *principal* and *agent* which underpins the idea of representation loses its foundation. Körösényi's (2005) analysis of leadership and the changing meaning of representation may usefully be expanded into this direction: While the principal disintegrates, the agent adopts the role of the responsible leader. And this analysis also sheds light on the transformation of political parties which has been highlighted by Crouch (2004) and many others: It is in response to these changes, that political parties are abandoning any comprehensive ideologies, shedding any narrow orientation towards particular social classes, milieus, or groups (social identities), and adopting strategies which try to identify, stimulate, and surf sporadic waves of concerns and preferences in the political catch-all market.

In the sense that the dissolution of the autonomous Self and its immersion into the consumer market is the distinctive and defining criterion of *late* or *de-nucleated* modernity (Blühdorn 2006), simulative democracy is the form of democracy that is particular to this state of modernity and that takes account of its specific needs and problems. In the same way in which the emergence of representative democracy addressed the evolving insufficiencies of direct democracy (problems of size; complexity increases emerging from social stratification), the emergence of simulative democracy addresses the evolving insufficiencies of representative democracy (evaporation of a stable identity; complexity increases emerging from the internal differentiation and temporalization of identity claims). The models of direct democracy and representative democracy corresponded to the needs of traditional subject-centered modernity. Simulative democracy is democracy beyond the abdication of the idealist autonomous subject and is particular to contemporary system-centered modernity. The distinctive character of the three forms of democracy may be illustrated by comparing the ways in which each of them performs the three major tasks of democratic systems which are, firstly, to facilitate the self-determination and self-realization of citizens, secondly to formulate the public good and make binding decisions about its implementation, and, thirdly, to provide the executive organs of the state with legitimacy.

With regard to the first of these three tasks, direct democracy centers on and emphasizes the role of the public-minded *citoyen*. Representative democracy centers on and calls upon the citizen as *voter*. And simulative democracy centers on the citizen as *customer* and consumer of options provided by the political and economic markets. In terms of the formulation and implementation of the public good, direct democracy places the primary emphasis on practices of public deliberation. In representative democracy these tasks are delegated to elected representatives and their agents. And in simulative democracy the emphasis is on practices of persuasion by means of which political elites advertise and sell their interpretations of systemic imperatives. As regards the source of legitimacy, finally, the model of direct democracy relies primarily on physical presence and immediate participation in processes of deliberation and decision making. In representative democracy, in contrast, legitimacy derives primarily from the transparency of nonparticipatory decision-making procedures and from the accountability of elected representatives who are judged by their empirically measurable performance (effectiveness). And in simulative democracy, legitimacy turns into an issue of performance in a different sense: it derives from the performed persona of politicians and performance criteria such as efficiency and competitiveness which are purely formal categories but are presented as substantive values. These distinctive features of the three types of democracy are tentatively summarized in table 12.2. In each case, the illustration flags up only those elements which are new and which distinguish a state of democracy from its predecessor. Just like representative democracy retains and reinterprets, rather than abandons, the key elements of participatory democracy, this also applies for the transition from representative democracy in simulative democracy. In each transformation of democracy constitutive categories such as autonomy, participation, or legitimacy are reinterpreted so that the conceptual shells can be retained, and be used as *signs* which regenerate the belief in referents which have long since disappeared. In the third transformation, in particular, they turn into what Beck (2002) has called *zombie categories*, but like stars whose light can be seen long after they have ceased to exist, they extend the lifetime of traditional modernity well beyond its factual decline.

The concept of simulative democracy should not be understood as a primarily normative concept that is used, first and foremost, with critical intentions. In this term, the emphasis is not on highlighting that in this form of politics democratic values and practices are *merely* simulated. Nor does it aim to signal that unreal or unauthentic democratic beliefs, institutions, and procedures should be replaced by something different which is closer to the democratic ideal. In particular practices of simulation must not be interpreted restrictively as strategies deployed by social elites as means of deceiving, ruling, and

Table 12.2. Three Historical Forms of Democracy

	Direct Democracy	Representative Democracy	Simulative Democracy
distinctive understanding of the citizen	autonomous citizen	autonomous voter	autonomous consumer: *presents political and economic customer as autonomous subject*
distinctive pattern of decision making	deliberation	delegation	persuasion: *presents systemic imperatives as public good and political choice*
distinctive source and form of legitimacy	participation, input legitimacy	effectiveness, output legitimacy	efficiency, performance legitimacy: *presents formal economic efficiency as grounded social efficiency*

exploiting the masses.[10] Any interpretation along such lines would—as was outlined in the critique of the neomodernist approaches earlier in this chapter—once again fail to grasp the distinctive character of the emerging third historical form of democracy. Instead, simulative democracy ought to be taken as a primarily descriptive concept that, first and foremost, aims to flag up the distinctive characteristic of late-modern democracy, which is its concern with the performative regeneration of the modernist foundations of democracy which in *denucleated* modernity have become dangerously weak. What is being performed or simulated is not primarily *democracy*, but that the consumer-citizen still has the status of autonomy that was ascribed to the idealist subject. In terms of the public good and its implementation, what is being regenerated by means of simulation is the belief in the existence of a public good and the belief in political decidability. And with regard to the source of legitimacy, what is being simulated is that economic competitiveness and efficiency are not just abstract and formal criteria, but that they are grounded in substantive social needs and values (see chapter 3). At the center of all three of these dimensions is the simulative regeneration of the autonomous subject which was the very center of traditional modernity and of the idea of democracy, and whose abdication is the distinctive feature of *denucleated* modernity.

THE PERFORMANCE OF DEMOCRACY

The notion of simulative democracy sheds a new light onto the concept of democratic performance. As we noted in the introduction to this volume, questions about the performance of democracy have recently shifted into the very center of the study of democratic systems (e.g., Eckstein 1971; Gurr and McClelland 1991; Fuchs 1998; Lijphart 1999; Roller 2005). For the measurement and evaluation of the performance of democratic systems, Fuchs distinguishes between *systemic performance* and *democratic performance*. With the first of these concepts he aims to capture all those functions which any political system is expected to perform (e.g., security, stability, material provision). The second concept, democratic performance, is intended to measure and assess the achievement of objectives which are particular to democratic political systems. These are the goals of self-expression, self-determination, and self-realization, i.e., the implementation of the modernist-idealist vision of the autonomous self, subject, and citizen. Insofar as, ultimately, Fuchs's two dimensions are both measuring the fulfillment of human, i.e., *subjective* rather than *systemic* needs, their distinction is not fully convincing or useful. In the *late-modern* condition, however, i.e., after the abdication of the autonomous subject and after the transition from subject-centered autonomy-oriented modernization to system-centered efficiency-oriented modernization (see chapter 3), Fuchs's two concepts can usefully be redeployed: *systemic performance* may now be understood as the effective execution or implementation of systemic imperatives, i.e., as the responsiveness of the political system to systemic requirements such as innovation, competitiveness, efficiency, or growth. And *democratic performance* may now be read as the performative stabilization or regeneration of the idea of the autonomous subject and citizen, its self-determination, its political participation and efficacy, and of the belief in grounded social efficiency, bottom-up legitimacy, and so forth.

The strategies and practices which late-modern society has developed for this purpose, i.e., for the performative regeneration of the modernist belief system and the stabilization of its own foundations, are manifold and diverse. The most prominent ones include:

(1) the celebration of the institutions and procedures of representative democracy which is becoming ever more dogmatic as depoliticization and the rise of the metaphysics of efficiency (see chapter 3) incrementally turn these institutions and procedures into purely managerial bodies and formalized rituals;

(2) the cultivation of the conceptual shells of modernist democratic thought whose content, however, is being redefined in such a way that, as Tony Blair (2005) has diplomatically put it, "the values we believed in, become relevant to the time we live in";

(3) the launch of well-mediatized government campaigns for social inclusion, democratic renewal, corporate responsibility, environmental

sustainability, and so forth, which accompany the adamant defense of the agenda of growth, competitiveness, social inequality, and unsustainability (Blühdorn 2007c);

(4) the articulation of radical opposition to corporate globalization or military conflict, and the pursuit of social movement action for a new democracy, global justice, environmental integrity, etc., which are, as Furedi notes, forms of "disengaged protest" (Furedi 2005: 42–47) that is "motivated by the impulse to find meaning" (ibid.: 47) and as such "no longer an means to an end but an end in itself" (ibid.: 46) (also see Blühdorn 2006);

(5) and the development of academic narratives about democratic deficits, emerging grassroots revolutions, responsible government, cosmopolitan democracy, and so forth, all of which contribute more to the campaign for the neomodernist and neodemocratic turn than to conceptualizing the specific condition of late or denucleated modernity.

What all of these strategies have in common is that they make use of signs whose referents (autonomy, equality, inclusion, representation, democratic self-rule, environmental integrity, etc.) have in the late-modern condition become unstable and questionable, and that if only by continuing to use these signs, they regenerate the belief in their referents. Of course any suggestion that late-modern society is a unitary entity which has acquired, or can acquire, consciousness of its late-modern predicament and is able to take coordinated remedial action would be sociologically indefensible. Nonetheless, it is perfectly possible to say that these diverse social practices, knowingly or unknowingly, all contribute to the recreation of modernist narratives which—even though they have in many respects become counterproductive—are still an indispensable source of meaning.

On the basis of this analysis of late-modern society's politics of simulation, we may, in conclusion to this chapter, consider an explanation for the widely recognized decline in confidence in, and satisfaction with, the performance of democracy that is very different from the one offered by Dalton and many others who argue along similar lines (e.g., Cain et al. 2003). As was noted in the introduction to this chapter, Dalton suggests that due to the "deepening commitment to democratic principles" (2004: 192), democratic "expectations have risen faster than performance" (ibid.: 199), and he believes that this has given rise to the perception of performance gaps and democratic deficits, which, in turn, are presented as a major cause of the "dissatisfaction with contemporary governments" (2004: 192). This chapter has developed a very different argument: It has suggested that in a third transformation of democracy, late-modern societies have moved beyond Dalton's modernist democratic ideals which are, arguably, increasingly perceived as inefficient and counter-productive, but which can, nevertheless, not be abandoned. Trying to manage this dilemma, individuals and social institutions in late-modern societies have become, to use Hendriks and Tops' words, *"masters of ambiguity*, conciliators of apparent contradictions" (1999: 150). They have developed strategies which enable them to pursue their late-modern ideals and at the same time cultivate their traditionally modern opposites. Yet, their practices of simulation can at best pacify, but never resolve the incompatibility between efficiency and democracy which have been explored throughout this book. Ultimately, the (self-)hypnotizing oratory of democratic renewal and civic empowerment never gets beyond the status of "non-convinced political communication" (Luhmann 1992), and the need to constantly increase its volume is a permanent reminder that the late-modern preference for efficiency does not allow for—and perhaps not even require—more than the performance of democracy.

Thus widespread dissatisfaction with democratic systems is not simply the result of a performance gap in Dalton's sense, but of the gap that remains between the indispensability and the counterproductiveness of the traditional modernist belief system. Dissatisfaction with the performance of democracy is the irremovable predicament of late-modern society. Dalton believes that "the contemporary situation is a pattern of *dissatisfied democrats* or *critical citizens* who want to improve the democratic process" (2004: 200). The analysis of the third transformation of democracy throughout this chapter suggests that the contemporary condition may be described more appropriately as a pattern of *simulative democrats* who, rather than trying to "move democracy closer towards its theoretical ideal" (ibid.: 205), have firmly embraced the late-modern metaphysics of efficiency, and who keep trying to patch up its unsustainability with inevitably insufficient strategies of simulation. Any claim that late-modern societies have reached a final form of politics or even the end of history would undoubtedly be very short-lived, but it may become increasingly difficult to describe the further evolution of western political systems in terms of the transformation of *democracy*.

NOTES

1. This does not mean to say that democratic parliaments cease to be important or even cease to exist, but merely that in advanced modern democracies parliaments no longer are—if they ever have been—the main forum of substantive political negotiation and decision making. For the purposes of this chapter, the terms *post-parliamentary democracy* or *post-parliamentary politics* are therefore understood to

denote that while parliaments may stay in place and retain their formal functions, substantive politics has relocated into other arenas.

2. Warren counts the transition from Greek direct democracy towards modern representative democracy as the *first* transformation.

3. In his famous *Ruckrede* speech of 1997, Federal President Roman Herzog declared: "In times of existential challenges only those will win who are genuinely prepared to lead" (Herzog 1997). More recently, the "anti-Führer-state" and the participatory consensus culture have explicitly been branded as the "German defect" which renders the country "inefficient, slow and unwilling to reform" (Steingart 2004: 135ff/153).

4. Indeed Körösényi does not make any such claim.

5. This does by no means preclude the *short term* mobilization of social protests such as the east-German Hartz IV protests of 2004.

6. *Greed is cool!* is the motto of an extended and very successful advertising campaign of German electronics retail chain SATURN; *Cheap is what I want!* is the slogan of German food retailer PLUS.

7. This obviously also includes the formation of new social organizations or institutions which are established for the pursuit of specific political values and goals.

8. In this context, *nonpolitical* must be understood as self-centered and uninterested in the elaboration and implementation of social alternatives. The *nonpolitical* pursuit of personal affairs may well entail the uncompromising exploitation of all available means in the fight for perceived rights and entitlements.

9. *Delegation* is the key strategy for the depoliticization of issues. It implies the transfer of decision-making powers and responsibilities to scientific experts, economic markets, courts of justice, transnational regimes, or any other institution or authority that seems more or less insulated from the problems that tend to befall pluralist democratic politics.

10. This is, of course, part of what the concept seeks to capture, but in order to escape modernist-Marxist patterns of analysis and grasp the specific condition of late-modernity, practices of simulation should more suitably be described as "societal strategies of societal self-deception" (Blühdorn 2007c).

REFERENCES

Bauman, Zygmunt (1999): *In Search of Politics*. Cambridge: Polity.
—— (2000): *Liquid Modernity*. Cambridge: Polity.
—— (2005): *Liquid Life*. Cambridge: Polity.
Beck, Ulrich (1992): *The Risk Society. Towards a New Modernity*. Cambridge: Polity.
—— (1997): *The Reinvention of Politics. Rethinking Modernity in the Global Social Order*. Cambridge: Polity.
—— (2002): "The Cosmopolitan Society and its Enemies." *Theory, Culture & Society* 19, no. 1–2: 17–44.
Benz, Arthur (1998): "Postparlamentarische Demokratie. Demokratische Legitimation im Kooperativen Staat," in: Greven, Michael Th., ed.: *Demokratie—eine Kultur des Westens*. Opladen: Leske and Budrich, pp. 201–22.

Blair, Tony (2005): "We are the Change-Makers." Speech to the Labour Party conference, Brighton, 27 September 2005.

Blumenthal, Julia von (2003): "Auswanderung aus den Verfassungsinstitutionen. Kommissionen und Konsensrunden." *Aus Politik und Zeitgeschichte* B43/2003: 9–15.

Blühdorn, Ingolfur (2002): "Unsustainability as a Frame of Mind. And How We Disguise It. The Silent Counter Revolution and the Politics of Simulation." *The Trumpeter* 18, no. 1: 59–69.

—— (2003): "Inclusionality—Exclusionality. Environmental Philosophy and Simulative Politics," in: Winnett, Adrian and Warhurst, Alison, eds.: *Towards an Environment Research Agenda*. Volume II. Houndmills/New York: Palgrave Macmillan, pp. 21–45.

—— (2004a): "Future-Fitness and Reform Gridlock. Towards Social Inequality and Post-democratic Politics?" *Debatte. Review of Contemporary German Affairs* 12, no. 2: 114–36.

—— (2004b): "Post-Ecologism and the Politics of Simulation," in: Wissenburg, Marcel, and Yoram, Levy, eds.: *Liberal Democracy and the Environment. The End of Environmentalism?* London/New York: Routledge, pp. 35–47.

—— (2005): "Social Movements and Political Performance. Niklas Luhmann, Jean Baudrillard and the Politics of Simulation," in: Haas, Birgit, ed.: *Macht— Performanz. Performativität, Polittheater*, Würzburg: Königshausen & Neumann, pp.19–40.

—— (2006): "Self-Experience in the Theme Park of Radical Action? Social Movements and Political Articulation in the Late-modern Condition." *European Journal of Social Theory* 9, no. 1: 23–42.

—— (2007a): "The Participatory Revolution: New Social Movements and Civil Society," in: Larres, Klaus, ed.: *A Companion to Europe Since 1945*. London: Blackwell (forthcoming).

—— (2007b): "Symbolic Politics and the Politics of Simulation: Eco-political Practice in the Late-modern Condition." *Environmental Politics* 16, no. 2 (forthcoming).

—— (2007c): "Self-Description, Self-Deception, Simulation. A Systems-theoretical Perspective on Contemporary Discourses of Radical Change." *Social Movement Studies* 6, no. 1 (forthcoming).

Boggs, Carl (2000): *The End of Politics. Corporate Power and the Decline of the Public Sphere*. New York/London: Guilford Press.

Buller, Jim, and Flinders, Matthew (2005): "The Domestic Origins of Depoliticisation in the Area of British Economic Policy." *British Journal of Politics and International Relations* 7, no. 4: 526–43.

Burnham, Peter (2001): "New Labour and the politics of depoliticisation." *British Journal of Politics and International Relations* 3, no. 2: 127–49.

Cain, Bruce, Dalton, Russell, and Scarrow, Susan, eds. (2003): *Democracy Transformed? Expanding Political Opportunities in Advanced Industrial Democracies*. Oxford/New York: Oxford University Press.

Carter, April (2005): *Direct Action and Democracy Today*. Cambridge: Polity.

Crouch, Colin (2004): *Post-Democracy*. Cambridge: Polity.

Czada, Roland, Lütz, Susanne, and Mette, Stefan (2003): *Regulative Politik. Zähmungen von Markt und Technik*. Opladen: Leske and Budrich.

Dahl, Robert (1994): "A Democratic Dilemma: System Effectiveness versus Citizen Participation." *Political Science Quarterly* 109, no. 1: 23–34.

Dahrendorf, Ralf (2000): "Afterword," in: Pharr, Susan, and Putnam, Robert, eds.: *Disaffected Democracies*. Princeton: Princeton University Press.

Dalton, Russel (2004): *Democratic Challenges—Democratic Choices. The Erosion of Political Support in Advanced Industrial Democracies*. Oxford/New York: Oxford University Press.

Diani, Mario, and McAdam, Doug (2003): *Social Movements and Networks. Relational Approaches to Collective Action*. Oxford/New York: Oxford University Press.

Dryzek, John (2000): *Deliberative Democracy and Beyond. Liberals, Critics, Contestations*. Oxford/New York: Oxford University Press

Du Gay, Paul (1996): *Consumption and Identity at Work*. London/Thousand Oaks/New Delhi: Sage.

Eckstein, Harry (1971): *The Evaluation of Political Performance: Problems and Dimensions*. London/Thousand Oaks/New Delhi: Sage.

Falconer, Lord (2003): *Speech to the Institute for Public Policy Research*. London.

Flinders, Matthew (2004a): "Distributed Public Governance in Britain." *Public Administration* 82, no. 4: 883–909.

—— (2004b): "Distributed Public Governance in the European Union." *Journal of European Public Policy* 11, no. 3: 520–44.

Fuchs, Dieter (1998): "Kriterien demokratischer Performanz in Liberal Demokratien," in: Greven, Michael Th., ed.: *Demokratie—eine Kultur des Westens?* Opladen: Leske + Budrich, pp. 152–79.

Furedi, Frank (2005): *Politics of Fear: Beyond Left and Right*. London: Continuum.

Gamble, Andrew (2000): *Politics and Fate*. Cambridge: Polity.

Giddens, Anthony (1990): *The Consequences of Modernity*. Cambridge: Polity.

—— (1991): *Modernity and Self-Identity. Self and Society in the Late Modern Age*. Cambridge: Polity.

Gurr, Robert, and McClelland, Muriel (1991): *Political Performance: A Twelve-Nation Study*. London/Thousand Oaks/New Delhi: Sage.

Hendriks, Frank, and Tops, Pieter (1999): "Between Democracy and Efficiency: Trends in Local Government Reform in the Netherlands and Germany." *Public Administration* 77, no. 1: 133–53.

Herzog, Roman (1997): "Aufbruch ins 21. Jahrhundert." Speech delivered in the Adlon Hotel in Berlin on 26 April 1997 (widely referred to as *Ruckrede*), Bundespressearchiv.

Klingemann, Hans-Dieter (1999): "Mapping Political Support in the 1990s," in: Pippa Norris, ed.: *Critical Citizens*. Oxford/New York: Oxford University Press, pp. 31–56.

Körösényi, András (2005): "Political Representation in Leader Democracy." *Government & Opposition* 40, no. 3: 358–78.

Lees-Marshment, Jennifer (2001): *Political Marketing and British Political Parties*. Manchester: Manchester University Press.

Lijphart, Arend (1999): *Patterns of Democracy: Government Forms and Performance in Thirty-Six Countries*. New Haven: Yale University Press.

Luhmann, Niklas (1992): "Ökologie des Nichtwissens," in: Luhmann, Niklas: *Beobachtungen der Moderne*. Wiesbaden: Westdeutscher Verlag, pp. 149–220.

Moran, Michael (2003): *The British Regulatory State. High Modernism and Hyper-Innovation*. Oxford/New York: Oxford University Press.

O'shaughnessy, Nicholas, and Henneberg, Stephan, eds. (2002): *The Idea of Political Marketing*. Westport/London: Praeger Publishers.

Poguntke, Thomas, and Webb, Paul (2005): *The Presidentialization of Politics. A Comparative Study of Modern Democracies*. Oxford/New York: Oxford University Press.

Power, Michael (1997): *The Audit Society. Rituals of Verification*. Oxford/New York: Oxford University Press.

Roller, Edeltraud (2005): *The Performance of Democracies. Political Institutions and Public Policy*. Oxford/New York: Oxford University Press.

Sarcinelli, Ulrich (2003): "Demokratie unter Kommunikationsstress? Das parlamentarische Regierungssystem in der Mediengesellschaft." *Aus Politik und Zeitgeschichte* B43/2003: 39–46.

Sennett, Richard (2004): "The Age of Anxiety." *The Guardian*, 23 October 2004.

Steingart, Gabor (2004): *Deutschland. Der Abstieg eines Superstars*. München: Piper.

Strøm, Kaare, Müller, Wolfgang, and Bergman, Torbjörn, eds. (2003): *Delegation and Accountability in Parliamentary Democracies*. Oxford/New York: Oxford University Press.

Thatcher, Mark, and Stone Sweet, Alec (2002): "Theory and Practice of Delegation to Non-Majoritarian Institutions." *West European Politics* 25, no.1: 1–22.

Walter, Franz (2005): "Die Alternativlosen." *Der Spiegel* 16/2005: 54–56.

Warren, Mark (2003): "A Second Transformation of Democracy?" in: Cain, Bruce, Dalton, Russell, and Scarrow, Susan, eds.: *Democracy Transformed? Expanding Political Opportunities in Advanced Industrial Democracies*. Oxford/New York: Oxford University Press, pp. 223–49.

About the Contributors

Lewis Baston is Research Officer of the Electoral Reform Society, London. Prior to that he was Research Fellow at Kingston University. His principal research interests include elections, electoral systems and voting behavior, and contemporary history. He is author (with Simon Henig) of two editions of the *Politico's Guide to the (UK) General Election* and *The Political Map of Britain*, and has been an election commentator for RTE, BBC Radio, the Financial Times, and Guardian Online. He is also author of *Reggie: The Life of Reginald Maudling* (Sutton 2004).

Ingolfur Blühdorn is Reader in Politics and Political Sociology at the University of Bath (UK). His research specialisms include social and political theory, political sociology, as well as environmental sociology. He has published widely on social movements and their organizations, Green Parties, and the transformation of politics in advanced European democracies. His forthcoming publications include the monograph *Reinventing Green Politics: The Repositioning of Green Parties in a Changing Political Landscape* (Berghahn 2007) and *The Politics of Unsustainability: Eco-Politics in the Post-Environmental Era* (Routledge 2007, coedited with Ian Welsh).

Frank Decker is Professor of Political Science at the University of Bonn (Germany). His research focuses on political parties and institutional problems of Western democracies. Recent publications include a widely acknowledged book on right-wing populism (Leske and Budrich 2004) as well as edited volumes on populism (VS Verlag für Sozialwissenschaften 2006) and German federalism (VS Verlag für Sozialwissenschaften 2004). His *Encyclopedia of German political parties* (coedited with Viola Neu) is due for release in 2006.

Matthew Flinders is Reader in Parliamentary Government and Governance and Deputy Dean of the Faculty of Social Sciences at the University of Sheffield (UK). His research interests span governance and public policy, control and accountability frameworks, executive-legislative relationships, and constitutional reform. His forthcoming publications include the monograph *Walking Without Order: Delegated Governance and the British State* (Oxford University Press 2007), and *The Oxford Handbook of British Politics* (Oxford 2008, coedited with Andrew Gamble, Milke Kenny, and Colin Hay).

Sven Jochem is Junior Lecturer in Political Science at the Universities of Konstanz (Germany) and Bern (Switzerland). His research includes political theory as well as the comparative analysis of contemporary welfare state reforms. He has published on welfare state reforms in Germany as well as in other European countries. His forthcoming publications include *Reformpolitik im Wohlfahrtsstaat. Deutschland im internationalen Vergleich* (Reforming the Welfare State. Germany in a Comparative Perspective) and *Skandinavien. Politik, Geschichte, Wirtschaft* (Scandinavia. Politics, History, Economy; Beck 2007).

Uwe Jun is Professor of Political Science at the University of Trier (Germany). His research focus is on political institutions in western democracies, political communication, and parliamentarism. He has widely published on political parties and on contemporary developments in European political systems. He is author of *Wandel von Parteien in der Mediendemokratie* (Parties in Media Democracy; Campus 2004), as well as editor of *Politische Theorie und Regierungslehre. Eine Einführung in die politikwissenschaftliche Institutionenforschung* (Political Theory and Government. An Introduction to Political Research into Institutions; Campus 2004) and *Kleine Parteien im Aufwind* (Small Parties on the Rise; Campus 2006).

Josef Schmid is Professor of Political Economy and Comparative Policy Studies at the University of Tübingen (Germany). His research interests are social and economic policy and political organizations. He has published widely on comparative social policy and welfare state as well as on trade unions and political parties in Germany. He is currently working on monographs on political economy and on leadership in political organizations.

Christian Steffen is research manager of the Otto Brenner Stiftung (Otto Brenner Foundation, Frankfurt, Germany). Prior to this he was Junior Lecturer in Politics at the University of Tübingen. His research areas include the transformation of the welfare state and political organizations. He has published on trade unions and political parties and is currently working on a book on political economy organizations.

Ian Welsh is Senior Lecturer in Sociology at the University of Cardiff (UK). His research spans social and political theory with a focus upon environment, social movements, and the sociology of science. He is currently Principal Investigator on the Emergent Politics of Genomics project within the ESRC-funded CESAGen research center. He has published widely on social movements and political and technological change. His publications include *Complexity & Social Movements: Multitudes on the Edge of Chaos* (Routledge 2006, with Graeme Chesters) and *Mobilising Modernity: The Nuclear Moment* (Routledge 2000). He is coeditor of *The Politics of Unsustainability: Eco-Politics in the Post-Environmental Era* (Routledge 2007, with Ingolfur Blühdorn).

Elmar Wiesendahl is Professor of Political Science at the University of the Armed Forces Munich (Germany). His principal research interests include political theory, party theory, party change, and political elites. He is author of *Parteien in Perspektive* (Parties in Perspective; VS Verlag für Sozialwissenschaften 1998), *Mitgliederparteien am Ende?* (The Decline of Member Parties; VS Verlag für Sozialwissenschaften 2006), and *Parteien* (Political Parties; Fischer Verlag, forthcoming).